What they're saying about

The Learning Revolution

by Gordon Dryden and Dr. Jeannette Vos

"This is the book that I wish I had written."

> Sir Christopher Ball, Director of Learning, The Royal Society for the encouragement of Arts, Manufactures and Commerce, and author of *Start Right. the importance of early learning*, and *More Means Different*

"Absolutely outstanding. The entire book is the most inspiring and comprehensive pulling together of all the various strands of learning research that I have ever seen."

> Colin Rose, England, author of *Accelerated Learning*

"With this book, *The Learning Revolution*, Gordon Dryden and Jeannette Vos establish themselves as world leaders in that same revolution. *The Learning Revolution* is what books on education should be: a masterful blend of knowledge, care, optimism and very practical advice. It provides a superb tour of the main advances and main concepts that will affect education and learning in the 21st century. It is also a *tour de force!*"

> Tony Buzan, England, originator of Mind Mapping®™ and author of *The Mind Map Book—Radiant Thinking; Use Your Head; Use Your Memory;* and *Make The Most of Your Mind.*

"This book will do for lifelong learning what *In Search Of Excellence* and *Up The Organization* did for business: take it brilliantly into the 21st century. And it's as valid for every business as it is for every parent, student and teacher."

> Reg Birchfield, publisher, *Management* magazine, New Zealand

"As soon as I took it out of the mail, *The Learning Revolution* became a desktop resource in our office. The book provides information and perspective that have been tremendously beneficial to me personally and to hundreds of others receiving parts of it in shared presentations. Its format makes the book easy to use and enjoyable to handle. One can pick it up for a minute or several hours and be informed, challenged and inspired. In just a couple of months this book has already contributed to the hopeful vision for education the authors propose."

Dr. Jeanne Forrester, Education Advisor to the Governor of Mississippi, USA

"If today every parent and every teacher alive read this book, the world would change for the better by tomorrow. I know only one other thing which has that power."

Glenn Doman, Philadelphia, USA, author of *Teach Your Baby To Read*

"With the publication of *Common Sense,* Thomas Paine launched a revolution in the 13 American colonies. May this wonderful book launch The Learning Revolution throughout the world. It is a masterpiece of research . . . not about what might be done someday, but what is being done and can be done now. It brings together some of the 20th century's great scholars on enhanced intelligence and accelerated learning, and provides us with a blueprint for the 21st century—now."

Steven Snyder, President, Steven Snyder Seminars, California

"An inspiring book. An easy-to-read-and-grasp outline of tomorrow's world and the learning methods needed to make the most of it. We're already planning to use it as the catalyst to make 1994 The Year Of The Learning Revolution in Scandinavia."

Ingemar Svantesson, publisher and author, Sweden

"This book is terrific, and the left-right page format, with poster and text, is outstanding. A 'must' for school board members especially. Congratulations on a fine production."

Lyelle L. Palmer, Professor of Education, and Special Education Chair, Winona State University, Minnesota, USA

"This book addresses the most primary problem facing both adults and youth, and that is: how to learn more in less time, enjoy it, and retain it. This enormous and much-needed volume hands us the key to unlocking that mysterious yet relatively simple process of learning how to learn. A must."

Bettie B. Youngs, Ph. D., Ed. D., Del Mar, California, USA, author of *The 6 Ingredients of Self-Esteem*

"For more than 40 years I've searched for a theory of learning which works when you put it into practice. *The Learning Revolution* convinces with crisp summaries of new and still developing theory and a treasure-house of applications. A truly remarkable book."

"Congratulations on your superb effort to bring present views about learning and education together . . . a very positive message of our potential, toward learning specifically and toward life in general."

"It's great to read a book that presents the world's best learning and teaching breakthroughs in such a straightforward and easily read manner."

"A masterful job of covering all the basics of learning, using a practical, hands on approach which is relevant to all students, regardless of skill level or subject."

"The best in learning from around the world . . . catapults the reader into the possibilities of education's future. An important book . . . invaluable for anyone interested in learning."

"At last, a 'textbook' with immediate and relevant practical application! Anyone should be able to apply what he or she has read within minutes. The authors demonstrate a creative, playful approach to the learning process . . . They wish to make it a truly enjoyable journey for the student—and they succeed magnificently."

"Dozens of books have spelled out the revolution in technology, information and communications sweeping the world. One of the great needs now is for a learning revolution to enable us all to take advantage of those changes. And here, at last, is a book that writes the script: succinctly, simply, enthusiastically, honestly. A well-aimed challenge for all of us to rethink entirely everything we were ever taught about learning and teaching."

Mike Moore, former New Zealand Prime Minister

"The best thing I have read in years. Both professionally (as a management trainer) and personally (as a parent), I have learned so much from this book that it astounds me — not that I learned it, but that it was there to learn."

Linda Thomas, management trainer, Georgia, USA

"A delight to read. A smorgasbord of delicacies that will light up every reader: parent, teacher, administrator and student. The range and richness of the concrete examples make a compelling argument for change."

Norm Erickson, President, Society for Accelerative Learning and Teaching, former corporate trainer for IBM, Rochester, Minnesota, USA

"As with individuals, for businesses to be successful they must exercise the learning process, and this book provides the ideal formula. Two chapters alone are worth the price of the entire book: *The 15 major trends that will shape tomorrow's world* and *How to think for successful ideas.* The rest is a bonus—and for students, a considerable one."

Charles G. Lamb, Senior Lecturer in Marketing, Lincoln University, New Zealand, organizer of the 1993 Marketing Education Conference

"Everyone who expects to live, work and learn in the 21st century should read this book . . . inspirational . . . a blueprint for success."

Sylvia W. Peters, Edison Project, Knoxville, Tennessee, USA

"At last! An exciting and practical exploration and description of the learning possibilities available to all—young and old. This definitive work can free us to create a vision and a plan to build the kind of schools that will produce self-directed learners, perceptive thinkers, quality producers, effective communicators, collaborative contributors, creative problem solvers and conscientious achievers."

Don Lucas, Principal, Trona High School, Trona, California, USA

But does it work?

We've been careful to include in this book only results that have been proven. Here are some:

■ In Flaxmere, New Zealand, 11-year-olds up to five years behind at school are catching up in under ten weeks, using a tape-assisted reading programme. Details, pages 378-381

■ In a United States Army trial, soldiers using the techniques recommended in this book have achieved 661 per cent better results when learning German: more than twice the results in one-third the time. Details, pages 331-333

■ Bridley Moor High School, Redditch, England, has made a careful comparison of results with accelerated learning techniques. They've compared one class which has used the new methods to learn a foreign language—for only ten weeks—and one learning by conventional methods for a year:

	Using new methods	Using normal methods
80% pass mark or better	65%	11%
90% pass mark or better	38%	3%

Thus, using new techniques, ten times as many students achieved a 90 percent pass mark. Details, page 330

■ Bell Atlantic have cut staff training times by 42, 57 and 50 percent, with big reductions in costs and dropout rates. Details, pages 466-467

How to read this book in one-tenth the time

1 Skim-read the contents pages to get an overview.

2 Read the summary of main points at the start of each chapter.

3 Read the first three pages of the Introduction.

4 Quickly glance at the left-hand "poster pages" throughout the book.

5 These steps will tell you which chapters you must read thoroughly and which you can "skim."*

6 Read the "must-read" chapters first, "highlighting" key points with a coloured marker pen or pencil.

7 Skim the other chapters to refresh yourself on important points, again highlighting key information.

8 If you're not trained in rapid reading, turn to page 151 for some simple tips.

* *If the total subject-matter is new to you, you're welcome to read every chapter thoroughly and at your own pace.*
But we still recommend steps 1, 2, 3 and 4 above—
before you read the whole book. They will provide a "big picture" overview in advance. And that makes it much easier to remember the main points.

How to remember the main points from this book: make a Mind Map®

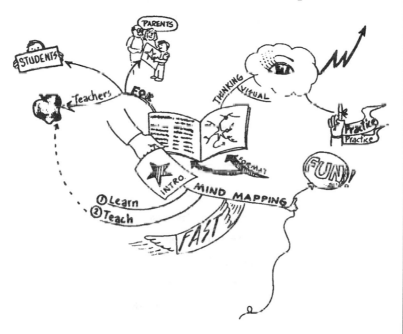

Your brain has 100 billion active cells. And each one can grow up to 20,000 connections, like branches on a tree.

Each of those branches stores information about associated topics—and good memory is based on association.

You'll recall things easier if you record information as your brain does. So don't take linear notes. Draw Mind Maps.®

Start with a sheet of A-3 paper and make a Mind Map of the information you want to remember. See pages 158-161 for simple tips; starter map on page 20.

Mind Mapping is a registered trade mark of Tony Buzan. Illustration above from *Mapping InnerSpace,* by Nancy Margulies, published by Zephyr Press, Tucson, Arizona.

———

Also by Gordon Dryden

Book:

Out Of The Red

Television documentaries in
the *Where To Now?* series:

The Vicious Cycle
Right From The Start
The Vital Years
Back To Real 'Basics'
The Chance To Be Equal
The Future: Does It Work?

Also by Jeannette Vos

Book:

Hot Minds (in production)
Doctoral dissertation:
An Accelerated/Integrative Learning Model Programme

The Learning Revolution

A lifelong learning programme for the world's
finest computer: your amazing brain

Gordon Dryden and
Dr. Jeannette Vos

**accelerated
learning**

The Learning Revolution

A lifelong learning programme for the world's
finest computer: your amazing brain

Accelerated Learning Systems Ltd., 50 Aylesbury Road, Aston Clinton,
Aylesbury, Bucks, HP22 5AH, United Kingdom.
Telephone (0296) 631177. Fax (0296) 631074.

Dryden, Gordon, and Vos, Jeannette
The Learning Revolution
Includes bibliographical references.
Summary: A detailed report on how to achieve the learning revolution that is urgently required to match the revolution in information and technology. A working guide for everyone, with special interest to teachers at all school and college levels.

ISBN: 0-905553-43-8

Published by Accelerated Learning Systems
The Learning Revolution
Written by: Gordon Dryden and Jeannette Vos
Typeset in New Zealand, printed and bound in England by
Unwin Brothers Limited, The Gresham Press, Old Woking, Surrey,
a member of the Martins Printing Group.

Contents

Contents

Contents

Notes:
1. Financial figures throughout are in United States dollars. Conversions, where required, have been done at approximate August 1993 rates, unless otherwise stated.
2. Billions are also in American terminology; thus one billion is 1000 million, and a trillion is a million million.
3. The source for each left-hand "poster page", where needed, is given at the bottom of the page. Other sources, where not obvious, are cited in the chapter reference notes.

This book will change the way you think, live, learn, work and act

Every so often comes a book that changes the way we think and act.

Some have been scientific works to alter our view of the world.

Others have crystallized changing times: books like Alvin Toffler's *Future Shock,* John Naisbitt's *Megatrends* and Tom Peters' and Robert Waterman's *In Search Of Excellence.*

Some have been stirring calls to action: pamphlets like Thomas Paine's *Common Sense,* with its challenge to revolution.

Now comes a book with all three elements. *The Learning Revolution* will change the way you think, live, learn, work and act.

It summarizes research from a wide range of disciplines, and synthesizes it into a new theory of learning and a learning society.

It reports succinctly how that knowledge is already bringing about revolutionary breakthroughs in learning and education.

And it sounds a challenging call to action: for a revolution in learning and thinking to match the soaring changes in technology, information and in our ability to produce an abundance of goods and services.

Co-authors Jeannette Vos and Gordon Dryden represent an unusual blend of international talent.

The first: a Netherlands-born American citizen with a doctorate in education earned from seven years' research into the world's best methods of rapid, effective learning; an educator who grew up in the Canada but has spent most of her life teaching in the United States: at early-childhood, elementary, high school and university levels.

Her career includes teaching America's first Masters Degree where 75 per cent of course work uses "integrative accelerated learning"—at Cambridge College, Massachusetts.

The second: a New Zealand-based high-school dropout at age 14; yet a man who has since become an award-winning broadcaster, journalist and television producer and one of the South Pacific's foremost seminar presenters for such companies as General Motors and McDonald's. His career also spans management in advertising, broadcasting, publishing, public relations, consulting and international marketing.

As a top radio and TV talkshow host, he was already reading an average of 15 books a week before the research on this book. He now says his earlier methods were inefficient!

While Jeannette Vos was completing her doctorate, her co-author was touring the globe with a television crew, capturing on 130 hours of videotape some of the world's best breakthroughs in education and the links between brain research, diet, health, parenting, child abuse, crime and the needs of a rapidly changing world. As he toured in particular through Sweden, the United Kingdom, the United States and New Zealand, the simple truth struck him: not only had most of the world's learning problems been solved, but they had been solved in pockets in each of the countries visited. Yet many of the solutions remained unheralded; and often the more thorough the research, the less it was known.

The co-authors met almost by accident in 1991 at the annual conference of the American-based international Society for Accelerative Learning and Teaching: a convention that showcased new learning and teaching ideas from business, school, university and home.

Six months later they swapped their output: six one-hour television documentaries from New Zealand, the doctoral research from America. The confirmation was amazing. What Jeannette Vos had summarized in painstaking and ground-breaking research, Gordon Dryden, the succinct communicator, had captured in action on video-camera.

Now they've combined their abilities to record those breakthroughs and show how anyone can benefit: a personal passport to the future for students, parents, teachers and lifelong self-educators. The result is a book that combines unusual talents: meticulous, documented academic research, linked with a writing and communications style that is as crisp and clean as an electronic beep; a book whose very presentation epitomizes the dramatic message it conveys.

The Publisher

Some see things as they are and ask why. I dream of things that never were and ask why not.

GEORGE BERNARD SHAW
Back to Methuselah, Act 1

Handbook for a gentle revolution: to turn despair to hope

This is a book about the coming revolution: the one we'll make together.

It can be a gentle, positive learning revolution[1] to take advantage of the current explosions in technology and communications. Or it can continue its present eruption in violence, drugs, dropouts and despair.

The need for drastic change is clear:

■ Of the 65 million Americans under 18, 13 million live in poverty, 14.3 million live in single parent homes, and almost two million live with no parent at all.[2]

■ In a world that spends $83 million[3] every hour on "defence," a bipartisan National Commission on Children can still report that addressing the unmet needs of American youngsters "is a national imperative as compelling as an armed attack or a natural disaster."[4]

■ More than half of America's young people leave school without the knowledge or foundation required to find and hold a good job.[5]

■ And each one of us knows that America is in the midst of a raging epidemic of juvenile homicide, suicide, drug abuse and violence. Our kids are killing, dying and bleeding in the streets. The searing 1992 riots in Los Angeles are only a taste of what is to come unless we find some answers. And similar problems are emerging in many other countries.

This book is about practical, proven alternatives: actions and programmes that work, effectively and simply, to build a decent future for our children and our families. We've called this book *The Learning Revolution* because true education for all is a major part of the answer. But we're not talking here only about *academic* education. We're talking

How to start your own Mind Maps®

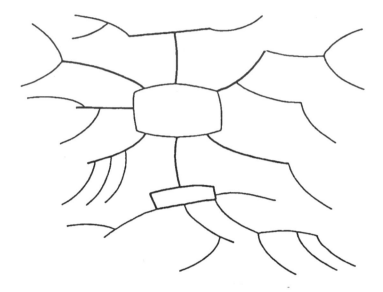

Mind Maps® provide an excellent way to make visual notes.

If you're new to the technique, enlarge this one and use it as a model.

Duplicate copies on A-3 pages, and use one for each chapter.

Mind Maps can branch out in any direction. Curving the lines makes it easier to write every word right side up.

See pages 158-161 for more instructions.

This page is reproduced from *Mapping InnerSpace,*
by Nancy Margulies, published by Zephyr Press, Tucson,
Arizona, 1991, and reprinted here with permission.

Mind Map® is a registered trademark of Tony Buzan.

about personal growth (which includes self-esteem), life-skills and learning-to-learn. Once you know *how* to learn, you can accelerate learning. We've found it's simple for most people to learn anything at least five times better, faster, easier—and to keep on learning throughout life. That's the easy part of the equation. The need is not only to absorb *information* in new and exciting ways, it is to build the confidence needed to benefit fully from an era in which anything is now possible.

This is a handbook for that revolution. In it you'll find simple tools that are already turning around health systems, preschools, elementary schools, high schools and businesses, in America and around the world.

It's also a book with a different format. Many great teachers believe that most learning is subconscious.[6] We also know that we learn more efficiently by *doing*. So the format aids both processes:

1. Key points and quotations are summarized on all left-hand pages. These are designed for "skim re-reading"—a learning technique that helps "store" and retrieve information much more efficiently.

2. Many of the quotations and summaries are designed to be enlarged into posters. We've printed some in shadow letters so the posters can be coloured-in. These posters, which help set the subconscious atmosphere for learning, can be used at home, school and work.

3. Other posters are check-lists. These contain simple tips to use for a variety of results, and are a constant reminder of main principles.

4. We've also included many practical do-it-yourself pointers. These include music you can play, and games and techniques you can use immediately.

5. You're also invited to make your own Mind Map of each chapter. If you're new to the technique, enlarge the sample map opposite, and start filling it in for practice.

6. In the text, we've summarized the best ideas we've found around the world. We've also recommended other books and contacts for those who want more detailed information in specific areas.

Above all, this book is a call to action. The problems are urgent. The answers are here. If not now, when? If not us, who?[7]

Jeannette Vos, Ed. D.
San Diego, California, USA

Some main themes of this book

■ The world is racing through a revolution that will change life as much as the alphabet, printing and steam-power.

■ For the first time in history, almost anything is now possible. We are the first people to live in an age of potential plenty.

■ Nearly every problem in the world has been solved—somewhere in the world.

■ Any society that picks the best of those solutions will lead the world in any field it chooses.

■ Many have yet to learn how to make those choices.

■ We therefore need a learning revolution to match the explosion in technology, knowledge and communications.

■ Fortunately that revolution, too, is gathering pace: a revolution of the mind; a revolution in the way we learn how to learn, and how to find brilliant new solutions.

■ This is a handbook for that gentle revolution.

Time to raise your vision in a world where almost anything is possible

This book is based on eight main beliefs:

1. The world is hurtling through a fundamental turning point in history.

2. We are living through a revolution that is changing the way we live, communicate, think and prosper.

3. This revolution will determine how, and if, we and our children work, earn a living and enjoy life to the fullest.

4. It is a world where almost anything we want to achieve is now possible.

5. Probably not more than one person in five knows how to benefit fully from the hurricane of change.

6. Unless we find answers, an elite 20 percent could end up with 60 percent of the nation's income, the poorest fifth with only 2 percent.[1] That is a formula for guaranteed poverty, school failure, crime, drugs, despair, violence and social eruption.

7. We need a parallel revolution in lifelong learning to match the information revolution, and for all to share the fruits of an age of potential plenty.

8. Fortunately, that revolution—a revolution that can help each of us learn anything much faster and better—is also gathering speed.

This book tells its story. It also acts as a practical guide to help you take control of your own future.

For the first time in our two million or more years we have the possibility of enough to go around.

RODERIC GORNEY
The Human Agenda*

*Published by the Guild of Tutors Press, Los Angeles, California.

The Learning Revolution has come not a moment too soon.

We are now in an age of instant communication. *We have the ability to store all the world's information, and make it available almost instantly, in virtually any form, to almost anyone anywhere on earth.*

Using that ability to the fullest will change your world at least as much as the alphabet, the printing press, the steam engine, the automobile or television. Its impact will be greater than the silicon chip, the personal computer, the voice-activated word-processor, fibre optics, satellites and interactive compact video disk—even though it will make use of all these.

At last we are also learning to make use of the most brilliant human resource of all: the almost limitless power of the trillion cells and billions of connections that make up the average human brain.

It's an era where all of us need to rethink the meaning of words like "work," "unemployment," "retirement" and "education."

We are racing into an age dominated by a one-world economy. As American Secretary of Labour Robert B. Reich[1] says, this world will have no *national* economies, products, technologies, corporations or industries. But we will still have *national societies*. And a prime task of each society is to prepare all its members to reshape their own future; to develop the skills and abilities needed to flourish in that one-world economy.

To prosper in the new one-world economy, would you like to learn to speak a foreign language fairly competently in only four to eight weeks?*

In a world where school dropouts have no future, would you like to be guaranteed that your children will catch up at school in under ten weeks—even if they are now three years behind?

In a world where knowledge is exploding, would you like to be able to skim through four books a day—and remember what you read?

In a world of instant communication, would you like to be able to tap into the combined knowledge and talents of humanity—on your own personal computer or TV screen?

In a world where perhaps only a quarter of all people will have

* Breakthroughs summarized early in this book are explained fully later, and chapter notes are sourced to those fuller explanations.

Millions saw the apple fall, but Newton was the one who asked why.

BERNARD M. BARUCH*

*Adviser to every U.S. President from Woodrow Wilson
to Dwight D. Eisenhower.

fulltime jobs as we now know them, **would you like an effective method to relearn anything you want?**

In a world where education systems are under severe criticism, **would you like some guaranteed methods to reduce the current failure rate?**

In a world where 12,000 babies will be born each hour, **would you like to know how to make sure each baby has a bright beginning?**

In a world where everyone will have to plan for several different careers in a lifetime, **would you like to learn the key principles about any new job simply and easily?**

In a world where 20 percent of the population will soon be over 60, **would you like to know how you can go on enjoying life well into your 80's or 90's?**

In a world which calls for radical new solutions to old problems, **would you like to know how we can each learn simple ways to create new ideas?**

And in a world where soaring taxation and deficits threaten to strangle democracies, **how can we achieve these results without spending an extra cent?**

If these questions sound like the start of a glowing advertisement, relax. Every one of these results is possible right now, and all are being achieved somewhere in the world. Some of them come from new breakthroughs in brain research, some from soaring advances in technology. Others come from new insights that link science and philosophy. Fortunately, they come at a time that makes changes in *learning* even more urgent than changes in *technology.*

Already only 20 percent of Americans are earning over 50 percent of the nation's income.[3] Most of these top earners are skilled in identifying and solving problems, and linking together new opportunities and answers. Harvard Professor Reich estimates that by the year 2020 the top fifth of America's earners will account for more than 60 percent of all the income earned by its citizens. The bottom fifth will take home two percent—unless we change our priorities and educate and retrain *most* of our people so that they develop the skills and abilities currently used by only the most affluent. An increasing array of forecasters say that dramatic new forms of education provide the key.

British professor and consultant Charles Handy in *The Age of Unreason* says the overwhelming pace of change demands "completely re-

Apocalypse or Golden Age. The choice is ours.

JOHN NAISBITT and
PATRICIA ABURDENE
Megatrends 2000*

*Published by William Morrow and Company Inc.,
105 Madison Avenue, New York, NY 10016.

thinking the way in which we learn." He says education, however, will not be education as most of us have known it. "Education needs to be reinvented. Education will not finish with school, nor should it be confined to those who shine academically at 18. Learning . . . happens all through life unless we block it."

Handy calls for *upside-down thinking* on every major issue that confronts the world today. Among dozens of ideas (some of which we will explore later), he says, "upside-down thinking suggests that, instead of a *national* curriculum for education, what is really needed is an *individual* curriculum for every child."

Achieving this would change entirely most concepts about schooling. It means completely rethinking not just the role of schools, but the role of business as well.

Handy also paints the grim alternative. "The danger of doing nothing is that the underclass (that new alarming word), excluded from the world we are moving into, takes its own initiatives, substituting terrorism for politics and bombs for votes, as their way of turning the world upside-down."

John Naisbitt and Patricia Aburdene paint a similar picture. "We stand at the dawn of a new era," begins their book *Megatrends 2000.* "Before us is the most important decade in the history of civilization, a period of stunning technological innovation, unprecedented economic opportunity, surprising political reform, and great cultural rebirth."

They also pose the alternative: "Apocalypse or Golden Age. The choice is ours."

In *Odyssey,* Apple Computers former C.E.O. John Sculley criticizes a school system that is "preparing our children for the same old repetitive jobs in the industrial age—the very jobs that are disappearing daily. Instead we should be preparing them for the jobs of the future, jobs that will require thinking skills, not rote memorization and repetition."

He says product planning today should start with "unconstrained dreaming." That change demands an entirely new set of creative skills for most people—skills currently not taught at most schools. At Apple, he says, "we believe that the best way to predict the future is to invent it. We feel the confidence to shape our destiny."

American business consultant Tom Peters believes new information systems are greatly reducing jobs in "middle management" and that every

Human history becomes more and more a race between education and catastrophe.

H.G. WELLS
The Outline of History

worker now needs to become a "self-acting manager." In *Liberation Management,* he gives this advice to students: "Remember that (1) education is the only ticket to success and (2) education doesn't stop with the last certificate you pick up. Studenthood for life is a necessity, by definition, in a knowledge-based society. You need to take your education—and the education of all others—very seriously. Education is the 'big game' in the globally interdependent economy. Period."

Says Scandinavian Airline Systems Chief Executive Jan Carlzon, in *Moments Of Truth:* "An employee without information cannot take responsibility. With information he cannot avoid taking it."

The Learning Revolution points the way to success.

It's already helping teenagers to dramatically lift their school marks after only ten days at a live-in *SuperCamp.*[4]

It's enabling Australian high-school students to learn a three-year foreign language course in eight weeks, and English adults to learn German in under four weeks of home study.

It's helping 11-year-olds in New Zealand close five-year reading gaps in under ten weeks.

It's lifting some of the sons and daughters of America's poorest workers into "gifted children's" classes as soon as they start school.

It's a revolution that enables anyone to learn anything much faster. More effectively. More enjoyably. And throughout life—from the very earliest years until well into your eighties, or even longer.

As co-author, over the past 40 years in a career that spans business, marketing, advertising, public relations, journalism, radio and television, I've developed some simple beliefs:

1. Virtually anything is now possible. We can achieve almost all the things that utopians dreamed about when I was a boy in the 1930s.

2. Nearly every problem has been solved, in part, somewhere in the world. And the first to pick the best of the world's best solutions—and join them to their own achievements—will lead the world.

3. Where problems have not been solved, we now have simple techniques to produce great new solutions. In fact, most new answers are simply new combinations of older elements, new ways of linking the combined wisdom with the resources of the world. Motivating people to define problems and opportunities, and to seek out new solutions, is one of the keys to success.

No army can withstand the strength of an idea whose time has come.

VICTOR HUGO

4. You don't have to be a giant country, a giant state, a big company or a large school to lead the world. Early history abounds with the record of small cities and states—Athens, Rome, Holland, Portugal, Spain, Britain—that have done just that. So does recent history: Taiwan, with the world's biggest foreign exchange reserves; resource-barren islands like Hong Kong and Singapore which have swept past resource-rich countries like New Zealand in total income per person; tiny Malaysia which is now the world's biggest exporter of silicon chips.

5. We are now at a key historical turning point. Around 10,000 years ago our ancestors first learned to grow crops and put animals to work. This ushered in the agricultural revolution. Around 250 years ago they unleashed the power of steam, and pioneered the industrial revolution. Over the past 20 years we've entered the age of instant information, and the world will never again be the same.

This book is based in part on these beliefs. But it's also based on a remarkable coincidence. In the late 1980s and the early 1990s, co-author Jeannette Vos and I were completing different projects, in different parts of the world. We had never met.

After a working life in teaching at preschool, elementary, high school and college-university levels in the United States, Jeannette was handling a seven-year research project for her doctorate in education. Her subject: big improvements in learning methods; techniques that saw high-school under achievers making dramatic turn-rounds in only ten days at *SuperCamp*.

Around the same time I was completing a major research, writing and videotaping project for a six-part series of television documentaries looking, in part, at new educational breakthroughs around the world and around my own home country in New Zealand.

Our early backgrounds were also similar: my own at ten different elementary schools before quitting formal "education" at age 14 and starting a roving career that was to take me into journalism, advertising, radio, television, public relations and business management. Dutch-born Jeannette: moving to Canada with her family at the end of the second world war and attending 12 different schools before graduating from high school and a career in teaching.

The two authors first met briefly at the 1991 American convention of the Society for Accelerative Learning and Teaching. When the TV series and doctoral dissertations were finished, we swapped copies and back-

Emblazon these words on your mind: learning is more effective when it's fun.

PETER KLINE
*The Everyday Genius**

*Published by Great Ocean Publishers Inc., 1823 North Lincoln Street, Arlington, VA 22207.

ground research. The similarities were amazing. The television and academic research dovetailed. The findings were dramatic. The truth was also simple:

It *is* possible for anyone to learn almost anything much faster—often anywhere from five to 20 times faster—and often ten times to 100 times more effectively, at any age. Those learning methods are simple, fun-filled, common sense—and they work.

Together, they provide the basis for the learning revolution that is needed to match the technology, information and communications explosion that is transforming all our lives.

Hopefully you will find in these pages the simple tools to reshape your future.

Gordon Dryden, Auckland, New Zealand

The 15 key trends to shape your future

1. The age of instant communications.
2. A world without economic borders.
3. Three steps to a one-world economy.
4. The new service society.
5. From big to small.
6. The new age of leisure.
7. The changing shape of work.
8. Women in leadership.
9. The decade of the brain.
10. Cultural nationalism.
11. The growing underclass.
12. The active aging of the population.
13. The new do-it-yourself boom.
14. Cooperative enterprise.
15. The triumph of the individual.

The 15 major trends that will shape tomorrow's world

A revolution is changing your life—and your world.

You are part of the first generation to live in a new age: an age that offers an unlimited choice of futures in an era where virtually all things are possible.

Each of us can make those choices—and go on making them throughout life—only if we can grasp the scope of those changes, see their potential, and seize the opportunities.

Your children's world will be like none other before. Their future, too, depends on the ability to grasp new concepts, make new choices, and go on learning and adapting throughout life.

Developed countries have already made the leap from an industrial society to an age of information: an age where human brainpower and knowledge will continue to replace machinery and buildings as the main capital in society.

The new age is also one of stark alternatives. For those with the new knowledge: a world of opportunity. For those without: the prospect of unemployment, poverty and despair as the old jobs disappear, the old systems crumble.

The main thrust of this book is that new methods of learning are urgently needed if most people are to benefit. And not just for a new generation, but for those who are already adults.

But learning can be fully effective only if it enables each of us to link directly to the needs of the new age. Of all the trends, we believe at least 15 main ones should dictate the shape of our new learning systems and methods:

A single optic fibre will conceivably deliver hundreds of television stations, as well as give each home access to a video library containing, potentially, every movie you'd ever want to see.

WILL HIVELY
Incredible Shrinking Optical Act*

*An article published in *Discovery* magazine, February, 1993.

1. The age of instant communication

The world has developed an amazing ability to store information and make it available instantly in different forms to almost anyone. That ability will revolutionize business, education, home life, employment, management and virtually everything else we take for granted.

Our homes will re-emerge as vital centres of learning, work and entertainment. The impact of that sentence alone will transform our schools, our businesses, our shopping centres, our offices, our cities— in many ways our entire concept of work.

Instant communication is the *dominant* technology. And as Stewart Brand says in *The Media Lab: Inventing The Future at M.I.T.:* "Communications media are so fundamental to a society that when their structure changes, everything is affected."

Or as Neil Postman and Charles Weingartner write in *Teaching As A Subversive Activity:* "When you plug something into the wall, someone is getting plugged into you. Which means you need new patterns of defence, perception, understanding, evaluation. You need a new kind of education."

It's been almost 30 years since author-teacher John Holt in *How Children Fail* issued this vital challenge: "We must ask how much of the sum of human knowledge anyone can know at the end of his schooling? Perhaps a millionth. Are we then to believe that one of these millionths is so much more important than another? Or that our social and national problems will be solved if we can just figure out a way to turn children out of schools knowing two millionths of the total, instead of one?"

Holt argued even then that "since we can't know what knowledge will be most needed in the future, it is senseless to try to teach it in advance. Instead, we should try to turn out people who love learning so much and learn so well that they will be able to learn whatever needs to be learned."

We don't accept all of Holt's thesis. Of course everyone has to share in basic knowledge. And sure, as H.D. Hirsch Jr. argues in *Cultural Literacy,* there is a core of information that should be part of everyone's essential understanding of the world and one's own society. But the information explosion underscores the heart of Holt's argument. Today's technology provides us with many of the tools to deliver that information, and any other factual data, direct to your home, as you require it. New learning techniques can help you absorb that knowledge much faster, better, smarter. And new thinking styles can help you

History's landmarks

The world	**4.5 billion years old**
Life	**3.5 billion years ago**
Humans	**2 million years ago[1]**
'Modern' humans	**35,000 to 50,000 years ago[1]**
Farming	**12,000 years ago**
The plough	**5,000 years ago**
The wheel	**5,000 years ago**
Steam-power	**250 years ago**
Computers	**40-50 years ago**
And now	**The age of instant communications**

Communications

First brains	**500 million years ago[2]**
Speech	**35,000 to 50,000 years ago[3]**
Writing	**6,000 years ago**
Alphabet	**4,000 years ago[4]**
Printing	**1040 AD in China, 1451 AD in Europe**
Telephone	**1876**
Moving pictures	**1894**
Television	**1926**
Transistor	**1948**
Fibre optics	**1988: 3,000 messages at once**
	1991: 80,000
	2000: 10 million (prediction)

Main sources: *Reader's Digest Book of Facts, The Inventions That Changed The World* and *The World Book Encyclopedia.*

1. Most anthropologists differentiate between *homo habilis (handy man),* dating back 1.5 to 2 million years, *home sapiens (wise human beings)* and *homo sapiens sapiens,* our own species, whose earliest remains have been dated to 35,000 years ago.

2. Early "brains," of course, were very simple nervous systems.

3. No one knows for certain when understandable speech developed. But the latest brain research has identified the parts of our brain that deal with speech, thought and reasoning: all are in our forebrains which are most fully developed in *homo sapiens sapiens.*

4. The earliest alphabet emerged about 1700 B.C., but the more modern Greek version was not introduced into Europe until around 1000 B.C.

restructure it in new ways—to take advantage of the changing times.

Our ability to communicate is one of our key human traits. Most scientists say the world has existed for 4,500 million years,[1] and that humans in somewhere near their present form have been here for maybe two million years, and as "modern humans" for 35,000 to 50,000 years. Yet our ancestors—whatever arguments exist over their origins—did not invent any form of writing until 6,000 years ago.

It took another 2,000 years before they created the first alphabet—the amazing development that eventually enabled all knowledge to be recorded by rearranging only 26 symbols. But not until the 11th century AD did the Chinese start printing books. And it was not until 1451 that German inventor Johannes Gutenburg printed the first European book: transforming our ability to store and communicate knowledge by making the printed word more accessible.

Not until the last hundred-odd years did we start to speed up the process: the first typewriter in 1872, the first telephone message in 1876, the first typesetting machine in 1884, silent movies in 1894, the first radio signals in 1895, talking movies in 1922, infant television in 1926 and the computer microprocessor and pocket calculator in 1971.

Since then the communications explosion has rocked the world. By 20 years ago most developed countries had the choice of at least two national television networks, perhaps three or four. By the late 1980s most American viewers could choose 50 or more.

The day these words were first typed the co-authors sat in their homes on opposite sides of the Pacific and watched President Clinton's inauguration speech live. And so did millions of other people in over 200 countries and territories now reached by the international Cable News Network service. Yet even this technology is outdated: we still largely choose on our TV screen from the information others have pre-selected. *Tomorrow we will be able to choose whatever we want and need.*

The world is becoming one gigantic information exchange. By 1988 a single fibre optic "cable" could carry 3,000 electronic messages at once. By 1991: 80,000. By 2000 the prediction is 10 million.[2]

The impact on employment alone has been staggering. Not too many years ago most of our phone calls went through manual exchanges. Today you can dial the world at the touch of a few buttons. To handle all the world's telephone calls today in the old way, possibly a quarter of the adults on earth would need to be employed in manual phone ex-

Today we are at the start of another media revolution: the fusion of television and the computer.

CD-I Producers' Handbook*

* Published by Philips Interactive Media Systems, Los Angeles, 1991.

changes. Instead, all those jobs have been eliminated, but the efficiency of our phone systems has soared.

The demand for people with skills—to make, install, service and use the new technologies—has also soared. This is especially true for those who can come up with new ways to turn combinations of technologies into new individual solutions.

Visit the Smithsonian Institute in Washington DC and you could easily spend a week absorbed in its displays of history, technology, science, space and art. Now the Smithsonian has compressed virtually all of that on to one CDI—an interactive compact video disc, ready for instant replay on any television screen. And not just as a videotape, but a videodisc where you use your remote control to select and replay anything from the Smithsonian's menu. Your own individual curriculum. Instantly. Whenever you want to use it. At a tiny fraction of the cost of a seven-day visit to Washington.

Or take a typical printed home encyclopedia. Brilliant—but out of date as soon as it is produced. Now visit a model school of the future (as we will do later) and you'll find a complete encyclopedia available to every student, electronically networked to dozens of personal computers. Regularly updated, and completely interactive. You choose what you want to use—and a CD-ROM delivers it, instantly, with the ability to print-out anything you need, or store it on your individual computer-console memory. CD-ROM stands for Compact Disc, Read Only Memory. It looks the same as an audio compact disc but is formatted for computer data instead of sound. And on one CD "you've got a cheap little parking place for 250,000 pages of text, the equivalent of 500 books, instantly computer-searchable and publishable at one-fiftieth the cost of printing on paper."[3]

This year alone the world will produce over 800,000 different book-titles.[4] If you read one a day, it would take you well over 2,000 years to complete them all. But what if you could automatically select only the information you want, when you want it, and have it fed to you through one of those 10 million messages that we will soon be able to transmit at the same time on one fibre optic "cable"?

And what if you could reproduce that information at home in any form: on computer, videotape, compact disc or on your home printer? The technology is already in place. Today's newspaper summarizes the world amid standardized advertisements. Headlines and special sections help you skim and select. The classified advertisements appear alpha-

In the near future most homes and businesses will be linked together by a global fibre optic-based phone network, and effectively interconnected to the whole of recorded media.

NEW MEDIA: CD-I TO VIRTUAL REALITY*

*From the Introduction to a symposium, organized by the
Department of Computer Science, University of Auckland, New Zealand,
June 16, 1993.

betically—for the same reason. But tomorrow's technology will analyse your individual interests, and deliver your own personal printout direct to you, through your home electronic multi-media system—what some are calling *The Daily Me.*

Or take office work. Even 20 years ago some of the most highly skilled typists in the world could find guaranteed work in legal offices, to type out wills, the land transfer forms and thousands of other forms of modern society. Today most of that basic information can be stored on a computer—and a few sentences tapped into a word processing programme can personalize those legal documents almost instantly.

But soon even word processing will be outdated. American educationalist Dr. Willard Daggett[5] tells how he had to fill in unexpectedly as a guest speaker at a European conference. He spoke from notes, without a written speech. But within 90 seconds of him finishing, copies of his full speech, edited and spelling-checked, were delivered to every delegate—in four different languages. All through a voice-activated word processor.

Or take management. Even ten years ago most manufacturing companies needed several layers of management and supervisory staff to run the traditional industrial factory and the offices accompanying it: to pass down the instructions, order supplies, oversee output. Today's computers deliver the vital information where it is needed. So more and more workers have to become self-managing. Around the world large numbers of "middle" managers have lost their jobs. Many more will be lost as "staff" specialists disappear and every worker has access to the knowledge the "experts" once possessed.

So what should be demanded of an education system? Should it provide for everyone the training and skills previously the domain of the few? Should you learn to read only one book of "literature" in a year, or to devour computer manuals? Or both? Do you learn algebra—which only about 17 per cent of school graduates ever use? Or do you learn other forms of thinking and problem solving?

2. A world without economic borders

We are moving inevitably to a world where most commerce will be virtually unrestricted.

Ignore the short-term moves to protect some countries' farming incomes. The genie is out of the bottle: the instant transfer of money

(In the coming century) there will be no national products or technologies, no national corporations, no national industries. There will no longer be national economies . . . All that will remain rooted within national borders are the people who comprise a nation. Each nation's primary assets will be its citizens' skills.

ROBERT B. REICH
The Work of Nations*

* Published by Simon & Schuster, New York, London and Sydney.

around the globe has altered the very nature of trade and world commerce.

The world now trades $7.6 trillion[6] a year in goods and non-financial services. But by 1990 the world's money markets traded $114 trillion in "electronic funds": 15 times the amount of other trade.

Megatrends 2000 co-author John Naisbitt lists a global economy as his main prediction for the nineties. "That's the undoubted direction the world is going—towards a single-market world economy. Sure, we have the counter-trends of protectionism along the way, but the main overarching trend is to move to a world where there's free trade among all countries."[7]

And President Clinton's first Secretary of Labour, Robert B. Reich, writes at the start of his outstanding book *The Work Of Nations— preparing ourselves for the twenty first century:* "We are living through a transformation that will rearrange the politics and economies of the coming century. There will be no *national* products or technologies, no national corporations, no national industries. There will no longer be national economies, at least as we have come to understand that concept. All that will remain rooted within national borders are the people who comprise a nation. Each nation's primary assets will be its citizens' skills."

And those will depend above all else on the ability of a nation's population to learn those new skills, particularly in defining problems, creating new solutions and adding new values. Certainly a nation's education system can no longer be based simply on remembering a limited core of information.

3: The three steps to a one-world economy

While international finance has spurred the growth of the one-world economy, three enlarged trading blocs are the stepping stones: a more united Europe, the Americas and the Asian-Pacific rim.

Despite setbacks, a European Community has emerged, with completely interlinked economies, and trade between America, Canada, Central and South America is growing.

But undoubtedly one of the main energizers of the coming century is the rise of the Asian-Pacific rim, with Japan the first leader and China now emerging as a potential giant. If the 19th was the British century and the 20th the American, many are forecasting that we are now entering the Asian-Pacific age.

We live in the first era in human history when our species' entire heritage of knowledge, wisdom and beauty is available to each of us virtually on demand.

ROBERT GROSS
*The Adult Learner**

*An article in *New Horizons for Learning,* published by New Horizons for Learning, 4649 Sunnyside North, Seattle, WA 98103 (Spring 1993).

John Naisbitt travels to Asia regularly, and talks glowingly of the production, consumer and educational revolutions that are transforming South Korea, Taiwan, Hong Kong, Singapore, Malaysia and Thailand. "By the year 2000," he says, "Europeans will constitute six percent of the world's population and they will have grown in the nineties by only 11 million. But the richest countries in Asia—their consumer-driven countries—will have grown by 200 million customers. So the Asian-Pacific rim is where the economic centre of gravity will be."

And you don't have to be a giant to participate. "Singapore is a wonderful example," says Naisbitt. "It has only 2.6 million people. It's only about the size of Manhattan Island. But look at their record. When they started Singapore Airlines they had 1.9 million people—yet it's now one of the largest airlines in the world. It's one of the most popular airlines in the world. And Singapore Airlines is the most profitable airline in the world. So you don't have to be a big country or a big company to participate in the global economy.

"To underscore that, the United States is the largest exporter in the world, but 50 percent of our exports are created by companies with 19 or fewer people. Only seven percent of U.S. exports are created by companies with 500 or more people. And in Germany, the second largest exporting country in the world, the profile for its exports is almost exactly the same."

Leading Japanese management consultant Kenichi Ohmae, in *The Borderless World,* underlines another factor. "If you look at the prosperous nations today—Switzerland, Singapore, Taiwan, South Korea and Japan—they are characterized by small land mass, no resources, and well-educated hard-working people who all have the ambition to participate in the global economy. Having an abundance of resources has truly slowed down a country's development, because bureaucrats there still think that money could solve all problems. In a truly interlinked, global economy, the key success factor shifts from resources to the marketplace, in which you have to participate in order to prosper. It also means people are the only true means to create wealth."

Robert Reich argues that the competitiveness of Americans and other rich industrial countries in the new global market no longer depends on national corporations or national industries. It depends on the new functions that its citizens perform to add value within a global economy.

More and more the living standards of all people, particularly in

There is more to life than increasing its speed.

MOHANDAS GANDHI

developed countries, will depend on their entrepreneurs' ability to find value-added niches and develop them internationally. And the stepping stone will generally be first through associated trading blocs.

Naisbitt calls education "the Asian-Pacific Rim's competitive edge." And he points to the signposts: The Japanese have the highest proportion of science degrees of any country—69 percent of degrees awarded, compared with America's 25 percent (although Japan's educational system, like many others, is planning many big essential changes). Japanese attend school 257 days a year, compared with America's 180. Half of Seoul's adult population either attends a university or has graduated from one. South Korea has the highest number of Ph. D.s per person in the world. And it turns out 32,000 applied-science graduates a year in areas like engineering—proportionately more than America and nearly as many as Japan. Naisbitt also points to a possible trend of the future: 206 of Korea's 256 universities are owned by companies like Hyundai, Daewoo and Korean Air.

Four separate but interrelated facts spell out even more of the resulting educational imperatives:

1. In California—America's richest state and major gateway to the Asian-Pacific Rim and the new Mexican partnership—by the year 2000 50 percent of the population will be Asian or Hispanic. Does anyone sincerely believe that a mono-cultural, single-language educational system will satisfy the needs of such a society?

2. Across the Pacific, tiny New Zealand lives by trade. Forty years ago almost 80 percent of it was with Britain. Today its biggest trading partners are the Pacific rim countries, Australia and Japan. Its fastest-rising partners are Taiwan and Korea. Yet despite many of its other great innovations in education, 34 percent of its high school foreign language students are still studying French—a legacy of former European ties. Less than three percent are studying Japanese or other Asian languages.

3. New Zealand has 60 accountants for every one in Japan.

4. Seventy percent of the world's attorneys are in the United States. And there are three times as many lawyers on Manhattan Island, New York, as in all of Japan.

Do you think some of our priorities might be wrong? Robert Reich is only one who has questioned whether more accountants have given us a better financial system and whether more lawyers have created more justice. So what should the new priorities be?

By the year 2000 under two percent of Americans will work on farms, and ten percent in manufacturing.

JOHN NAISBITT
author of *Megatrends* *

*Forecast in author interview, Cambridge, Mass, 1990.

4. The new service society

Peter Drucker, Naisbitt, Ohmae, Reich and many other forecasters all agree the next trend: the move from an industrial to a service society.[8]

Naisbitt again: "When I got out of college in the fifties, 65 percent of the workforce in America was blue-collar. Now it's down to about 13 percent, and its falling. That doesn't mean we're producing less. In fact, around 24 percent of America's gross national product is in manufacturing, about the same as it has been every year for 40 years. The difference is that 40 years ago 65 percent of the workforce was manufacturing these products, and today only 13 percent. Now obviously that 24 percent represents many more products as our economy has grown tremendously. The big change is: we're now manufacturing with information, rather than people. With computers, automation and robots instead of workers.

"And that industrial workforce will continue to shrink, just as the agricultural base has shrunk. A couple of hundred years ago 90 percent of the people in North America were farmers. As recently as a dozen years ago it was about three and a half percent. Now it's way below that."

Both Naisbitt and Drucker predict that by the year 2000 only ten percent of the workforce in affluent developed countries like America will be working in direct manufacturing. And the figures back them up. Almost half of all routine American jobs in steel-making disappeared between 1974 and 1988—from 480,000 to 260,000. General Motors alone wiped out 150,000 American production jobs in the 1980s.

So if all a developed country's manufacturing can be done with ten percent of its workers, and all its farm products produced by another two percent, what will the other 88 percent of us do?

Some are calling our future "the new service economy." But the very terms "manufacturing" and "service" are becoming obsolete. More and more, manufacturing will be combined with service: customized for individuals—in the same way that computer hardware now represents a very small part of the total service supplied by a computer company. By far the biggest part is in specialist consulting: customized software systems and training.

The demands on education systems will be phenomenal. Most of the world's schooling methods were developed to service the fairly rigid structures of an industrial economy. Most developed countries did an excellent job of providing the basics for perhaps the top 20 percent of our population to become managers, lawyers, doctors, accountants, academ-

The best way to predict the future is to invent it now.

ARTHUR L. COSTA
Creating The Future*

*Edited by Dee Dickinson and published by Accelerated Learning
Systems, Aston Clinton, Bucks, England. Dr. Costa is a professor
of education at California State University, Sacramento, California.
He is a former President of the Association for Supervision
and Curriculum Development.

ics and other professionals. We also did well in educating perhaps another 30 percent to become tradespeople, the skilled and semiskilled. And, depending on the country, our primary schools did provide a good basic understanding of reading, writing and arithmetic to all our youngsters, including the 50-odd percent who would go out and get unskilled work.

Today most of those unskilled jobs no longer exist. Reich puts it succinctly: "Twelve thousand people are added to the world's population every hour, most of whom, eventually, will happily work for a small fraction of the wages of routine producers in America." He argues that three broad categories of work are emerging around the world: *routine production services, in-person services* and *symbolic-analytical services.*

Routine production services involve the repetitive tasks typical of smokestack industries: on the industrial assembly lines, and the routine supervisory jobs performed by low- and mid-level managers

Many of those routine manufacturing and assembly services are now being done either by robots in developed countries or by more traditional methods in low-labour-cost countries. For the unskilled in rich countries, the immediate result is disastrous, specially for some minority groups. For many years, during the height of the industrial boom, waves of migrants flowed into the cities of America, Britain, parts of Europe, Australia and New Zealand. Many of them started in the manual jobs of an unmechanized or semi-mechanized economy. This was the first rung up the ladder to a better future. But now, as many unskilled workers are ready to grasp the bottom rung of the ladder, the ladder itself has been taken away.

In-person services are also often repetitive: serving in fast-food outlets, bars and restaurants or working in supermarkets. These will continue as major job providers: for the chefs, waiters, check-out workers, taxi-drivers, hostesses, child-care centre operators and many more. Often these are lowly-paid and part-time—unless the "servers" can link with other technologies to provide exceptional levels of service.

Symbolic-analytical services involve the people who "solve, identify and broker" problems by *manipulating symbols:* the research scientists, design engineers, software engineers, civil engineers, biotechnology engineers, sound engineers, public relations execu-

$1.9 billion retailer Nordstrom gets by with a one-sentence policy manual: 'Use your own best judgment at all times.'

TOM PETERS
Thriving on Chaos*

* Published by Alfred A. Knopf, New York.

tives, investment bankers, lawyers, real estate developers and even a few creative accountants, management consultants and tax consultants.

This is the group that already in America makes up 20 percent of society—and earns around 50 percent of total annual income. A few, such as Apple Computer pioneer Steve Jobs, may be school dropouts, but overwhelmingly the successful symbolic-analysts have graduated from the top colleges and universities.

Reich says the major high-paid growth alternatives in developed countries revolve around this same third category. He spells out some of the demands these changing opportunities will place on education: "Every innovative scientist, lawyer, engineer, designer, management consultant, screenwriter or advertiser is continuously searching for new ways to represent reality which will be more compelling or revealing than the old. Their tools may vary but the abstract processes of shaping raw data into original patterns are much the same."

He thinks we all need to learn how to conceptualize problems and solutions, using at least four basic skills: abstraction, system thinking, experimentation and collaboration. "For most children in the United States and around the world," says Reich, "formal education entails just the opposite kind of learning. Rather than construct meanings for themselves, meanings are imposed upon them. What is to be learned is prepackaged into lesson plans, lectures and textbooks. Reality has already been simplified; the obedient student has only to commit it to memory. An efficient educational process, it is assumed, imparts knowledge much as an efficient factory installs parts on an assembly line."

Much education, in fact, still resembles the declining industrial method of production: a standard assembly-line curriculum divided into subjects, taught in unit, arranged by grade, and controlled by standardized tests. This no longer reflects the world we live in. And traditional educational systems can no longer cope with the demands of the new realities.

5. From big to small

In the traditional industrial economy, bigness ruled. GM, Ford and Chrysler dominated world car production for almost half a century; IBM towered over computers; and so on through dozens of different industries.

90 percent of new jobs are in companies with under 50 people.

JOHN NAISBITT
co-author of *Megatrends 2000**

* In author interview, 1990.

Even 25 years ago only big companies could afford the giant computers that were then the peak of electronic achievement. That technology helped spur the ride to centralized bureaucracy, takeovers, acquisitions and mergers.

Today most of those giant computers are obsolete. The world of the mini has arrived. Sure, the big companies are still there. But their vast air-conditioned computer rooms lie empty or transformed.

And their organizational structure is changing fast. Where the giant companies are still prospering, they have generally been split into dozens of small project teams, each self-acting and self-managing, cutting through the old specialization, the old business pyramid-style hierarchies, the old army-style management.

Tom Peters gives dozens of examples in his 834-page book *Liberation Management.* But to cite just one: Zurich-based ABB Asea Brown Boveri is now one of Europe's giant companies, with revenues of $28.9 billion in 1991. But it now operates as 1,300 independent incorporated companies and some 5,000 autonomous profit centres. Most of these are split into ten-person, multi-function teams. And it has slashed its "head office" staff by 95 percent.

The giant Japanese companies have pioneered "just-in-time" production systems, buying thousands of products from small production units, delivered exactly when they are needed.

And in other fields—notably retailing—franchising and computerization make it possible for small distribution outlets to link with major international systems-suppliers, from McDonald's to computer and software manufacturers.

Some analysts[9] say that by the year 2000 50 percent of all retailing will be through franchises (mostly self-operating small units linked to giant systems) and direct-marketing networks (mainly individuals linked to world suppliers).

But for employment the big growth industries are the ones dominated by small companies. Says John Naisbitt: "It's the young entrepreneurial companies that are creating nearly all the new jobs in the United States. In the 1980s America created 22 million brand-new jobs; there were that many more people in paid employment at the end of the eighties. And 90 percent of those 22 million jobs were in companies of 50 or fewer employees. That is the new economy. That is what's creating the new wealth-creating capacity. So if you want to see what the new company

The new age of leisure

1930: life expectancy at birth
60 years—525,000 hours

Sleep:
175,000
hours

Work:
100,000
hours

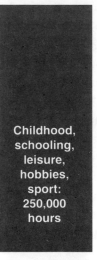

Childhood,
schooling,
leisure,
hobbies,
sport:
250,000
hours

The year 2000:

**life expectancy at birth
75 years—657,000 hours**

Sleep:
219,000
hours

Work:
50,000 hours

Childhood,
lifelong
education,
leisure,
hobbies,
sport,
travel:
388,000
hours

* Calculations based on *The Age of Unreason,* by Charles Handy,
published by Century Hutchinson, London, England.

looks like and what's going on in new companies, you look at the young companies, not the old household-word companies that are shrinking and are very slow to change."

In many of these companies, the educational need is for thinking and conceptual skills, risk-taking, experimenting, and an openness to change and opportunity. How much of that is taught at schools?

6. The new age of leisure

British educator, broadcaster and business consultant Charles Handy puts the figures neatly in *The Age of Unreason*. When he first started work in the 1940s it was standard for each person to spend 100,000 hours in his or her lifetime in paid work, although we never thought of it in those terms. But we generally worked around 47 hours a week, for 47 weeks of the year for 47 years—generally from age 16, 17 or 18. And that worked out at just over 100,000 hours. Handy predicts that by the turn of the century—at least in developed countries—we will each need to spend only around 50,000 hours of a lifetime in paid work. And he thinks we will each split that into different and convenient "chunks."

The average male now lives to at least 70 years—a total of over 600,000 hours. And if we sleep for 200,000 hours and spend only 50,000 hours in paid employment, we will have over 350,000 hours to spend on leisure, education, travel, hobbies and everything else.

Leisure, tourism and lifelong education will be among the major growth industries. Already some of the trends are obvious. Half a billion tourists travel each year. By the year 2000, the prediction is a billion.[10]

Overcrowded Japan set goals in the mid-1980s to have 10 million of its citizens taking holidays abroad by 1991.[11] The target was achieved. Over 90 percent of Japanese newlyweds honeymoon in other countries.

New Zealand's tourist targets are typical: a firm plan to increase overseas tourists from one million in 1992 to three million by the year 2000.[12]

Tourism is one of the few industries capable of creating vast numbers of new jobs. Achieving that will require big increases in foreign language training, culture-knowledge, hospitality service skills and the creation of exciting new leisure experiences.

And not the least of education's tasks will be to help prepare each country's citizens for a stimulating age of leisure.

Tomorrow's employees will be doing what robots can't do, which means that their work will call for sophisticated intelligence.

RENATE NUMMELA and GEOFFREY CAINE
Making Connections*

*Published by the Association for Supervision and Curriculum Development, 1250 N. Pitt St., Alexandria, VA 22314-1403.

7. The changing shape of work

Handy forecasts that by the turn of the century a minority of working-age adults will be employed in full-time permanent employment by traditional-style companies. Those will generally be highly-trained people, probably not starting work until their mid-twenties—with graduate and post-graduate qualifications. They are likely to provide the essential core management services.

The rest will work in three separate clusters:

Cluster one will involve project groups: people coming together for specific projects, often for short periods. This will probably be the dominant high-paying work method of the coming decade. And its requirements will provide some of education's biggest challenges.

Says Handy: "The upside-down school would make study more like work, based on real problems to be solved or real tasks to be done, in groups of mixed ages and different types of ability, all of them useful. Not only would people learn more in such a school, because they would see the point and purpose of what they were doing, but it would give them a better idea of the world they would be entering."

It is impossible to overstate the importance of the growing *project-group* nature of work, each person an open-minded self-acting specialist collaborating with an open-minded team to produce new solutions.

The second cluster will be part-time and seasonal workers: those who work two or three days a week in supermarkets, or weekends or summers in the tourist industry. It will be one of the few outlets for the unskilled or semi-skilled. And those filling these positions are already the new-poor of the working population: the low-paid check-out cashiers, the peak-time, part-time fast-food servers.

The third cluster will be those who work individually or as a family group —often doing things they love to do. Here the potential is great. Norman McCrae, longtime deputy editor of *The Economist* spelled it out around ten years ago in a book called *The 2024 Report*—looking back from the year 2024 over the previous 50 years. Since then, virtually everything he forecast has come about: the fall of the Berlin wall, the revolt in eastern Europe, the collapse of the Soviet empire. He says he was too optimistic about the number of people who would by now be working from home. "I thought it would be over 50 percent, but we now might have to wait a few years for that."[13]

But he's adamant on one of the major predictions: that a single,

The women's movement is the West's secret weapon . . . the first country or culture that truly blends men's and women's strengths will be the next world power.

ROBERT T. KIYOSAKI
If You Want To Be Rich And Happy
Don't Go To School?

* Published by The Excellerated Learning Publishing Co.,
P.O. Box 7614, San Diego, CA 82107.

efficient worldwide electronic communications system will enable competent people in any country to sell goods and services to anyone else—and to use data bases to identify those services. He believes that families will use such services to swap everything from holiday-houses to ideas.

This will also enable skilled teachers to sell their services worldwide: the choice of the world's best educators in everyone's homes. As part of the research for this book, we visited the University of California at Berkeley where 600 students regularly pack into the lectures and brain dissection demonstrations by Professor Marian Diamond. Not too far ahead, all the world will be able to receive the same lectures—at home.

Like most of the other changes coming up, this one will demand education that encourages people to be their own managers, marketers and world communicators.

8. Women in leadership

Of the 22 million new jobs created in America in the eighties, two thirds were taken by women. Naisbitt says that the increase of women in leadership positions in America is now reaching critical mass. "Forty percent of all managers are now women. Thirty-five percent of the computer scientists are women. Half the accountants are women, as are an increasing number of lawyers and doctors. If you go to medical schools or business schools, half of the freshman class are women. And women are creating new companies at twice the rate of men."[14]

Naisbitt predicts that by the year 2000, America will have up to 24 women as state governors—"the best training ground for president." He points to Houston, Texas: "what would be regarded as a good conservative 'old boy' city. Houston is the fourth largest city in the United States. It has a woman as mayor, a woman chief of police, a woman superintendent of schools, a woman superintendent of hospitals, a woman president of the Chamber of Commerce, and a woman president of the University of Houston."

The trend is growing elsewhere. Pittsburgh, the former dirty, dingy steel capital of the world, is now regularly voted as among the most liveable cities in America—sparked by a brilliant woman mayor. In New Zealand, the cities of Wellington, Christchurch and Hamilton currently have women mayors. And the former mayor of the biggest city, Auckland, has become the first female Head of State, the Governor General.

If I had to name a driving force in my life I'd plump for passion every time.

ANITA RODDICK,
founder of The Body Shop,
*Body and Soul**

* Published by Ebury Press, London, England, in
association with The Body Shop International.

There is no doubt that in many cases women provide a new perspective. Anita Roddick is an outstanding example. In 1976 she opened her first retail venture, The Body Shop, in Brighton, England. By 1991 her world-wide chain had 709 shops, sales of $238 million and profits of $26 million. By 1993, 893 shops and a new one opening every two and a half days—nearly all of them franchises.

In her book *Body and Soul,* Roddick's perspective comes through on almost every page. "The great advantage I had when I started The Body Shop was that I had never been to business school . . . If I had to name a driving force in my life, I'd plump for passion every time . . . The twin ideas of love and care touch everything we do . . . For me there are no modern-day heroes in the business world. I have met no captains of industry who made my blood surge. I have met no corporate executive who values labour and who exhibits a sense of joy, magic or theatre. In the 15 years I have been involved in the world of business it has taught me nothing. There is so much ignorance in top management and boards of directors: all the big companies seem to be led by accountants and lawyers and become moribund carbon-copy versions of each other. If there is excitement and adventure in their lives, it is contained in the figures on the profit-and-loss sheet. What an indictment!"

Just as women are changing business, so will philosophies like this change education. But how will we teach "love," "care" and "compassion?"

9. The decade of the brain

Some say the 1970s provided the decade of space exploration; the eighties, the decade of greed; and the nineties will be the decade of inner-space: the decade when we finally appreciate and come to utilize the tremendous potential of the human brain.

Tony Buzan puts it into perspective. To anyone studying education, he would seem a typically bright product of an excellent education system. He graduated in 1964 from the University of British Columbia, Canada, achieving double honours in psychology, English, mathematics and general sciences. But looking back today, he is staggered as what he *wasn't* taught.

"At school I spent thousands of hours learning about mathematics. Thousands of hours learning about language and literature. Thousands of hours about the sciences and geography and history. Then I asked myself: How many hours did I spend learning about how my memory

Your brain is like a sleeping giant.

TONY BUZAN
author of *Use Your Head*

* In author interview, Marlow, England, 1990.

works? How many hours did I spend learning about how my eyes function? How many hours in learning how to learn? How many hours in learning how my brain works? How many hours on the nature of my thought, and how it affects my body? And the answer was: none, none, none, none.

"In other words, I hadn't actually been taught how to use my head."[15] Well after leaving university, he went into a library and asked for a book on how to use his brain. "The librarian said: 'The medical section's over there.' I said: 'I don't want to take my brain out; I want to use it.' And she said: 'Oh, there are no books on that.' And I thought: No books on how to use your most valuable tool. I must write one. And I did."

Since then he has written eight books. One of them, *Use Your Head*, has sold over a million copies. It is a recommended introductory text for Britain's Open University. It and the other simple Buzan techniques are essential for anyone joining The Learning Revolution.

10. Cultural nationalism

The more we become a one-world economy, the more we develop a global lifestyle, the more we will see an equal counter-movement for what Naisbitt calls cultural nationalism.

"The more we globalize and become economically interdependent," he says, "the more we do the human thing; the more we assert our distinctiveness, the more we want to hang on to our language, the more we want to hold on to our roots and our culture.

"Even as Europe comes together economically, I think the Germans will become more German and the French more French."

Again, some implications for education are obvious. The more technology thrives, the more the striving to capture our cultural heritage, in music, dance, language, art and history. Where individual communities are inspiring new directions in education, particularly among so-called minority groups, we're seeing a flowering of cultural initiatives—and a tremendous rise in self-esteem.

11. The growing underclass

You don't have to move too far from the centre of the city in places like New York, Chicago, Philadelphia and Los Angeles to see the grim signs of a soaring underclass—predominantly associated with colour and educational failure. Statistic after statistic shows that members of this

Over one-fifth of all children (in the U.S.), and over half of all minority children, live in poverty.

THE NATIONAL COMMITTEE FOR
PREVENTION OF CHILD ABUSE *

* Quoted in *Healthy Start*, a manual produced by the
Hawaii Family Stress Centre on behalf of the State of Hawaii
Department of Health, 1991.

underclass are often trapped in a self-perpetuating cycle. Back in 1970 Alvin Toffler predicted in *Future Shock* the era of the *fractured family:* more divorces, changing lifestyles, the breakdown of the nuclear family. Most of his predictions have come true. And where the fractured family has coincided with unemployment, the ingredients have formed the recipe for social disaster.

Says African-American researcher Karen Pitman, Director of the Centre for Youth Development and Policy Research at the Academy for Educational Development: "In the U.S. about four out of every ten women become pregnant before they get out of their teens, and for black and Hispanic youth it's about seven or eight out of ten."[16]

Why? "Pregnancy tends to occur earliest in young people when they do not see a long life course; when they are about to drop out of school; when they are not doing well in school; when they don't see that their lives are going to be very different in a positive way five years, ten years down the road . . . What it seems to boil down to is this: if you think you have a future, you are more likely to delay parenthood."

Washington, D.C.'s Lisbeth Schorr, author of *Within Our Reach— breaking the cycle of disadvantage,* sums up the problems: "More and more families are getting stuck at the bottom of the heap. And that of course has a lot to do with the fact that we are in a post-industrial society, where it is almost impossible for a youngster without skills, without school skills, to get a job with which to support a family."[17]

Pitman concurs: "As we've moved from a manufacturing economy to a service economy, there has been a real erosion of wages of young men: the people who should be starting families. So we've seen a sharp decline in the earning power of young men, and in particular young black men."

Those who lack earning power, who lack self-esteem, those who get pregnant young and don't marry, those who marry young but don't have training in parenthood, and those who are poor are those most at risk of failing as parents. In turn their children have the hardest time breaking out of the poverty trap.

More reasons why, in every successful school system we have found around the world, self-esteem is a major starting point in the curriculum.

12. The active aging of the population

Just as economies are dramatically changing, so are demographics. And the most striking trend in developed countries is the active aging of

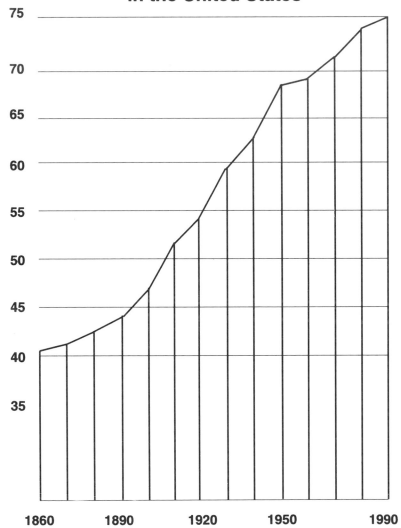

The new third age

Life expectancy at birth
in the United States

Data compiled from U.S. National Centre for Health Statistics,
updated from a graph which appeared Ken Dychtwald's book,
Age Wave, published by Bantam Books, 666 Fifth Avenue,
New York, NY 10103.

the population. A hundred years ago only 2.4 million Americans were over 65, under four in every 100. Today there are over 30 million— around one in eight. By 2050: over 67 million— almost 22 percent of the population.[18]

Since 1920 in America, average life expectancy has increased from 54 years to 75. In most developed countries, the average male reaching 60 can also expect to live to at least 75, and the average woman over 80.

At current rates of growth, by the year 2025, the world's over-60 population will have increased to one billion. Little wonder that many are calling 60-plus *"The Third Age."* Others are challenging us to abolish the word "retirement" from our vocabularies.

Says Faith Popcorn, in *The Popcorn Report:* "Sixtyfive is now the beginning of the second half of life, not the beginning of the end "

As we'll explore later, the over-60's generation represents one of the greatest untapped resources for the future of education.

13.   The new do-it-yourself boom

The industrial age also gave birth to another phenomenon: the confusion of structures with reality. Just as giant corporations arose to provide standardized mass-produced products to millions of people, so giant organizations arose to "deliver" health and education.

And so we came to confuse education with schooling; health with sickness-treatment and hospitals; law with lawyers. We came to regard education as something someone else provided for you; we believed that health was something you purchased from doctors, specialists and hospitals. Today that concept is changing rapidly. The new do-it-yourself revolution involves more than painting your home and doing your gardening. It involves taking control of your own life.

Personal computers can now provide the basis for much of what we pay experts to do: prepare wills, handle accounts, buy stocks and bones, and figure taxes.

Every sensible person now accepts that health also comes from what you do personally: what you eat and drink, and how you exercise. The high cost of "health care" is highlighting the need to do so.

But in "education" the change is slow to come. Californian educationalists Renate Nummela Caine and Geoffrey Caine explain in their book *Making Connections: teaching and the human brain:* "One function of schooling should be to prepare students for the real world.

One of the only places operating largely as it did more than 50 years ago would be the local school.

RENATE NUMMELA and GEOFFREY CAINE
*Making Connections**

* Published by the Association for Supervision and Curriculum
Development, 1250 N. Pitt St., Alexandria, VA 22134-1403.

They need to have a sense of what will be expected of them, how they will be challenged, and what they are capable of doing. The assumption is that, by and large, schooling as we know it meets those goals. The reality is that it does not. On the contrary, it fosters illusions and obscures the real challenges. In particular, it fails to deal with the impact of electronic media.

"Take a close look at American teenagers. For a moment, let time run backwards to deprive teenagers of gadgets that are in some way dependent on electricity. One by one, we remove the television, the CD players, the computer, the videodisc, the radio, tape player, record player, electronic games, airplanes, air conditioning and automatic heating, shopping in large malls, and the opportunity to acquire large numbers of possessions. How well do you think our teenagers would cope? How would their lives be different? And what about our own?

"One of the only places that would reflect scarcely any difference in the scenario we've painted—and that would be operating largely as it did more than 50 years ago—would be the local school."

Obviously that criticism does not apply to those schools that are rapidly changing, and encouraging students to take control of their own world. But does it not apply to most?

14. Cooperative enterprise

The 1990s started with the collapse of Soviet-style communism, and we hope that the new decade has also heralded the decline of gambling-casino capitalism.

Our own view is that both are rapidly being superseded by new concepts of *cooperative enterprise*.

In *The 100 Best Companies To Work For in America,* nearly every company listed has pioneered new forms of staff involvement: partnerships, stock-holding, profit-sharing, continuing education, job-sharing, flex-time, project teams and many more.

"If you want to see what the new company looks like," says John Naisbitt, "you look at the young companies, not the old household word companies that are shrinking and are often slow to change. And in the new companies you find a high degree of participative management and decision-making. You find everyone being involved in sharing the profits, including the people in the mailroom and the receptionist. You can't work for many of these new model companies unless you own

We can no longer shortchange our brains and impoverish our spirits.

JEAN HOUSTON
Educating The Possible Human*

* Reprinted in *Creating The Future,* edited by Dee Dickinson,
and published by Accelerated Learning Systems Ltd,
Aston Clinton, Bucks, England.

stock. If you don't have the money, they lend you the money interest-free to buy stock, because you have to have literal ownership. And the company's daycare is often built in right from the very beginning. They pay for any kind of education courses the people take in order for them to grow personally. And they create environments where people can nourish personal growth and educational growth."

15. The triumph of the individual

Around the world we're also seeing a revival of individual power and responsibility.

For around 200 years, national governments and then industrial giants have dominated almost every aspect of society.

Now the individual consumer is king—and queen—with the right and ability to choose from the best products and services around the world. This will also involve each one of us in taking the responsibility for choosing our own education—and in selecting the very best educational systems from around the world.

*

Obviously there are many other important trends. John Naisbitt and Patricia Aburdene in *Megatrends 2000* list five that we have not mentioned: a renaissance in the arts, the emergence of "free-market socialism," the privatization of the welfare state, the "new age of biology" and "the religious revival of the new millennium."

Grasping all the opportunities will change not only the face of government and industry, but the very nature of the world we live in, and the very nature of the educational and learning systems that will groom us for the future.

A continuing theme in this book is that we cannot achieve the educational breakthroughs we need unless we make an increasing investment in new *methods* of education and learning. *No one would think of lighting a fire today by rubbing two sticks together. Yet much of what passes for education is based on equally outdated concepts.*

Thirteen steps to a great education system

1. Rethink the role of electronic communications in education.

2. Everyone a computer expert.

3. A dramatic improvement in parent education, especially for new parents.

4. A major overhaul of early childhood health services to avoid learning difficulties.

5. Quality early childhood development programmes for all.

6. Catch-up programmes at every school.

7. Define individual learning styles—and cater for each one.

8. Learning how to learn and how to think should be on everyone's agenda.

9. Redefine what should be taught at school.

10. A four-part curriculum, with self-esteem and life-skills training as key components.

11. A three-fold purpose for most study.

12. Redefine the best teaching venues—not just at school.

13. Keep it simple and cut out the jargon.

The 13 steps needed to create the world's best education system

The race is on to design the world's best education system

Former President George Bush challenged America in 1990 to produce the world's best schools by the year 2000.

Three other major countries have specific plans to achieve the same goal. Each plan has a similar label: Japan 2000, Germany 2000, Russia 2000, America 2000. Another detailed report has urged Britain to provide "higher education" for 50 percent of its population by 2000.[1]

New Zealand, with its three million population, has introduced *Tomorrow's Schools*.[2] Its stated goal: excellence in education. The government has turned educational funding over to every community in the country—and invited each community to rethink entirely the future of schooling. Some of the results have already turned many traditional forms of school organization upside down.

But if your aim is only to create the world's best *schools,* then the answer is surprisingly simple: you need only to identify the best ideas already operating in your own country and around the world, and select the ones that fit your own community or your personal needs.

But the real revolution is not only in schooling. It is in *learning how to learn,* in learning new techniques that you can apply to any problem, any challenge.

A full *learning revolution* will thus involve much more than schooling. In fact, we challenge the idea that traditional classrooms should remain as the main medium of education. Fortunately, most of the learning breakthroughs have already been made. Many of them have come from able teachers. Many from business. Many from sports

We do know that everyone's potential goes far beyond anything ever realized.

PETER KLINE
The Everyday Genius*

*Published by Great Ocean Publishers Inc., 1823 North Lincoln Street, Arlington, VA 22207.

psychology and coaching techniques. Many from research into the human brain. Some from studies in nutrition. Others from health programmes. And many from linking communities, schools and businesses together to replan the way ahead.

In Sydney, Australia, Beverley Hills High School is now teaching students to speak reasonable French in eight weeks—a course that normally takes three years. Their teachers are convinced that the same "accelerated learning" techniques can be applied successfully to all other forms of learning. *

In America, Bell Atlantic, Kodak and other big companies are cutting training costs in half by using similar methods.

In Sweden, migrants from 114 different countries are learning to speak three languages fairly fluently before they turn five—including their parents' own language. And nearly every Swedish adult speaks excellent English—partly because 60 percent of the country's television programmes are broadcast in English, with Swedish subtitles.

In Needham, Massachusetts, John Eliot School has soared to the top of the state testing programme by using accelerated, integrative learning techniques and teaching social competency skills and thinking skills.

In New Zealand, primary school pupils up to five years behind in their reading age have caught up in as little as eight weeks, using a "tape assisted" reading programme that matches their reading age to their interest level. It's one of several simple programmes that have given New Zealand one of the world's best elementary schooling systems—the best in the world for basic literacy, according to *Newsweek*.

In California, some of the sons and daughters of America's poorest workers have been quickly selected for gifted children's classes when they enter school. This has resulted from a pilot programme which linked a 90-year-old Italian early-childhood development model with a "total immersion" language system.

As Europe has moved to integrate, thousands of adults have been learning second and third languages at home in a few weeks by following the systems pioneered over 30 years ago by Bulgarian psychologist Georgi Lozanov.

In the mid-Pacific, the tiny Cook Islands capital of Rarotonga has been able to reduce child hospital admissions by over 90 percent—by linking

As in the Introduction and Chapter one, examples cited briefly in this chapter are covered and fully sourced in later chapters.

It is possible to speed-up the learning process anywhere from five to 20 times.

CHARLES SCHMID,
American accelerated learning pioneer*

*Author interview, San Francisco, 1990.

preschool education with parent education and by regular screening for infant health problems.

Thousands of Missouri youngsters are now getting a great start in life because of that state's pioneering programme, Parents as Teachers. This programme educates new parents in their own homes and corrects any possible learning difficulties before each child reaches three years of age.

Enrol in Britain's Open University—and its TV and radio courses— and you'll be encouraged first to "learn how to learn" by using new techniques in rapid reading, memory training and information retention.

In New Zealand migrant children starting school at age five up to three years behind their peers in English-language reading skills, are catching up rapidly—thanks to a "four-minutes-a-day" programme that enlists volunteer parents as teachers. The same programme is also being used to help 11-year-olds close three-year reading gaps.

Japanese schools have little vandalism and graffiti—partly because pupils have become their own self monitoring janitors and cleaners. And several New Zealand families have solved the Asian-Pacific Rim's biggest language-training problem by inviting Japanese teenagers to live in as family members for a year. The visiting Japanese learn English, and the New Zealand infants learn Japanese.

In California, Texas and Pennsylvania, ten-year-olds who were previously up to three years behind are now doing advanced high school mathematics. They're learning from a system where the teachers hardly ever provide answers but are specially trained to ask questions.

In New Zealand, high school students in Palmerston North have increased their average grades in national examinations by up to 30 percent as a result of an "integrated studies" programme. They spend a large part of their school year on "field study trips" around rivers and mountains—and doing the same kind of case-study projects pioneered by the Harvard Business School. Several New Zealand schools now run farms, and one runs a forestry plantation and a trout hatchery.

Another New Zealand high school has scored spectacular results by splitting all subjects into six-week "modules." Each student—teenage or adult—can do a six-week introductory or advanced course in a variety of subjects. These range from accounting to computers, welding to wood-work, motor mechanics to videotape production. They also study "core subjects" and take challenging or catch-up modules where needed. And students of almost any age can be in the same class.

Children can learn almost anything if they are dancing, tasting, touching, hearing, seeing and feeling information.

JEAN HOUSTON
Educating The Possible Human*

*Reprinted in *Creating The Future,* edited by Dee Dickinson and published by Accelerated Learning Systems, Aston Clinton, Bucks, England.

In Ontario, Canada, one elementary school has introduced what is possibly North America's finest array of electronic, computerized learning tools, with spectacular results. It is used as a model interactive school-of-the-future.

In Indianapolis, Indiana, an unusual inner-city public elementary school has been proving in practice the theories first propounded by Harvard Professor Howard Gardner: that we all have at least seven different forms of intelligence: linguistic, logical-mathematical, visual-spatial, musical, kinesthetic, intrapersonal and interpersonal. One of its key principles: that every child should have his or her "multiple intelligences" stimulated every day.

A Seattle, Washington, primary school has also effectively catered to all learning styles by setting up seven different activities in each classroom, to cover each one of those seven intelligences

In Alaska, one high school has based its entire structure around the same quality management concepts that have turned Japan from a devastated country into a world power. Among many other new ideas, it has set up four pilot companies. One of them sells smoked salmon to Japan and Korea, while its students learn about Pacific-Rim marketing and the languages of the region. The students have become "co-managers" of their own education, setting and achieving their own high goals.

A primary school in Greensboro, North Carolina, has doubled its pupils' test scores in mathematics and reading after introducing a system to check each student's learning style and catering to it. This is one of dozens to record similar increases in the United States.

Kristin private school in Auckland has produced some great results by involving parents from the start of each year in an overview of what their children will be learning. In addition, each 17-year-old at Kristin acts as a personal mentor for a kindergarten pupil. Thinking-skills and Mind Mapping are taught and used extensively. And in some classes the year starts with a one-week motivational course.

The SuperCamp programme, which has now spread from America to other countries, has consistently created a marked increase in teenagers' test results after only ten days in a highly motivated, active, integrated learning environment. One key: a dual curriculum that builds self-esteem and at the same time academic knowledge and other skills.

In Germany, fully half the teenagers undergo apprenticeships, and use

Today a single hair-thin optical fibre can transmit . . . the contents of the *Encyclopedia Britannica*— all 29 volumes— from Boston to Baltimore in less than a second.

WILL HIVELY
Incredible Shrinking Optical Act*

*Article in *Discovery* magazine, February 1993.

them as the base to tackle higher education. It is one of many tmoves to return learners to work alongside those with experience.

In Venezuela and in Seattle, Washington, parent-education programmes have started with new mothers in maternity hospitals, linking closed-circuit training videotapes with one-to-one discussions.

In path-finding New Zealand, Maori (Polynesian) grandparents have sparked the world's fastest-growing preschool movement by becoming teachers in "nga kohanga reo" or language nests. Introduced first to save the native language, these "nests" are now starting to serve as models for cooperative parent education and child development. But more importantly, they are showing every country how to utilize one of our most under-used resources: the skills and abilities of people aged 60 and over.

And yet another New Zealand area has designed its own "school of the future"—turning it into a lifelong community learning resource.

Later we will spell out the specifics of some of these programmes—and show how the *principles* can be adopted by anyone wishing to improve learning skills. We summarize them here to prove the point that the world abounds with educational answers. Put all the best ones together—join them with specific community, family and student needs—and the result could be the best school system in the world.

That would be a great start. But we are convinced that much more is needed to produce the world's best *educational* and *learning* systems. To be specific, such systems would see firm action in 13 separate but interrelated areas.

1. The role of electronic communications

Sure, Japan's University of the Air already offers 234 courses to 25,000 students. One million Chinese students take courses through their TV university. Eighty thousand students are enrolled in Britain's Open University, which uses TV and radio as tools. America has its Public Broadcasting Service and *Sesame Street*. And several other countries use "educational" television in limited ways. But generally television is a one-way medium. And no country has yet placed a national programme to link all its citizens into an *interactive electronics instant communications network*. France probably comes closest.

Just think for a moment about the phenomenon of talkback radio—and the limited technology on which it is based. Over 100 years have passed since Alexander Graham Bell invented the telephone. Around 90

Truly interactive video and TV will be available in the home and office in three to five years— and I've always guessed too conservatively.

DR. ARZNOI PENZIAS,
Nobel Prize-winner
and Vice President, Research, at
Bell Research Laboratory, New Jersey*

*Speaking on New Zealand's TV3 television network, direct from New Jersey, U.S.A., on the opening of the new Pac-Rim-East fibre optic link, June 17, 1993. The picture was carried on a bandwidth equivalent to only two telephone lines.

have gone by since Marconi sent the first radio message across the Atlantic. Slightly more since J. J. Thompson, professor of physics at England's Cambridge University, ushered in the electronic era. By discovering that the atom is not the smallest particle, Thompson set off a chain reaction. By discovering that tiny particles whirl at fantastic speed around the nucleus of the atom, Thompson was to bring about a revolution in communications. By discovering further that electrons, when pushed, can hop from atom to atom even faster, Thompson and those who built on his work were to bring us transistorized radio, television, atom bombs, computers, space travel, laser beams, satellite communications and everything that has become known as the electronic revolution.

Yet how much of this has been linked interactively? In the main, only talkback radio. And that links only two of the oldest bits of instant technology. What would happen if we linked all the new tools?

Electronics now provides the tools to communicate instantly with almost any person on earth. The first nation to fully realize that power and link it with new learning techniques could lead the world in education.

But most governments could not even say which Minister would be responsible for such an idea. Ministers of Education generally concentrate on schooling, and not on interactive electronics; Ministers of Health on hospitals—and not on using TV for health education.

New Zealand would be typical. It is a world pioneer in "distance" education—and for years has used radio to connect its "Correspondence School" to isolated farm-houses. For over a quarter of a century it has also been a world leader in electronic banking transfers; checks drawn on any trading bank can be cleared overnight through a centralized electronic system. Around 20 years ago, its government set up four different inquiries into the future of television, including educational TV. The practical result? Nothing. And when the government did set up its wide-ranging school reforms-review in the mid 1980s, the otherwise-excellent result concentrated mainly on school management.[3]

Fortunately in virtually every developed country individual schools are leading in the drive to link computers with studies. The big computer, electronic and photographic companies are also showing the way. The giant telecommunications companies are setting up the networks that can later be used as the basis for many forms of interactive learning.

School will either change very rapidly or it will collapse.

SEYMOUR PAPERT
Obsolete Skill Set: The 3 R's*

*Article in *Wired* magazine, May-June, 1993.

One big need right now is to use the existing and growing volume of interactive technology to help solve some of our major educational problems. Nintendo-type interactive video games are only the forerunners to big breakthroughs in making learning fun through electronics.

Says Gil Simpson, head of New Zealand's main computer software firm, the Aoraki Corporation: "It's a crying shame to see a 15-year-old dropout spending hours a day at a video games parlour, very enthusiastic about what he is doing, and not making the connection that he has started to learn the basics of computer programming. Not knowing that he can go down to a Polytechnic Institute and enter an introduction-to-computers course that could spark a new career."[4]

Not to make full use of instant electronic communications in education would be like our ancestors failing to use the alphabet, refusing to produce typeset books or rubbing sticks together to start a fire.

2. Everyone computer-smart

We do not place much emphasis on the need to learn too many specific trade skills too early in life. But computers are to the 21st century what telephones have been to the 20th. Everyone should become computer-smart. And computers are easy to master if you learn at an early age.

So don't wait for government action. Don't wait for the voice-activated word processors of tomorrow. Start with a course in touch-typing on a word processor. Try to integrate computer work with everything else you're learning, and build on your knowledge from there.

3. Dramatic improvement needed in parent-education

Most brain researchers are convinced that 50 percent of a person's ability to learn is developed in the first four years of life.[5] Not 50 percent of one's knowledge, nor 50 percent of one's wisdom. But in those first four years the infant brain makes around 50 percent of the *brain-cell connections*—the pathways on which all future learning will be based.

If this is true, then home, not school, is the most important educational institution in the land. And parents, not teachers, are the main first educators. Yet even in many advanced countries, fewer than 50 percent of mothers-to-be—and a much lower percentage of fathers—attend any form of prebirth classes. And even those are often restricted to lessons about birth itself. There is an almost total lack of education for parenthood: no training in such areas as the diet necessary for brain growth, or

Every child has, at birth, a greater potential intelligence than Leonardo Da Vinci ever used.

GLENN DOMAN
author of *Teach Your Baby To Read**

*Author interview at The Institutes for the Achievement of
Human Potential, 8801 Stenton Avenue, Philadelphia,
PA 19118, December, 1992.

the best types of stimulation required by young learners.

If the present authors had to pick any priority for targeted education, and especially for educational TV, it would be parent education.

4. Early childhood health service priorities

If the first few years are vital for *learning,* the nine months before birth and the first five years of life are probably the most important for *health.* Good diet and sound nutrition are essential for learning, and so are regular health check-ups.

For example, even in an advanced society such as New Zealand, up to 20 percent of infants suffer from ear infection.[6] If undetected and untreated, it can lead to "glue ear"—where a main hearing "tube" becomes blocked with a sticky composition that looks like glue. If that happens in both ears, a child can hardly hear. And if an infant can't hear in the years that are vital for language development—from birth to four years—he can be handicapped for life.

British research scientist Professor Michael Crawford has spent more than ten years researching the impact of diet on pregnant women and their babies. He's horrified at the overwhelming ignorance about the impact of nutrition on the developing brain, especially before an infant is born.

"Every farmer and every gardener knows perfectly well," he says, "that if he's going to have a good crop of potatoes, or if he wants to grow great roses, he's not going to run out and put some fertilizer on them the day before he wants to dig or pick them. He knows he's got to prepare the roots, almost a year before, to get beautiful roses. It's common knowledge. Everyone understands this as far as cabbages and roses are concerned. But mostly we don't even think about it when it comes to preparing to have a baby."[7]

One university study also shows that 22 percent of new mothers are "at risk"—and nine percent could present a big physical danger to their babies unless they receive extra support and education.[8] Generally they don't get it. And the self-perpetuating cycle of disadvantage continues. When they do get practical help, tied in with parent education, the change in attitudes is dramatic. A few million dollars in prevention saves billions later—in the cost of prisons and psychiatric care.

5. Early childhood development programmes

If 50 percent of the ability to learn is developed in the first four years

Second chance must not mean second best.

NEW ZEALAND MINISTRY OF EDUCATION
Education for the 21st Century*

*A discussion document for public debate,
published by Learning Media, June, 1993.

of life and another 30 percent by age eight, then early childhood development programmes should also be top priority. Most countries reverse this.

Even in New Zealand, for instance, where the level of preschool education is high, each year the government spends $5758 from taxation for every university student, $2481 for each secondary school student, $1694 for each primary school pupil, but only $783 for each three- and four-year-old at kindergarten.[9]

6. You can catch up at any stage

Good catch-up programmes abound. Many, as we will see, are at elementary or primary school. But even at the start of high school it is not too late for most. And many of the new learning techniques can also be used effectively for adult learning and teaching.

7. Catering to every individual learning style

We all know instinctively that some of us learn better one way, some another. Some love to read by themselves. Others can learn best in groups. Some love to study while sitting in chairs, others lounging on a bed or a floor.

Each of us has a preferred learning style and a preferred working style. Some of us are mainly visual learners: we like to see pictures or diagrams. Others are auditory: we like to listen. Others are haptic learners: we learn best by using our sense of touch (tactile learners) or by moving our bodies (kinesthetic learners). Some are print-oriented: we learn easily by reading books. Others are "group interactive": we learn best when interacting with others.

Our traditional secondary school has done a great job in appealing to two of our seven "intelligence centres": linguistic intelligence (the ability to speak, read and write) and logical-mathematical intelligence (the type we use in logic, maths and science). Most of our examination systems are based on testing those limited academic intelligences.

But many of our current high school dropouts do not learn best by those methods. And the high school classroom techniques used to teach so-called academic learners are NOT the best methods to lift the standards of those who make up our high dropout rate.

And sure, it is probably impossible to cater to every individual learning style all the time. But it is possible to design school curricula

We learn ten percent of what we read, 15 percent of what we hear, but 80 per cent of what we experience.

GLOBAL VILLAGE IN ACTION*

*Article in *On The Beam,* winter 1992 edition, published by New Horizons for Learning.

so that all learners are tested to determine their preferred learning style—
and for all the main styles to be catered to at school.

Equally important, it is now simple and inexpensive to provide printouts of preferred learning and work styles for everyone to plan his or her
own education and future working career.

8. Learning how to learn and learning how to think

This means learning how your brain works, how your memory works,
how you can store information, retrieve it, link it to other concepts and
seek out new knowledge whenever you need it—instantly.

Some of these specific techniques are named "accelerated learning,"
"super learning," "suggestopedia," "whole-brain learning" and "integrative learning." But it's unfortunate that such labels imply complexity.
The best learning systems are simple. Better still, they are fun. Generally
they have this in common: they encourage you to use all your "intelligences" and senses to learn much faster: through music, rhythm, rhyme,
pictures, feelings, emotions and action. Overwhelmingly the best learning methods are similar to those we use as infants.

Thinking skills are also easily learned, and proven methods include
Edward de Bono's *Lateral Thinking,* Alex Osborn's *Brainstorming,*
Donald Treffinger's *Creative Problem Solving,* Robert Fritz's *Technol-
ogy For Creating,* Stanley Pogrow's *HOTS (Higher Order Thinking
Skills)* and Calvin Taylor's *Talents Unlimited.* Again, the best techniques
are simple and fun.

9. Just what should be taught at school?

The co-authors believe *how* we learn is more important than *what* is
learned. Learn to study five times faster, better and easier and you can
apply the principles to any subject. But everyone needs a common core
of knowledge, and maybe that core is changing.

Dr. Willard Daggett, Director of America's International Centre for
Leadership and Education, is well placed to compare countries. He has
served on school reform commissions in Russia, Germany and Japan—
and is well versed in the American system.

He says, "The world our kids are going to live in is changing four times
faster than our schools."[10] And he says American schools cannot meet
those changing needs, for two reasons: "One, they don't have the
capacity. And two: much of what we teach in American schools is

The world our kids are going to live in is changing four times faster than our schools.

DR. WILLARD DAGGETT
Director of International Centre for
Leadership and Education*

*Address to Colorado school administrators, 1992.

irrelevant. It relates to nothing but schools. We don't have an education system with the relevancy to enable us to compete against the most advanced countries of Europe and Asia. We have been consumed by institutional issues and not by the needs of our children."

He challenges all of us to think from a child's point of view. "I'd like my children to be lifelong learners," he says. "Wouldn't you? Well, what math and science do we use in lifelong learning? What English language? If we can't answer that question, then how can we truly say we are preparing our children for lifelong learning."

Daggett says the last wave of school reform in America came after the end of the second world war. "Our parents wanted a better future for their children, and saw higher education as the key. So the pressure was put on schools to prepare youngsters for college. That was the demand that drove school reform. But we have looked to what the colleges want, not on the changing needs of the real world."

Daggett quotes a Carnegie Foundation international survey that tested people's ability to use simple technology. "The results were the same in every state of America. The people who could best follow an instructional manual and programme a videotape unit to record TV programmes in advance: ten-to-12-year-olds. They were better than 18-year-olds except for one group: 18 year-olds who had dropped out of school. Dropouts were better than high school graduates. High school graduates were better than college graduates.

"And one group was even worse than college graduates: those holding masters degrees!"

On international math scores, says Daggett, three Asian nations and three European nations share the top six places. America is last of all developed countries. "Yet Carnegie found in those six top nations, the higher your education, the more likely you are to be able to read the manual and programme your VCR. Why? Because they teach it, and we don't." Daggett says most other advanced nations are adding four years of technical reading and writing to their school curricula. He asks another key question: "In the world of work, which of these skills do you use the most: reading, writing, or speaking and listening? Speaking and listening. Which do we teach the least? Speaking and listening." He says many European and Asian schools spend an hour a day teaching listening and speaking.

Daggett says a third of all new jobs in the United States are for

What we know today will be obsolete tomorrow. If we stop learning we stagnate.

DOROTHY D. BILLINGTON
*Adults Who Learn and Grow**

*Article in *New Horizons for Learning*, Spring 1993.

technicians or technical repairers. The most common: auto technicians. "What skills do they require? Not simply mechanical. Today's auto motors run from computers, microprocessors and electronic circuits. In 1990 General Motors' manual was 476,000 pages long—on a computer. To be able to define problems that you can't see, you have to be able to communicate with the computer. You have to be able to frame the language that will get the computer to tell you precisely what needs fixing. Do you learn that language through a curriculum that is literature-based?

"Little wonder that over 80 percent of U.S. auto dealers are hiring foreign-born technicians because they have been trained in those skills. They have been trained in applied physics. Seventeen other nations have now added two years of applied physics to their secondary school curriculum. Four nations have added three years—and Germany and Japan have added five years. Most other advanced nations are adding four years of technical reading and writing."

Daggett certainly does not argue that schools should stop teaching literature. So how do you add in those extra subjects? One answer, he says, is to extend the time spent each year at school.

"In America," says Daggett, "the traditional school year still has 180 days, five and a half hours a day. Japan up until recently has had 243 days and eight and a half hours a day—and now it has moved to 257 days a year and nine and a half hours a day. Why? Because they want to keep up with South Korea, which has moved to 270 days a year, ten hours a day. By 1996, all the nations in Europe will have moved to a 240-day school year."

More days? More hours? Or *more effective learning techniques?* Or both? And for what purpose? Says Daggett: *"We should get all our seventh-graders to encourage their teachers to ask the same question every day: 'Where will you ever use what I am teaching you today?'"*

10. Learning on four levels

Whatever subject or subjects a youngster learns, the real test of tomorrow's education system will come from its ability to excite them with the utter joy of learning. That means encouraging every student to build the self-esteem that is vital for everyone to grow and develop.

In every successful system we have studied around the world, self-esteem ranks in importance ahead of course-content.

Equally important for those who would otherwise drop out is the need

Children Learn What They Live

If a child lives with criticism, he learns to condemn.

If a child lives with hostility, he learns to fight.

If a child lives with ridicule, he learns to be shy.

If a child lives with shame, he learns to feel guilty.

If a child lives with tolerance, he learns to be patient.

If a child lives with encouragement, he learns confidence.

If a child lives with praise, he learns to appreciate.

If a child lives with fairness, he learns justice.

If a child lives with security, he learns to have faith.

If a child lives with approval, he learns to like himself.

If a child lives with acceptance and friendship,

  he learns to find love in the world.

Dorothy Law Nolte

to learn the skills of coping with life. That means a four-pronged curriculum is needed—one that stresses:

* Self-esteem;
* Lifeskills training;
* Learning-how-to-learn;
* As well as building specific basic academic, physical and artistic abilities.

Fortunately, all aspects can be blended to reinforce each other.

11. A three-fold purpose for study

Studying should generally also have a three-fold purpose:

1. To learn skills and knowledge about the specific subjects—and how you can do that faster, better, easier.

2. To develop general conceptual skills—how you can learn to apply the same or related concepts in other areas. And:

3. To develop personal skills and attitudes that can also easily be used in everything you do.

12. Just where should we teach?

In the history of the world, classroom schooling is very new. And the time has come to ask if it is the best and if it should remain the main learning forum.

We see schools being changed into community resource centres for lifelong learning—and probably health and parent education centres as well. To use them for under 200 days a year for only a few hours a day is a tremendous waste of valuable assets, and amounts to less than 15 percent of total time. And to use them largely for one-sided lectures is largely to waste even that 15 percent. In later chapters we will explore the likely mix of future "schools." But for now it's vital to restress that most of us learn best by doing and participating through all our senses. It's also amazing what emerges when entire communities rethink their learning needs and start to redesign their schools around those needs.

For almost two years the Lincoln Unified School District in Stockton, California, has done just that.[11] School administrators, parents, students, staff and consultants have all been involved. And the district's 13 school sites are now being redesigned as thematic learning centres, each linking an integrated-studies curriculum with core subjects. A pilot project at

Perhaps schools won't look like schools. Perhaps we will be using the total community as a learning environment.

ANNE TAYLOR
*Creating The Future**

*Edited by Dee Dickinson and published by Accelerated Learning
Systems, Aston Clinton, Bucks, England.

The Pacific School has included six thematic programmes. And the school is developing a 40-acre environmental learning centre.

New Orleans architect Steven Bingler has been one of the consultants. And he's thrilled at the scope. "So far," he reports, "recommendations include a working farm—possibly for endangered species; organic and hydroponic gardens; an environmental research facility; and a boat moored on an adjacent canal to ferry students on study missions into the thousand miles of waterways in the San Joaquin river delta region."

Bingler also stresses the practical life-skills involved. "The primary ingredient of the new Lincoln Plan is its focus on students. As the system develops, each student will be given the opportunity to develop his or her own personal educational plan (PEP) in consultation with an adult mentor and an educational professional. As the twelve other sites expand to include more thematic opportunities, like health and fitness, performing arts or business, students will have even more choices in their learning path. And because each site will be connected to a network of community resources, the learning process will also be integrated with everyday commerce and community affairs."

Kimi Ora Community School in New Zealand shows a similar approach. The whole community has designed it—with administrators, architects and staff. Now the entire complex pulsates with life from 8 a.m. to 10 p.m., with youngsters from two to 82 years old attending.[12]

Where other communities might revolve around shopping or business centres, this community revolves around its school. It's a preschool centre, a health centre, a multi-cultural centre, a retraining centre and much more. It operates parenting courses, computer classes and a gymnasium. The health centre includes a public health nurse, physiotherapist, dental nurse, naturopath and doctors' rooms. And from preschool onwards Kimi Ora Community School offers a choice of learning in English, Maori or bilingual classes.

Similar multi-faceted educational resource centres are growing wherever communities are being challenged to reinvent their future—in an era where almost anything is possible.

13. Keep it simple and cut out the jargon

We are great admirers of top teachers. Many of the best ideas we've seen have come from teachers, educators and educational researchers.

But many leaders in higher education share one major failing: they

To write simply, check your Fog Index*

To write clearly and well, generally use short words and short sentences.

To check your own clarity in writing:

1   Count how many words you use in an average sentence.

2   To do that, check any 100 words you have written, in a report or letter.

3   Divide that 100 by the number of sentences used.

4   Then count how many "complex" words you have used for every 100 words you have written (a "complex" word is one with three syllables or more—not counting words with capital letters).

5   Add the two totals together, and then take four-tenths of the total. That is your Fog Index.

For example: if you average 20 words to a sentence, and ten complex words in every 100 words, your total is 30. Four-tenths of this is 12. That is your Fog Index.

Reader's Digest has a Fog Index of between 8 and 9. *Time* magazine is about 11. If you're higher than 13 you're hard to read. Churchill's quote opposite has a Fog Index of 3.2.

*Joseph Peart and Jim R. McNamara, in *The New Zealand Handbook of Public Relations,* published by Mills Publications, Lower Hutt, New Zealand (1987), attribute the invention of the Fog Index to Robert Gunning, an American businessman.

write in university jargon. We are convinced that the greatest truths are the simple truths. The greatest lessons are easy to understand. But when a simple truth is clothed in verbiage, that often stops it from breaking through to those who need it most.

Most good learning methods are common sense. Every infant learns by many of these methods. Yet when parents or students start reading the jargon they "switch off." They start doubting their own common sense, because "the experts" make it complicated.

In researching this book, we have re-read hundreds of others and hundreds more speeches and articles. Here are just some of the words used on one page of one article: pedagogical dimensions, epistemology, pedagogical philosophy, constructivism, cognitive, instructional sequencing, experiential value, equalitarian facilitator, instructivists.*

Sure, we know that every discipline has its jargon. But every first-year journalist learns to read "lacerations, contusions and abrasions" from the hospital records and record it as "cuts, bruises and scratches." Every junior advertising copywriter grows up with KISS implanted on her brain: Keep It Simple, Stupid. Nearly every professional writer is taught the Fog Index—to make his writing easy to read. To write using short words, terse sentences.

Every good public speaker grows up with former British Prime Minister Winston Churchill as a model. He "hurled words into battle" to rally an entire nation during the second world war. And the words were simple and direct: "We shall go on to the end. We shall fight in France. We shall fight in the seas and oceans. We shall fight on the beaches, in the fields, in the streets and in the hills. We shall never surrender."

So we make a sincere plea to those who have made or researched the changes that are needed in learning: please remember Churchill, and hurl your words into action—simply, crisply—to rally a world for change.

Fortunately, some of the most succinct scientific communicators are probing the most important learning weapon of all: the human brain.

We are not criticizing the research. Often it is brilliant. But we are criticizing the failure to communicate that research to the people who need it. Here is one example from a recent New Zealand publication: "Early writers called these abilities learning how to learn. More contemporary writers call them metacognitive or decontextualized skills."[13] You are reading two contemporary writers who, when we mean learning how to learn, will write "learning how to learn."

Your magic brain:

■ Has a trillion brain-cells, including:
- 100 billion active nerve-cells.
- 900 billion other cells that "glue," nourish and insulate the active cells.

■ Can grow up to 20,000 "branches" on every one of those 100 billion nerve-cells.

■ Has three distinct brains in one:
- An instinctive brain.
- An emotional brain.
- And your amazing cortex.

■ Has two sides that work in harmony:
- Your left "academic" brain.
- Your right "creative" brain.

■ Runs a "telephone exchange" that shuttles millions of messages a second between the left and right sides.

■ Has seven different "intelligence centres."

■ Operates on at least four separate wavelengths.

■ Controls a transmission system that flashes chemical-electrical messages instantly to every part of your body.

■ And it holds the key to your own personal learning revolution.

You're the owner of the world's most powerful computer

It's not much bigger than a large grapefruit.

It's much smaller than the heart of a lettuce. You could hold it easily in one hand. It generally weighs under 1,500 grams (three pounds). Yet it's thousands of times more powerful than the world's most powerful computer. And it's all yours. Your magic brain.

Nearly everything we know about it we've learned in only the last 25 years. Amazingly, most of that information is not taught at school. Yet it's the knowledge that can change your life, the way you learn, the way you think, the way you solve problems, the way you create.

British author, psychologist and educator Tony Buzan puts it succinctly: "Your brain is like a sleeping giant." Among other things, he's psychology coach for the British Olympic rowing team. Talk to him in his office overlooking Britain's River Thames at Marlow, near Henley, and you catch the enthusiasm:

"Your brain is made of a trillion brain-cells. Each brain-cell is like the most phenomenally complex little octopus. It has a centre, it has many branches, and each branch has many connection points. And each one of those billions of brain-cells is many times more powerful and sophisticated than most of the computers around the planet today. Each one of these brain-cells connects, embraces—cuddles, in a sense—hundreds of thousands to tens of thousands of others. And they shuttle information back and forward. It's been called an enchanted loom, the most astoundingly complex, beautiful thing in existence. And each person has one."[1]

Of those trillion brain-cells, probably 100 billion are active neurons or nerve-cells. Each one is capable of making up to 20,000 different

Your brain has 100 billion active cells, each with up to 20,000 connections

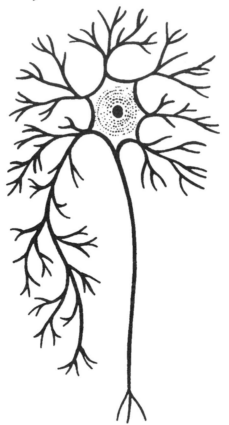

Your brain has about100 billion active neurons or nerve-cells.
Each one grows branches like a tree, to store information:
up to 20,000 branch-like *dendrites* with each cell.
Each neuron is like a powerful computer.
And each connects to other cells by sending
electrical-chemical messages along a long axon.

Illustration from *Make The Most Of Your Mind,* by Tony Buzan, published by Pan, London, and reprinted here with permission from Tony Buzan.

connections with other cells.   Stanford University Professor Robert Ornstein says, in *The Amazing Brain,* that the possible number of connections is probably bigger than the number of atoms in the universe.

Doubt it? Then consider what happens if you took only ten everyday items—like the first ten things you did this morning—and combined them in every possible sequence. The result would be 3,628,800 different combinations. Take 11 items, connect them, and the number of possible combinations is 39,916,800! So now try combining 100 billion cells in every possible way—when each one can make up to 20,000 different connections—and you get some idea of the creative capacity of your own brain.

And how do you make the most of its great ability? Says Buzan: "You make the most of your mind by first studying what it is. The first thing you do is find out what it's made of. Then how it works. How does the memory work? How does concentration work? How does the creative thinking process work? So you literally start to examine and explore yourself." Start that exploration and you come up with some surprises:

Your three brains in one

First, you've got three distinct brains in one—on three different levels, from top to brain-stem.

Next, your brain has two sides. Each controls different functions and processes information in different ways. *These sides are linked by an amazing electronic and chemical relay-system that itself has 300 million operating nerve-cells.* This shuttles information around instantly like a multi-national automatic telephone exchange.

We also now believe that each of us has at least seven different "intelligence centres" in the brain. But very few of us develop more than a small part of that latent ability.

Your brain also works on at least four different electrical wavelengths—like four different radio or television channels.

The most advanced part of your brain has six distinct layers.

You also have an active conscious brain and a subconscious brain. And much of the knowledge you take in is learned subconsciously.[2]

At the great risk of over-simplifying:

Your lower brain—or brain-stem—controls many of your instincts, such as breathing.

A simplified overview of how your brain works

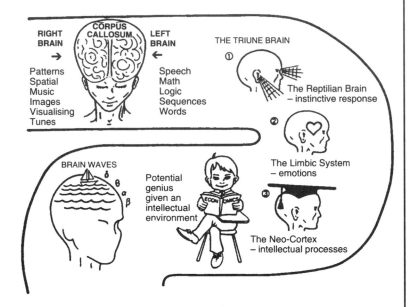

From top left in sequence:

(a) The left and right-hand sides of your brain process information in different ways, but they are linked by the 300 million nerve cells of your corpus callosum.

(b) Of your "three brains in one," the first is your "reptilian brain," which controls many of your instinctive responses.

(c) Your limbic system or "old mammalian brain" is the emotional centre of your brain.

(d) Your neo-cortex makes you uniquely human.

(e) The more you stimulate the brain, the more its connections grow.

(d) Your brain works on four different wavelengths. Tuning-in to the "correct band" can help you to learn much faster.

Illustrations from *Accelerated Learning,* by Colin Rose, published by Accelerated Learning Systems, Aston Clinton, Bucks, England, and reprinted here with permission.

The central part of your brain controls your emotions. Scientists call it the *limbic* system—from the Latin word *limbus* or "collar"—because it wraps around the brain-stem like a collar.

Your upper brain enables you to think, talk, reason and create. Scientists call it the *cortex*—the Latin word for "bark."

You use many different parts of the brain together to store, remember and retrieve information.

Each one of these factors has an important bearing on how you use your inbuilt personal computer.

It is not the role of this book to indulge in religious debate. But the awesome power of your brain may well provide common ground for creationists and evolutionists. Those with deeply-held fundamental religious beliefs could well argue that the complexity of the human brain and mind, with the soul, represents a pinnacle of creation. All other creatures have brains that are puny by comparison.

Many scientists, on the other hand, say that humans are the end result of over four billion years of evolution.[3] They say that's how long the earth has existed. In this theory, the first primitive forms of life did not emerge for the first billion years.

Scientists now believe it wasn't until 500 million years ago that creatures started to develop brains, along with backbones and the nervous systems that link them. Even today, semi-primitive creatures like oysters or lobsters—without backbones—have very simple nervous systems, with only a few thousand nerve-cells.[4] But in creatures with backbones the nervous-brain system is much more complex. Even a rat's brain has millions of cells: highly developed, incidentally, where they are linked to his whiskers.

If you dissected your brain, at the base of your skull you would find a segment almost identical to that found in a lizard, a crocodile or a bird. Because of this, some scientists have dubbed it the "reptilian"[5] brain. This part of the brain controls very simple but important functions: like our breathing, heart rate and many basic instincts. Turn a light on and any insect nearby will stop dead still. The bright light will send an instant signal to its tiny reptilian brain. Drive toward a bird sitting on the road and it will fly off an instant before you hit it; its reptilian brain has an inbuilt programme to flee. Think of that next time you go to swat a fly—and it escapes a split second before the swat lands.

Above your brain-stem is your second-tier brain. This limbic system

Three brains in one

At bottom: Your brain-stem, near the top of your neck, is also called the "reptilian" brain—because it is similar to the brains of cool-blooded reptiles. It controls many of your body's instinctive functions, such as breathing.

In the centre: Your "old mammalian" brain— which is similar to the brains of other warm-blooded mammals. It controls your emotions, your sexuality—and has a key role to play in your memory.

At top: Your "cortex" (bark), which you use for thinking, talking, seeing, hearing and creating.

The illustration is from *Your Child's Growing Mind,* by Jane M. Healy, published by Doubleday, 666 Fifth Avenue, New York, NY 10103, and reprinted here with permission.

is also often called the "old mammalian" brain—because it is similar to a major part of the brains of other mammals.

Scientists say it started developing with the first warm-blooded mammals—or breast-feeding animals—between 200 and 300 million years ago. They say mammals still kept their "reptilian" brain, but added to it.

It's the part of the brain that is programmed to instruct a baby—or a lamb or pup—instinctively to suckle its mother almost instantly after birth. And, as we'll find out later, it's significant that the emotional and sexual centre of your brain is very closely connected with parts of the brain that deal with memory storage. You can remember things better when you are emotionally involved—like your first love affair.

Sitting on top of the limbic system is the two-sided cerebrum and its cortex which caps everything else like a crumpled blanket. This cortex is only about 30 millimetres thick (about an eighth of an inch). But it has six layers, each with different functions. It is the part of our brain that makes humans a unique species. And, depending on your beliefs, it is one of the phenomenal achievements of either creation or evolution.

Your neurons, dendrites, glial cells and insulating system

Each of our 100 billion active neurons is a virtual computer in itself. Each is capable of sprouting between 2,000 and 20,000 branches, called dendrites—very much like the branches of a tree. Each of these stores information, and receives input from other cells.

Each neuron in turn transmits its own messages around the brain, and around the body, along major pathways known as axons. Each axon in turn is covered with a "myelin" sheath. This is much like insulation around electric wires. The better the sheathing or insulation, the faster messages will speed along the "wires": up to 100 meters a second.

All the dendrites, in turn, are surrounded by up to 900 billion "glial" cells which "glue" the parts of the brain together.

And all these parts link to make up the most unique natural computer the world has ever known.

Learn how to use all parts of your amazing brain—and the results could astound you. "For a start," says Tony Buzan, "if you really set your mind to it you could easily read four books a day. And not just read them, but remember what you've read. Now four books a day is what the average student reads in a year—or is supposed to read in a year.

Your seven intelligence centres, and maybe an eighth

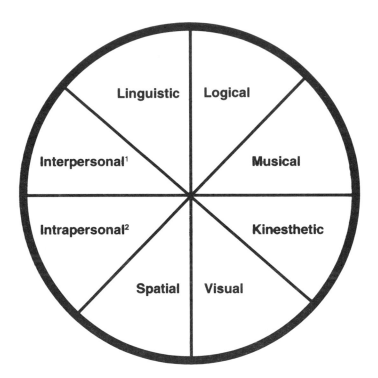

These are the seven different "intelligences" identified by Professor Howard Gardner of Harvard University, except that he brackets "spacial" and "visual" intelligence. Some others believe these are two separate but closely related functions.

Note:
1. Interpersonal intelligence is the ability to relate with others.
2. Intrapersonal intelligence is the introspective ability to know one's self.

Professor Gardner's theory is outlined fully in his book *Frames of Mind* and expanded for school use in *The Unschooled Mind,* both published by Basic Books, a division of HarperCollins, New York.

"Now imagine for a moment that four members of the one family start to study the same subject—and they each read four books on it in a day. Then they each put the main information together on a colorful "Mind Map"* so the main points are easy to remember. They swap Mind Maps—and at the end of the day each of those four people could have absorbed the information from 16 different books: as many as the average student would read in four years."

And how hard is it to do that? Buzan again: "Not hard at all—if you learn how the brain works. It really is a fantastic tool. Let's take the human eye—only one small part of the brain. Like the brain itself, the eye is much more powerful than we've ever realized. We now know that each eye contains 130 million light receivers which can take in trillions of photons per second. It's like: bang! I see a new mountain scene, and I can take it in, in its entirety, in a second. So a single page in an ordinary old book is nothing for the eye-brain combination. It's just that we haven't been taught how to use those same visual skills for reading."

Your seven different "intelligence centres"

Ask Harvard psychologist Professor Howard Gardner, and he'll tell you that visual ability is only one of your many "intelligences."[6] He's spent years analysing the human brain and its impact on education. And his conclusions are simple but highly important.

Gardner says we each have at least seven different types of intelligence. Two of them are very highly valued in traditional education.

He calls the first one linguistic intelligence: our ability to read, write and communicate with words. Obviously this ability is very highly developed in authors, poets and orators.

The second is logical or mathematical intelligence: our ability to reason and calculate. This is most developed in scientists, mathematicians, lawyers, judges.

Traditionally, most so-called intelligence tests have focused on these two talents. And much schooling around the world concentrates on those two abilities. But Gardner says this has given us a warped and limited view of our learning potential. He lists the other five distinct intelligences as:

Musical intelligence: obviously highly developed in composers, conductors and top musicians;

* *Mind Map is a trademark registered by Tony Buzan.*

The two sides to your brain

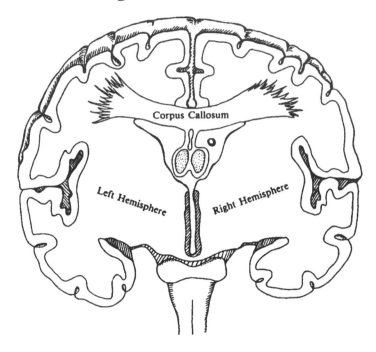

Corpus Callosum

Left Hemisphere   Right Hemisphere

The left side emphasizes	The right side emphasizes
Language	Rhyme
Logic	Rhythm
Numbers	Music
Mathematics	Pictures
Sequence	Imagination
Words	Patterns

The corpus callosum links both.

Illustration from *Unicorns Are Real,* by Barbara Meister-Vitale, published by Jalmar Press, 2675 Skypark Drive, Torrance, CA 90505, and reprinted here with permission.

Spatial or visual intelligence: the kind of ability used by architects, sculptors, painters, navigators and pilots;

Kinesthetic intelligence or physical intelligence: very highly developed in athletes, dancers, gymnasts and perhaps surgeons;

Interpersonal intelligence: the ability to relate to others—the kind of ability that seems natural with salesmen, motivators, negotiators.

And *intrapersonal intelligence* or introspective intelligence: the ability of insight, to know oneself—the kind of ability that gives some people great intuition. The kind of ability that lets you tap into the tremendous bank of information stored in your subconscious mind.

But these are not merely arbitrary functions that Professor Gardner has invented for a Ph. D. thesis. He says brain surgery and research have shown that each of these "intelligences" or abilities is located in a distinct part of your brain. Severely damage that part and you're in danger of losing that particular aspect of intelligence. That's what happens if you have a stroke. In layman's terms a stroke is caused by a blood clot that blocks the oxygen supply to the brain, causing damage. And depending on which part is damaged, so it will affect the body-function controlled by that part of the brain: speech or the movement on one side of the body.

The two sides of your brain

Look at an electronic scan of your brain and you'll see how different parts of it process different types of information. We take in that information through our five major senses: by what we see, hear, touch, smell and taste.

In general terms the left-hand side of your brain plays a major part in processing language, logic, mathematics and sequence—the so-called academic parts of learning.

The right-hand side of the brain deals with rhythm, rhyme, music, pictures and day-dreaming—the so-called creative activities.

The split is not, however, as simple as that. Both sides of the brain are linked by the corpus callosum, the highly complex switching system with its 300 million active neurons. It is constantly balancing the incoming messages, and linking together the abstract, holistic picture with the concrete, logical messages.

British businessman and researcher Colin Rose, author of *Accelerated Learning* and developer of several rapid-learning foreign language

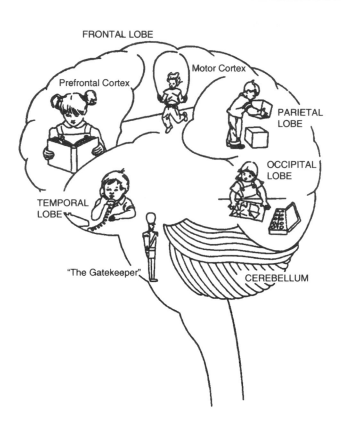

The parts of the brain that deal with different functions:

THE PREFRONTAL CORTEX: which deals with thinking.

THE TEMPORAL LOBE: the speech centre of the brain.

THE MOTOR CORTEX: which controls activity.

THE PARIETAL LOBE: which handles your spacial ability.

THE OCCIPITAL LOBE: your visual centre.

THE CEREBELLUM (or little brain), which plays a key part in adjusting posture and balance. It also acts like an "automatic pilot" when we perform learned functions like riding a bicycle or using a typewriter.

THE "GATEKEEPER" is a simple name for the "Reticular Formation" which acts like a control-centre for the brain, switching messages to the right destination.

Illustration from *Your Child's Growing Mind,* by Jane M. Healy, published by Doubleday, 666 Fifth Avenue, New York, NY 10103, and reprinted here with permission.

courses, gives a simple example of how different aspects of the brain can work together in an integrated way. "If you're listening to a song, the left brain would be processing the words and the right brain would be processing the music. So it's no accident that we learn the words of popular songs very easily. You don't have to make any effort to do that. You learn very quickly because the left brain and the right brain are both involved—and so is the emotional centre of the brain in the limbic system."[7]

The emotional centre of your brain is also very closely connected with your long-term memory storage system. That's why we all remember easiest any information with a high emotional content. Almost anyone can remember his or her first major sexual experience. All adults over 50 can recall precisely where they were when they heard the news of the death of President John F. Kennedy. Music and the words to songs trigger deep memories— if the music is associated with personal elation or pleasurable experiences. Discovering how the brain processes such information is a vital key to more effective learning.

Leading brain researcher Professor Marian Diamond[8] took a day out at the University of California at Berkeley to demonstrate precisely how the brain works; and how it's much more complex than any simple left-side-right-side explanation. Slicing into a human brain delivered from a nearby morgue, she starts with the stem or base. "This little area here is called the medulla," she explains. "It regulates your heartbeat and respiration, so it's essential to your life. It's only an inch long in the human brain, and the same length in a chimpanzee's brain." But the medulla in a human develops to three times the capacity of the chimp.

"Next to it is the cerebellum. Literally that means 'little brain.' It's responsible for coordination and balance. And only recently have we found out how important it is for learning and for speech."

She then holds up the top half of the brain, the part that looks like a giant wrinkled walnut: the cortex. "If it wasn't folded, it would be about two and a half feet square." Why is it folded? "Well, we believe it developed over thousands of centuries. Basically, to go through the human birth canal this part of the brain had to fold in upon itself." According to many scientists, the brain developed new capacities as our ancestors came down from the trees, started to walk upright, learned to use fire, started to use and make tools, and learned to speak.

Says Professor Diamond: "You'll find the most recently-evolved part

Your brain can keep learning from birth till the end of life.

Marian Diamond
Professor of Neuroanatomy and
Director of the Lawrence Hall of Science
University of California at Berkeley*

*Author interview in Berkeley, 1990.

of the brain right behind your forehead: your frontal lobe. It's essential for your personality, for planning ahead, for sequencing ideas. It's this part primarily which makes modern man differ from his earlier ancestors."

Behind that she points to the area just behind the forehead. "For me to be talking to you right now, it's this part of my brain that's firing. We call it our motor speech area. For one to understand the words I'm saying (pointing to an area further back), this is the part of your brain that would be in action."

And not surprisingly you don't process sight only through your eyes. Professor Diamond points to the back of her head. "You'll find your visual cortex back here. When you're hit on the back of the head, that's why you see stars. You've jarred your visual cortex."

As she slices through the brain, she explains each part: the small areas that move your arms, legs and fingers; the parts that control feeling, pain, temperature, touch, pressure and hearing.

And as she moves down into the limbic system, Professor Diamond starts delving into even deeper secrets: the parts of the brain that deal with fear, rage, emotion, sexuality, love, passion. The tiny pituitary gland that secretes hormones. The ability of the brain to register and cut off pain. And the almost magical way the brain sends messages around itself and around your body: messages that are constantly changing from electrical impulses to chemical flows.

But to Dr. Diamond all these elements together simply prove the great untapped potential of the human brain. We ask her what message she would communicate about the brain if she could talk individually with every person on earth. And her reply comes back clear and succinct: "I'd let them know how dynamic their brains are. And the fact that they can change at any age, from birth right to the end of life. They can change in a positive manner, if one is exposed to stimulating environments. Or they can change in a negative manner if they do not receive stimulation."

To her one of the key abilities that separate the human race from animals is our ability to communicate. And especially our ability to communicate in so many ways: in words, pictures, songs, dance, rhythm and emotion.

Not surprisingly, scientists are now finding out what many societies seem to have known instinctively for thousands of years.

Over 2,000 years before Christopher Columbus sailed across the

The learning style of a typical student

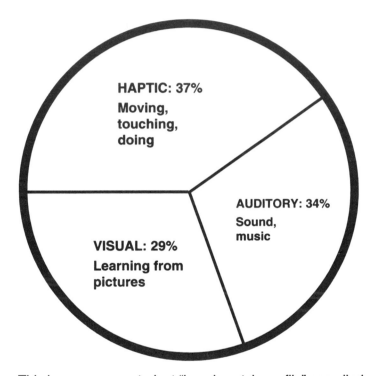

HAPTIC: 37%

Moving, touching, doing

AUDITORY: 34%

Sound, music

VISUAL: 29%

Learning from pictures

This is an average student "learning style profile" compiled by Specific Diagnostic Studies, of Rockville, Maryland, from 5300 students, grades 5 through 12, who have undergone SDS's Learning Channel Preference Checklist, in the United States, Hong Kong and Japan.

SDS, however, stresses that it would be statistically incorrect to deduce from this that 37 percent of students are solely haptic (or tactile-kinesthetic) learners, that 34 percent are auditory and that 29 percent are visual.

Every student profile showed a certain percentage in each of the three categories, and the percentages in the graph above represented the mean average.[11]

Atlantic to "discover" the New World, the ancestors of today's Polynesian societies sailed the much bigger Pacific.[9] They navigated by the sun, the moon and the stars—using what Professor Gardner would today call spacial or visual intelligence. Not surprisingly, when his researchers tested Solomon Islanders they found the part of the brain dealing with "spatial intelligence" highly developed.

Those same Pacific explorers, with their fantastic navigational feats, would probably have failed a modern "intelligence test" because they never developed a written language. Even today Polynesian youngsters from their earliest years learn through dance, rhythm and song.

Language itself sets up different patterns in your brain—and different patterns in your culture.

If you grow up in China or Japan, you learn to write a "picture" language—and this is largely learned through part of the right-hand side of your brain.

Grow up in one of the Western "alphabet" cultures, and you learn how to take in information through all your senses but to communicate in *lineal* writing. The English language, for instance, has about 600,000[10] words, yet each one is made up of variations from only the 26 letters of the alphabet. Communicate in alphabet languages, and you will largely be using a section of the left-hand side of your brain.

But if you grew up in a traditional Polynesian, Melanesian or Micronesian culture in the Pacific, without either a picture or a "sequential" written language, then your main verbal communication would be through sound alone—reinforced through rhyme, rhythm, song and dance, and of course by your holistic sense of sight.

Researchers will now tell you that there are at least three main learning-style preferences:

1. Haptic learners, from a Greek word meaning "moving along": people who learn best when they are involved, moving, experiencing and experimenting; often called kinesthetic-tactile learners.

2. Visual learners, who learn best when they can see pictures of what they are studying, with a smaller percentage who are "print-oriented" and can learn by reading.

3. Auditory learners, who learn best through sound: through music and talk.

Lynn O'Brien, Director of Specific Diagnostic Studies Inc., of Rock-

**Some students are
very visual: they have
to see everything.
Others don't want
to see something
written down:
they're more
auditory types.
Others are kinesthetic:
they have to stand
and move. They learn
even abstract things
by moving their bodies.**

CHARLES SCHMID
founder of the LIND Institute*

*Author interview, San Francisco, 1990.
LIND stands for "Learning In a New Dimension."

ville, Maryland, has found most elementary and high school students learn best when they are involved and moving, while most adults have a visual preference.[11] But most of us combine all three styles in different ways, as we explore later. We all learn best and fastest when we link together many of our brain's great abilities. Of those attributes, three are extremely important for learning:

1: How you store and retrieve information—quickly, thoroughly and efficiently.

2: How you can use it to solve problems.

3: How you can use it to create new ideas.

For the first two, you use the brain's unique ability to recognize patterns and associations. For the third, we learn how to break the patterns—how to recombine information in a new way.

How your brain stores information

As a patterning device, the brain almost certainly has no equal. It is capable of sorting and storing virtually every major piece of data it takes in.

Learn to identify and recognize a dog, for instance, and your brain sets up a storage file for dogs. Every other type of dog you learn to recognize is stored in a similar *patterning system*. And the same with birds, horses, cars, jokes or any other subject. Many scientists now believe we store many of those interconnected subjects like branches on a tree.

But it's much more complex than that. If we asked you to name the apples you know, you'd start to rattle them off: red delicious, golden delicious, Granny Smith and so on—from your "apple" memory-tree. If we asked you to list all the fruits you know, you'd have apples stored with oranges, pears and grapes on your "fruit" memory tree.

And if we asked you to name round objects, you'd include oranges from your "round objects" memory-tree. So your brain classifies information in many different storage-files—like a library cross-references books, or a book index.

The brain, however, is much more efficient. It stores this information by making great use of associations. Every person's brain has an association cortex. It can link up like with like, from different memory banks.

As a simple experiment, take public speaking. Most people list it as

If you want to remember anything, all you have to do is to associate (link) it with some known or fixed item.

TONY BUZAN
Use Your Perfect Memory*

*Published by Plume, The Penguin Group USA Inc.,
375 Hudson Street, New York, New York 10014,
and reprinted with the permission of Tony Buzan.

one of their greatest fears. Ask anyone on the spur of the moment to make a spontaneous speech in public, and the first reaction will almost certainly be to clam up.   Adrenalin flashes through the brain-cells. The brain "downshifts" into a primitive mode. Fear blots out your memory banks. You're scared! Yet let someone else start by telling any sort of joke, and almost immediately each person in the group will start to remember an *associated* humorous story. Or gather round the piano at a party. As each person starts a song every one else remembers it almost instantly.

It's as if each of us has a tremendous ability to store information—and to remember it when we trigger off the right *association*. And in fact that is exactly correct.   Surgeons who have applied electrodes to parts of a brain during operations[12] have been amazed to find their patients, on awakening, have total recall of specific events, even right back to their early childhood.   And that, of course, is what often happens under hypnosis A hypnotist "unlocks our minds" and enables us to recall information that has been stored away for years.

Learning to store information in patterns and with strong associations is probably the first step toward developing your brain's untapped ability.

It's one of the first keys to improving your ability to remember anything: by *associating* it with a strong *image* and using one or more of your brain's abilities. How else do you easily remember that April has 30 days, if not by the rhyme that begins *Thirty days hath September, April, June and November*—all stored through the section of your right brain that deals with rhymes?

Your four separate wavelengths

The second step is learning to use your subconscious mind.

And here's where we meet up with brain-waves.   Link yourself up to an electronic scanner and you'll soon find out that parts of your brain can send and receive information on different frequencies. In one sense they're similar to television signals.   Tune in your TV set to channel 2, or 22, and you'll be able to receive messages sent out on that wavelength.

Scan your brain when you're wide awake and it will be transmitting a certain number of cycles per second.   Scan it when you're dozing and it will be transmitting on a "different frequency." Likewise when you're in the early stages of sleep and dreaming, and later when you're in deep sleep.

You are what you eat.

BRIAN AND ROBERTA MORGAN
Brain Food*

* While this quotation has been used many times before,
it forms a key theme of the Morgans' excellent book,
published by Michael Joseph Ltd. in 1986, and by
Pan Books, London, in 1987.

*Many researchers are now convinced that we can absorb informa-
tion much more quickly and effectively when our brains are in a state
of "relaxed alertness."**

That's the state we often achieve with certain types of meditation. Or
listening to relaxing music. Some of the "accelerated learning" techniques to be explored later in this book are based on experiences with
"baroque" music. The pace of many baroque compositions is similar to
the "wavelength" you'll find in your brain when it's in that same state of
"relaxed alertness." If information is read to you in time with that music,
it "floats into your subconscious" and you can learn much faster.

But whether or not you use music, the logic is very simple. You'd find
it impossible to make any sense out of a radio receiver if you were tuned
in to four stations at once. Likewise in learning. You need to clear your
wavelengths—and tune in to only one station.

That's why nearly every successful learning session starts with relaxation: clearing your mind so your subconscious can receive uncluttered
messages—and store them in their right "file."

Your brain runs on oxygen and glucose

Like any other complex machinery, your brain needs energy. Basically, it gets that from the food you eat. If you're an adult, your brain
makes up only about two percent of your total weight. But it uses about
20 percent of the energy you develop.

Feed it a low-energy diet, and it won't perform well. Feed it a high-
energy diet, and your personal computer will work smoothly, efficiently.

*For energy, the brain needs plenty of glucose. That's why fresh
fruit and vegetables are so essential to your diet. They're rich in
glucose.*

Your brain also has a unique way of transmitting messages—around
its billions of cells and to the rest of your body. Each message flows
around your body *electrically* and *chemically,* and it keeps switching
from one form to the other.

Each message travels like electricity along a brain-cell's axon, then
turns into a chemical flow when it jumps across the connecting-point to
another cell. Scientists call these gaps *synapses.* These synaptic

** See next chapter, page 162, for an illustration of brainwaves in action.
This subject is handled in much more detail in chapter 9.*

How diet affects your transmission system

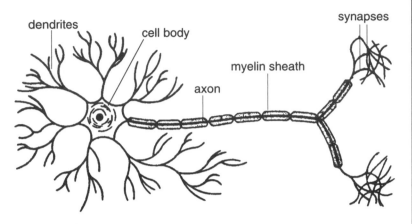

Each of your 100 billion active neurons or brain-cells stores information on its thousands of *dendrites,* like branches.

It then transmits that information to other cells, and other parts of the body, by electrical impulses, along a major pathway called an *axon* (for axle or axis).

When it reaches the synapse (connecting gap) to another brain-cell, each electrical impulse triggers a chemical reaction—a neurotransmitter which jumps across the gap to transfer the message.

Each axon is insulated by a myelin sheath, which acts as an insulator. The better the insulation, the more efficient the message is transmitted. The brain has at least 70 different types of neurotransmitters, and each is affected by diet.

The entire "communication system" is surrounded by *glial* cells (for "glue"), which lay down the myelin sheathing and generally nourish the active nerve-cells. The right diet is also vital for this nourishment (see more detail in chapter 6).

Illustration is from *Accelerated Learning,* by Colin Rose, published by Accelerated Learning Systems, of Aston Clinton, Bucks, England, and reprinted here with permission.

connections are another key to brain function. To send those messages, your brain first has to generate electricity. If you could test it now, you'd probably find it generating about 25 watts. That's the amount needed to run the smallest light-bulb in your home.

And the source of that brain-electricity: good food combined with oxygen. Obviously you get oxygen through breathing. That's why deep breathing is highly recommended before and during study: to oxygenate your blood. And that's why exercise is not only good for your body, it's good for your brain. It enriches your blood with oxygen.

Cut off the supply of oxygen and you destroy brain-cells. Stop it completely and you die.

Your brain needs the right type of energy to produce those chemical flows—what the scientists call *neurotransmitters*. And these in turn depend on a balanced diet, one that includes plenty of protein. Scientists have identified around 70 different types of neurotransmitters, including adrenalin and endorphins, the brain's natural painkillers or opiates. And, as Brian and Roberta Morgan point out in their excellent book *Brain Food:* "Any deficiencies in nutrients can reduce the levels of certain neurotransmitters and so adversely affect the types of behaviour they are responsible for. Conversely, a physical or mental problem can be corrected by boosting the level of the relevant transmitter and this can be done by making a simple alteration in the composition of your diet."

As an example, they point to the big increase in Alzheimer's disease among elderly people, and add: "Another characteristic of senility is the reduced ability of the brain—by as much as 70 or 80 percent—to produce acetylcholine, the neurotransmitter responsible for memory." Dr. Brian Morgan, formerly a Professor at the Institute of Human Nutrition at Columbia University in New York, recommends a diet rich in lecithin to help improve everyone's memory, but especially that of older people. Foods rich in lecithin include peanuts, soya beans and wheat germ. He also recommends lecithin and choline chloride dietary supplements to boost the neurotransmitters that are needed to improve your memory.

The Morgans also spell out other dietary deficiencies that impair mental performance, including a polyunsaturated fat called *linoleic acid* which the body itself cannot manufacture. "Fortunately," say the Morgans, "it is also extremely easy to find: one teaspoon of corn oil is enough to supply an adult with all he needs. But that teaspoon is crucial for proper brain operation. Without it, the brain cannot repair its myelin sheaths, and

Brain functioning depends very much on what you've eaten for breakfast.

RICHARD M. RESTAK
The Brain: The Last Frontier*

*Published by Warner Books, in arrangement with Doubleday & Co., 245 Park Avenue, New York, NY 10017.

the result may be a loss of coordination, confusion, memory loss, paranoia, apathy, tremors and hallucinations."

They also point to iron deficiency as a major cause of poor mental performance. They say this probably affects more people in Western society than any other single deficiency. And that it "decreases attention span, delays the development of understanding and reasoning powers, impairs learning and memory, and generally interferes with a child's performance in school."

The brain also needs a constant supply of other nutrients. Among the main ones are sodium and potassium. Each of your 100 billion neurons has up to one million sodium pumps. And they're vital for transmitting all your brain's messages. Sodium and potassium supply those pumps with energy. Like glucose, potassium is found mainly in fruits and vegetables. And sodium is found in most foods.

Put simply, reduce your sodium intake and you reduce the movement of electrical current around your brain; you reduce the amount of information the brain can receive. Reduce your potassium intake drastically and you risk anorexia, nausea, vomiting, drowsiness and stupor. All could be symptoms of your brain's vital pumps not working.

Simple tips on brain food

Fortunately, nearly all fruits are rich in potassium, especially bananas, oranges, apricots, avocados, melons, nectarines and peaches. So are potatoes, tomatoes, pumpkins and artichokes.

We'll deal with some aspects of diet in later chapters, particularly for pregnant women and children. But for now, if you want your brain to be working efficiently for all forms of learning and work:

1. Eat a good breakfast every morning, preferably with plenty of fresh fruit. Include half a banana for its potassium content—and a whole one if you're pregnant—with an orange or kiwi fruit for vitamin C, and any other fresh fruit in season. If you have children, make sure they do too.

2. Eat a good lunch, preferably including a fresh vegetable salad.

3. Make fish, nuts and vegetable "fats" key parts of your diet. Fish and vegetable oils have a vital role in nourishing the brain's billions of glial cells. And nuts and vegetable oils are major sources of that linoleic acid, which the brain needs to repair the myelin insulation around your brain's "message tracks."

The greatest unexplored territory in the world is the space between our ears.

BILL O'BRIEN
Chief Executive Officer, Hanover Insurance*

*Quoted by Peter M. Senge, in *The Fifth Discipline,* published by Random House, 20 Alfred Street, Milson Point, NSW 2061, Australia.

4. Exercise regularly to oxygenate the blood.

If tapping into your amazing brain provides the first magic to learning, then a sensible diet and exercise are two of the magician's wands.

In a very real sense, you are what you eat. Knowing the correct "brain food" to fuel your brain is one of the first steps to improving your learning ability. But your potential is to be much more than your diet.

Says Oxford University Professor Colin Blakemore in **The Mind Machine:** *"The human brain is the most complex piece of machinery in the universe."*

Says Bill O'Brien, president of America's Hanover Insurance Company: "The greatest unexplored territory in the world is the space between our ears."

That challenging exploration starts with learning how the brain works. But it continues most effectively by using it regularly. The words of the old axiom—"If you don't use it you lose it"—apply even more to your brain than your muscles.

And just as simple dietary steps can help improve your mental powers, your memory and your learning ability, so too there are other keys to help you learn much faster and better. And most of them are simple.

20 easy first steps to better learning

1   Start with the lessons from sports.

2   Dare to dream.

3   Set a specific goal—and set deadlines.

4   Get an enthusiastic mentor—fast.

5   Start with the big picture first.

6   Ask!

7   Seek out the main principle.

8   Find the three best books written by practical achievers.

9   Relearn how to read efficiently.

10   Reinforce with pictures and sound.

11   Learn by doing.

12   Don't take linear notes—draw Mind Maps.

13   Retrieve what you've learned—through the same senses you stored it with.

14   Learn the art of relaxed awareness.

15   Practise.

16   Review and reflect.

17   Use linking tools such as memory pegs.

18   Have fun, play games.

19   Teach others.

20   Take an accelerated learning course.

The first 20 steps to learn anything five times faster, better, easier

Try to forget everything you've ever thought about education.

If school was a bore, forget it. If you dropped out early, forget that too. If you flew through college exams, fine; this chapter should help you do even better. But even if you flunked school, accept that lifelong learning is now needed. And this chapter is an introduction to simple do-it-yourself learning methods—even if you don't have access to a teacher skilled in all aspects of accelerated learning.

If you're a professional teacher, we still think you'll pick up some new tips. But we handle new styles of teaching in later chapters. This is mainly for self-starters and those who'd like to be.

In brief, this chapter will help you develop new skills or abilities. It will pass on simple tips to absorb information easier, retain it in your memory, and recall it when you need it. It will especially help you to use your new-found brain-power to achieve those results.

And the 20 simple tips:

1. Start with the lessons from sports

Sports probably provides a much better learning model than many schools. There are at least eight lessons you can learn from it:

1. All sports achievers have a dream. They dream the impossible and make it happen.

The champion wants to break the 3 minute 50 second barrier for the mile. Or take the Olympic gold. Or be in a world series winning team.

All sports achievers, at every level, have dreams. It may be to break

Relaxed concentration is the key to excellence in all things.

W. TIMOTHY GALLWEY
*The Inner Game Of Tennis**

*Published by Random House, New York (1974).

100 at golf, then 90, then 80. Or to become the club tennis champion. Or to run the New York marathon at age 65.

2. All have specific goals. And they break those goals down into achievable steps. So while the dream is always there, they build on their successes. You can't become a world champion overnight; you have to tackle hurdles regularly along the way—and celebrate each success as it is achieved.

3. All sports achievers combine mind, body and action. They know that their goals can be achieved when they link the right mental attitude, fitness, diet and physical skills.

4. They all have vision; they learn to visualize their goal. To *see* their achievements in advance. To play through their next football match like a video of the mind. Jack Nicklaus, possibly the greatest golfer of all time, says 90 percent of his success has come from his ability to visualize where every individual shot is going to land.

5. They all have passion. They have an overwhelming desire to succeed.

6. Each one has a coach, a mentor, a guide. In fact, we can probably learn more about real education from the success of the American college coaching system than we can from most college classes. If you doubt it, how many Olympic athletes, basketball and football stars have emerged from colleges—where the coaches are mentors, friends and guides?

7. All sports achievers have a fantastically positive attitude toward mistakes. They don't even call them mistakes; they call them *practice*. Even Bjorn Borg, John McEnroe and Martina Navratilova belted balls into the net thousands of times on their way to the top in tennis. No teacher marked those shots as failures. They were all essential parts of learning.

8. They all achieve by doing. Sport is a hands-on operation. You don't get fit by reading a book—although that may help with the theory. You don't develop the right muscles staring at a television set. You don't long-jump over 28 feet in a classroom. All sports achievements result from *action*.

Former American Olympian pentathlete Marilyn King says all astronauts, Olympic athletes and corporate executives have three things in common:

"They have something that really matters to them; something they really want to do or be. We call it *passion*.

Passion
+
vision
+
action
is the
equation
for
success.

MARILYN KING
U.S. Olympic pentathlete*

*Article in *On The Beam,* published by New Horizons for Learning
(Vol. X11, No. 1, Fall 1991), and adapted from the *Dare To Imagine*
seminars, presented by Marilyn King, Beyond Sports,
484 Lake Park Ave., Oakland, CA 94610.

"They can see a goal really clearly, and the 'how to' images begin to appear like magic. While the goal may seem farfetched, they can imagine doing all these little steps on the road to that goal. We call it *vision*.

"Finally, they are willing to do something each day, according to a plan, that will bring them one step closer to their dream. We call it *action*.

"Passion + vision + action is our equation for success."[1]

Marilyn King runs courses and seminars teaching "Olympian Thinking" to corporate executives. She has also launched a "Dare To Imagine" project to pass on the same techniques to at-risk young people in her home city of Oakland, California.

So how can you apply the same principles to anything else you want to achieve and learn—and how can you do it faster, better, easier?

2. Dare to dream—and imagine your future

If, as we believe, nearly all things are now possible: what would you really like to do? What's your real *passion?* The thing you'd like to do more than anything else? Make great wine? Become the district golf champion? Get a doctorate? Start a new career?

Nearly every major achievement in the world has started with a vision: from Ford to Disneyland, Sony to Apple. So take up the King challenge—and *dare to imagine what you'd like to achieve.*

3. Set a specific goal—and set deadlines

Ask yourself first: What specifically do I want to learn? Why do I want to learn it?

If it's a new job, a new skill, a new hobby, a trip overseas, a new sport, a musical instrument or a new challenge, what will you need to know?

It's easier to learn anything if you have a set goal. When you've done that, break it down into achievable bite-sized pieces. Then set realistic deadlines for each step, so you can see your success from the start.

4. Get an enthusiastic mentor—fast

Whatever you want to learn, many others have already learned it. When you've set your goals, find an enthusiast you can come to for specific advice. And if you can swap skills, even better.

Let's say you're a printer who wants to learn word processing. Obviously you'll be skilled in typography. So find a word processing

Remember
jigsaw
puzzles:
they're much
easier when
you can see
the whole
picture
first.

specialist in a computer publishing field. You teach them typography while they teach you word processing. If you're new to a firm, do the same thing. Find someone who can help, regularly. Someone in the office or only a phonecall away.

If you want to play golf, take professional lessons—certainly. But find a good player whose style you admire, and ask if you can play a game or two together.

The same principles apply if you're learning new technology. No one ever learned to operate a computer solely from a 700-page manual. Each student learned hands-on, with a coach.

5. Start with the big picture first

Learn from the marketers of jigsaw puzzles. If you started to assemble 10,000 pieces of a giant jigsaw puzzle one by one, it might take you years to finish. But if you can see the total picture on the package, you'll know exactly what you're building. Then it's much easier to fit each piece into place.

We're amazed at how often common sense disappears in educational systems. Subjects are taught in isolation. They're often taught in small segments, without students knowing the big picture first.

In real life, that's not the best way. It would take you years to discover New York by walking down every street. So what do you do as a tourist? You go to the top of the Empire State Building. Preferably with a New York guide. And you put yourself in the big picture. You can see Central Park, the Staten Island Ferry, the Statue of Liberty, Wall Street, the two main rivers, the key bridges, Broadway, Greenwich Village, the United Nations headquarters and the way the city is laid out in numbered avenues and streets. Then when someone tells you an address is 10 blocks south of Central Park on Sixth Avenue, or four blocks east of the Lincoln Tunnel, you have a mental picture of where to go. You can build on your overall image Mind Map.

Many traditional schools still introduce subjects through textbook lectures spread over months. You're taught to read each chapter slowly and deliberately—a week at a time—without ever having the "big overview." That's crazy. It's inefficient.

Instead, try this simple experiment. Next time you're planning anything, seek out the simplest overview. If you're visiting a new city, get the colour tourist brochures in advance. They'll show you the main

I keep six honest serving men, they taught me all I knew: their names are What and Why and When and How and Where and Who.

RUDYARD KIPLING

highlights. Or go to your public library, seek out an encyclopedia summary and duplicate it. Then when you've got the big picture, build up the details. You'll know where they fit. Remember that jigsaw puzzle.

6. Ask!

It's the best three-letter word in the learner's dictionary. Never be afraid to ask. And never be afraid to ask the best experts you can find—even if you've never met them before.

We hope it won't be long before each of us has a home computer/video terminal linked with international data banks. But even then you'll have to ask for what you want. So begin now.

Start with your public library. It's not merely a book centre. It's a learning resource. Librarians are trained to help you. Call them before you visit; tell them specifically what you want to do; and ask them for the best beginner's guide. Use that for your overview; then build on it. But be specific. If you're a business executive planning a visit to Japan, ask them for simple guides to the country, its business, its culture, and the industry you're involved in.

If you learn easily by reading, that overview will probably be a book, a booklet or an article. If you learn best visually, seek out a videotape, or at least a book with plenty of coloured pictures and graphics. If you learn best by listening, get some audio tapes and play them in your car.

But don't stop at the library. Find someone from the university who's studying the field you're interested in. Ask the name of the best professor—the one who's the best simplifier. And ring him.

Or ring the university library, the nearest research institute, the best firm in the business. And don't be afraid to go to the top. At the very least, ask for the Human Resources Manager or the person in charge of staff training and development. And ask for the company's most helpful simplifier.

If you want to learn about another country, call its embassy or consulate. Or its trade or tourist office. Or one of its major companies.

To learn about radio, ring a radio station and ask if you can sit in on a recording session. If you're a student and think you'd like a career in a specific field, ring the best company and ask if you can come in and work free of charge for a week during the holidays.

In fact, make asking a habit. It's probably the simplest thing you can learn from journalism. How do you think all that information gets into

Nothing is more dangerous than an idea when it's the only one you have.

EMILE CHARTIER
as quoted in *The Creative Whack Pack**

* © 1989 Roger von Oech, Box 7354, Menlo Park, CA 94026.
Each *Whack Pack* card has a different suggestion to stimulate
ideas, and Emile Chartier is quoted under the heading:
Find the Second Right Answer.

newspapers, on to television and radio every day? By journalists calling "sources." And everybody else has the same right. Generally people love to help; they enjoy being asked about their specialty.

7. Seek out the main principle

In nearly every field you'll find one main principle for success. Or perhaps two or three. Find them out first—before you fill in the details.

In photography, the first principle for an amateur: never take a photo more than four feet from your subject. Second principle: preferably shoot without a flash, with a semi-automatic camera. On those two principles, one of the co-authors paid for a world trip as a photographer!

In cost accounting, the main principle: there's no such thing as an accurate cost, unless your business is running 24 hours a day, 365 days a year, on automatic equipment and with a guaranteed market for all you produce. Second principle: find the break-even point. Below that you're losing money. Above it you're making a profit.

In talkback radio, the main principle: no matter how big or small the city, if the host asks only for *opinions* he'll get the same 30 uninformed callers every day; if he asks for *specific interesting experiences* he'll get new interesting callers, with stimulating new information.

In education, a main principle: people learn best what they passionately want to learn, and they learn fastest through all their senses.

In journalistic interviewing, the first principle: ask *what* and *why.*

How do you find main principles? First you ask. Then:

8. Find the best three books written by practical achievers

Don't start with academic textbooks. In the area of your interest, find the three best books written by people who've *done it.*

If you want to study advertising, call Saatchi & Saatchi or a top agency and ask their creative director what to read. She'll almost certainly recommend *Ogilvy on Advertising* as an overview. And if you want to study copywriting: John Caples' *How To Make Your Advertising Make Money* and *Tested Advertising Methods.*

To study management, start with Robert Townsend's *Further Up The Organization,* Tom Peters' *Thriving on Chaos,* Peter M. Senge's *The Fifth Discipline,* and Stephen R. Covey's *The 7 Habits of Highly Effective People.*

Seven simple steps to learn a computer

1   Read a simple guide book on computers, one with plenty of pictures. Perhaps The *Personal Computer Book* by Peter Williams.

2   Ask some knowledgeable friends.

3   Limit yourself to one application until you get the hang of it, perhaps word processing.

4   Spend some time around computer stores until you find someone who knows what he's talking about, uses simple language and doesn't mind you phoning to ask questions.

5   Get him to demonstrate the word processing kit and to tell you the key points.

6   Write down the key points and affix them to your computer.

7   Start right away on word processing, and also take four half-day hands-on classes.

Summarized from
ROBERT TOWNSEND
*Further Up The Organization**

*Published by Michael Joseph, London, and used here to show how tips from hands-on books can crystallize main principles.

To practise new skills in thinking, start with the best book we know on the subject, Michael Michalko's *Thinkertoys*. Then deal yourself a hand of cards from Roger von Oech's *Creative Whackpack*—a brilliant ideas-starter. His first book, *A Whack On The Side Of The Head*, is also good.

If you want three other books on effective learning, try Tony Buzan's *The Mind Map Book—Radiant Thinking* and *Use Your Head*, and Colin Rose's *Accelerated Learning*.

If you're a teacher and want to add to those techniques, read *The Everyday Genius* by Peter Kline, *School Success* by Kline and Laurence Martel, and *SuperTeaching* by Eric Jensen.

For more about your brain, try *The Amazing Brain* by Robert Ornstein and Richard F. Thompson, *Brain Food* by Brian and Roberta Morgan, and *The Mind Machine* by Colin Blakemore.

More books are suggested at the back of this book. But in your own field ask the nearest expert to suggest a beginner's guidebook.

9. Relearn how to read—faster, better, easier

Amazingly, few people know how to read properly. And we're not talking about *mirror-reading* at thousands of words a minute.

Let's start with two questions: Do you think you could regularly read four books a day and absorb the main points?* Have you read a newspaper this week? If you answered the first question no, and the second yes—think again. If you read a daily newspaper in any city, you've read the equivalent of at least four books. And the Sunday editions of the *New York Times* or *Los Angeles Times* are equal to dozens of volumes.

And how do you read a newspaper? You read only those things you are interested in. And how do you know? Because newspapers are divided into sections, so you only read the sports pages if you're interested in sports, the business pages for business. But even then you don't read every sports story or every business article. Newspaper headlines highlight the main points, and make it easy for you to select. Even the writing style of newspapers makes it easy to glean the main points. After each headline, you'll generally find them summarized in

* *In almost eight years as a radio talkshow host, Gordon Dryden read, on average, 15 new books a week—well over 6,000 in total—and generally skim-read two or three others a day, using the techniques covered here.*

If you can
read a
newspaper
in an hour,
you already
know how
to read
at least
four books
a day.

the first paragraph. So you can either read the summary or devour the whole story.

Over half of a newspaper is advertising. But you don't read every ad. Advertisers flag your attention with headlines and pictures. Classified ads are in alphabetical order. So even if you want to buy a house, you don't read all the *Houses for sale* pages. You select those in your preferred suburb.

Very simply, *you've cracked the newspaper code.* You know the formula. You know how to skim-read a newspaper every day. So you already know how to skim-read four books or anything else in print. The secret is to crack their code, to find each publication's formula. Court reporters, for example, know the standard format for written judgments. The judge normally reviews the case and the main arguments for many pages, then delivers his or her finding in the last paragraph. So reporters never start reading a court judgment from the front. They start on the last page—generally at the last paragraph—because they are reading the judgment to report the verdict.

And the same principle applies to all non-fiction reading. First ask yourself: *Why am I reading this? What do I want to get out of it? What new information will I want to learn? Then find the book's formula.*

Nearly every non-fiction book will state its main purpose in an introduction—as this book has done. This will tell you whether the book can provide the answers you want. Then you have to decide whether you need to read every chapter. You've almost certainly come to the subject with some basic knowledge which you're looking to extend. So you don't have to read all the material unless you want to refresh your memory.

Generally, non-fiction authors write books like speeches: the introduction "tells 'em what you're going to tell them; then you tell 'em; then you summarize." And often each chapter is written in a similar way: the chapter title and first paragraph or paragraphs indicate the theme, the chapter amplifies it, and it may end with a summary. If the book has sub-headings, they'll help as well.

Many books have other pointers. With colour pictures, skim them and their "captions." Tom Peters' *Thriving on Chaos* summarizes each chapter on a separate page at the start of each chapter. In the book you are now reading, key points and telling quotations are highlighted on every other page.

In brief, read every non-fiction book like a recipe book. If you want

How to skim-read a book*

■ **Try and define first what information you are seeking.**

■ **Then hold your book about 20 inches away from your eyes: far enough to see the whole page.**

■ **Run your index finger down the centre of the page, with your eyes looking just above your fingertip.**

■ **Move the finger so fast that you do not have time to stop at each word and pronounce it to yourself.**

*Generally, this advice applies to non-fiction reading, where you are reading to gain information for a specific purpose. The same techniques can be used to read fiction, but even most good readers prefer to read fiction more slowly, so they can savour the atomsphere, the plot and the word-pictures.

to cook pork chow mein tonight, you don't read every page in *The 1,000 Recipe Chinese Cookbook*. You read only what you need to know. This tip alone will enable you to read four books in the same time it takes to skim a newspaper.

Another tip: do NOT read "slowly and deliberately." Look out your window right now. Then reflect on your brain's fantastic ability to take in all that information instantly. Remember those 130 million light receivers in each of your eyes, and their magic ability to flash that scene to your visual cortex. That's your brain's holistic ability to "photograph" a complete picture. Learn to use it.

Even those pages you think you need to read will include much information that can be skimmed. Remember your purpose, and the key answers you are seeking. For instance, school teachers, business executives and people approaching "retirement" are probably reading this book for different reasons.

So learn to skim for the points you want. Start by holding this book in one hand far enough from your eyes to see the entire page—generally about 18 to 20 inches. With your other hand use your index finger or a retracted ball-point pen. Practise running either your finger or the pen quite quickly down the centre of each page, with your eyes looking just above the point of your pen or finger, following it down. You'll be amazed at what you can take in, if you know specifically what you are looking for.

This is not just speed-reading. It's sensible skim-reading and selective reading. If you're looking for main principles, then that skim-reading may be all you'll need. If you're looking for specific information and quotes to include in a report, article or book, you'll need to stop and note them. If you own the book, use it as a dynamic resource. Mark key information with a highlighter. If the book is not yours, write down page numbers. Return to them and write or type out the key points. The physical act of writing or typing will help embed them in your brain's memory-vaults—learning through the sense of touch as well as sight. Better still, highlighting will make it easy to refresh your memory when you want to retrieve the information later.

10. Reinforce with pictures and sound

Because you've read this far, you're obviously a print-oriented learner, and a linguistic learner. But you can also learn better if you

How to count in Japanese—and learn by doing

English	Japanese	Sound	Action
one	ichi	Itchy	Scratch your
two	ni	knee.[1]	knee.
three	san	Sun,	Point to sky.
four	shi	she	Point to girl.
five	go	go	Walk.
six	rocko	rock.	Rock 'n' roll.
seven	shichi	shi-chi	Double sneeze.
eight	hachi	hat-chi	Put on funny hat.
nine	kyu	coo	Coo like a dove.
ten	ju	ju	Don Jewish hat.

*Adapted from an accelerated-learning
Japanese language-training course,
demonstrated by Creative Learning Company,
P.O. Box 5422, Wellesley Street Post Office,
Auckland 1, New Zealand.

1. Say, "Itchy knee" and "Sun, she go rock," as sentences
while you mime the actions.

reinforce the message with pictures and sound. So check out whether simple video or audio tapes are available on the subject you're studying.

And if you have family members who are not great readers, encourage them to *start* with their preferred learning style. If one's an auditory learner, make her car into a university with a cassette-player. If one has a visual learning style, then seek out picture books, videos, CD-I's (compact discs with interactive videos) and interactive computer programmes.

11. Learn by doing

We can't stress enough the need to engage all your senses. We give practical suggestions in other chapters.

But for do-it-yourselfers, when you check out introductory courses—or advanced ones—make sure they provide hands-on experience.

You learn to cook by cooking. You learn to play tennis by playing tennis. And even when you take golf lessons, every good professional gets you right into action. Education is generally ineffective when it separates theory from practice.

So make an effort to learn through more than one sense. If you're learning a foreign language, try to picture the scene you're learning, try to imprint the information through other senses.

To learn to count to ten in Japanese, for instance, try miming the words with actions (see routine opposite).

Good teachers and accelerated learning courses use many other techniques, as we'll explore later. But for do-it-yourselfers, interactive technology can now help greatly. Let's take two of the most complicated non-physical games: bridge and chess. You can learn both by playing—especially with a good coach.

But bridge or chess masters don't really want to spend hours playing with a novice. So some of them have now worked with software programmers to put their knowledge into interactive computer games. So, as well as playing with your friends, you can "play the computer." At bridge, you can see your cards on the screen and, if you win the bidding, you can see your partner's hand to play it. The computer will play your opponents' hands. And when each hand is over you have a choice of seeing all hands—and checking how the cards should have best been played.

In most computer chess games, you can choose your level of compe-

Don't take linear notes: draw Mind Maps

An adaptation of the Mind Mapping principle originated by Tony Buzan, and drawn here by Nancy Margulies,* of St. Louis, Missouri, U.S.A. Note how:

1. The main theme is in the centre.

2. There is a main branch for each sub-theme.

3. Single words are used for each concept.

4. Where possible, each concept has a picture.

In the accompanying text, Nancy Margulies also recommends setting aside 30-minute periods of uninterrupted time to practise Mind Mapping— and her illustration summarizes that reminder.

* Taken from *Mapping InnerSpace,* by Nancy Margulies, published by Zephyr Press, P.O. Box 13448-C, Tucson, Arizona 85732-3448, and reprinted with permission. A videotape is also available.

tency, from novice to advanced; the computer will play at the same level.

12. Don't take linear notes—draw Mind Maps

There's no use taking in important information if you can't recall it when you need it. And here traditional schooling methods are archaic. Tens of thousands of students around the world right now are taking notes. They're writing down words line by line. Or in some languages, column by column. But the brain doesn't work that way. It does not store information in neat lines or columns. The brain stores information on its tree-like dendrites. It stores information by *pattern and association.* So the more you can work in with the brain's own memory-method, the easier and faster you'll learn.

So don't take notes, make Mind Maps. And make them with trees, with pictures, with colours, with symbols, with patterns and associations. Mind Mapping is a method devised by Tony Buzan. His excellent new volume, *The Mind Map Book—Radiant Thinking,* is a good introduction.

Swedish publisher Ingemar Svantesson has produced *Mind Mapping and Memory.* And in the United States the finest book on a similar theme is Nancy Margulies' *Mapping InnerSpace.* Margulies has also written a great accelerated-learning book *Yes, You Can Draw!* and produced a first-class video to go with it.

Those books, and some of the Mind Maps in this one, demonstrate the principles in practice. The main points are simple, even if you are not yet a pictorial artist:

1. Imagine your brain-cells are like trees, with each one storing related information on its branches.

2. Now try arranging the key points of any topic on a sheet of white paper in the same tree-like format.

3. Start with the central topic—preferably with a symbol—in the centre of the page, then draw branches spreading out from it. If you're Mind Mapping New York, use the Statue of Liberty as the centrepoint. If it's Sydney, use the harbour bridge. If it's our chapter on the brain, sketch a two-sided brain.

4. Generally record only one word and/or symbol for each point you want to recall—one main theme to each branch.

5. Put related points on the same main branches, each one shooting off like a new sub-branch.

The principles of smart reading in map form

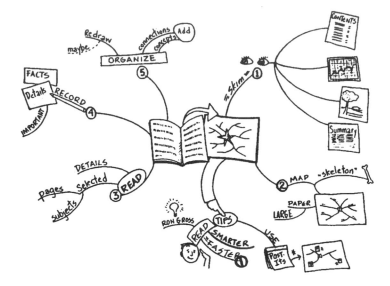

In her book, *Mapping InnerSpace,* Nancy Margulies* draws this map to illustrate the key concepts of "smart reading:"

1. Skim-check the main points first.

2. Prepare a large map skeleton (our sample is on page 20 if you want to start with a pre-prepared map).

3. Read not merely faster, but smarter.

4. Record key facts and important details on your map.

5. Organize concepts together, and when you've finished the book or other reading matter, redraw your Mind Map if you feel it needs to be simplified.

* From *Mapping InnerSpace,* by Nancy Margulies, published by Zephyr Press, Tucson, Arizona, and reprinted here with permission.

6. Use different coloured pencils or markers for related topics.

7. Draw as many pictures and symbols as you can.

8. When you've completed each branch, enclose it in a different coloured border.

9. Add to each map regularly. In this way it's easy to start with the overview and then build up your Mind Map as you learn more key points about each subject.

13. Easy ways to retrieve what you've learned

If the brain stores information by patterns and associations, and Mind Maps record it in the same way, then it's sensible to use the same methods for easy recall.

Here some more brain-knowledge will come in handy. Your brain has both a short-term and a long-term memory. And that's fortunate. You come to an intersection as the traffic light is turning red, and you stop. The lights turn green and you go. Your long-term memory has learned and remembered the rules about traffic lights. But your short-term memory doesn't have to remember each of the thousands of times you stop for the red light.

So how do you store and retrieve the information you need for long-term use? Partly by patterns and associations.

Mind Mapping is just one method. Another is to use all your intelligence-centres, including those involved with rhyme, rhythm, repetition and music. You don't have to spend hours on boring rote memory. As you've read this book, highlighted key phrases and sub-headings and made a Mind Map of the main points, we suggest you do two things immediately you've finished:

1. Immediately reskim the key points you've highlighted.

2. Re-do your Mind Map. This will also help you link your main lessons: by pattern and association. Almost certainly, if you're new to Mind Mapping, you'll have found it difficult to list each key point in only one word. But try to do so. It's very important.

Then tonight, not too long before you're thinking of sleeping, play some relaxing music. Take another look at your Mind Map. Try to think of the main lessons you have learned; try to visualize them. Think of the associations—because that state of almost reverie, just before sleep, is a vital part of the learning process.

Your brainwaves

1. Beta

2. Alpha

3. Theta

4. Delta

These are actual recordings of human
brain-waves—from top:
1. When wide awake—the conscious mind,
operating at 13 to 25 cycles per second,
the so-called beta state.
2. The ideal learning state of "relaxed alertness,"
8 to 12 CPS— alpha.
3. The early stages of sleep, 4 to 7 CPS—theta:
the mind is processing the day's information.
4. Deep sleep, 0.5 to 3 CPS—delta.

14. Learn the art of relaxed alertness

Up to now, most points we've summarized are logical, "left brain" activities. But to make use of the extraordinary powers of your right brain and your subconscious, *the real key to effective learning can be summed up in two words: relaxed alertness—your state of mind, especially when you start any learning session.*

We've already mentioned brainwaves. Now let's start to put them to use. Your brain operates, like a television or radio station, on four main frequencies or waves. We can measure them with an EEG machine (electro-encephalograph).

If you're wide awake and alert at the moment, or if you're talking, making a speech or working out an involved problem in logic, your brain is probably "transmitting" and "receiving" at 13 to 25 cycles per second. Some call this the beta level.

But that's not the best state for stimulating your long-term memory. Most of the main information you learn will be stored in your subconscious mind. Many researchers and teachers believe that the vast bulk of information is also best learned subconsciously. And *the brainwave activity that links best with the subconscious mind is at 8 to 12 cycles per second: alpha.*

Says British accelerated learning innovator Colin Rose: "This is the brain wave that characterizes relaxation and meditation, the state of mind during which you daydream, let your imagination run. It is a state of relaxed alertness that facilitates inspiration, fast assimilation of facts and heightened memory. Alpha lets you reach your subconscious, and since your self-image is primarily in your subconscious it is the only effective way to reach it."[2]

When you start getting sleepier—the twilight zone between being fully awake and fully asleep—your brain-waves change to between 4 and 7 cycles a second: theta.

When you're fully into deep sleep, your brain is operating at between .5 and 3 cycles a second: delta. Your breathing is deep, your heartbeat slows and your blood pressure and body temperature drop.

And the impact of all this on learning and memory? American accelerated learning pioneer Terry Wyler Webb says beta waves—the very fast ones—are "useful for getting us through the day, but they inhibit access to the deeper levels of the mind. Deeper levels are reached in the

Music can do in minutes what weeks of meditative practice strive towards.

COLIN ROSE
Accelerated Learning*

*Published by Accelerated Learning Systems,
Aston Clinton, Bucks, England.

alpha and theta brain-wave patterns, which are characterised by subjective feelings of relaxation, concentrated alertness and well-being. *It is in the alpha and theta states that the great feats of supermemory, along with heightened powers of concentration and creativity, are achieved."*

And how do you achieve that state? Thousands of people do it with daily meditation, or relaxing exercises, especially deep breathing. But more and more teachers are convinced that some types of music can achieve the results much quicker and easier. Says Webb: "Certain types of musical rhythm help relax the body, calm the breath, quiet the beta chatter and evoke a gentle state of relaxed awareness which is highly receptive to learning new information."

Of course many types of music can help you remember messages when it's accompanied by words—as television and radio advertising prove every day. But researchers[3] have now found that some baroque music is ideal for rapidly improving learning, partly because its main 60-to-70 beats-to-the-minute is identical to the alpha brainwaves.

Skilled teachers are now using this music as an essential ingredient of all accelerated-learning teaching. But for do-it-yourself learners, the immediate implications are simple: play the right type of music at night when you want to review your material, and you'll dramatically increase your recall.

In part that's because of how your brain works most efficiently when you're dropping off to sleep. Some call it R.E.M. sleep. The initials stand for *rapid eye movement*. And EEGs tell you why: it's almost as if your mind—even with your body asleep—is using its visual cortex to take quick frame-by-frame photographs of the day's main events.

Many researchers believe that in this state the brain is sorting out new information and storing it in the appropriate memory banks. And quiet relaxation as you review your Mind Maps, and reflect on the day's main points, opens up the pathways to those subconscious storage files.

That probably also explains why you dream: your subconscious is "dialing up" your old memories to collate the new information. And if you're thinking through a problem, your subconscious sifts through some alternative solutions, as we'll discuss in the next chapter.

The alpha state is also ideal for starting each new specific study period. Quite simply, it makes great sense to clear the mind before you start. Take your office problems on the golf course and you'll never play great golf. Your mind will be elsewhere. And the same applies to study. Come

Music suggestions

Use different music for different purposes.

For creating a calm atmosphere

Relaxing music, like *Watermark* by Enja, non-vocal music such as *The Lonely Shepherd* by Samphir, *Andante* from the Lind Institute, or some of the tracks from Ray Lynch's *No Blue Thing.*

For getting in the mood

Especially for cooperative learning activities, *Deep Breakfast* by Ray Lynch.

For "clustering" and fast writing

Antarctica by Vangelis or *Brazilian* in the *Invisible Touch* album by Genesis (the latter is specially popular with teenagers).

For "poetry writing"

December by George Winston.

For putting poems and whole language to raps

A selection of Hammer's tapes, but just the instrumental part.

For "state changes"

Vary the music depending on the age groups, but generally any upbeat instrumental music, such as *Switched On Beatles* by Chase and Rucker for those who grew up in the Beatles era; C C Music Factory for today's teenagers, and Elvis Presley music for those from an earlier era.

For getting started with teenagers

Right after a break, *Strike It Up* by Black Box.

For goal setting

Chariots of Fire by Vangelis.

For "visualizations"

Slow music such as Kitaro's *Silk Road,* Michael Jones' *Sunsets,* and George Winston's *December.*

*These are from selections used by Jeannette Vos in class. See page 174 for specific "active" and "passive" concert music. See also our resource lists at end of book for music catalogues and training manuals. Unfamiliar terms above are covered in later text.

straight from a high school French class to a mathematics lecture and it can be hard to "switch gears." But take a few moments to do deep breathing exercises, and you'll start to relax. Play some relaxing music, close your eyes and think of the most peaceful scene you can imagine—and soon you'll be in the state of relaxed alertness that makes it easier to "float information" into your long-term memory.

15. Practise, practise, practise

If you're learning to speak French, speak it. If you're learning about computers, use them. If you've taken a course in Asian cooking, cook an Asian feast for your friends. If you're studying shorthand, write it. If you want to be a public speaker, join Toastmasters—and speak publicly. If you want to be a writer, write. If you want to be a bartender, mix drinks.

Remember the sporting maxim: it's not a mistake, it's practice.

16. Review and reflect

When you're learning a physical-mental skill, like typing or cooking, you can practise it with action.

But in gaining other types of knowledge, make sure you review regularly. Look again at your Mind Map and review the main points immediately you've finished it. Do it again in the morning. And again a week later. Once more a month later. Then review it, and other associated data, before you have specific need for it: for an examination, an overseas trip, a speech or whatever. Before reading a new book, for instance, many people find it helps to first look at their existing Mind Maps on the subject, or skim-read the highlighted parts of three of four books that they've already read on the subject.

17. Use linking tools as memory pegs

Since the memory works best by association, develop your own "memory pegs." Associate newly acquired knowledge with something you already know.

The association can be physical: such as learning to count in Japanese by scratching your knee (see page 156).

It can be visual: like visualizing scenes to remember names—forging gold in a blacksmith's shop to remember Mr. Goldsmith, a picture of a crocodile under a McDonald's arch to remember founder Ray Krok.

It can be a strong visual story: like picturing a sequence to remember,

You can remember any new piece of information if it is associated to something you already know or remember.

HARRY LORAYNE and JERRY LUCAS
The Memory Book*

*Published by W.H. Allen, London.

say, the planets in order from earth—the hot sun shining so strongly it breaks a thermometer, and all the Mercury spills out; this runs outside where a beautiful woman, Venus, is standing on the Earth; it keeps running over the earth into the next-door neighbour's red-earth garden; a warlike neighbour, Mars, appears and starts hurling abuse. But just then a smiling giant appears, Jupiter—the biggest planet—and on his superman-type chest he has the word SUN emblazoned, for Saturn, Uranus and Neptune, and running alongside him is a happy dog, Pluto.

It can be rhyming and visual: like memorizing numbers with rhyming pictorial words, and linking them up with the items to be memorized: so that **one** becomes **sun; two, shoe; three, tree; four, door; five, hive; six, sticks; seven, heaven; eight, gate; nine, mine;** and **ten, hen.** To remember ten items, such as on a shopping list, link each one *visually* with the numbered sequence—so that if your first three items are butter, cheese and milk, you visualize butter being melted with the sun (one), cheese in a shoe (two), and milk being poured over a tree (three).

It can use the initial letter principle: as marketing people remember the key elements of advertising by AIDA: *attract Attention, arouse Interest, create Desire* and *urge Action.*

But whichever association method you use, *try to make it outlandish, funny and preferably emotional—because the "filter" in the brain that transfers information to your long-term memory is very closely linked with the brain's emotional centre. And link your associations with as many senses as you can: sight, sound, smell, touch and taste.*

18. Have fun, play games

Ask a friend what images flash to mind when you mention education or study. Now see how they tally with Tony Buzan's experience. "In my 30 years of investigating people's associations with the word 'study,'" he says, "ten major words or concepts have emerged. They are: boring, exams, homework, waste of time, punishment, irrelevant, detention, 'yuck,' hate and fear."[4]

But ask a four-year-old fresh out of a good preschool centre and she'll talk about the fun she had. So nearly all progressive educators now stress the need to recapture the fun-filled joy of early learning. And humour itself is a great way to learn. So try to link humour with study. Think up games to play to reinforce the key points with someone who's studying the same subject—even Trivial Pursuit-type quizzes.

ACT I ACTE 1
Scene I Scène I

Philip arrives in Paris (Monday). **Philip arrive à Paris (Lundi).**

Philip looks at the house. **Philip regarde la maison.**
It is big and beautiful. **Elle est grande et belle.**
Philip goes up to the **Philip s'approche de la**
front door. **porte d'entrée.**
He rings the bell and waits. **Il sonne et attend.**
An old lady opens the door. **Une dame âgée ouvre la porte.**

Mme Brossetout:	What do you want, young man?	**Qu'est-ce que vous voulez jeune homme?**
Philip:	Hello.	**Bonjour madame.**
	Is this Mr Dubois' house?	**C'est ici la maison de Monsieur Dubois?**
Mme Brossetout:	Yes it is.	**Oui, c'est ici.**
Philip:	I have an appointment with Mr Dubois.	**J'ai rendez-vous avec Monsieur Dubois.**
Mme Brossetout:	Who shall I say it is, please?	**C'est de la part de qui, s'il vous plaît?**
Philip:	Mr West.	**Monsieur West.**
Mme Brossetout:	Ah yes, Mr West. Please come in.	**Ah oui, Monsieur West. Entrez, s'il vous plaît.**
Philip:	Thank you.	**Merci madame.**

Philip goes into the house. **Philip entre dans la maison.**
Madame Brossetout calls **Madame Brossetout appelle**
Mademoiselle Dubois. **Mademoiselle Dubois.**

Mlle Dubois:	Who is it?	**Qui est-ce?**
Mme Brossetout:	It's Mr West.	**C'est Monsieur West.**

This is a typical written page from a good accelerated learning language course. Note:

1. Each "act" is written like the act of a 12-act play, so you can visualize what you are doing.
2. Your own language version and the foreign version are written side by side, line by line.
2. You can read the foreign language version, accompanied by music, while listening to it through headphones—and still be aware of the translation.
3. No sentence is longer than seven words, a good "chunking" principle as it is easier to remember concepts with no more than seven items.

*Reprinted from a French course for English-speakers, produced by Accelerated Learning Systems, Aston Clinton, Bucks, England, and reprinted here with permission. Turn the next page to see a pictorial version of the same material.

19. Teach others

"Each one—teach one." That's the recommended theme for the nineties from California brain-researcher Marian Diamond.

As well as being professor of neuroanatomy, she's Director of the Lawrence Hall of Science, a fun-filled resource and learning centre attached to the University of California at Berkeley.

"I want to introduce the concept," she says, "that everyone can learn to be a teacher. One has to be accurate with the facts as a teacher, yet imaginative with creative ideas for new directions in the future. As we learn the facts, we can turn around and share with the next person so that the 'association cortices' can create the new ideas."[5]

Diamond believes that even a child in kindergarten can learn to be a teacher. And she asks: "Why spend the next 12 to 15 years in only being taught? What one learns the first day of school can be shared not only with other schoolmates but with parents as well."

And whatever your age there are few better ways to crystallize what you've learned than to teach the principles to others, to make a speech or to run a seminar.

20. Take an accelerated learning course

This chapter has concentrated on simple, do-it-yourself tips. It would take many books this size to cover every point in detail. But the best way to learn all the principles is to take a specific accelerated learning course. Inquire what's available at your school or college. Seek out a private tutor. Or consider taking a do-it-yourself course.

Many of these courses are now available for learning a new language. The best do-it-yourself courses we have seen are from Accelerated Learning Systems in England.[6] The Australian high schools covering a three-year French course in eight weeks are also using the same methods. Here are the basic principles, and how they're used in a typical foreign language learning kit:

a. There are 2,700 languages in the world. English has about 600,000 words. German has under 200,000.[7] But linguists agree that about *90 percent of all speech uses only about 2,000 words.[8] Understand these fluently, speak them fluently, and you'll be able to converse reasonably well in your new language. In fact, even 1,000 words learned fluently may enable you to get by.*

Illustrations from a typical accelerated learning foreign language course* workbook. Each picture depicts the same sequence as the written dialogue. Students are encouraged to duplicate and enlarge the illustrations, to use them as posters and to colour them in. The illustration above is the pictorial version of the wording reproduced on page 170.

*Published by Accelerated Learning Systems, Aston Clinton, Bucks, England, and reprinted here by permission.

b. An accelerated learning language course therefore builds the basic 2,000 words into, say, 12 different "plays" or scenes—like a 12-act drama. [9]

c: An attractive workbook helps. On some pages *the script for each act is written in both English and, say, French or Spanish, line by line. But no sentence is longer than seven words*, because your short-term memory can absorb information easiest in "seven bit" bites. That's why phone numbers are generally easy to remember; over seven digits, and they switch to a separate area code. Teachers call this seven-bit principle "chunking."

d. Many acts involve you as a visitor to a new country, and weave a story around the typical events a tourist would find. So *the workbook also illustrates each act with pictures—stimulating the visual sense.*

e. Each scene is also recorded on an audio tape, in the foreign language, so the student can learn by listening while reading the foreign language and visualizing it.

f. Before starting each lesson, the student plays relaxing music from a special tape—through headphones—and follows suggestions for breathing and relaxation exercises. The aim is to tune out other distracting thoughts, and to place the brain in a state of "relaxed alertness"—so the new language can "float" into the brain.

g. That's where *music plays its three-part role: (1) it helps you relax; (2) it activates your right-brain to receive the new information; and (3) it helps move the information into your long-term memory-storage banks.* Lozanov* teachers believe a well-orchestrated music concert can in effect do most of the teaching in a greatly-reduced time. [10] The student first listens to the words of the foreign language while reading the text, with specific music in the background—and the words read in time and

---

* There is much more depth to the Lozanov method of teaching and learning than we can cover in this brief introduction to the technique. Music selection, in particular, is critical for the "active" and "passive" concerts. In chapter nine, we link the main principles of Lozanov with many other proven techniques, but for those experimenting with music in preparing their own accelerated learning programmes, we strongly recommend studying the music principles first with a publication such as "Accelerated Learning with Music—Trainer's Manual," published by Accelerated Learning Systems, of Norcross, Georgia. Relaxing music from one's own culture has a definite part to play in the learning process, but it is NOT a substitute for the specific music recommended by Lozanov.

Georgi Lozanov's music for easier learning

The Georgi Lozanov technique uses music in three distinct ways to accelerate learning:

1. **Introductory music, along with deep breathing exercises, to relax participants and achieve the optimum state for easy learning.**
2. **An "active concert," in which the information to be learned is read in time to expressive music.**
3. **A "passive concert" in which the learner hears the new information read softly against a background of baroque music, to help move the information into the long-term memory banks.**

Here are a few typical selections:*

FOR ACTIVE CONCERT	FOR PASSIVE CONCERT
Beethoven, Concerto for Violin and Orchestra in D major, Op. 61.	Corelli, Concerti Grossi, Op. 6, No. 2, 8, 5, 9.
Tchaikovsky, Concerto No. 1 in B flat minor for Piano and Orchestra.	Handel, The Water Music.
Mozart, Concerto for Violin and Orchestra, Concert No. 7 in D major.	J.S. Bach, Fantasy in G major, Fantasy in C Minor and Trio in D minor; Canonic Variations and Toccata.
Haydn, Symphony No. 67 in F. major; Symphony No. 69 in B. major	Corelli, Concerti Grossi, Op. 4, No. 10, 11, 12.
Beethoven, Concerto No. 5 in E flat major for Piano and Orchestra, Op. 73 ("Emperor").	Vivaldi, Five Concertos for Flute and Chamber Orchestra.

*Selections are from *Language Teacher's Suggestopedic Manual,* by Georgi Lozanov and Evalina Gateva (1988), and *Suggestology and Outlines of Suggestopedia,* by Lozanov (1978), both published by Gordon and Breach, New York.

tone to the music. The first "active concert" is then followed by a so-called "passive" concert, in which the student sits with eyes closed while more music is played in soft tones and the language is effectively "surfed" under it. This is a key element of the Lozanov technique, and the music is almost invariably baroque to maintain, and synthezize with, the most effective learning state: alpha.

h. Students are also encouraged to replay the baroque music before they go to bed at night, and to look through their workbook pictures of the "act" they're studying. In that way, the subconscious keeps filing the new information overnight.

i. Next day the student plays games, supplied in his kit, to reinforce some of the main words learned.

j. The kit* includes other suggestions, including pictures and words for common clothes and household items—and a physical learning video. This teaches you in the same way you learned your own language as an infant—although much faster. The presenter mimes each word or phrase, while you learn to say "sit" *(asseyez-vous* in French), "walk" *(marchez)* or "touch your elbow" *(touchez votre coude).*

k. Apart from the 2000 main words, *most other words can be worked out if you understand the "keys."* In Japanese, for example, most female first names end in "ko," so if you know that and see the name "Michiko" you know the person is probably female. *So a typical do-it-yourself kit includes a guide to all the main principles of the new language.*

*

These simple methods will help you remember anything much faster, better, easier, even without making a detailed study of integrative accelerated learning techniques. But the real challenge is to use your ability to create new solutions. To use your brain-power to think for successful new ideas. And here, too, The Learning Revolution provides some easy answers.

*Not all foreign language programmes are the same. With the development of these techniques, some language programmes around the world have merely been "put to music." The method we have outlined here is that used by Accelerated Learning Systems, of Aston Clinton, Bucks, England, which is the system we have found most effective around the world for "teaching yourself." We acknowledge, with thanks, their permission to summarize their main points, and to use illustrations from one of their typical language courses.

Your checklist for producing ideas

1. Define your problem.

2. Define and visualize the ideal solution.

3. Gather the facts: specific, general.

4. Break the pattern.

5. Go outside your own field.

6. Try new combinations.

7. Use all your senses.

8. Switch off — let it simmer.

9. Use music or nature to relax.

10. Sleep on it.

11. Eureka! It pops out.

12. Recheck it.

A 12-step creative process for business, school and life

Ideas change the world.

They determine the success of every company, the way of life of every country. Virtually every nation that has flowered into world leadership has done so on the strength of its ideas—and its ability to put them into practice. India, Persia, China, Egypt, Mesopotamia (now Iraq), Greece, Italy, Britain, Holland, Portugal, Spain, Mexico, Peru, America: all at times have had outstanding civilizations based on the power of ideas.

The ideas of Socrates, Aristotle and Plato helped turn tiny Athens into the world's first democracy, even if a limited one. The brilliant discoveries of Newton and Britain's Golden Age of Science in the 17th century paved the way for England's industrial revolution and the way of life that went with it.

And so it has continued. Henry Ford's mass-production principles set the American economy on its 20th-century burst. Ernest Rutherford's brilliance ushered in the atomic era. Keynes' theories in the 1930's gave governments the economic theories needed then to transform society. Jean Piaget, John Dewey, Maria Montessori, Lozanov and dozens of others have given us ideas for new educational insights.

Thomas Edison held 1093 patents,[1] and electrified the world. Walt Disney and Apple Computers' Steve Jobs[2] each founded giant commercial empires on the power of a new idea—and a different make-believe mouse. Ray Krok[3] was a middle-aged milk-shake machine seller when he first visited the California hamburger bar of Dick and Maurice McDonald. He was to take their basic concept, mix it with others, and turn the result into the world's biggest fast-food chain.

An idea
is a new
combination
of old
elements.

*There is nothing
new under the sun.
There are only
new combinations.*

GORDON DRYDEN
Out Of The Red*

*Published by William Collins, Auckland, New Zealand.

All the great ideas in history, all the great inventions, obviously have one thing in common. All have come from the human brain. Just as the brain has fantastic ability to store information, it has an equal ability to re-assemble that information in new ways: to create new ideas.

And very simply, *an idea is a new combination of old elements.* Write that down, underline it, reinforce it. It could be the most important sentence you ever write. It contains the key to creating new solutions. There is *nothing new under the sun. There are only new combinations.*[4]

Think for a moment of the thousands of different cookbooks around the world. Every recipe in every book is a different mixture of existing ingredients. Think of that example whenever you tackle a problem.

And all the breakthroughs everywhere—radio, television, the internal combustion engine— are new combinations of old bits. A push button shower combines at least three "old" elements: hot and cold water and a mixing valve. Nylon and other "new" synthetic fibres are new combinations of molecules that have existed for hundreds of centuries. In nylon's case: recombined molecules from coal.

Since an idea is a new mixture of old elements, *the best ideas-creators are constantly preoccupied with new combinations.*

In most management courses, you learn the overriding need to define correctly the problem you want solved.

But now a new revolutionary element has emerged. We can now define the ideal solution in advance—and start creating it.

This is a revolutionary change. Whereas previously we organized our existing knowledge to solve a problem, within the limits of that knowledge, today we start by defining what we would like to achieve. And then we organize the things we don't know in order to achieve it.

Sixty years ago clothing manufacturers were stuck with such basic yarns as wool, cotton and silk. Then Wallace Corothers synthesized nylon in 1935. Today we can define the ideal garment, and then produce the fibres and mixtures to create it. Families became tired of darning socks, so science created a blend of nylon and wool to give us the benefit of both: a new mixture of old elements.

Iron-weary mothers wanted shirts that would drip-dry without creases. So science created polyester fibres: a new combination of old elements.

Fashion-conscious women liked the easy-care properties of nylon but pined for the fluffiness of wool. So science created acrylics—by recom-

Children enter school as question marks and leave as periods.

NEIL POSTMAN
co-author of
*Teaching As a Subversive Activity**

*Published by Dell, New York.

bining the elements of natural gas. Peter Drucker, in *The Age of Discontinuity*, has crystallized the new innovative technique in a graphic way. He calls it "a systematic organized leap into the unknown." Unlike the science of yesterday, he says, "it is not based on organizing our knowledge, it is based on organizing our ignorance."

But amazingly these techniques are not taught in most schools, yet in many ways they are the key to the future.

Even worse: school tests are based on the principle that every question has one correct answer. The great breakthroughs in life come from entirely new answers. They come from challenging the status quo, not accepting it.

Courses in thinking would be one of our top priorities in every school. Otherwise, as American educator Neil Postman has suggested in *Teaching As A Subversive Activity:* children may "enter school as question marks but leave as periods."

California creative consultant Roger von Oech says, in *A Whack On The Side Of The Head:* "By the time the average person finishes college he or she will have taken over 2,600 tests, quizzes and exams. The 'right answer' approach becomes deeply ingrained in our thinking. This may be fine for some mathematical problems, where there is in fact only one right answer. The difficulty is that most of life isn't that way. Life is ambiguous; there are many right answers—all depending on what you are looking for. But if you think there is only one right answer, then you'll stop looking as soon as you find one."

So how do you use your own brainpower to make Drucker's systematic organized leap into the unknown? These are the steps we've found most useful:

1. Define your problem

One first step is to define in advance your problem—specifically but not restrictively.

2. Define your ideal solution and visualize it

Step 2 is to define what you would like to achieve—ideally. And then you organize your 100 billion active brain neurons to bridge the gap between where you are and where you want to be. It also helps greatly to visualize the ideal solution, to picture "in your mind's eye" the best possible result.

Vertical thinking is digging the same hole deeper. Lateral thinking is trying again elsewhere.

EDWARD de BONO
originator of Lateral Thinking*

*Author interview, Radio i, Auckland, New Zealand, 1976.

Let's use New Zealand as an example again. For over a hundred years it has been largely a one-crop economy. That crop: grassland farming. Virtually every other one-crop economy has remained an undeveloped, poor country—whether the crop be bananas, sugar, coffee or pineapples. But New Zealand has remained prosperous because of the ideas it has created or adapted to build the world's most efficient grassland farming industry and market its products around the world.

It didn't invent refrigeration or refrigerated shipping. But no nation has used that more to build living standards. Still with only three million people, New Zealand is the world's largest exporter of butter and cheese, the largest of lamb and one of the two top exporters of meat and wool.

For more than a century it has lived off the sheep's back. But how to get the maximum return? A century ago Australian farmers bred merinos for fine wool, other breeds for meat. New Zealand cross-bred to produce both good wool and good meat. A new combination of old elements.

Part of that cross-breeding process produced a genetic freak: a sheep that grew long wool like coarse hair: the ideal wool for carpets. Elsewhere in the world, inventors developed "tufting" machines to turn synthetic fibres into carpets up to 50 times faster than the old weaving process. New Zealand technicians adapted these to handle coarse wool. And the country is now the world's largest exporter of carpet wool—and probably the largest exporter of tufted woollen carpets.

New Zealand didn't invent flying, although a south Canterbury farmer, Richard Pearse,[5] made an abortive attempt with a home-made model around the same time as the Wright Brothers. Nor did New Zealand invent "crop-dusting," the spreading of farm fertilizer by air. But again no country has developed the concept more: for more than 50 years it has used what it calls "aerial top-dressing" to spread super-phosphate fertilizer on mountainsides to make them suitable for grazing sheep. A problem defined—and a new mixture of old elements to solve it.

New Zealand has also lived off cow's milk. And again the new ideas have flowed: cross-breeding for maximum meat and milk production; circular herring-bone "sheds" for the world's most efficient on-farm milking; milk-tankers to take the milk to cooperative dairy companies, including the world's first automated processing plant; a research institute to produce instant milk powder; a cooperative Dairy Board for international marketing. Little wonder that New Zealand can produce a ton of butter for $1,239, compared with America's $2,148, the Nether-

The only dumb question is a question you don't ask.

PAUL MacCREADY
Inventor

lands' $2,829 and Japan's $4,929.[6] Problems defined. Vision set. And the two linked by new mixtures of old elements. Result: a prosperous farming-based economy.

3. Gather all the facts

If a great idea is a new combination of old elements, then the next step is to *gather all the facts* you can. ***Unless you know a big array of facts on any situation or problem, you're unlikely to hit on the perfect new solution.***

Facts can be *specific:* those directly concerned with your job, industry or problem. And they can be *general:* the facts you gather from a thousand different sources. You will only be a great idea-producer if you're a voracious seeker of information. A questioner. A reader. A challenger. And a storer of information, in notebooks and dendrites.

There is no substitute for personalized, purposeful homework. What comes out must have gone in. The key is to somehow link information filed in, say, "brain-cell number 369,124" on "dendrite 2,614," with another stored on "cell number 9,378,532"—or wherever.

Here your brain's patterning ability creates both problems and opportunities. Each one of us uses our brain for every waking minute to take action in a pre-patterned way—from walking to running, from reading to watching television, from driving a car to stopping at red lights. Your brain tends to store information in narrow channels, on associated "branches" for easy and quick retrieval, so we normally come up with the same answers.

4. Break the pattern

To solve problems creatively, however, you've got to *open up new pathways, find new cross-over points, discover new linkages. You've got to break the pattern.*

And the easiest way to do that is to *start with questions that redirect your mind.* What would happen to your problem if you doubled it, halved it, froze it, reconstituted it, reversed it, adapted it, rearranged it, combined it? What if you eliminated it—or part of it? If you substituted one of the parts? If you made it smaller, shorter, lighter? If you recoloured it, streamlined it, magnified it? If you repackaged it? Distributed it in a different way? What if you applied all your senses—and added scents or fragrances, added sounds or made it different to see or touch?

Go outside your own field

- ■ The inventors of Kodachrome colour film, Leopold Mannes and Leopold Godowsky, were musicians.

- ■ George Eastman (of Eastman Kodak) was originally a book keeper in a bank.

- ■ Ladislo Biro, the inventor of the ballpoint pen, was in turn a sculptor, a painter and a journalist.

- ■ King Camp Gillette (the inventor of the safety razor) was a travelling salesman in bottletops.

- ■ John Boyd Dunlop (inventor of the pneumatic tire) was a veterinary surgeon.

GORDON RATTRAY TAYLOR
in *The Inventions That Changed The World**

*Published by Reader's Digest, 26 Waterloo Street, Surry Hills, NSW 2010, Australia.

Three excellent books on idea-creation are Michael Michalko's *Thinkertoys—a handbook for business creativity in the 90s,* James L. Adams' *Conceptual Blockbusting* and Roger von Oech's *A Whack On The Side of the Head.*

And von Oech has used one of his own techniques to reproduce his book as a pack of playing cards: his *Creative Whack Pack.* Every card provides a challenging new starting point.

This present book is another example of a new combination in practice. The large-type quotations on each left-hand page are intended to reitcrate main themes for easy skim-reading, to refresh your memory—and for easy enlarging into posters. The book itself has been adapted in part from a television series, *Where To Now?*

5. Go outside your own field

Try to put your existing preconceptions aside. The elements you use to solve problems should not only be those that are specific to the industry or process you're involved in. Use only those and you'll come up with the same old solutions.

Ask a teacher to redefine education, and generally he'll start thinking about school, and not about interactive videodiscs or life in 2010. Ask your brain to add 1 plus 1 and it will automatically answer 2. It's programmed that way.

But your brain has also stored facts about thousands of different interests: from recipes to football. The answers to problems in farming may well come from meanderings in space research. So all good inventors, innovators and creators develop an insatiable appetite for new knowledge. *Always remember to ask.*

6. Try various combinations

Next: since an idea is a new combination of old elements, try various combinations. Jot them down as they come to you. Try different starting points. Choose anything at random—a colour, an animal, a country, an industry—and try to link it up with your problem and solution.

Work at it. Keep your notepad full. But a word of caution: don't concentrate too closely on your specific field or you'll be limited by your own preconceptions. Read as widely as you can—particularly books on the future and challenging writings away from your own specialty. Keep asking: *What if?* "What if I combined this with that? What if I started

Who said this?

1. "The horse is here to stay, but the automobile is only a novelty—a fad."

2. "Heavier-than-air flying machines are impossible."

3. "Video won't be able to hold on to any market it captures after the first six months. People will soon get tired of staring at a plywood box every night."

4. "Everything that can be invented has been invented."

5. "Who the hell wants to hear actors talk?"

ANSWERS:

1. President of the Michigan Savings Bank, advising Henry Ford's lawyer not to invest in the Ford Motor Company.

2. Lord Kelvin, 1985.

3. Daryl F. Zanuck, head of 20th Century Fox movie studio, commenting on television in 1946.

4. Charles H. Duell, commissioner of the U.S. Office of Patents, in a 1899 report to President McKinley— arguing that the Patents Office should be abolished.

5. Harry M. Warner, president of Warner Bros. pictures, in 1927.

from here instead of there?" And keep asking.

7. Use all your senses

It also helps greatly to consciously try to engage all your senses. If your problem has been defined mathematically, try to visualize some answers. Remember how Albert Einstein's theory of relativity came to him after he'd been day-dreaming, imagining that he was travelling through space on a moonbeam.

Mind Mapping, too, is an excellent creative tool—to link information together in new ways, on new branches, in new clusters, so your ideas are not merely listed in one-dimensional lines.

Work at it until your head swims. Then . . .

8. Switch off—let it simmer

Like good food after you've eaten it, let your digestive juices take over and do the work—in this case the digestive juices of your own subconscious. Note the relaxation techniques we've touched on in accelerated learning, to put your brain into its most receptive and creative mode.

9. Use music or nature to relax

Many people find it pays to play relaxing classical music, visit an art gallery or go for a walk by a river or the sea. Anything that opens up the mind to new combinations.

Different techniques work for different people. One of the present authors has always found chess a positive creative stimulant—mainly because of the way every move opens up new possibilities. Other people find chess too focused. The other co-author finds swimming and walking more effective.

10. Sleep on it

Just before going to sleep at night, remind yourself of the problem—and the ideal solution. If you have a set deadline, feed that into your "brain-bank" too. And then *your subconscious mind will take over.* But as advertising leader David Ogilvy puts it: "You have to brief your subconscious. Then you have to switch off your thought processes and wait for something, for your subconscious to call you and say, 'Hey, I've got a good idea!' There are ways to do that. A lot of people find that to take a long hot bath produces good ideas. Other people prefer a long walk.

If you do not live in the future today, you will live in the past tomorrow.

PETER ELLYARD
Executive Director, Preferred Futures,
of Australia

*Speech to New Zealand school principals, 1992.

I've always found that wine produces good ideas—the better the wine the better the idea."[7]

11. Eureka! It pops out

The next step is the easiest of all: it pops out. You'll be shaving, or taking a shower, or sleeping—and suddenly the answer is there.

In part the process works because it's similar to the way your brain processes information in the first place. Just as you can use your subconscious to file information in patterns, so you can use your subconscious to deliberately break up those patterns and find new combinations. But only if you state your vision and your goal *specifically*. *It also pays to set a deadline, so your subconscious can feed that, too, into its data banks.*

12. Recheck It

When the new answer has popped out, *recheck it.* Does it fully solve your problem? Can you amend it or improve it?

The system we've just highlighted could be called the problem-solving way to creativity.

An alternative is a vision or mission approach. That's the same as problem-solving—except you don't start with the problem. You start with a vision of a future where virtually every dream is now possible.

Australian futurist Dr. Peter Ellyard is one of many who favour this approach. He feels that starting with a problem often limits the solution. "The dangers of a problem-centred approach can be best seen," he says, "in the inappropriately named 'health care' industry. In most first-world countries 'health care' is virtually out of control. The words 'health care' actually mean 'illness cure.' The industry consists of the activities of doctors, hospitals and pharmacies. The size of our health care budget has become an index of the nation's sickness, rather than its health. This forgets that the basic state of humans is to be healthy, not ill. We have adopted a problem-centred approach to health, largely defining health as an absence of illness, and a healthy future as an illness-free one. A *mission-directed* approach to promoting and maintaining health would be very different. It would concentrate on nutrition, exercise, good relationships, stress management and freedom from environmental contamination. This is a totally different agenda. However, the current problem is that we now pour so much money and effort into the problem-

I'd rather know some of the questions than all of the answers.

JAMES THURBER

centred, technology-driven approach that there are very few resources available for a mission-directed approach."[8]

The current authors certainly wouldn't disagree with this analysis—except to say that the "problem" was not correctly defined. And Ellyard makes a vital point: generally we all try to define a problem too narrowly. Define your problem as "unemployment," for example, and you may restrict your answers to new jobs—and not consider retraining leave or the desirability of leisure and study-time.

When consulting engineer William J.J. Gordon was given the task of finding a new way to open cans, he deliberately didn't use the word "can-opener" when briefing his engineers and designers. Instead they toyed with such notions as a banana and its easy-peel abilities. Their eventual solution: the ring-pulls you now see on most tear-tab cans. A "can-opener" approach would have limited the result.[9]

Whether you use the problem-solving or mission-directed approach, you generally won't come up with a great idea unless you define a specific goal in advance.

There are, of course, many exceptions. Bacteriologist Alexander Fleming stumbled on penicillin when confronted with a strange mould growing at St. Mary's Hospital in London.

And when Massachusetts inventor Percy Spencer was working on a novel radar system in 1945, it struck him that the radiation it emitted could have a culinary use. So he hung a pork chop in front of the magnetron machine he was working on. And, as British BBC presenters Peter Evans and Geoff Deehan report, he "produced the first microwave meal in history."[10] In another of history's quirks, it was the Japanese who capitalized on the invention. "When a Japanese firm started to manufacture magnetrons, it was forbidden under the peace treaty to undertake military contracts. Therefore it concentrated on peaceful uses of microwave technology; now Japan leads the world in microwave sales." Or at least it did until the Koreans caught up.

But most breakthroughs come from a firm vision of the future: a specific goal. Ellyard, in fact, consistently challenges school principals and administrators to visualize the 21st century and then look at the tasks of the education system to help make the dream a reality.

Many of those creative techniques can be adapted from other fields. Advertising, for example, has given us "brainstorming"[11]—the original idea of Alex Osborn, one of the founders of Batten, Barton, Durstine and

Creative futures:

Test yourself, your family or your class

1. Describe your professional situation four years from now.
2. Describe your personal situation five years from now.
3. Describe your holiday travel in 1999.
4. Describe your interests, desires and aspirations in 2002.
5. Describe your home in 2004.
6. Describe what you think your place of work will be like in 2007.
7. Describe a party with friends in 2009.
8. Describe a weekend in 2011.
9. Describe your house in 2012.
10. Describe your personal experiences in 2014.
11. Describe what you do in your spare time in 2015.
12. Describe your memories in 2017.

PETER EVANS and GEOFF DEEHAN
*The Keys To Creativity**

*Published by Grafton, London, but dates (above) are updated.

Osborn. Osborn has outlined a checklist of questions for producing new ideas in advertising and marketing.

Here it is in part (with some of our ideas-starters in brackets, to show that the same questions can be used for any subject, including education):

Can you put it to other uses?

New ways to use as is? (School computer classrooms for evening adult training? Restaurants as off-hours cooking schools?)

What other uses if modified? (National parks as "schoolrooms"?)

How can you adapt it?

What else like this? (Schools as public libraries, for books, interactive video, paintings and magazines?)

What other idea does this suggest? (Schools as community movie theatres, for joint-class viewing, freeing teachers for one to one help?)

What could we copy? (Iceland's example in using schools as backpackers' hostels for overseas tourists during summer vacations?)

What if we modified it?

What new twist can you think of? (Every student a teacher too, paired with someone else? Night-school classes targeted at specific learning styles?)

What if you changed the meaning? (Sweden has *parental* leave on almost full pay for one year after the birth of a baby—instead of *maternity* leave—so fathers can share responsibilities.)

What if we changed the colour? (And turned school corridors into community art galleries?)

What if we considered motion and sound? (Training classes in video and baroque music, maybe?)

What if we modified shape? (Look what a unique bottle did for Coca Cola—separated it from all other softdrinks in the world. Maybe schools with adjustable walls, designed like convention-centres for multiple-purpose use).

And if we magnified it?

What could you add? (Grandparents as school mentors? Parent volunteers for lunches, office work, field trips, reading programmes?)

More time? (School hours, with after-school hobby and homework facilities, as in Russia?)

Greater frequency? (Schools working shifts, like Singapore?)

Have you ever thought of this?

All the literature that has ever been written in the modern English language consists of patterns of only 26 letters.

All the paintings ever made are patterns of only three primary colours.

All the music ever written consists of patterns of no more than 12 notes.

All the arithmetical expressions we know of consist of only 10 symbols.

And for the vast computations of digital computers, everything is made up of patterns of only two components.

Thus, whenever we speak of something as being "new" we are really talking about original patterns of already existing components.

DON FABUN
*Three Roads To Awareness**

*Published By Glencoe Press, Beverly Hills, California.

Longer? (School year? How would you organize teachers' preparation and training time if schools worked the same hours as businesses?)

What could you multiply? (Link English, geography, history, biology, science, ecology and computers into integrated studies programmes, as Freyberg High School does in New Zealand?)

What could you exaggerate? (One of the keys to memory-training: big, humorous, ludicrous images linked to the information you need to remember.)

What should you minify?

What to subtract? (Algebra from the syllabus—with ideas-creation as the replacement?)

What can you make smaller? (Schools themselves, maybe? Or split into small project groups, like industry?)

Miniature? (Each school with its own small community newspaper, or its own radio station—with every student a reporter?)

Shorter? (Summer holidays? Or link them with Outward Bound or SuperCamp-style adventure projects?)

Omit? (Teachers as first exam assessors, maybe? Try getting individual students to set their own goals, do their first assessments, then discuss them with classmates. We've found that most people will actually over-achieve targets they set themselves.)

What can you substitute?

Who else instead? (Students themselves to plan their own personalized curriculum—as they do at New Zealand's Tikipunga High School?)

What else instead? (A tourist industry based on home-swaps, home-stays, farm-stays, student and teacher interchanges? What better way to build multi-cultural understanding?)

What other ingredients? (Schools designed as business communities, with their own banks, stores, courts, lawyers and police, operated by students? One Boston school has been doing this for years.)

Other power? (Solar-heating units for sale from engineering classes?)

What other place could be used? (Children's museums as joint-venture school projects? Local businesses as study centres?)

What can you rearrange?

What components can you interchange? (Teaching by TV, maybe.)

Other patterns? (What goods or services can school sell?)

SCAMPER

**is a checklist
of ideas-spurring questions.
Some of the questions were first
suggested by Alex Osborn,
a pioneer teacher of creativity.
They were later arranged
by Bob Eberle into this mnemonic:**

S = Substitute?

C = Combine?

A = Adapt?

M = Modify? Magnify?

P = Put to other uses?

E = Eliminate or reduce?

R = Reverse? Rearrange?

**To use SCAMPER:
1. Isolate the challenge or subject
you want to think about.
2. Ask SCAMPER questions about
each step of the challenge
or subject and see what new ideas emerge.**

MICHAEL MICHALKO
Thinkertoys*

**Published by Ten Speed Press, Berkeley, California.

Other layouts? (Just what *would* students come up with if asked to design the ideal learning resource of the future?)

Other sequences? (Same teacher for each year throughout school—like in the Rudolph Steiner system? Or immersion into one global unit of study at a time, instead of a host of separate subjects all in one day?)

Can you transpose cause and effect? (Maybe running every class like an open-line talkback show: based solely on students' questions?)

How about a change of pace? (At least four student exchanges with other areas every year: city for country, culture for culture? If you're a teacher, run a student poll on the past year's highlights. We'll be surprised if field-trips and town-country and inter-country swaps are not tops.)

What can you reverse?

What if you transposed positive and negative? (That Japanese system of wiping out litter and graffiti by making students double as janitors?)

How about opposites? (A lesson from supermarkets, maybe? For years grocery shops assumed they had to serve customers. Then someone thought of customers serving themselves. And supermarkets were born. So how about the school as a smorgasbord, giving the choice to pupils?)

Can you turn it back to front? (Another business lesson—from the assembly line: Henry Ford did much the same as the supermarket pioneers. Says American creativity consultant Michael Michalko: "Instead of asking the usual question, 'How can we get the workers to the material?' Ford asked, 'How can we get the work to the people?' With this reversal of a basic assumption, the assembly line was born.")

Can you reverse roles? (Michalko again: "Alfred Sloan took over General Motors when it was on the verge of bankruptcy and turned it around. His genius was to take an assumption and reverse it into a 'breakthrough idea.' For instance, it had always been assumed that you had to buy a car before you drove it. Sloan reversed this to mean you could buy it while driving it, pioneering the concept of instalment buying for car dealers." So what can school financing learn from that?)

What can you combine?

How about a blend, an alloy, an assortment, an ensemble? (A school as a farm?)

Combine units? (Schools as health centres?)

Combine purposes? (Colleges as community fitness centres?)

If you learn only one word of Japanese make it KAIZEN

KAIZEN strategy is the single most important concept in Japanese management—the key to Japanese competitive success. KAIZEN means improvement. KAIZEN means *ongoing* improvement involving *everyone:* top management, managers and workers.

MASAAKI IMAI
*Kaizen: The Key To Japan's Competitive Success**

*Published by Random House, 201 East 50th St., New York, NY 10022.

Combine appeals? (Regular ethnic dinners as part of each school's multi-cultural curriculum? A Japanese, Hispanic or Italian week?)

Combine ideas? (Why not your own community programme to plan its future for the next century?)

Don Koberg and Jim Bagnall, in their book *The Universal Traveller,* have added such words as: multiply, divide, eliminate, subdue, invert, separate, transpose, unify, distort, rotate, flatten, squeeze, complement, submerge, freeze, soften, fluff-up, by-pass, add, subtract, lighten, repeat, thicken, stretch, extrude, repel, protect, segregate, integrate, symbolize, abstract and dissect.

Stanford University engineer James Adams[12] suggests thinking up your own favourite "bug list"—the things that irritate you—to start you thinking. And he lists among his own: corks that break off in wine bottles, vending machines that take your money with no return, bumper stickers that cannot be removed, crooked billiard cue sticks, paperless toilets, dripping faucets and "one sock." "If you run out of bugs before ten minutes," says Adams, "you are either suffering from a perceptual or emotional block or have life unusually under control."

Another technique is to focus on 1,000 percent breakthroughs. What can you do ten times faster, better, cheaper? Given the tremendous increase in technology, in almost any field 1,000 per cent improvements are possible: in some operations. Learning to typeset magazine advertisements and newspapers, for instance, once took a six-year apprenticeship. To "make-up" pages took five years of training. Today, with desktop computerized publishing, any competent typist can compress much of that 11-year training into a week. What would it take to achieve similar breakthroughs in your field?

At the other extreme, *if you learn only one word of Japanese in your life, make it Kaizen. It means continuous improvement.*

But it means much more than that. *It means a philosophy that encourages every person in an industry—every day—to come up with suggestions for improving everything:* themselves, their job, their lunchroom, their office layout, their telephone answering habits and their products. Matsushita, the giant Japanese electronics company, receives about 6.5 million ideas every year from its staff.[13] And the big majority are put into operation quickly. Says Toyota Motor chairman Eiji Toyoda: "One of the features of the Japanese workers is that they use their brains as well as their hands. Our workers provide 1.5 million suggestions a

At Matsushita Electric
in recent years employees have submitted about
6.5 million ideas annually.

TOSHIHIKO YAMASHITA
The Panasonic Way*

*English-language edition published by Kodansha International,
114 Fifth Avenue, New York, NY 10011.

year, and 95 per cent of them are put to practical use."[14] And at Nissan Motors "any suggestion that saves at least 0.6 seconds—the time it takes a worker to stretch out his hand or walk half a step—is seriously considered by management."[15]

It is beyond the scope of this book to cover the total secret of Japan's Quality Management and Kaizen movements.[16] But to test, in part, the effectiveness of their method, try an introductory "Kaizen" on anything you're involved in. If you're a teacher, genuinely encourage your class to write down and then discuss every specific suggestion they can make to improve their school and their education. Schools that have tried this have been amazed at the results—as we'll report later. Or if you're in business, apply Kaizen to even one company operation—like answering outside phone-calls, speeding up service in the firm's cafeteria or making sure all orders are delivered on time.

Many universities, of course, would say they have always taught thinking as part of logic, psychology and philosophy. But most schools don't teach what Edward de Bono[17] has termed *lateral thinking:* the ability to open-mindedly search for new ideas, look in new directions, challenge existing concepts.

Roger von Oech thinks even the terms logical and lateral thinking are too restrictive. He says we're also capable of conceptual thinking, analytical thinking, speculative thinking, right-brain thinking, critical thinking, foolish thinking, convergent thinking, weird thinking, reflective thinking, visual thinking, symbolic thinking, propositional thinking, digital thinking, metaphorical thinking, mythical thinking, poetic thinking, non-verbal thinking, elliptical thinking, analogical thinking, lyrical thinking, practical thinking, divergent thinking, ambiguous thinking, constructive thinking, thinking about thinking, surreal thinking, focused thinking, concrete thinking and fantasy thinking.[18]

But most people unwittingly limit their thinking potential. One reason is the brain's ability to file material inside existing patterns. When a new problem is tackled, we're conditioned to go down the track of previous answers. We all have preconceptions, taboos and prejudices, though few of us ever admit them. They can be emotional, cultural, religious, educational, national, psychological, sexual or culinary.

We are also preconditioned from school to come up with "the right answer"—not the open-minded challenge for a better way. Probably every adult, for instance, would claim to have an open mind. But ask

<u>Do a "PMI" on this proposition:</u>

"That all teaching should be done by computers."

<u>Write three separate columns,</u>
one headed Plus, one Minus
and one Interesting.

<u>Now list all the "plus" points</u>
(like: All study could be
interactive; you'd get
instant feedback).

<u>Then all the "minuses"</u>
(No personal relationships;
and how could a computer be
a field-trip guide?).

<u>Then all the "interesting" ideas</u>
that occur to you
(How would a computer handle
discipline? How would a
computer be paid?
Could you make computer study
a joint-venture between home
and school?)

PMI is one of Edward de Bono's
suggestions for teaching thinking

anyone to open-mindedly create a new religion—with the freedom to choose ideas out of all the world's great religions and schools of philosophy, and the story could be different. Why? Simply because you are challenging a very fundamental belief.

Or ask a trained medical doctor to analyse the lessons to be learned from yoga, acupuncture, chiropractic, osteopathy, ayurvedic health or homeopathy—and again open-mindedness could be lacking.

The same applies to education. Almost every adult who has succeeded at high school or college will have firm ideas on the best educational system. And it will generally be the system that he succeeded in. Listen to anyone praise a "good school" and you will almost certainly find a school that suits that particular person's learning style.

Now that's not unusual. You could probably go through life and never find a person totally objective about everything. And fortunately, no one system of education, or religion, or health, suits all. So perhaps the first step in "conceptual blockbusting"—to use James Adams' term[19]—is to accept that we all have fears, we all have biases. The best way we know to start overcoming them is to combine fun and humour. That often works for students in particular. A fun-filled atmosphere can lead to high creativity. If you're not used to "far-out" brainstorming sessions, probably a good warm-up exercise is to start with a humorous challenge. Try inventing a new golfball— one that can't get lost. Or planning what you'd do with a holiday on the moon. Or ask some "What if?" questions. Like what would happen if pets became school teachers? Or if computers ran the government? Then use some of de Bono's techniques, such as PMI, CAF, C&S, APC and his "Six Thinking Hats."[20]

PMI standards for Plus, Minus and Interesting. Here the students are asked to choose a fairly outlandish statement, and in three columns write down all the points they can think of to be "plus" factors, then all the "minuses," and lastly all the reasons the proposition could be "interesting."

CAF means Consider All Factors. And again write them down, searching for new factors that don't spring immediately to mind.

C & S stands for Consequences and Sequel. Logically, both should be listed under CAF, but de Bono says that most people just do not consider all the consequences unless their attention is specifically drawn to them.

APC stands for Alternatives, Possibilities and Choices. And again

**When Bell first offered
his telephone for sale
it was turned down because
"there was no need for it."**

**When Edison undertook the
development of the
electric light, a body
of distinguished experts
agreed that his efforts were
"unworthy of the attention
of practical or scientific men."**

**The Xerox copying process
was available for four years
before a backer could be found.**

DON FABUN
Three Roads To Awareness*

*Published by Glencoe Press, Beverly Hills, California.

the reasons are obvious: a list that encourages you to speculate.

As de Bono summarizes one of his other techniques: "The theme of my book *Six Thinking Hats* is simple. There is the white hat for neutral facts, figures and information. There is the red hat to allow a person to put forward feelings, hunches and intuitions—without any need to justify them. The black hat is for the logical negative, and the yellow hat for the logical positive. For creativity there is the green hat. The blue hat is the control hat, and looks at the thinking itself rather than at the subject—like an orchestra conductor controlling the orchestra. The purpose is to provide a means for rapidly switching thinkers from one mode to another—without causing offence."[21]

All are excellent classroom techniques. Especially the "six hats"—when you go to the trouble to obtain some bizarre models, in colours and odd shapes, and pass them around as each person acts the part.

But the simple ideas we have suggested earlier in this chapter are the ones we have found to work effectively in virtually any situation: in advertising, business, marketing, selling, exporting, market research and all aspects of learning and education. They work, we believe, because they show the logical links between sequential and creative thinking. Your critical "left-brain" logic sees the common-sense in the step-by-step approach to the "right-brain's" creative ability.

They start, of course, by tapping into the outstanding power of the brain. And the brain's potential, as we'll turn to next, is grounded in processing which goes back to the start of life—even well before birth itself.

Checklist for new mothers

1 All the active braincells a child will ever have are present by birth.

2 A well-nourished fetus during pregnancy will develop an average of 250,000 new brain cells every minute.

3 Smoking, alcohol and drugs can severely affect that brain-growth.

4 Poor diet during vital periods can cause lifelong learning disabilities.

5 Eat plenty of fish, green-leaf vegetables, fruit, nuts and vegetable oil.

6 Have a banana a day when pregnant, for potassium and folic acid.

7 Iron- and zinc-rich foods are essential for baby's brain-growth.

8 Breast-feed if possible—to add the vital "coating" to the main braincells.

9 After birth, make sure to get baby's hearing and eyesight checked regularly.

A sensible guide to producing better, brighter babies

Your body is more fascinating than any machine.

Every day about two million of its cells wear out. But the body replaces them automatically.

Every 15 to 30 days your body completely replaces the outermost layer of your skin. What you see in the mirror today is not the same skin you had a month ago.

But some cells your body will never replace: the 100 billion active nerve-cells, or neurons, that make up your brain's cortex.[1]

Every one of them was present the day you were born. In your mother's womb you were growing them at an average of 250,000 cells every minute.

Each one continues to grow in size over the first few years of life. Each one, as we've seen, is capable of sprouting up to 20,000 dendrites. But after birth you never gain another active neuron as long as you live.

What happens to each brain in the nine months before birth is therefore vital to later learning ability. When pregnant women are severely under-nourished, their children can be born with fewer than half the brain-cells of a healthy child.

As we've seen, neurons are not the only cells in the brain. We each have up to 900 billion *glial* cells to nourish the neurons. These glial cells also develop *myelin,* the sheathing that wraps around our *axons.* These are the nerve pathways that speed messages from neuron to neuron and around our bodies—like electrical transmission wires. Both of these cell groups start growing in the womb, and continue during the first few years of life.

Within the next minute an average of 250,000 brain-cells will have multiplied in each and every well-nourished growing fetus in the world.

RICHARD M. RESTAK
The Infant Mind*

*Published by Doubleday & Company, 666 Fifth Avenue,
New York, NY 10103.

If the baby is poorly fed in those vital early years, it will not produce all the nourishing glial cells it needs. *And if some foods are missing from the expectant mother's diet, the nerve pathways around the brain and body will not be efficiently insulated.*

As American researchers Brian and Roberta Morgan put it in their highly-recommended book *Brain Food:* "The human brain begins growing in the womb, and the majority of this development does not slow down until the age of six. Growth in the brain of the fetus, infant and young child is time-dependent. This means that the brain grows in specific stages at specific times. If it does not have all the nutrients essential for its growth at those times, damage or malformation can result which cannot be corrected at a later date. A developing infant who is fed poorly during its period of brain growth may be left with learning disabilities which will remain for the rest of its life, no matter what is done at a later date to correct the nutritional deficiency."

Scottish Professor Michael Crawford sums up ten years of research into the impact of nutrition on infant and fetal brain growth: "Wherever we've found low birth-weight babies, small head circumference and intellectual deficits in infants, we've found that right across the board the mothers concerned had diets before and during pregnancy that were deficient in a large number of nutrients."[2]

Even in developed societies such as Britain, the United States and New Zealand, at least ten percent of babies continue to arrive with low birth-weights. Generally that results from the mother's poor diet, smoking, taking drugs or being affected by toxic substances such as lead.

Crawford is amazed at the lack of education on diet and nutrition. And he says poor diet before birth affects more than the brain. Seven separate studies indicate that later heart problems, high blood pressure and many strokes have their roots in poor diet before birth.

Perhaps surprisingly, one of the major deficiencies is fat. But a special kind of fat. "Unfortunately," says Crawford, "we've come to think of fat as lard and dripping. *But what the fetus really needs is a highly specialized fat—the essential fats we call them, because you really do need to have them in your diet. They're the fats you need to build cells, especially brain-cells, and not the sort of fats that animals and humans dump on their waistlines.*

"Many of those fats come from marine life. Now of course it's an old wives' tale that fish is good for the brain. It happens to be that we now

If a pregnant woman smokes one cigarette, her fetus will stop breathing for five minutes.

RICHARD M. RESTAK
The Infant Mind*

*Published by Doubleday & Company, 666 Fifth Avenue,
New York, NY10103.

have absolute scientific evidence for this. *We find that the fats found in fish and seafood of all sorts are especially relevant to the growth and development of the brain." And those same fats are vital for developing the body's immune system.*

They are also needed to build and maintain the myelin insulation.

Crawford wishes everyone would return to "the unsophisticated foods of nature": plenty of green leafy vegetables, fruit, nuts and vegetable oil.

If Crawford and his dietician, Wendy Dole, could get one message through to every potential mother in the world, it would be simply this: *the most important time for your child's brain-growth is before you become pregnant.*

Women who have used oral contraceptives should be especially careful of their diet before pregnancy. "The pill" reduces your body's stores of pyridoxine (one of the B vitamins) and folicin or folic acid, a vitamin needed for neural development. Severe folic acid deficiencies can cause serious malformations of the brain and other organs.

Crawford says pregnant women in particular should include bananas in their regular daily diet. "Not only are they a good source of potassium, they also contain good supplies of folic acid."

Zinc and iron are minerals essential for early brain growth. Where pregnant monkeys have been fed a diet low in zinc, their infants later play less with others, act withdrawn and have difficulty learning complex tasks. Iron is needed for all cell growth and multiplication. It also influences the oxygen supply to the blood.

Most dietary experts say that a simple, sensible diet is best before and during pregnancy: three meals a day, plenty of fruit, vegetables, nuts, fish and lean meat. An iron supplement during pregnancy is highly recommended. The diet should be high in foods that are rich in iron and zinc, such as beans, peas, broccoli, carrots, whole wheat bread, berries and brown rice. And don't try any special diets to keep you slim.

The other "no-no's" during pregnancy? "Smoking, alcohol and drugs,"[3] says New York researcher Ian James, Professor of Paediatrics, Obstetrics and Gynaecology at Columbia University's Presbyterian Medical Centre. *He says "for every one cigarette the mother smokes, the baby smokes two." Smoking starves the fetal brain of oxygen—at a time when oxygen is vital for cell formation.*

Pregnant women who smoke 15 to 20 cigarettes a day are twice as likely to miscarry as non-smoking mothers. In the first few weeks after

Drugs are most dangerous to the fetus during the first three months of pregnancy, when the heart, brain, limbs and facial features are forming.

THE READER'S DIGEST BODY BOOK*

*Published by The Reader's Digest.

birth, smokers' infants die at a rate 30 percent higher than non-smokers' infants. Babies also absorb poisonous nicotine through breast milk. And they are later more prone to respiratory infections, and they also have a higher rate of pneumonia.

Alcohol can also damage the growing brain. And heavy drinking can cause what has become known as "fetal alcohol syndrome," which results in reduced brain size, distorted facial features, poor coordination and hyperactive behaviour.

James describes the effects of cocaine or heroin as devastating, especially for young pregnant women and their babies. Educational psychologist Jane M. Healy, of Vail, Colorado, says research estimates show that at least one of every nine babies born in the United States is drug-affected. "Many authorities warn," she adds, "that growing cocaine use by pregnant women will soon flood the schools with children who have attention, learning and social problems. And these children are not even included in our already declining test scores."[4]

After birth, diet is still vital for all cell growth. And the importance of myelination cannot be stressed too much. Some of it is in place before birth: around the nerve pathways that enable a newborn baby to suck, cry and move its fingers. But at birth the pathways needed for walking, talking and bladder control are not yet myelinated.

"Common sense tells us that it is useless to try and get a newborn to walk alone," says Healy, "but at about one year, when those connections have myelinated, it may be difficult to prevent."

About 75 percent of myelin comes from fat—from what Crawford calls "essential fats." And the other 25 percent comes from protein. Breast feeding by a healthy mother is the best source of both. And of zinc, which is also vital to form glial cells. Breast milk also contains specific antibodies which coat the baby's intestines and respiratory tract and fight off infection. It also helps protect the baby from ear infections, eczema and other allergies. And it provides calcium and phosphorous needed for rapidly growing bones. In fact, the only thing lacking in a healthy mother's breast milk could be vitamin D. That's why many doctors recommend a vitamin D supplement. A well-balanced milk "formula" can also be used in place of breast milk—but it must be one that tries to duplicate the essential elements of mothers' milk.

All this sounds like elementary common sense. And about four mothers out of five seem to "do the right thing—naturally." But even in

Understanding a child's brain and the way it develops is the key to understanding learning.

JANE M. HEALY
Your Child's Growing Mind*

*Published by Doubleday, 666 Fifth Avenue, New York, NY 10103.

many "developed" countries around 20 percent of mothers can't cope without some form of help. And around ten percent of mothers are at "high risk."

Researchers at the Otago University School of Medicine in New Zealand, for instance, have completed a ten-year study of women having babies at the nearby Dunedin maternity hospital. Before a baby is born, hospital staff ask the mothers some simple questions, such as age, marital status, employment and home addresses over the previous year. And the figures have been consistent year by year: 78 percent of mothers can cope adequately. But 22 percent need some form of help. And nine percent of all babies are considered high risk.[5] They could be seriously abused or maltreated unless their mothers are helped.

It's not hard to identify the risk factors: young, single mothers, moving around a lot. No job. Parents who've already split up. A history of foster homes. Maybe a background of drugs. Mother suffered parental violence as a child.

Unfortunately, a similar pattern exists in many countries. The United States has 22 million children under six. Five million of those are living in poverty and about half that number again are just above the poverty line.[6] And guess who'll be the educational failures of the next century unless that poverty trap is broken?

That's why we've listed parent education and early childhood health programmes as vital first priorities in any sensible education system.

Dozens of research projects show the vital connection between good nutrition and other brain-developing activities in the first five years of life.

Ideally most early brain development happens in sequence. A child learns to see before it learns to talk. It learns to crawl and creep before it walks. Walks before it runs. Learns to identify simple objects before it learns to reason. If an infant misses out on one of those steps—like walking without ever crawling or creeping—learning problems can result. To use computer terms, that's because the early activities lay down the "hard-wiring" or "hardware" of the brain—in a set sequence. When the hardware is in first-class condition, it can be used to "run" any software program: like learning a foreign language or a new subject. But if any of the "hard-wiring" has been skipped, the brain could have difficulty running some programmes.

The early-development timetable is set in part by the sequence of

**In one survey of 200 inmates
of Mt Eden prison
in Auckland, New Zealand:**

■ **All 100 Maori (Polynesian)
prisoners checked
had hearing loss
ten times worse than the
national average.**

■ **Eighty-two percent of
non-Maori prisoners had
the same degree of hearing
loss.**

■ **Most of it stemmed from lack
of hearing checks and
treatment in early childhood.**

Pacific Network magazine*

*Published by the Pacific Foundation, Auckland, New Zealand,
February 1992 edition.

myelination. A thin spiral of sheathing around axons is present at birth, but the full insulation is then laid down around the body, and the brain, in sequence. Overall, in the body that starts at the top and works down. That's why you can make sounds before you learn to walk—the long axons transmitting messages to your toes and calf muscles take longer to coat than the axons to your tongue and larynx.

In the brain, full myelination starts at the back and moves to the front. That's why you learn to see before you learn to talk and reason: your optical nerve-centre is at the back of the brain, your speech-centre is further forward, and your reasoning-centre is at the front. The process is completed in the centre of the brain—what scientists call the "association cortex": the part you use to sort incoming information and blend it with data already in your storage files.

When axons are fully covered by their myelin sheath, they can transmit messages around the body up to 12 times faster than they could before. In fact, the speed of transmission around the body can vary from one mile an hour to 150 miles.[8]

Just as the fetus grows in spurts, so does the new infant brain. And the timing of those bursts can be vital.

Close one eye of a two-year-old for as little as a week, for instance, and you will almost certainly damage its ability to see.[8] This is because the growing brain is laying down its main visual pathways from the eyes to the vision-centre at the rear of the brain. The two separate pathways are competing for dominance. Shut one eye for any length of time and the other one will lay down the dominant pathway. Close one eye for a week when you're 20 and it won't matter, because by then your basic pathways have been laid down.

Says Stanford University human biology professor Robert Ornstein: "The critical period during which the two eyes establish their zones of dominance seems to be about the first six years in humans, six months in monkeys, and perhaps three months in cats. It is a very sensitive period. If one eye of a kitten is kept closed for only one day, it will have poor vision in that eye as an adult.

"There is a very important practical lesson from this basic work on the visual brain. Do not ever keep *one* eye of a human infant closed for an extended period of time. Keeping both eyes closed is better; after all, infants sleep a good bit of the time."[9]

It is the same with hearing. Your inner ear is no bigger than a small

If you want to help children, you have to start looking at the brain; after all, they don't read with their kidneys!

DR. DEBORAH WABER
of Harvard University*

*Quoted by Jane M. Healy, in *Endangered Minds,*
published by Simon & Schuster, 1230 Avenue of the Americas,
New York, NY 10020.

nut, but it contains as many circuits as the telephone system of many cities. The ear also contains another tiny vital structure called a cochlea. It looks like a snail shell and works like a piano keyboard. But a piano has only 88 keys, while the cochlea has 20,000 hairlike sensory cells which pick up sound impulses and transmit them to the brain.

The whole intricate hearing mechanism is obviously vital for learning language. As with sight, the basic language pathways are also laid down in the first few years of life. Some experts say the full English language has only around 40 different sounds—and all the world's languages probably between 60 and 70. Hear all those sounds clearly in the vital first few years of life, learn to pronounce and use them, and you'll be able to pronounce other languages much better if you learn them later in life.

Most healthy children in a well rounded environment also learn to speak fluently at least the 2,000 basic words of their language in the first four years of life. But if they can't hear, they'll find it much more difficult to speak fluently. And if they can't hear or speak, they'll have difficulty learning. Several surveys in New Zealand, for instance, found 20 percent of preschool children with hearing problems in one ear, and ten percent with severe hearing loss in both.[10]

That's just one more reason that the most effective early childhood development programmes include regular hearing and sight checks, along with major attention to nutrition and parent education.

We are indeed what we eat and what our mothers ate. We are also very much the result of what we do and what we think. And just as the right nutrition and exercise can provide the nourishment for a young brain's "nerve highways" and developing dendrite branches, so the right activity, involving all five senses, can produce more dendritic connections. All future learning will be based on those connections—and the early nourishment that went into their development.

All the best educational programmes around the world combine elements that stimulate both a child's physical and mental development—for in truth there is no split between the two.

We are all a combination of what we eat, think and do. And, after good care in the nine months before birth, the best programmes concentrate next on the most vital years of life: from birth to eight.

How to make the most of the vital years: from birth to eight

■ Fifty percent of a person's ability to learn is developed in the first four years of life.

■ Another 30 percent is developed by the eighth birthday.

■ Those vital years lay down the pathways on which all future learning is based.

■ Youngsters are their own best educators, parents their best first teachers.

■ Youngsters learn best by what they experience with all their senses, so stimulate them.

■ Our homes, beaches, forests, playgrounds, zoos, museums and adventure areas are the world's best schools.

■ Simple physical routines can help infants explode into learning.

■ Infants grow in a patterned way, so learn to build on that growth pattern.

■ Learning anything, including reading, writing and math, can be fun—so long as it is treated like a game.

How to enrich your child's intelligence from birth to eight

Most mothers seem to know it intuitively.

Now researchers have proved it beyond doubt: you develop around 50 percent of your ability to learn in the first four years of life. And you develop another 30 percent of that ability before you turn eight.[1]

This does not mean that you absorb 50 percent of your *knowledge* or 50 percent of your *wisdom* by your fourth birthday. It simply means that in those first few years you form the main learning pathways in your brain. Everything else you learn in life will be built on that base. You also take in a fantastic amount of information in those early years. And all later learning will grow from that core.

Says British psychologist Tony Buzan: "At the moment a child is born it's already really brilliant. It picks up language, much better than a doctor of philosophy in any subject, in only two years. And it is a master at it by three or four."[2]

Buzan says every child born, unless it has severe brain damage, is a budding genius.

He demonstrates that early rage to learn with a piece of paper. "Imagine I am now a three-month-old baby," he smiles. "You've given me this piece of paper. You know it's not going to last long. Now do I do it like this?" (He mimes a small child looking passively at the paper and then ignoring it.)

"Or do I do it like this?" (He then tries to tear the paper, crumple it, rattle it, and even stuff it in his mouth.) "It's obviously the second way. And what that little baby was doing was being a little Isaac Newton—the perfect scientist.

All children are born geniuses, and we spend the first six years of their lives degeniusing them.

BUCKMINISTER FULLER

"What kind of musical instrument can I make from this material (shaking it)?

"What is the sociological, economic value of this material (putting it in his mouth)?

"Anybody want some (offering it around)?

"What is the engineering, mechanical, tensile strength of the material (pulling it apart)?

"Stick it in the chemical laboratory (chewing it)?

"Check the musical instrument—and on to the next experiment.

"Now the baby is using all of its brain. Logic? Yes. Analysis? Yes. Rhythm? Yes. Everything? Yes."

Scientists have tested this infant ability in many ways. In 1964, Benjamin S. Bloom, Professor of Education at the University of Chicago, published a summary of major research findings. In it, he studied five main human characteristics between birth and age 17 and 18: height, general learning ability, school achievement, aggressiveness in males and dependence in females.[3]

Overwhelmingly, he found that development soared in the first few years—then tapered off. Generally it reached its halfway point before the fifth birthday. He found boys reached 54 percent of their maximum height by their third birthday, another 32 percent between three and 12, and the last 14 percent by the 18th birthday.

He also concluded that among both girls and boys, about 50 percent of intelligence, as measured in tests at 17, took place between conception and age four, about 30 percent between four and eight, and the final 20 percent between the ages of eight and 17. Even researchers who question the validity of standardized intelligence tests would probably endorse this overall finding—so long as the words *learning ability* are substituted for *intelligence.*

Bloom also analysed vocabulary, reading comprehension and general school achievement between birth and age 18. This convinced him that 33 percent of an 18-year-old's academic skills are achieved by age six, 42 percent between six and 13, and 25 percent between 13 and 18.

Bloom's research covered an age where male-female roles were very stereotyped—and encouraged early by training. He concluded that 50 percent of the aggressiveness that males showed at age 18 or 20 had developed by age three. And 50 percent of the "passivity" that females

Education
must
start
at
birth.

NEW ZEALAND MINISTRY OF EDUCATION

*Education for the 21st Century**

*Published by Learning Media Ltd., Box 3293, Wellington, New Zealand.

exhibited by 18 or 20 had developed by age four. Bloom's findings came from analysing many different *longitudinal* studies, which check the progress of the same people over many years.

Two of the most thorough analyses since Bloom's have been done in the South Island of New Zealand.

The first is through the Otago University School of Medicine in Dunedin, a city of around 100,000 people. In 1972, 1,661 babies were born in Dunedin. Their progress has been checked regularly ever since. And more than 1,000 of them are still being surveyed.

Research director Dr. Phil Silva says that the survey underlines the vital importance of the first few years of life.[4] "That doesn't mean that the other years are unimportant, but our research shows that children who have a slow start during the first three years of life are likely to experience problems right through childhood and into adolescence and early adult life."

He says it's also vital to identify any special problems in the first three years, such as hearing or eyesight defects, "because if we don't help them at the early stages then it's likely that they are going to experience long-lasting problems throughout their lives."

The other survey has checked the progress of 1,206 infants born in the city of Christchurch in 1977. One of its key findings: between 15 and 20 percent of youngsters fall behind because they don't get the necessary early-childhood health-checks and developmental experience.[5]

Buzan agrees. "Make sure that the child, from as early as possible, gets as much exercise as its wants, with as much of a free body as possible: hands free, feet free, able to crawl a lot, climb a lot. Allow it to make its own mistakes so that it learns by its own trial and error."

There are only five main pathways into the brain, the five senses of sight, hearing, touch, taste and smell. Youngsters obviously learn through all of them. Every day is a learning experience. They love to experiment, to create, to find out how things work. Challenges are there to be accepted. Adults and older children to be imitated.

Most important, a child learns by doing. He learns to crawl by crawling. He learns to walk by walking. To talk by talking. And each time he does so he either lays down new pathways in the brain—if his experience is new—or he builds on and expands existing pathways—if he is repeating the experience.

Youngsters are their own best educators, parents their best first teach-

In one American survey, children received six negative comments for every positive comment.*

*Survey carried out by Jack Canfield in 1982 and reported by Bobbi DePorter in *Quantum Learning,* published by Dell.

ers. And our homes, beaches, forests, playgrounds, adventure areas and the whole wide world our main educational resources—as long as children are encouraged to explore them safely through all their senses.

Researchers stress the need for positive encouragement. Says British accelerated learning pioneer Colin Rose: "It's true throughout life that if you think you are a poor learner, you'll probably be a poor learner."[6] But the real question is how that thought pattern is programmed. American research has shown that most children, from a very early age, receive at least six negative comments to every one of positive encouragement.[7] Comments like "Don't do that," or "You didn't do that very well," are where the problem starts.

Research has also established beyond doubt the importance of every child growing in an enriched environment.

Berkeley scientists in California have been experimenting for many years with rats—and comparing their brain growth with humans. "Very simply," says Professor Marian Diamond, "we've found with our rats that all the nerve cells in the key outer layers of the brain are present at birth. At birth the interconnecting dendrites start to grow. For the first month the growth is prolific. Then it starts to go down.

"If we put the rats in enriched environments, we can keep the dendrite growth up. But if we put them in impoverished environments, then dendrite growth goes down fast.

"In enrichment cages, rats live together and have access to toys. They have ladders, wheels and other playthings. They can climb, explore and interact with their toys. Then we compare them with rats in impoverished environments: one rat to a cage, no toys, no interaction. Again very simply: we've found that the rat brain-cells increase in size in the enriched environment—and the number of dendrites increases dramatically. In the impoverished environment, the opposite."[8]

The rats then take an "intelligence test": they're put in a maze, and left to find food in another part of the maze. The "enriched" rats do so easily. The others don't.

Obviously, scientists can't cut up human brains to test the impact of early stimulation. But they can check with radioactive glucose. "And these checks," says Diamond, "show that the vital glucose uptake is extremely rapid for the first two years of life—provided the child has a good diet and adequate stimulation. It continues rapidly until five years. It continues very slowly from five to ten. By about ten years of age, brain-

Even 15 minutes of rocking, rubbing, rolling and stroking a premature baby four times a day will greatly help its ability to coordinate movements and therefore to learn.

RUTH RICE*

*Summarized from her dissertation, *The Effects of Tactile-Kinesthetic Stimulation on the Subsequent Development of Premature Infants,* University of Texas (1975).

growth has reached its peak—although the good news is this: the human brain can keep on growing dendrites till the end of life, so long as it is being stimulated. Very simply, the human brain-cell, like the rat's, is designed to receive stimulation—and to grow from it."

That doesn't mean turning an infant's home into a formal school classroom. The reverse, in fact: infants learn by play and exploration. It's the formal classroom that needs redesigning.

"We used to think that play and education were opposite things," say Jean Marzollo and Janice Lloyd in their excellent book *Learning Through Play.* "Now we know better. Educational experts and early childhood specialists have discovered that play *is* learning, and even more, that play is one of the most effective kinds of learning."

The key: turning play into learning experiences—and making sure that all learning is fun.

In fact, things that good parents take for granted provide some of the best early learning. But we don't mean "academic" studies. *Scientists have proved, for instance, that regularly rocking a baby can help greatly in promoting brain growth.* It stimulates what they call *the vestibular system.* This is a nerve-system centred in the brainstem and linked very closely with a baby's inner-ear mechanism, which also plays a vital part in developing balance and coordination. Scientists say this is one of the first parts of the brain to begin to function in the womb—as early as 16 weeks after conception.

"It is this early maturity that makes the vestibular system so important to early brain development," says Richard M. Restak, M.D., author of *The Brain: The Last Frontier* and *The Infant Mind.* "The fetus floating in its amniotic fluid registers its earliest perceptions via the activity of its vestibular system. In recent years evidence has accumulated that the vestibular system is crucial for normal brain development. Infants who are given periodic vestibular stimulation, by rocking, gain weight faster, develop vision and hearing earlier, and demonstrate distinct sleep cycles at a younger age." [9]

Dr. Ruth Rice, of Texas, has shown in controlled tests that *even 15 minutes of rocking, rubbing, rolling and stroking a premature baby four times a day will greatly help its ability to coordinate movements and therefore to learn.* [10]

And Dr. Lyelle Palmer, Professor of Education at Winona State University in Minnesota, has completed extensive studies at kindergarten

Helicopter spin

For ages three years and above, provided they can walk and run

Have children balance themselves by extending hands out from the sides of their body.

Invite them to spin as fast as possible, in a standing position, for 15 seconds. Say: "We are helicopters flying to the airport." Play loud music while spinning.

Then say: "STOP and close your eyes. Keep your balance. Remain standing." (Do not say: "Don't fall down." Emphasize what to do, not what not to do.) The children stand for 25 seconds until they no longer feel dizzy. The process is then repeated.

Spin ten times. This will take about five minutes. Spin 15 seconds, rest 15 seconds, spin 15 seconds and so on. Speed is important. It keeps the ear fluids moving.

Eventually children will spin with eyes closed, opening them occasionally in order to check on safety. (Do not spin one way and then immediately spin the other way because it is important that the fluid in the semicircular canals of the ear keeps moving. When you start spinning the other way, the fluid movement stops and stimulation is reduced.)

For children having difficulty, the adult stands over the child and assists by grasping one hand and quickly pulling the child's arm around the body and creating a continuous spinning action.

This is one of the routines used by Professor Lyelle Palmer with great success to improve the learning ability of young children.

level to demonstrate the vital importance of such simple stimulation for five-year-olds.[11] Every day youngsters have attended a gymnasium as a key part of early schooling. There they are encouraged to carry out a simple series of routines: spinning, rope jumping, balancing, somersaulting, rolling and walking on balance beams. On the playground, they are encouraged to swing on low "jungle gyms," climb, skate, perform somersaults and flips. And in classrooms they play with a wide range of games, also designed to stimulate their sense of sight, hearing and touch. All activities are designed to increase in skill-levels during the year, and to help stimulate overall brain development.

At the end of each year, many of the children undergo the Metropolitan Readiness Test to measure whether they've developed enough to start first-grade schooling. Nearly all have passed the tests in the top ten percent for the state—and most have been in the top five percent. Nearly all of them come from working-class backgrounds.

Palmer, a former president of the Society for Accelerative Learning and Teaching, emphasizes that the children are not simply walking, running and skipping the normal "motor" activities. "The stimulation activities we recommend," he says, "are specifically designed to activate the areas of the brain we know will promote their sense of sight, touch and hearing—as well as their ability to take in knowledge."[12]

Most parents, for instance, seem to learn instinctively that infants love to be held firmly by their hands and spun around like a helicopter blade. Palmer's Minneapolis public school research at New Vision School has shown that such activities result in important brain growth. And the greater the intensity of the activity the greater you see the results of the brain-growth in areas that are receptive to further learning.

The overall result is a big gain in competence, self-confidence, increased attention, faster responses and the ability to tackle learning activities of increasing complexity.

Palmer stresses that the activities are not what many schools would regard as "academic." But any classroom visit shows the youngsters "exploding" into true learning. Early reading is taught with word-card games. The youngsters get an early introduction to mathematics by playing with dominos and big cards with dots instead of numbers. And they play games to develop pre-writing skills.

Does it help "academic development?" You bet! In another study of at-risk youngsters who were not doing well at school, Palmer's methods

I learned the way a monkey learns: by watching its parents.

QUEEN ELIZABETH II*

*Quoted by John-Roger and Peter McWilliams, *Do it! Let's Get Off Our Buts,* Prelude Press, 8165 Mannix Drive, Los Angeles, CA 90046.

produced dramatic gains in reading ability. The children of the experimental group read three to ten times faster than the control group.[13]

Significantly, all activities in Palmer's experimental classes are presented in what he describes as "a context of fun."

Again, that is a recurring message throughout our research. As another American accelerative-learning pioneer, Peter Kline, puts it in *The Everyday Genius:* "Emblazon these words on your mind as the most important ones in this book: **Learning is most effective when it's fun.**"

And that learning can start from the moment of birth. Hundreds of books are available to help parents choose fun-filled activities for infants. Again, the main points are simple:

1. The vital importance of step-by-step movement

Infants grow in a patterned way. They're born explorers. So encourage them to explore in a safe but interesting environment. So long as they are warm, don't limit their movements with too much clothing.

"Give them the chance to crawl from as early an age as possible," says Janet Doman, director of The Institutes for The Achievement of Human Potential in Philadelphia, which runs regular week-long international parent-education courses. "Babies can actually crawl from birth, but generally they are restricted by so much clothing that they don't develop this ability till later. Very simply, the more they crawl the sooner they're going to creep, and the more they creep the more they'll be able to walk. And each of these stages ensures that the next stage comes at the right moment—and that they have completed the neurological maturation that goes with it.

"If babies are bundled up for so long that they don't really crawl much at all, but go straight to creeping, then they may well pay a price for that five years later when they get to the point where they need to be able to converge their vision perfectly."[14]

But how on earth can creeping affect a baby's *eyesight?* "Basically, a newborn baby has no ability to converge its two eyes. But when the baby starts to crawl, the need to use two eyes together is born—because all of a sudden the baby is moving forward in space and he begins to hit the sofa or the chair. Nature's a little bit of a tough teacher, and whenever this happens the baby says: 'Wait a second; I'd better see where I'm going.' And that's when the baby begins to pull in those two roving eyes and

Nature has built the brain in such a way that during the first six years of life it can take in information at an overwhelming rate and without the slightest effort.

GLENN DOMAN
author of *Teach Your Baby To Read**

*Author interview, Philadelphia, PA, 1990.

begins to say: 'Where am I?' After that, every time the baby is moving he will turn on his vision, look to see where he's going, and bring those two eyes together. As they converge their vision, it gets better and better. But if you miss that vital stage of development you're missing out a vital stage of brain development."

Part of the reason is very simple: to creep and crawl, a baby needs to use all four limbs. And this movement strengthens the 300 million nerve-cell pathways that link both sides of the brain through the corpus callosum. Children who skip creeping or crawling—common in youngsters with severe brain damage from birth—thus find it impossible to fully coordinate both hemispheres.

2. Simple tips from the start

Everything we learn about the world comes in through our five senses. From the very earliest days infants try to touch, smell, taste, hear and look at whatever surrounds them. So encourage them from the outset.

Says Janet Doman: "A baby is born into a world in which, essentially, he is blind, can't hear very well and his sensation is far from perfect. And that's a very uncomfortable place for a baby to be. He's trying to figure out: 'Where am I? What's going on? What's gonna happen next?' Because he can't see, he can't hear and he can't feel very well. So I think the job of a parent is very clear: to give enough visual, auditory and tactile stimulation so that the baby can get out of this dilemma of not being able to see, hear or feel.

"That doesn't have to be complicated. For example, often new parents put children in a pastel environment. And this for baby is a disaster. The baby needs to see contrast, needs to see outlined shapes and images, needs to see black-and-white contrasts. If you put him in a room of pale pinks and pale blues, it's like putting him in a world where there's nothing to see—so he can't see it."

The institutes' courses recommend new parents to "checkerboard" one wall of a baby's bedroom, with big black and white squares of poster-board. "When you do this simple thing," says Doman," you see an instant reaction from baby. All of a sudden, he can see contrasts, and it turns on his vision. When baby is able to see outline consistently, then we would go back to the checkerboard and put a red triangle in a black square, a bright green circle in a white square, a blue star in a black square. Again simple things that provide contrast."

A baby in his first few months would probably taste only milk and vomit. Now that's not a very interesting taste variety!

JANET DOMAN
Director of The Institutes for the
Achievement of Human Potential*

*Author interview, Philadelphia, PA, 1990.

Or take taste. Doman says it is one of the most neglected senses. "In the normal course of events, a baby in his first few months of life would probably taste only two things: milk and vomit. Now that's not a very interesting taste variety! So we encourage our mothers to introduce some variety: a little taste of lemon or orange or nutmeg."

And sound: "Mothers intuitively speak in a slightly louder, clearer voice to babies—and that's great," says Doman. "And it's even better if you constantly tell baby what's happening: saying 'Now I'm dressing you,' 'I'm putting your right sock on,' 'Now I'm changing your diaper.'"

Playing soothing background music is also recommended. It's significant that youngsters in the Pacific islands of Polynesia, Melanesia and Micronesia almost invariably grow up with the ability to sing in harmony—an almost perfect sense of pitch. Every Polynesian also seems to be a natural dancer. Every New Zealand Maori seems to be able to sing in perfect tune. Again, experts will tell you it's because of what they did well before they went to school. They grew up in a culture where singing and dancing play a major part. And they patterned all that information in the vital early years.

In a similar way thousands of three- and four-year-olds around the world can now play the violin—many in their own orchestras—thanks to programmes pioneered by Japan's Shinichi Suzuki.[15]

3. Build on the five senses

As an infant gets older, many parents feel it's even easier to encourage learning through all the senses—because you see the instant feedback.

In *Learning Through Play,* Marzollo and Lloyd stress that children learn from experiences that are concrete and active. "For a child to understand the abstract concept of 'roundness,' he must first have many experiences with real round things. He needs time to feel round shapes, to roll around balls, to think about the similarities between round objects, and to look at pictures of round things. When children are at play, they like to push, pull, poke, hammer and otherwise manipulate objects, be they toy trucks, egg cartons or pebbles. It is this combination of action and concreteness that makes play so effective as an educational process."

Their book suggests hundreds of simple activities:

To develop the sense of touch:

Cut two round holes on opposite sides of a large cardboard box—then fill the box with small objects of different textures: a stone, sandpaper, a

In the Anang society in Nigeria . . . by the age of five the children can sing hundreds of songs, play numerous percussion instruments and perform dozens of complex dances.

THOMAS ARMSTRONG
*In Their Own Way**

*Published by Jeremy Tarcher, Los Angeles..

silk scarf, felt, a sock, a plastic toy, a piece of wood and a spoon. Encourage your infant to put both hands in the box and see if he can identify each object. But make it a guessing game, not a test.

To develop a sense of smell and taste:

Prepare a lunch that has several distinct tastes and smells: from ingredients such as peanut butter, tuna fish sandwich, chocolate milk, toast, a hot dog with mustard, a cheese sandwich, lemon cookies, an egg salad sandwich. Prepare lunch each day while he's watching. Then at lunchtime ask him if he'd like to play the guessing game. If he says yes, blindfold him with a handkerchief—and he can try to guess what food he's eating.

To develop hearing:

If you have a tape recorder, use it to make a tape of sounds for your child to identify. Let him watch as you make it—this way he'll understand where the sounds come from. Record interesting voices, including his; clocks ticking, water running, refrigerator door being shut, footsteps, an egg beater, electric shaver, an alarm clock going off, a telephone ringing, dog barking, a horn blowing.

To encourage acute sight:

Get some different coloured cardboard and cut it into three-inch by five-inch cards. Then play your own junior card games: naming colours, matching colours, laying them out in different patterns.

4. Use the whole world as your classroom

With a little thought, it's easy to turn every outing into a learning experience.

You can search for shapes

"They're all around you," say Marzollo and Lloyd. "Point them out to your child and soon he'll point them out to you." Circles, such as wheels, balloons, the sun, the moon, eye glasses, bowls, plates, clocks, coins. Rectangles, such as doors, windows, apartment houses, cereal boxes, books, beds and delivery trucks. Squares, like paper napkins, handkerchiefs, windows and tabletops. Triangles, like rooftops, mountains, tents, Christmas trees and sails.

You can see opposites everywhere

And this is a great way to learn words—by association: if a ball goes up it must come down. So do seesaws at the park. Lights go on and off, doors get open and closed, night turns into day.

If, as it is said, the Battle of Waterloo was won on the playing fields of Eton, the great discoveries and new options of the 21st century may well be won in the nurseries of the 20th.

PETER KLINE
*The Everyday Genius**

*Published by Great Ocean Publishers, 1823 North Lincoln Street, Arlington, VA 22207.

Every supermarket trip is a learning journey

Before you shop, ask your youngster to help you check through the refrigerator and pantry to see what you need: for your infant and the rest of your family. Then in the supermarket, the search is on: to find what the child wants and talk about where it comes from. But again, make it a game.

Learn to count with real things

Start with the things your child can touch: "This is one spoon; and these are two spoons." Then make it a natural fun game: "You've got one nose but how many eyes? You've got one mouth but how many ears? And how many fingers?" Involve him as you set the table for two, three or four people. Let him count the money at the shopping counter.

Make it fun to classify

As we've already discussed, the brain stores information by association and patterns. So start the process early. On laundry day, perhaps, he can sort socks into pairs, shirts for ironing, shirts for folding and storage.

5. The great art of communication

Language, of course, is a unique human ability. And infants learn by listening, imitation—and practice. So talk to them from the start. Tell them what you're doing. Introduce them to their relatives. Read to them regularly. Above all, remember the importance of positive encouragement. If she says "I goed to the store," don't tell her that's wrong. Instead, try: "You went to the store, didn't you? And I went too. Tomorrow we'll go to the store again."

Again: make everything a fun language lesson by introducing a subject, then turning it into a guessing game: "These are my eyes, and this is my nose. Have you got eyes ? Where are they? Have you got a nose? Where is it?"

Nursery rhymes are great—simply because they do rhyme, and rhymes are easy to remember. Every child should be exposed to books from the start—and should be read to regularly.

Learning to read is also simple, if it's treated like fun and as a game.

Glenn Doman has had many critics since he first wrote *Teach Your Baby To Read* in 1964. Yet most of the critics actually recommend many of the same techniques, and often they criticize Doman for things he has never recommended.[16]

More and more Malaysian village children between the ages of four to five are capable of reading in two languages.

DR. NOOR LAILY DATO' ABU BAKAR
and MANSOR HAJI SUKAIMI
The Child of Excellence*

*Published by the Nuri Institute, Malaysia.

Says Doman: "It's as easy to learn to read as it is to learn to talk. In fact it's probably easier—because the ability to see is developed before the ability to talk. But don't take my word for it. Ask any producer of television commercials. They use the same simple communication techniques. Look at TV any night, and you'll hear someone screaming COCA COLA, or ESSO or McDONALD'S—and at the same time the brand-names appear in large coloured words, often tied in with an easy-to-remember jingle. And two-year-olds have broken the code. Now they can read because the message is large enough to be interpreted."[17]

So Doman-trained parents not only talk new words to their youngsters—loudly and clearly—they show them the words in big type, just like TV commercials or company billboards do.

In many parts of the world parents have found it simple common sense to label as many things as possible, so children can recognize written words as well as those spoken, starting with all the names of important things: from baby's own name to mummy and daddy, parts of the body and everything around the house. Printed letters, two to three inches high, are recommended.

When preschools were combined with parent education centres in the Pacific island of Rarotonga over 20 years ago, they labelled everything in English as well as their native Polynesian language. They found it a great way to encourage youngsters to read and speak in two languages.

English-born teacher and author Felicity Hughes has used similar methods to teach young Tanzanian children to read in both English and Swahili.[18] And many of those children, in turn, have helped their parents to become literate.

In Malaysia, the Nury Institute has trained hundreds of parents to teach their three- and four-year-olds to speak and read in both Malay and English—specifically using the Doman technique.[19]

But is too much early learning robbing infants of their childhood? "If one insists that a happy childhood consists of sitting in a playpen playing with his nose," says Glenn Doman, "then we would certainly plead guilty to robbing a child of that. But if a happy childhood is having every kind of opportunity, then of course we're guilty of encouraging that.

"The people who criticize us are almost invariably people who have never set foot in our place, and have no idea what we're really saying.

"Indeed, we have a fail-safe law. We teach all mothers this law. When teaching your child, if you aren't having the time of your life, and

If you are forcing your infant, it is wrong. It is very wrong. And you should never do it.

BARBARA MONTGOMERY*

*Philadelphia mother who has enjoyed teaching her children the Glenn Doman way. By the age of three, her daughter was speaking and reading English, French and Japanese. From author interview in Philadelphia, PA, 1990.

the child isn't having the time of his life, stop, because you're doing something wrong. That's the fail-safe law."

Babies should also have colourful books as part of their home environment from the very start. Says New Zealand reading expert and author Dorothy Butler: "Keep the baby's books within reach, and make a practice of showing them to her from the day you first bring her home. The covers will be brightly illustrated, and at first you can encourage her to focus her eyes on these pictures. You can teach your baby a lot about books in the first few months."[20] Butler suggests showing even very young babies successive pages of suitable books: "Babies need people: talking, laughing, warm-hearted people, constantly drawing them into their lives, and offering them the world for a playground. Let's give them books to parallel this experience; books where language and illustration activate the senses, so that meaning slips in smoothly, in the wake of feeling."

The early years are also the ideal time to pick up more than one language, especially if you live in an area where other languages are spoken regularly. Says Doman: "All children are linguistic geniuses— witness their ability to learn to speak English in the first three years of life. If they live in a bilingual house, they learn two. And if they're born in a trilingual household, they learn to speak three."

Professor Diamond believes "love" is the most essential ingredient in early childhood education. "I think that warmth and affection is the prime consideration for healthy brain development. But from then on, expose them to a great variety of experiences. Let the child choose what interests her—and then move out from there."[21]

6. Parents as first teachers

So how can any parent become a better "first teacher?" Or better still, a first coach and mentor? Obviously you can read books on the subject, as you're doing now. But, like any other learning, hands-on experience with a mentor helps. And again the world provides many models.

In the United States, the Missouri Parents As Teachers programme is an excellent trailblazer.[22] It started in 1981 as a pilot programme—under the Parents as First Teachers title, and its early results were thoroughly researched. When all children in the pilot reached three, a randomly-selected group was tested against a carefully-matched comparison group. In all significant areas—language, problem-solving, health, intellectual

All parents want to be good parents. But most parents just don't have the information that they need to know how their children are growing and developing.

SUE TREFFEISON,
Training coordinator, Missouri
Parents as Teachers program*

*Author interview, St. Louis, Missouri, 1990.

skills, relating to others and confidence—the PAT group scored much better.

PAT is now a state-funded service provided by all 543 public school districts in Missouri. And more than 100,000 families with children under three have benefited from it.

Today about 60,000 Missouri families, with children from birth to three, are taking part in the program. They're being helped by about 1500 trained part-time "parent-educators." Every month, each parent is visited by a parent-educator, who offers timely information about the next phase of each child's development and suggests practical ways parents can encourage sound growth. Parent-educators also offer tips on home safety, effective discipline, constructive play and other topics.

At each visit, the parent-educator takes along toys and books suitable for the next likely phase of development, discusses what parents can expect, and leaves behind a one-sheet series of tips on how to stimulate the child's interest through that next stage.

"Families receive three types of service," says parent-educator Joy Rouse.[23] "The primary part is the monthly home visit. We also provide group meetings—a chance for parents to come together with other families who have children in the same age-group. Sometimes it will be for parent-child activities, others to hear a consultant talk about child development or parenting, and sometimes it's just a fun time. The third component is the screening that we do, and this is a key component. We screen for language development, general development, hearing and vision. We also have a network where we can refer families with special needs."

In Missouri, the programme is very much school-based, but in New Zealand the government has linked it with that country's Plunket programme (named after a former head of state), which has pioneered infant health-care checks, parent education and family assistance for most of this century. For many years the Plunket programme played a major part in achieving for New Zealand the world's lowest infant death rate. The government now intends to offer the Parents as First Teachers programme by 1998 to all parents who request it.[24]

Many Missouri schools link their PAT work with other programmes. The Ferguson Florissant School District, in St. Louis county, is typical.[25] It runs six separate preschool programs: PAT; a LINK program, with parents and infants together on courses; "Saturday School"—a half-day

This programme, in my judgment, is the best preschool programme on earth because it gives parents the chance to be their children's first teachers, no matter how meagre the education of the parent.

PRESIDENT BILL CLINTON*

*Commenting on HIPPY, the Home Instruction programme for
Preschool Youngsters, as introduced in Arkansas;
quoted in *Forward,* October 9, 1992.

for four-year-olds, with group visits at home; a programme for three-year-olds; a child-care centre, with youngsters from two to five, where parents pay; and education programmes for preschoolers with special needs. The day-care centre operates at the local high school, and is used as part of a training programme for teenage high-school pupils.

Thirty percent of Missouri families with youngsters under three are currently on the PAT program. The cost per family is approximately $250 a year, of which the state provides $180 and the school district finds the rest. So to provide that service to every American family with children up to three would cost $3 billion a year for 12 million youngsters. For the most needy third of all families, it would cost $1 billion a year.

Another home-based parent-education programme also has excellent results in correcting that problem. It's called HIPPY: Home Instruction programme for Preschool Youngsters.

It started in Israel in 1969, and is now operating in over 20 other countries or states, servicing about 20,000 families a year outside Israel. It has probably been given its biggest boost in America through its success in Arkansas, with the support of the former Governor and now President Clinton and Hillary Clinton. President Clinton is warm in his praise: "This programme, in my judgment, is the best preschool programme on earth, because it gives parents the chance to be their children's first teachers, no matter how meagre the education of the parent."[26]

HIPPY was designed by Professor Avima Lombard, initially for the nearly 200,000 refugees who came to Israel from Africa and Asia in the 1960s. They were poor and unsophisticated, and their children were sometimes neglected as their parents struggled to establish themselves in their new home. Like PAT, HIPPY takes training directly into the home, but for parents of children aged four and five. Mothers in the programme receive one visit every two weeks, and they meet with other mothers in group meetings every second week.[27]

Again, the results have been excellent—and in Arkansas, not only have children benefited but the programme has increased literacy among parents.[28]

In Malaysia, a parent-education programme has been taken out into the villages by Dr. Noor Laily Dato' Abu Bakar and Mansor Haji Sukaimi. They call it the Nury program—from a word that means "shining light." By mid 1992, they had trained 20,000 parents in Malaysia and 2,000 in Singapore. Of 15,000 children on the programme

In Venezuela: a programme to raise the intelligence of an entire nation, starting with videotapes in maternity hospitals.*

*As reported by Dee Dickinson in *New Horizons for Learning: Creating an Educational Network,* published by New Horizons for Learning, 4649 Sunnyside North,Seattle,WA 98103.

in 1992, 4,000 were able to attend 88 Nury child and parent-development centres in cities and villages.[29]

The world's most ambitious programme to raise the intelligence level of an entire country was started in Venezuela in 1979. A new government appointed Luis Alberto Machado, poet and philosopher, as the world's first Minister of State for the Development of Intelligence.[30]

Machado set out to choose from the world's best. He commissioned advice from such diverse sources as Harvard University, Edward de Bono and Glenn Doman's Philadelphia Institutes. His search was meticulous. His top assistants, for example, attended one of The Institutes' one-week *How to Multiply Your Baby's Intelligence* courses; and, financed by a grant from The Vollmer Foundation, Doman wrote for the Venezuela programme a book entitled *The Universal Multiplication of Intelligence.*

When the research was in, Machado started from the ground up· with pregnant women and new mothers. The programme included ten separate video programmes to educate parents. It continued with over 10,000 volunteers being trained to educate mothers, both in maternity hospital and at home.

Like Missouri, the programme concentrated on practical advice: how to create educational toys from household odds and ends, and how to involve the whole family in helping the new baby develop in every way.

Four commercial television channels added to the picture, each broadcasting 20 five-minute spots every day as a public service.

Then the project spread out into preschool, and on through elementary and high school, university and adult learning programs.

Seattle-based founder of the international New Horizons For Learning network, Dee Dickinson, later dubbed the whole project "an educational Amway"—after the highly successful home-based world-wide selling network. "In schools," she reported, "five psychologists trained 150 selected teachers, who in turn trained 42,000 other teachers, who then taught creative thinking and problem-solving processes to 1,200,000 children.

"Further additions to school programmes were created around the work of Reuven Feuerstein, an Israeli psychologist who is a pioneer in teaching intelligence; Jaacov Agam, the famous French graphic artist; Shinichi Suzuki, the Japanese musician who developed remarkable ways to teach very young children to play musical instruments; Edward de Bono, the prominent English creator of lateral thinking; Calvin Taylor,

Children's work IS their play. Children learn from everything they do.

CAROLYN HOOPER
New Zealand Playcentre Movement*

*Interviewed by Gordon Dryden in *Where To Now?* television series, reprinted in *Pacific Network* (February, 1992). Playcentre is a parents' cooperative movement in New Zealand that for over 50 years has been a world pioneer in combining parent education with early childhood development.

Utah psychologist and pioneer in the identification and teaching of creativity; and David Perkins, Harvard psychologist and major researcher in the assessment and development of creativity and intelligence.

"The Harvard Intelligence Project, designed specifically for Venezuela, focused on developing reasoning foundations, formal reasoning skills, inventive thinking, language comprehension, problem-solving and decision making."[31]

Among many strategies, 20 half-hour television programmes offered everyone *The Tools Of Thinking,* and Doman parent-training methods were introduced into even the poorest localities.

The full programme did not continue with a change of government, so it has not been possible to evaluate longterm benefits. But some of Machado's early childhood development work has continued through the Department of Education.

Dickinson was so inspired by the project that she vowed to introduce elements of it into the United States. So Seattle now has its own *Day One* programme that includes a parent-education videotape, volunteer training course and a manual—again with training starting in maternity hospital and continuing afterwards. The videotape has also been translated and is being used in Israel, Brazil, Guatemala, France, Canada, Mexico, Sweden, Germany and England—as well as in several areas of America.

7. Parents in preschool centres

Kindergartens*, of course, are not new. Friedrich Froebel started the first one in Blankenburg, Germany, in 1837. Its name summarized its theme: from the two German words that mean *garden of children.* Kindergartens were designed from the start to allow children freedom to explore—and certainly not as formal schools.

Since then many successful early childhood centres have been designed to include parent education.

Again in innovative New Zealand, a parents cooperative Playcentre movement has been operating since 1941. It was started as a project to provide support for mothers whose husbands were away at the war. The

* In the United States, kindergarten starts at age five. In New Zealand and some other countries, it is for children aged three and four.

Major child health problems in Rarotonga virtually disappeared through a simple programme of parent education and prevention.

BOB ELLIOTT,
Professor of Child Health, University of
Auckland School of Medicine, New Zealand*

*Author interview, Auckland, New Zealand, 1991.

women would take turns looking after a group of children to free the others for shopping or recreation. The movement quickly spread, and one of the early pioneers, Gwen Somerset, organized wider programmes to train the young mothers in child development skills. Today there are 600 playcentres throughout the country, catering to 23,000 children. And parent involvement is the key. They take turns in helping a trained, part-time supervisor run each centre. And their own training helps make them more competent parents.

Closely allied with New Zealand is the main Cook Island of Rarotonga, in the mid-Pacific, almost four hours away by jet. When Joseph Williams returned home with his medical degree from New Zealand and another one in health administration from the University of Hawaii, he found Rarotonga's small public hospital had 30 beds reserved for young children. And quite often there were two children to a bed: an average of 50 patients at a time, out of a total island population of only 10,000.

So as new Director of Health and later Minister of Health and Education, Williams took some simple steps. He opened preschool centres and used them for both parent education and child development. Elementary lessons in nutrition and child development, coupled with a series of early childhood checks, reduced Rarotonga's child admissions to the hospital by over 90 percent.[32]

Sweden is another country with highly advanced early childhood development programs—but with a tax-rate that most countries might find too high. For every child born in Sweden, one parent can have a year off work on almost full pay to be a fulltime parent.[33]

Later Sweden offers excellent preschool development centres. It also has one of the world's best refugee-support programs, with migrants from 114 different countries. By law, each preschool centre must employ adults who can speak both Swedish and the native language of each child. And generally they speak English as well.

But the prize for excellence in early childhood education could well go to aspects of a movement that was started over 90 years ago by Italy's first woman medical doctor, Maria Montessori.

When two television crews travelled the world in 1990 looking for the world's best ideas in creative education, they returned with similar findings. The American Public Broadcasting Service crew selected the Reggio Emilia Montessori "play school" in northern Italy as a model for preschool development, involving youngsters from two to six. It figured

Maria Montessori really was a pioneer in looking at the world from a child's perspective.

ANTONIA LOPEZ*

*The Education and Development Director, Foundation Centre
for Phenomenological Research, which operates
Montessori early childhood centres in California.
Author interview at centre near Stockton, California, 1990.

prominently in the PBS series *The Creative Spirit.* And as the producers later reported in a book of the same name: "Children there are given enormous scope in the resources they can draw on: they spend much time out of doors, visiting a variety of places—from farmers' fields to ancient piazzas—and they have a rich set of materials in the school itself.

One special aspect of the school is the total involvement of the parents. In fact, the Reggio Emilia school was created after World War II by a group of parents who joined together and took over an old movie theatre."[34] Reggio Emilia's activities are not built around subjects, but around collective projects—freely chosen by the youngsters and helped by the parents. These range from sculpture to trips around poppy farms to cooperative mural production.

A New Zealand TV crew searching out innovations came home bubbling with enthusiasm at a Montessori centre in California. Not that Montessori preschools are a complete novelty in America. There are over 450 in the U.S. But most of them are private, and often have high fees.

At French Camp near Stockton, California—an hour's drive from San Francisco—the New Zealanders found a Montessori centre catering to America's poorest working families, Mexican fruit and vegetable pickers.[35] Both parents work the fields from 4.30 or 5.00 each morning—for a family income of around $7,000 a year.

Yet their children are benefiting from preschool education that ranks with the top in the world—perhaps the top. Their centre is one of 18 run as a research experiment by the California-based Foundation Centre for Phenomenological Research. It should be a success model for the world, but is hardly known outside its own ranks.

In the grounds of the French Camp centre you'll see migrant youngsters dancing, singing and playing. Inside you'll see them engrossed in a wide variety of activities adapted from Montessori's original ideas.

They sit in child-sized chairs, at child-sized tables, use tools and implements specially designed for small hands. They also learn advanced mathematics the Montessori way, and are absorbed in it, using wooden rods of different lengths and colours to do decimals and numbers up to 2,000.

Among many other innovations, Montessori pioneered cut-out sandpaper letters so infants could learn by touch as well as sight. And at French Camp you'll find a full range of similar sensory experiences. Each room has a variety of live animals and fish that help the learning

If adults learned [to write] as easily as children under six years, it would be an easy matter to do away with illiteracy.

MARIA MONTESSORI
The Montessori Method*

*First published in English in 1912. Our quotation taken from
edition published in 1964 by Shocken Books Inc., New York.

process. Well-trained parents are always on hand to assist, but overall the youngsters are encouraged to be self-learners.

Says one of the Foundation's organizers, Antonia Lopez: "The major job of the adult is to provide the children with as many opportunities in all of their areas, whether it's cultural, or science, art, music, mathematics or language—to provide as many opportunities that are age-appropriate and sequentially developed."[36] Something to eat is served every two hours, with each meal a lesson in diet and nutrition: low-fat soups, whole-wheat tortillas instead of white-flour tortillas. Children set the tables as they learn to count the spoons and forks and plates. Each meal is a cultural delight.

And it doesn't stop with nutrition. All family members—male, female, siblings and children—get a physical examination each year.

Those who criticize Glenn Doman's early *reading* programme would probably gasp with amazement when they hear that French Camp children are *writing* fluently before they are five. Says Lopez: "Montessori tells us that children at about four and a half literally seem to explode into writing. Now that's the official 'I can-write-a-sentence-and-a-word' version of writing. But our children are really being introduced to writing and to reading much earlier. Even as young as two and a half, they're being introduced to pre-writing experiences: they're doing things left to right, top to bottom; learning relationships. And they're obviously exposed to rhymes and story-telling and all kinds of talking—so they're ready to explode into writing well before they are five."

It's perhaps significant that both Montessori's and Doman's initial research began with youngsters who were severely brain-damaged—and they then realized that these children, after multi-sensory stimulation, were often performing much better than "normal" children.

Montessori set out to fashion materials and experiences from which even "intellectually handicapped" youngsters could easily learn to read, write, paint and count before they went to school. She succeeded brilliantly; her brain-damaged pupils passed standard test after test.[37]

Under the Montessori method, however, a small child is not "taught" writing; she is exposed to concrete experiences that enable her to develop the "motor" and other skills that lead to the self-discovery of writing.

Auckland, New Zealand, Montessori specialist Pauline Pertab ex-

A five-year-old writes

Vogliamo augurare la buona Pasqua all'in= gegnere Edoardo, Talamo e alla principessa Maria? Diremo che conducano qui i loro bei bambini. Lasciate fare a me: Scriverò io per tutti 7 Aprile 1909.

A sample of hand-writing, done in pen, by a five-year-old
student of Italian educator Maria Montessori in 1909.
Translation: "We would like to wish a joyous Easter
to the civil engineer Edoardo Talamo and the Princess Maria.
We will ask them to bring their pretty children here.
Leave it to me: I will write for all. April 7, 1909."*

*Reprinted from *The Montessori Method,* by Maria Montessori,
published by Schocken Books, Inc., New York.

plains: "As early as two-and-a-half years of age, a child will be encouraged to pour water and do polishing, developing hand and eye coordination; to paint and draw, developing pencil control; and later to work with shapes and patterns, tracing the inside and outside of stencils and to work with sand-paper-covered letters about nine centimetres in depth—three to four inches—to get the feel of shapes."[38] The "explosion" occurs when a youngster discovers, by himself, that he can write.

At French Camp, all conversations are in Spanish—the language the parents brought in from Mexico. One specialist in indigenous languages, Professor Lily Wong-Filmore, of Berkeley, rates this programme first equal in the world for minority cultures. The other one: "The kohanga reo [Maori "language nests"], in New Zealand." Says Wong-Filmore: "The interesting thing is this: that if these children are as well educated as the graduates of our experimental preschool centres appear to be, they have no trouble learning English. English is a snap to learn when it is the dominant language. They pick it up in a year or so with no difficulty."[39]

The Foundation Centre was set up in 1975. It now serves over 1900 children at 18 locations in nine Californian counties. About 300 of those children are aged from six weeks to three years—looked after in separate buildings—and the rest are three to six years.

The research project actually started with English as the only language. But Lopez says that turned out to be disastrous. Then they tried a "bilingual" approach. And that didn't work either—probably because English is such a dominant language in America. But since then the results of the programme have been outstanding.

Says Lopez: "One principal at a Los Angeles elementary school came to us not too long ago and said: 'I have 22 youngsters whose kindergarten teachers have recommended them for the 'gifted' children's program. Looking into their background, we found they had some things in common: they were all from Central America, none of them spoke fluent English—and they all came from the Foundation Centre." So Wong-Filmore may be right. The French Camp Spanish-language preschool remains vividly imprinted in the TV crew's mind almost three years after their visit. So does the multi-language preschool in Sweden.

So perhaps it's not the choice of language that is vital. The answer to early childhood deprivation lies overwhelmingly in providing a total supportive environment for all children to develop their own talents.

In New Zealand 82 percent of all three and four-year-olds are in early

Ages five through eight are wonder years. We can put them in desks and drill them all day, or we can keep them moving, touching, exploring.

BARBARA KANTROWITZ and PAT WINGERT
*How Kids Learn**

Newsweek magazine (April 17, 1989).

childhood education programs, and the government's stated aim is to lift this total to 85 percent by 1995, 90 percent by 1998 and 95 per cent by 2001.[40] New Zealand's child-centred approach continues to make learning fun as students go on through primary school to achieve one of the world's highest rates of elementary-school literacy. Many European countries have similar high percentages of three- and four-year-olds in preschool.

But America's overall performance in early childhood education is appalling. In California—regarded as an American leader in public education—only 41 percent of English-speaking children and 15 percent of Mexican-American children come into kindergarten at age five with any experience of preschool centres.[41]

8. Continue the same fun-filled approach at school

Even worse: in many states "formal academic education" is the norm from the first elementary-school years. They don't get the chance for the fun-filled, experience-rich learning that is the basis for real growth. And all too often the joy of learning fades.

The alternatives are obvious:

■ Education programmes that encourage all parents to fulfil their important role as first teachers. Playcentre, Missouri and HIPPY already show how.

■ Preschool development centres to help every child become a "gifted child" in the vital years before five. They're already operating for California's poorest working families, with spectacular results.

■ Early childhood programmes to help every youngster, even from a deprived background, start school at a level equal to the current 20 percent top-achievers. Lyelle Palmer's results have shown the way.

■ And a complete rethink of how elementary schools are organized to provide fun-filled, experienced-based learning.

Fortunately examples also abound of what can happen at school when common sense is linked to good research and dedicated principals and teachers; and when schools take the simple step of programming for success instead of failure.

SELF-ESTEEM:

The secret heart of learning

| 1 | **Programme for success, not failure, for everyone.** |

| 2 | **Learn the lessons from the big achievers.** |

| 3 | **Concentrate on the six vital ingredients:*** |

■ **Physical safety.**

■ **Emotional security.**

■ **Identity.**

■ **Affiliation.**

■ **Competence**

■ **Mission.**

*From Bettie B. Youngs, *The 6 Vital Ingredients Of Self-Esteem: How To Develop Them In Your Students,* published by Jalmar Press, 2675 Skypark Drive, Torrance, CA 90505.

How to programme for success
in education as in business

Sometimes a great truth sears itself into your brain.

Or one crisp sentence telegraphs a truism more effectively than a thousand books.

Or you feel a mask has been whipped from shrouded eyes—as you see something so simple you wonder why you've never seen it before.

And the simplest truths have emerged from every success story we've analysed for this book:

■ *The best systems in the world are programmed to succeed.*

■ *Most current educational systems are programmed to fail.*

They're not programmed to fail everybody. But they are programmed to fail a large percentage of students. In some cases up to 50 percent. And whatever you programme you'll generally achieve.

The world's airlines plan to land their planes with 100 percent safety every time. A one-in-a-million failure rate would rightly be regarded as a tragedy.

The world's top car companies spend a fortune to reduce their manufacturing fault-rates from 2 percent to 1 percent.

But most school systems actually expect and plan for a reject rate that would send any business bankrupt.

Businesses use spell-checking computers so that every letter they write can go out word-perfect. Accounting firms use electronic calculators and computer programs to help make sure their clients' financial reports and tax returns are 100 percent accurate. Anyone in the real world who is learning a computer turns to a friend for advice when stumped.

If you refuse to accept anything but the best in life, you very often get it.

SOMERSET MAUGHAM

But in school examinations students using the same common sense techniques for excellence would be disqualified for cheating.

We stress that we are NOT opposed to evaluations and qualifications. Far from it. In our view, most school achievement standards are absurdly low.

A 20 percent product failure rate in any business, anywhere in the world, would be regarded as a financial disaster.* Schools are the only organizations to regard that result as a success.

■ More than half of America's young people "leave school without the knowledge or foundation required to find and hold a good job," says the SCANS** report on *What Work Requires of Schools.*[1] If you're an American reader, please stop and read that last sentence again—and weep for the future of half the children of the world's richest nation who can move out of a school system unfit to find a decent job.

■ "These young people will pay a very high price. They face the bleak prospects of dead-end work interrupted only by periods of unemployment"—from the same report.

■ "SCANS estimates that less than half of all young adults have achieved these (required) reading and writing minimums; even fewer can handle the mathematics; and schools today only indirectly address listening and speaking skills."

■ "Britain's workforce is under-educated, under trained and under-qualified," says a major similar study by Sir Christopher Ball, entitled *More Means Different.*[2]

■ Forty-seven percent of potential British employees in industry are unable to meet the skill needs required, Ball reports. If you're a British reader, please stop and read that sentence again—and weep.

The economic results are bad enough. But even worse, the angry human rejects of this crazy system often wear their rejection-slips as

The only business exception we know to this rule: the production of raw silicon chips. As each of these can be mass-produced for a few cents, some companies plan for a higher reject rate as the trade-off for speedy production. But they then test every chip to make sure that it works perfectly as the brain of the multi-thousand-dollar computer it will operate.

*** The Secretary's Commission on Achieving Necessary Skills, commissioned by the U.S. Secretary of Labour under the former President Bush's America 2000 Programme.*

Many more than ever face the crisis of childhood: violence, drugs, bad schools, poverty, divorce, or two parents working.
And no one seems to care.

*Fortune International**

*Main sub-heading for its *Children in Crisis* special report,
August 10, 1992.

lifelong badges of under-achievement, shame and despair.

But the answer, we're convinced, is not in more of the same. It is certainly not in a system that is actually programmed to produce failure.

And it would be a confidence trick of the worst type to suggest that even brilliant new learning techniques at school can completely compensate for *a society that itself is also programmed for many of its members to fail.* There is no way optimal learning can take place without physical safety and emotional security. And even the world's richest country is not providing that security for millions of its youngsters.

Of the 65 million Americans under 18, fully 13 million live in poverty—one in five. Around 14.3 million of them live in single-parent homes. Almost three percent live with no parents at all.[3]

Children of single parents are most at risk. In America three-quarters of them live in poverty during at least part of the crucial first eight years of their lives. And single-parent children are, on average, at least twice as likely to have behavioural and emotion problems, and 50 percent more likely to have learning disabilities, than two-parent children. They are also twice as likely to drop out of high school. Fully 3.4 million American school-age children are left to care for themselves after school each day.[4]

America has the developed world's highest rate of teenage pregnancy, followed closely by New Zealand. And New Zealand leads the U.S. in the proportion of children born to unmarried parents: 34 percent of all births, compared with America's 27 percent. The proportion soars in minority groups: two-thirds of African-American and New Zealand Maori babies are born to unmarried parents.[5] And most grow up in single-parent families. The self-perpetuating cycle of deprivation rolls on.

As *Fortune* reported in late 1992 in a major survey of *Children in Crisis:* "Obviously the most reliable predictor of crime is neither poverty nor race—but growing up fatherless."

Even in New Zealand—a much more egalitarian society than America—at least 15 percent of families are locked into the poverty cycle in some way: an unplanned teenage pregnancy to a mother who herself may have been a school failure and often physically abused by an under-achieving, frustrated parent; a single-parent, low-income home; a neighbourhood of poverty, frustration, crime and violence; children abused when the parent can't cope; early child-health needs ignored, leading to later learning difficulties; pre-programmed failure at school; drop out early; no skills, no job; crime, violence, prison.[6] As Lesley Max, author

If you think you can or think you can't, you're right.

HENRY FORD

of *Children: Endangered Species?* says: "If you have only one of those strikes against you, you might be able to break out of the cycle. But if you've got three or four it becomes increasingly difficult. If you're unemployed and always short of cash, if you're an unsupported teenage mother, and you've had a poor education—you've got problems, and so have your children." You're programmed to fail. "Multi-faceted problems," says Max, "require multi-faceted solutions."

Bulgarian psychiatrist and accelerated learning pioneer Dr. Georgi Lozanov puts it in academic terms: he calls it the "social suggestive norm"—the total social environment that conditions us all for success or failure.[7]

Henry Ford summarized part of the equation many years ago in simpler terms: "If you think you can, or think you can't, you're right." Others have restressed the message regularly: We are what we think we are. We become what we think we'll become.

And here we're not talking about the "touchy, feely, all-you-have-to-do-is-think-and-you'll-grow-rich" brand of fantasy. In our view, all self-esteem has to be firmly grounded in positive achievement. And real achievement is grounded in self-esteem. You have to achieve something specific to achieve full potential. "Feeling good about yourself" is not enough, although it's part of the secret. You have to ground your feelings in something you can do well: math, science, cooking, sewing, reading, accounting, karate, playing the piano, sport, singing, dancing—whatever.

But, as Lozanov argues, another aspect is equally vital: *too often we become what others expect.* And when those expectations are telegraphed daily by parents and teachers through word, attitude, atmosphere and body language, then *their expectations* become *students' limitations.*

Sports provide countless examples of the opposite effect. In the early 1960s three athletes living in one area of Auckland, New Zealand, won Olympic gold medals or broke the world record in every middle-distance event: 800 yards, 800 metres, 1,000 metres, 1,500 metres, one mile, 5,000 metres and three miles. Only one of them, triple gold medal-winner Peter Snell, was a natural athlete. One of them, Olympic 5,000 metres champion Murray Halberg, had a crippled arm. They succeeded because their coach, Arthur Lydiard, helped develop their confidence—and provided the training—to lead the world. "The talent wasn't exceptional," says Lydiard. "Anyone could do it. Motivation is the key."[8]

A well-developed mind, a passion to learn, and the ability to put knowledge to work are the new keys to the future . . .

SCANS REPORT*
What Work Requires of Schools

* U.S. Labour Secretary's Commission on Achieving Necessary Skills.

And sure: not every athlete can become a Carl Lewis, a John Walker or a Magic Johnson. But no one should be programmed to fail. Maybe—just maybe—society could tolerate such failure-based school systems 50 years ago. Then the world was a different place. Our schools served a different society.

In most developed countries they did a good job of preparing the people who would become our future managers and professionals: our accountants, lawyers, doctors, teachers, administrators, academics—perhaps 20 to 30 percent of the population.

They did a reasonable job of preparing those who would become the skilled or semi-skilled craftsmen and tradesmen, or the generally-female typists and accounts clerks who would support the mostly-male management teams. Many countries skimmed several groups off early into "technical education," to become the apprentice carpenters, plumbers, electricians, printers, engineers and other tradesmen.

At its best, the mid-20th-century elementary school also trained the rest of its youngsters to cope in the unskilled jobs that were then required. It taught them the basics of reading, writing and arithmetic—the so-called three R's. Our schools were programmed to produce the citizens needed for an industrial economy. And they produced what they programmed—what they expected. Their examination systems, too, were designed to produce the right professional-technical-labouring mix.

Even a much-praised early-education leader like New Zealand for years deliberately "scaled" the main high school examination to ensure that 50 percent of students failed. Even if the overall national average rose dramatically, 50 percent of students who lasted even three years at high school had built-in failure as a guaranteed result. Future generations will look back on that guarantee with horror and dismay.

But at least most of the "failures" could then get unskilled jobs, often highly paid. Today a soaring number can't. They're unemployed, disheartened, frustrated—often violent.

Every reliable "futures" forecast we have studied convinces us that this is not the only alternative. We live in a world where almost anything is now possible, where excellence is achievable. But for the vast majority of people to benefit from this new age demands from our educational systems *the same kind of educational results for most people that were previously guaranteed to the "top" 20 to 30 percent of students.*

Existing systems produce existing results. If something different is required, the system must be changed.

SIR CHRISTOPHER BALL
More Means Different*

* British report on *Widening Access to Higher Education*, published by
Royal Society for the encouragement of Arts, Manufactures and Commerce,
8 John Adam Street, London WC2N 6EY, England (1990).

As Ball puts it in his British report: "The nature of work is changing. It is becoming increasingly brain-intensive, value-laden and unpredictable. Skilled brain power is replacing disciplined muscle-power. Unskilled and low-skilled work is rapidly diminishing. In its place employers call for more people with professional, technical and managerial skills. Competitive economies in future will depend on the success of the education system in producing a high average level of education and training, rather than just a small leadership elite."

The Ball Report has called for Britain to increase the number of students in higher education—college, polytechnic and university—by a whopping 50 percent over this decade. And it has called for linking much more hands-on training with academic education.

Like Ball, we're convinced that "more means different." In later chapters we spell out many ways to achieve that type of result. But it will not be achieved in any school system that is programmed to fail even one person. As in sports, this does not mean that everyone will end up with first-class academic honours. But it does mean that *everyone should have the chance to excel at something— and to succeed regularly at something*.

Now obviously we're not criticizing the great schools that exist at every level around the world.

We are talking about the norm. And what societies or schools *expect*—what they programme themselves to *achieve* —they will normally get. Plan for "F's"—for failure—and you'll get them.

Compare this with other systems that are programmed to succeed— and where excellence results:

■ The U.S. armed forces, for instance, where a 50 percent failure rate would never be tolerated. Whatever your views on the 1991 Gulf War, the electronically-controlled rockets that rained down on Saddam Hussein's armed forces spelled out a message of excellence in military technology, planning, efficiency and competence.

■ Disneyland, where even a novice cleaner can't get to sweep a floor without a one-week extensive training course in the theme-park's philosophy, values and attractions.[9] And where every visitor is regarded as a guest and every employee as a partner committed to being a vital part of a daily extravaganza that smiles excellence at every corner.

■ Silicon Valley pioneer Hewlett Packard, where the lower-skilled computer assemblers work, eat, exercise and play alongside the Ph. D.

Create an institution where people aren't _allowed_ to be curious, and people _won't_ be curious.

TOM PETERS
Liberating Management*

*Published by Alfred A. Knopf, New York.

systems-designers; where all, without exception, are encouraged to take computers home to explore new ideas with their families; where all are partners in achieving excellence; and where most even have full authority to work their weekly hours at any time to suit them, without punching timeclocks.[10]

■ Japan's Matsushita-Panasonic, with its six million staff suggestions a year: 90 percent of them put into action in a day-by-day search to encourage all to share in a continuously-improving result.[11]

■ McDonald's, with its $40 million hamburger university, the training ground for the world's biggest fast-food chain.[12]

■ Japan's Sony, with its policy of disregarding every employee's former educational qualifications after he or she has been employed, because it wants everyone to be seen as an achiever, an innovator, a "seeker of the unknown" as part of a joint contribution to building a better world.[13]

■ Or Stew Leonard's famous dairy store in Norwalk, Connecticut, which averaged sales of $85 million a year on one site during the 1980's ($3,000 a square foot—compared with a national average of a little over $300)—and which sends every member of the staff who wants to go to a free 14-week, $600 Dale Carnegie course—including a 20-hour a week high school part-timer.[14]

Tom Peters, individually or with colleagues, has provided hundreds of other examples in his series of books starting with *In Search Of Excellence*. All tell stories of companies where staff are encouraged to exceed and excel—every day and every week.

Says Peters in his latest book, *Liberation Management:* "Create an institution where people aren't *allowed* to be curious and people *won't* be curious. Pretty soon bosses, with tons of corroborating evidence, will solemnly intone that 'most people aren't curious.'"

Or take any computer system as an example of striving for *excellence as the norm.* The programme that's being used to typeset this page, for example. This comes complete with an automatic "spell-checker." When each chapter is finished, the computer programme, if asked, automatically scans every word—and questions every possible mistake. The *expectation* is 100 percent excellence. And because of that expectation—and the system that produces it—nearly all books are printed with perfect spelling. Better still, the computerized spell-checker is a built-in, self-correcting educator. Even poor-spelling authors using it can check

Many of life's failures are people who did not realize how close they were to success when they gave up.

THOMAS EDISON

mistakes, and see correct or alternate versions instantly on the screen. So they learn by their mistakes. They expect 100 percent achievement. And because they expect it, and know how to get it, they succeed. They know they're a success by the final results they produce—and not the mistakes they learn on the way. And they learn to spell the successful way.

As Thomas Alva Edison put it when a friend tried to console him when about 10,000 experiments with a storage battery had failed to produce results: "Why, I have not failed. I've just found 10,000 ways that won't work."[15]

In most of today's school systems, Edison would have been graded a failure. In fact, he had only three months of formal schooling—but became probably the greatest inventor in history, with 1,093 patents to his credit.

Maybe not all of us can be an Edison. But each warmly-encouraged infant seems to have the same insatiable sense of adventure and exploration that motivates the great inventors and scientists.

Thomas Armstrong, author of *Awakening Your Child's Natural Genius,* talks about the child's "extraordinary" openness to new learning during the preschool years. At two or three, says Armstrong, the average child "explodes" into language and learning.

The infant learns best in an ideal atmosphere, with affection, warmth, encouragement and support. Where that same attitude continues in school, the same fun and speed of learning continues.

There are many ways to achieve this for major improvements in learning, as we'll cover later. But more important than all: every positive educational turn-around we've examined around the world starts with self-esteem—or self-image. That esteem is nurtured where a school, like the leading businesses, is also in search of excellence—where every student is encouraged to succeed.

Says Colin Rose, the British-based entrepreneur who has produced the world's fastest-selling foreign-language training programs: *"Of all the things thrown up by our research, probably the most vital is this: our self-image is probably the most important thing in determining whether we are good learners—or, frankly whether we are good at anything else."*[16]

Every school leader featured in this book would agree. All use a variety of techniques to make sure each youngster's self-image flowers and is grounded in practical achievement:

The six vital ingredients of self-esteem

Self esteem is a composite of six vital ingredients that can empower or detract from the vitality of our lives: The six are:

1 **PHYSICAL SAFETY**
Freedom from physical harm.

2 **EMOTIONAL SECURITY**
The absence of intimidations and fears.

3 **IDENTITY**
The "Who am I?" question.

4 **AFFILIATION**
A sense of belonging.

5 **COMPETENCE**
A sense of feeling capable.

6 **MISSION**
The feeling that one's life has meaning and direction.

BETTIE B. YOUNGS
The 6 Vital Ingredients of Self-Esteem
*How To Develop Them In Your Students**

*Published by Jalmar Press, 2675 Skypark Drive, Torrance, CA 90505.

■ When Dr. Dan Yunk arrived as new principal* at Northview Elementary School in Manhattan, Kansas, in 1983, he found low test scores, little discipline and a dispirited staff.

Visit the school today and you'll find a complete change in atmosphere—and results. You'll find fourth-graders learning fractions by making pizzas, learning Spanish by singing, learning American history through plays and songs.

You'll find fourth-graders paired with kindergarten buddies, acting as teachers themselves, and putting into written words the five-year-olds' stories.

You'll find youngsters in the school gymnasium from 7 a.m. You'll find all the different individual learning styles catered to: with plenty of sight, sound and action; a school where most pupils now play musical instruments, and the curriculum is rich with the arts.

In a workstyle that most teachers in other countries would find bewildering, in 1983 Yunk found teachers who "in 20 years had never been in each other's classrooms."[17] Today teacher cooperation is the norm.

When he first arrived, "parents didn't feel comfortable. Now they act as tutors, aides and mentors; one is even head of the computer club."

Of all elementary schools in the state in 1983, only about a third of Northview's fourth graders reached the expected competency levels.

By 1990: 97 percent—in the top three percent. And in some areas in the top 1 percent.

Yunk's recipe for success? The same as Bill Hewlett and Dave Packard's in business: "Management by walking around." "Empower pupils, parents and teachers; they have to feel that they own it."

■ The City Magnet School in Lowell, Massachusetts, is at the heart of a traditional Old England industrial town. It was set up early in the 1980s—planned by parents and educational leaders as one of the most unusual schools in the world.

For the school is much more than a school: it is a society in miniature. It has its own central bank, trading bank, courts, currency, lawyers, publishers and businesses. It publishes its own newspaper, magazines and yearbook, so its "staff" learn to write as reporters and editors, to produce as publishers and computer operators. Its "citizens" use their own currency to sell and buy each other's goods and services. And they

Dr Yunk is now Assistant Superintendent in the Manhattan School District.

Imagine
a school
with its own
bank, currency,
shops, traders,
lawyers,
courts and
newspaper:
a complete
micro-society.*

*The City Magnet School in Lowell, Massachusetts: a "normal" school
in the morning, a "society in miniature" in the afternoon.

learn all about interest rates, bank deposits, profit and loss accounts.

Parents are closely involved. One computer consultant is there two hours a day. But he doesn't think of it as a school. "We're a family," he says, "school and parents and students together."[18]

Says principal Sue-Ellen Hogan: "We want it to be an interactive society."

Regular classes take up four hours a day, before the school turns into a "Micro Society." But even the classes are geared to the real world. Says one teacher: "I teach publishing, not English." But the students learn both.

Discipline? Not surprisingly, the students handle that mostly themselves: run their own court cases, with charges, prosecution, defence and juries. Civics as a subject? "It's not just part of the curriculum; it's part of everyday life."

Its students perform well above grade levels on all standardized tests. But its parents, teachers and students think that's a minor part of the achievement. The school is based firmly on the principle that experience is the best teacher. And that education is grounding achievement and self-esteem in practice.

■ In the New Zealand city of Palmerston North, Monrad Intermediate* School is in the heart of a low-income district that only a few years ago was featured in a scathing television programme on glue-sniffing, drugs and social despair. Today the school is one of the most exciting in the country.

When Bruce Kirk arrived at the school as new principal soon after the TV programme, its staff turnover was shocking, its pupils despondent.

Today you'd hardly recognize the same place. It has one of the most sophisticated school computer set-ups in the country. Eleven-year-olds are learning every day to master computer skills like advanced desk-top publishing, scanning pictures from videotape and photography on to a computer-produced school newspaper. Others are using computer programmes to create music, solve problems and catch up if behind. Students turn up early each day to work at the computers—and may, if they wish, stay in at lunchtime to continue.

*Some schools in New Zealand take children from "primer one" to form two (what Americans would refer to as K-8 schools). Others go to "standard four" (equivalent to grade 6), and their children then spend two years at "intermediate" school before going to high school. Bruce Kirk has since moved in a different capacity to Freyberg High School, which is featured later in our story.

Motivation and productivity skyrocket when students reach their goals.

BETTIE B. YOUNGS
The 6 Vital Ingredients Of Self-Esteem
How To Develop Them In Your Students*

*Published by Jalmar Press, 2675 Skypark Drive, Torrance, CA 90505.

The school also has a wide range of Technic Lego. Walk into a Lego class and it's like entering a sophisticated workshop and laboratory. You're likely to find two 12-year-olds together designing an electric-powered washing machine, another two experimenting with hydraulic power.

Principal Kirk says it all brings up one very important point: "There is more than one way to learn."[19] The beauty of Technic Lego, he says, is that there is no recipe-book approach. "There is no one way of doing things, and the child finds out at his own rate to solve problems, to make discoveries about math, physics and concepts."

Computers and Technic Lego couldn't be bought out of the school's normal budget, and here Monrad has received a lot of help from one of its neighbours: the local branch of the international Glaxo pharmaceutical company. Glaxo has gone into partnership with Monrad. It provides about $35,000 a year in cash, but Kirk says "it's not just a dollars-and-cents exercise. Glaxo is saying, like us: put people first and everything else will fall into place."

Glaxo's recently-retired Chief Executive Tony Hewett says the partnership's success is "classic motivational technique. So much of it is just taking an interest in somebody. The mere fact that the children know somebody else is taking an interest in them is, I think, a major part of it."

And while the business help has been great, ask anyone at the school and they'll tell you the real change was one in attitudes.

When Bruce Kirk first arrived, he asked pupils and staff to tell him what was wrong with the school and how to change it.

"They told me in no uncertain terms that they wanted to feel better about their school. They didn't feel good about it."

In New Zealand most school pupils wear uniforms. At Monrad they wanted a new school uniform they could be proud of—so the children designed it, choosing the materials and patterns.

But probably the main changes at the school have been in the ways they've built links with parents and the local community. Of all the new technologies at the school, the most important is a mini-bus. With it come weekly visits to local senior-citizens' retirement homes and other community activities.

Every pupil now takes part in life-skills programs. From the Red Cross they learn how to handle babies. They learn the basics of car repair, how to mend their own clothes, to bake, and the principles of good

Often negative feelings stem from criticism suffered long ago. It's as if we had been hypnotized to accept our nonexistent limitations.

PETER KLINE
The Everyday Genius*

*Published by Great Ocean Publishers, 1823 North Lincoln Street, Arlington, VA 22207.

nutrition. The school caretaker even takes a class where the youngsters learn cleaning. And all these activities are hands-on. They learn to bath real babies, change tyres on real cars

Monrad is also a multi-cultural school—and so is its curriculum. About 25 percent of students are Maori—and its cultural enrichment groups have played a big part in bringing Maori parents into the school. Dozens of children regularly sing and dance in their own traditional Maori costumes.

Parents will tell how the biggest gain has been in self-esteem. "Several years ago," says Maori parent Debbie Green, "the kids never had self-esteem. They were wandering around the street sniffing glue, getting into trouble with the police. Now the kids don't feel they need to do those kinds of things to get attention. They know they can join the Maori club and that at school they're not being put down for being Maori."

Monrad, in fact, is a classic case study of the links between self-esteem, lifeskills study, and an overall curriculum that is also deeply embedded in a wide range of activities at the school and around the community.

■ But in many ways some of our most interesting research has been in Japan.* Japanese schools have the world's highest math and science test scores. More than 90 percent of students graduate from high school. And Japan has almost no illiteracy.

Yet Japan spends proportionately less on public education than most other developed countries: only 5.3 percent of the gross national product, as compared with 7.8 percent in Canada, 6.2 percent in Britain and 6 percent in the United States.[20]

Many "back to basics" Westerners attribute this success to an extremely rigid school system of long hours and rote learning. This is the major method of teaching at junior and senior high school, but visit any elementary school and you'll find the opposite.[21] In the primary grades there's an almost kindergarten atmosphere. In one second-grade classroom we found children on the floor playing with big globs of clay, beautiful artwork on the walls, and children who appear relaxed, physically safe and emotionally secure.

Co-author Vos acknowledges the assistance provided by the Stanford University Japan Project in sponsoring her educational research visit to Japan. Co-author Dryden's visits there have been to study commercial TV, educational television, economic planning and as an export and marketing consultant.

The school-day is eight hours in most of Asia, but about a quarter of that is devoted to after-school activities and clubs.

SCIENTIFIC AMERICAN*

*December 1992

Visit the children's lunchroom in Mito Municipal Oda Elementary School, and again comes the sense of social and emotional well-being: the beautiful classical music in the background, the children wearing hygiene masks as they serve lunch to other children in the line.

In fact, from kindergarten through third grade, one of the main Japanese school goals is social: teaching youngsters to be part of a group. After surveying 13 Tokyo elementary schools, American researcher Katherine Lewis reports that of all the goals and objectives displayed in classrooms, only 12 percent referred to academic work. The rest covered procedural skills, peer socialization, how children feel, personality development, physical energy, hygiene and personal habits. "The whole experience," says Lewis, "was at times more reminiscent of a scout meeting or a Sunday School than of a first-grade classroom."[22]

An overwhelming impression remains of early Japanese kindergarten and elementary schooling: that it is there *to lay the emotional and social groundwork for later academic learning.* In this way it may be one of the world's best bases for later accelerated learning.

To a degree that often amazes American teachers, Japanese elementary schools also seem to delegate class control to small groups of children, to encourage group self-discipline and responsibility, such as collective responsibility for cleaning up any graffiti. Result: no graffiti.

There is also no "tracking" in Japanese elementary schools. In every grade, slower learners are mixed with the more gifted. And promotion is automatic from grade to grade. Japan is very homogeneous—with a cultural climate that encourages a sense of community and family. So to "fail" youngsters at elementary school, to separate them according to ability, or any other criterion, would be regarded as anti-social.

Japan's teachers, too, enjoy, a public esteem that is missing in many countries. They also have a cultural tradition that sees them giving "life guidance" to students with special problems. Says former *Newsweek* foreign editor Robert C. Christopher, who lived in Japan for many years: "As Japanese teachers see it, their concern extends to the totality of their students' lives. If a Japanese youngster suddenly slumps academically, is caught smoking a cigarette or otherwise appears to be sliding into delinquency, his teacher will almost automatically call on the student's parents to find out what is troubling the child and to devise means of straightening it out."[23]

Japan, of course, is a consensus society—a land with few extremes of

Master the wonderful power of praise:

- ■ **Tell people they look good.**
- ■ **Say nice things about their family.**
- ■ **Recognize people's accomplishments.**
- ■ **Admire their possessions.**
- ■ **Compliment people for their ideas.**
- ■ **Commend people for trying even if they fail.**

DAVID J. SCHWARTZ
The Magic of Thinking Success*

**Published by Melvin Powers, Wilshire Book Company,
12025 Sherman Road, North Hollywood, CA 91605.*

rich and poor. Many outside its borders would say it is too conformist: that "the nail that sticks up gets pounded down," in the words of one of its most famous proverbs. But, says Christopher, "the manner in which consensus is achieved is known as *nemawashi,* or 'root-binding'—a term taken from *bonzai* culture, in which, whenever a miniature tree is repotted, its roots are carefully pruned and positioned in such a way as to determine the tree's future shape." Obviously that "root-binding" approach has a big bearing on Japan's early-education system. It is part of a total climate of group and family achievement—where Lozanov's "social suggestive norm" is a climate of security and nurturing.

As researchers, we, too, have reservations about some of Japan's later high school rote learning and regimentation. English is taught by methods that would be regarded as old-fashioned even by school systems who have not attained anywhere near the accelerated-learning results we detail in the next chapter. Japan's foreign-language results are as bad as its methods. The high-stress cramming for multiple-choice university entrance examinations is also a blot on a system whose early "root bind-ing" is an excellent model for the rest of the world.

We have similar reservations about many high school procedures in our own countries that stifle students into mediocrity. But we have only praise for every school that concentrates on self-esteem building and practical lifeskills training as the vital base for future learning.

When those basic principles of self-esteem are rediscovered, it's amazing how equally simple techniques can build on that *climate which makes learning possible;* methods that can lead to even more efficient learning.

Six steps to teach anything

1. THE RIGHT "STATE"

* Orchestrating the environment.
* Positive mood of teacher, student.
* Affirming, anchoring and focusing.
* Outcome and goal-setting: What's In It For Me?
* Visualize your goals.
* Regard mistakes as feedback.
* Peripheral posters.

2. THE RIGHT PRESENTATION

* Getting the Big Picture first, including field trips.
* Using all learning styles and all 7 intelligences.
* Drawing, Mind Mapping, visualizations.
* Active and passive music concerts.

3. THINK ABOUT IT

* Creative thinking.
* Critical thinking—conceptual, analytical, reflective.
* Creative problem solving.
* Deep memory techniques for permanent storage.
* Thinking about your thinking.

4. ACTIVATE TO DRAW OUT

* To access material and bring out of storage.
* Games, skits, discussions, plays, including all
  learning styles and all 7 intelligences.

5. APPLY IT

* Use it.
* Do it.
* Mind Map it.
* Combine it with what you already know.

6. REVIEW AND EVALUATE

* Know that I know.
* Self/peer/instructor evaluation.
* Ongoing review.

This is a Jeannette Vos checklist for teachers and trainers to set up
a model integrative accelerated learning system.

The fun-fast way to transform education at school and on the job

Fortunately, great teachers are fast changing the face of education.

So are some of the world's best business trainers. And they're doing it simply: by combining lessons learned from kindergarten, brain research, show business, advertising, television, music, dancing, the movies and sport.

Above all they're restoring fun to the learning process.

At Guggenheim School, 11-year-old students from the poorest district of Chicago, Illinois, are learning to speak fluent Spanish, through visualization, puppet shows and songs.[1]

Around America, business people are compressing an introductory accounting course into one day—by playing The Accounting Game.[2]

In Australia, secondary school students are appearing as French actors in their own videotape production— as a vital part of learning a three-year foreign-language course in eight weeks.[3]

In the tiny European State of Liechtenstein, one trainer has created over 240 games to teach virtually anything— from patent law to geography, history and physics.[4]

In Auckland, New Zealand, aspiring Polynesian company managers take only 90 minutes at a seminar to learn the main principles of marketing—playing the Great Pacific Century Marketing Game, with pineapples, bananas and gambling dice.[5]

IBM, Apple Computers, Shell Oil, Bell Atlantic, Air New Zealand and British Air are only five of the major companies using similar techniques to slash staff training time and costs: from teaching German

To learn anything fast and effectively, you have to see it, hear it and feel it.

TONY STOCKWELL
*Accelerated Learning
in Theory and Practice**

*Published by EFFECT (European Foundation for Education,
Communication and Teaching), Liechtenstein.

and Japanese to aircraft crews to training telephone linesmen—using music, relaxation, visualization and games.

At Mt. Eden Prison in Auckland, some convicted criminals are discovering the joy of true education for the first time—learning through music, song and dance.[6]

In New Zealand, too, all primary schools are using brightly coloured puzzles and games to learn elementary mathematics. And some unemployed high-school dropouts there are flying through advanced mathematics and literacy courses, using interactive computer games as their main learning tools.

At Cambridge College in Massachusetts, teachers are gaining a Masters Degree in education after only two semesters, including a five-week summer "intensive" that involves them directly in integrative accelerated learning techniques. Better still, they are seeing modelled in the classroom the techniques they're absorbing to earn their degree in record time.[7]

Some of the new techniques go by a variety of names: suggestopedia, neuro linguistic programming and integrative accelerated learning. But the best all combine three things: they're fun, fast and fulfilling. And the best involve relaxation, action, stimulation, emotion and enjoyment.

Says outstanding West Australian teacher and seminar leader Glenn Capelli: "Forget all the jargon. Forget all the big names. What we're really coming to grips with can be summed up in two words: true learning."[8]

Says British-born, Liechtenstein-based educational psychologist Tony Stockwell: "We now know that to learn anything fast and effectively you have to see it, hear it and feel it."[9]

Later we'll look at using the world as our classroom. But obviously much education will continue to revolve around schools, colleges and company training seminars.

And from our own research around the world, and practice in schools, colleges and business, all good training and educational programmes involve six key principles. As a lifelong learner of any age, you'll learn quicker, faster and easier if all six are organized brilliantly by a teacher who is an *involver*— not a *lecturer*— who, as a *facilitator,* orchestrates these factors:

1. The best learning "state;"

If it's not fun we're not interested.

JOHN-ROGER and PETER McWILLIAMS
Life 101:
Everything We Wish We had Learned About
Life In School—But Didn't*

*Published by Prelude Press, Inc., 8159 Santa Monica Boulevard, Los Angeles, CA 90046.

2. A presentation format that involves all your senses and is both relaxing, fun-filled, varied, fast-paced and stimulating;

3. Creative and critical thinking to aid "internal processing;"

4: "Activations" to access the material, with games, skits and plays;

5: Plenty of chances to practise;

6: Regular rehearse-and-review sessions.

1. The best learning "state"

Not surprisingly, each of those principles works best for an adult in almost the same way it works for a small child, when learning develops quickly and easily through exploration and fun.

Orchestrating the environment

Can you imagine a two-year-old youngster learning by sitting still on a classroom seat all day? Of course not. She learns through doing, testing, touching, smelling, swinging, talking, asking and experimenting. And she learns at a phenomenal pace.

She is highly suggestible, and absorbs information from everything that goes on around her—her total environment.

But once she gets past kindergarten, too often education starts to become boring. The fun disappears. In many classrooms around the world, youngsters are told to sit still, in straight rows, listening to the teacher and not exploring, discussing, questioning or participating.

Good teachers know that's not the best way to learn. So they plan a classroom setting that facilitates easy learning. They use fresh flowers for scent and colour. They cover the walls with colourful posters, highlighting all the main points of the course to be covered, in words and pictures—because it seems highly likely that most learning is subconscious.[10] Students absorb the lesson-content even without consciously thinking about it.

More and more teachers have music playing to establish the mood as students enter the classroom. Many use balloons and swinging mobiles to create an almost-party atmosphere.

"The total atmosphere must be non-threatening and positively welcoming,"[11] says Mary Jane Gill, of Maryland, U.S.A., formerly in charge of staff training for Bell Atlantic. Her techniques on one accelerated learning course cut training time by 42 percent, on another 57 percent. And the very first thing they did was change the atmosphere.

When I taught new safe driving techniques to truck drivers, we welcomed them with Dolly Parton music—and they loved it. It immediately told them they were welcome.

CHARLES SCHMID
founder of the LIND* Institute

*Learning in a New Dimension. Comment in author interview,
San Francisco, California, 1990.

Top Swedish high school teacher Christer Gudmundsson agrees: "The atmosphere from the time your students enter the classroom must be thoroughly welcoming."[12] And the late Charles Schmid, of San Francisco, California—a world pioneer in new teaching methods—found mood-setting music one of the major keys to achieving learning rates at least five times better than before. "And that applies everywhere, from preschool to a business seminar teaching computer technology."[13]

Liechtenstein's Stockwell—one of Europe's leading new-style trainers in both schooling and business—says the importance of well-designed colourful posters cannot be overstressed. "Overhead projector slides, 35mm slides and flipcharts are fine," he says, "but posters are miles better—and all should be up around the walls before any learning session begins. They're peripheral stimuli. Their constant presence engraves their content into your memory, even when you're not consciously aware of them."[14]

He also says colour psychology is important. "Red is a warning colour; blue is cool; yellow is seen as the colour of intelligence; green and brown have a pacifying effect and are warm and friendly.

"Never forget that effective posters make a strong impression on the long-term memory. They create memory pictures which can be called on when required although they were never consciously learned."

Stockwell even brings his own specially-designed chairs—ideal for relaxed learning—to seminars he runs in the United States.

It's the kind of lesson that all educational institutions can learn from the best businesses:

* The Seattle-based Nordstrom chain of clothing stores is used in dozens of management seminars as a model in profitable service—and it always has freshly-cut flowers in its customer changing rooms.

* Every international airline welcomes passengers on board with soothing, calming music—before presenting safety demonstrations.

* Visit Hawaii, the tourist capital of the mid-Pacific on a package tour and you'll soon slip into a welcoming vacation mood as you're greeted with a lei of island flowers.

* Visit Disneyland or Disneyworld and you're immediately struck by the cleanliness and total atmosphere.

* McDonald's has built the world's biggest fast-food chain through similar attention to atmosphere and welcoming detail.

Since the brain cannot pay attention

to everything . . . uninteresting, boring or emotionally flat lessons simply will not be remembered.

LAUNA ELLISON
*What Does The Brain Have
To Do With Learning?*

*Article in *Holistic Education Review* (Fall 1991).

Think of that the next time you visit a school or company seminar-room that persists with uncomfortable straight-backed wooden chairs and an atmosphere that is cold, lifeless and often colourless.

Setting the right mood

Canadian teachers Anne Forester and Margaret Reinhard, in their excellent book, *The Learners' Way,* talk of "creating a climate of delight" in every school classroom. They say variety, surprise, imagination and challenge are essential in creating that climate. "Surprise guests, mystery tours, field trips, spontaneous projects (old-fashioned days, pet displays, research initiated by the children) add richness to reading, writing and discussion. The production of plays and puppet shows is stimulated by the children's reading and is master-minded more and more fully by the children themselves.

"Your classroom will rarely be totally silent Sharing and interaction are the vital components of a climate of delight. Discoveries, new learning, the sheer joy of accomplishment demand expression."

If that "climate of delight" sweeps over you as you enter a well planned seminar room or classroom, it's the first step in setting the right mood for more effective learning.*

Early activity is vital

The next step is activity: precisely what students or trainees are encouraged to *do.* The colourful setting, posters and mobiles will already have started to stimulate those who are mainly *visual learners.* The music will have "touched base" with the mainly *auditory learners.* And early activity makes the *kinesthetic learners* feel instantly comfortable. Interspersing all three learning styles also makes sure that all three levels of the brain are activated: our *thinking* brain, our *feeling* brain and our *doing* brain.

But there are other good reasons for instant activity:

Jazzercise-type exercises to music encourage an increased flow of

---

* *Before starting any teacher-training session at the Californian State University at San Marcos, co-author Vos spends at least half an hour covering the walls with colourful posters, and making sure that all audio-visual equipment is working—including the tape-deck for the music that will welcome the class. Co-author Dryden always urges participants to have a brain-jogging breakfast of bananas, kiwi fruit, oranges and other fresh fruit before spending time at one of his Great Pacific Century Marketing Game seminars.*

Human Bingo

Find someone who has done the following
and write their name in the square

A kinesthetic learner	Owns a rowboat	Uses graphics in their workshops
Has a piece of the Great Wall	Plays an harmonica	A visual learner
Slept in an airport overnight	Has been to Bulgaria	Has taken part in a funny business luncheon
An auditory learner	Has taken a Dale Carnegie course	Is a good singer
Loves music	Is a great high school teacher	Is a fabulous cook

A Human Bingo Game: the type used by Libyan Labiosa-Cassone and Philip Cassone to break the ice in a seminar session at an annual conference of the Society of Accelerative Learning and Teaching.

Jeannette Vos uses the technique regularly, especially in social studies classes. Each student may receive a duplicated page of questions on a subject such as China or Japan, and each is encouraged to wander round the room at the start of class to find the answers from fellow students.

oxygen to the brain—and the brain runs largely on oxygen and glucose.

Other exercises to music—such as simple juggling and left-foot/ right hand, right foot/left-hand movements—can stimulate instant communication between the "right brain" and the "left-brain," as we cover in more detail in chapter 11. Others can loosen students up— mentally and physically: to help them relax. Canadian psychologist and astronomer Tom Wujec covers many in *Pumping Ions—Games and Exercises to Flex Your Mind.*

Other activities can break the ice and help participants get to know each other—and the talents that are available to be tapped, inside and outside the specific setting. Minneapolis accelerated learning trainers Libyan Labiosa-Cassone and Philip Cassone often start international seminar sessions with a pre-prepared game of "Human Bingo" (see opposite). Participants have two minutes to meet as many people as possible.

Other activities can put you in a positive mood. Australia's Capelli often gets his learners to:

* Sit in pairs—with someone they've never met before—and spend 45 seconds recounting the most interesting aspect of their background; so that each person starts the session by focusing on projects that have been personally successful (reinforcing self-esteem).

* Massage each other's neck and shoulder muscles to encourage relaxation.

* All sing a specially composed *Attitude song*—"The Big A in my life (students spell out each letter of A-T-T-I-T-U-D-E with their arms in time with the music)."[15]

Obviously the techniques will depend on whether you are taking a regular school class, running a specific-topic seminar, or introducing an international symposium.

Eric Jensen, author of *SuperTeaching* and co-founder of America's SuperCamps, believes two core elements affect learning: *state* and *strategy.* The third is obviously *content.* "State" creates the right mood for learning. "Strategy" denotes the style or method of presentation. "Content" is the subject. In every good lesson you have all three. *But many traditional school systems ignore "state." It is the most critical of the three. The "door" must be open to learning before true learning can happen. And that "door" is an emotional one—the "gatekeeper to learning."*

Is it possible to learn 1,200 foreign words a day?

The most remarkable claims for accelerated learning in foreign-language training have come from Dr. Georgi Lozanov.

He reports* that Bulgarian students have actually found it easier to remember between 1,000 and 1,200 new foreign words *a day* than 500 words.

Here are the results he records from 896 "suggestopedic" language-training sessions:

Number of of words given in session	Number of students in session	% of words memorized per session
Up to 100	324	92.3%
100 - 200	398	96.8%
201 - 400	93	93.1%
401 - 600	53	90.4%
1000 - 1200	28	96.1%

*Dr. Lozanov's results are reported fully in his book, *Suggestology and Outlines of Suggestopedy,* published by Gordon and Breach, New York (1978).

Both the current authors were present during Dr. Lozanov's keynote presentation to the Society for Accelerative Learning and Teaching in Seattle, Washington, in 1991.

It is fair to report, however, that in all our research we have not encountered results outside Bulgaria that come anywhere near matching the ones reported above. Dr. Charles Schmid, in San Francisco, has reported students being presented with 400 foreign words in a day and being able to use them in conversation within three days (see page 321), a remarkable enough feat.

The right brain wavelength

One of the main steps to achieve this is to get everyone working on the "right wavelength." *And here probably the most ironic contradiction occurs: to learn faster you slow down the brain.* One of your brain's "wavelengths" is obviously most efficient for deep-sleep. Another is more efficient for inspiration. And another, the one you're most conscious of: the wide-awake alertness of daily living. But many studies now reveal that a fourth brainwave is the most efficient "frequency" for easy, effective learning: what some call the alpha state.[16]

Bring on the music

Dozens of research projects have found that music is a very efficient dial to tune into that alpha frequency.[17]

"The use of music for learning is certainly not new," Californian accelerated-learning innovator Charles Schmid told us not long before his death. "We learned our alphabet to music—ABCD—EFG—HIJK—LMNOP. But in the last 25 years we've expanded our music knowledge tremendously. We've found out that in a special kind of relaxation our brain is most open and receptive to incoming information.

"That type of relaxation is *not* getting ready to fall asleep. It's a state of *relaxed alertness*—what we sometimes call *relaxed awareness.*"[18]

Much of our recent knowledge in this field has been built on the pioneering research started in the 1950s by Bulgarian psychiatrist and educator Georgi Lozanov. Lozanov set out to determine why some people have super-memories.

After years of research, he concluded that we each have an "optimum learning state." This occurs, he says, "where heart-beat, breath-rate and brain-waves are smoothly synchronized and the body is relaxed but the mind concentrated and ready to receive new information."[19]

In putting that research into practice, Lozanov achieved some amazing results, particularly in foreign-language learning. By the early 1960s Berlitz, then the world's largest language-training school, promised students could learn 200 words after several days' training—a total of 30 hours. But Lozanov's research reported Bulgarian students reported learning 1,200 words *a day* and remembering 96.1 percent of them.[20]

Many others have built on his research. According to Schmid: "We now know that most people can achieve that ideal learning state fairly

Music is the interstate highway to the memory system.

TERRY WYLER WEBB with DOUGLAS WEBB
Accelerated Learning with Music:
A Trainer's Manual*

*Published by Accelerated Learning Systems, 6193 Summit Trail, Norcross, Georgia 30092, in conjunction with the Accelerated Learning Systems Music Library.

easily—and quickly. Deep breathing is one of the first keys. Music is the second—specific music with a certain beat that helps slow you down: anywhere from 50 to 70 beats a minute." The most common music to achieve that state comes from the baroque school of composers, in the 17th and early 18th centuries: the Italian Arcangelo Corelli, the Venician Antonio Vivaldi, the French Francois Couperin and the Germans, Johann Sebastian Bach and George Frideric Handel.

Lozanov found baroque music harmonizes the body and brain. In particular, it unlocks the emotional key to a super memory: the brain's limbic system. This system not only processes emotions, it is the link between the conscious and subconscious brain.

As Terry Wyler Webb and Dougles Webb put it brilliantly in their highly-recommended *Accelerated Learning With Music: A Trainer's Manual:** "Music is the interstate highway to the memory system."[21]

Vivaldi's *Four Seasons* is one of the best-known pieces of baroque music used to start the journey along that highway. It makes it easy to shut out other thoughts and visualize the seasons of the year. Handel's *Water Music* is also deeply soothing. And for teachers trained in new learning techniques, Johann Pachelbel's *Canon in D* is a favourite to relieve tension.

Most of those teachers also use specially-prepared tapes to start each learning session—with soothing word-pictures to match the music and encourage relaxation.

Tapes can be either self-made, if you're competent in music, or bought. Their key first use in education is to put students into a relaxed, receptive state so they can focus on learning.

Break down the learning barriers

Lozanov says there are three main barriers to learning: the *critical-logical* barrier ("School isn't easy, so how can learning be fun and easy?"); the *intuitive-emotional* barrier ("I'm dumb, so I won't be able to do that"); and the *critical-moral* barrier ("Studying is hard work—so

* This book is a 200-page trainer's manual— ideal for school or business seminar facilitators. It is accompanied by The Accelerated Learning Systems Music Library: 11 double-sided stereo cassettes, of baroque, classical and romantic era music, plus one relaxation tape. The book provides detailed recommendations of how to use specific pieces of music in all learning situations, including recommendations for preschool and school-age children. See Recomended Resources at the end of this book for more details.

STEPPING OUT
MY OWN ACTION PLAN

GOAL: [   ]

ACTION:

    First step:

    Next step:

    Follow-up:

ANTICIPATED ROADBLOCKS:

MONITOR:

    How do I monitor? How am I doing?

    Who can mentor me?

SUPPORT:

    What support do I need?

REVIEW:

    **Do I need to adjust anything to
achieve my goal?**

COMMITMENT:

    **Am I willing to put forth all the effort
needed to achieve my goal?**

SELF ASSESSMENT:

    **To what degree did I achieve my goal
and how?**

*A simple checklist used by Jeannette Vos to
help students set and focus on their goals.*

I'd better keep my head down"). Understand where a student "is coming from" and you gain better rapport. Step into his world and you break resistance quickly, smoothly.

Encourage personal goal-setting and learning outcomes

Encourage students to set their own goals—and to plan their own future. If they know where they are going, then their path is focused. In our experience, *most people will over-achieve personal targets that they set themselves*—possibly the soundest principle to be applied in management.

In classroom settings, we both encourage the "Station WIIFM" game—to focus on "What's In It For Me?" Not in a selfish sense, but to get participants, perhaps in pairs, to tell each other what they specifically hope to get from the session, the day or the year.

The way this is introduced is vital, especially in school. Many at-risk students get very angry with the traditional "You-will-learn-this today" introduction. Instead, good teachers invite students to set their own goals, right from the outset, and the outcomes they would like from the session.

Often students come with "hidden agendas"—and they don't always "buy in" to the instructor's agenda. The key is to make learning a partnership, where the instructor prepares a smorgasbord of possible "curriculum pieces" and the students get a big say in what they want out of it.

Try visualizing your goal

Visualizing is a powerful learning tool. An ineffective teacher might well say: "Don't forget to study or you might do poorly in the upcoming test"—a negative reinforcer.

Eric Jensen suggests two better ways. One is to encourage students to visualize precisely how they would be using their new-found knowledge in the future. The other is to plant a positive thought that will encourage students to browse through their study-book looking for specific answers that might be used in the future.

We cannot stress this point too strongly: many teachers do not realize how damaging negative suggestions can be.

Trigger the emotions

Nor can we over-stress that the emotional "limbic" part of the brain is the gateway to long-term memory, so all good teaching encourages warm

Your most valuable asset [in learning] is a positive attitude.

BOBBI DePORTER
*Quantum Learning**

*Published by Dell Publishing, 666 Fifth Avenue,
New York, NY 10103.

emotions. This fuses what you have been learning into deep memory.

2. The keys to good presentation

Positivity and linking are the first ones

The presentation inputs the new learning. If you don't put it in you can't pull it out. And all good presentations must be learner-centred and linked to students' own goals and existing knowledge. "The more you link, the more you learn."

One technique to guarantee involvement from the start is for the learners and the instructor to toss a squashy, brightly coloured Koosh ball to volunteers to tell one main point they already know about a topic, and to draw Mind Maps covering the same points—from a pre-prepared map that lists the main "learning branches."

The sequence is designed to encourage the learners of every subject to start by identifying what they want to know, and then proceeding from what they already know—generally an amazing amount.

The entire presentation must also be positive. The facilitator should never suggest in any way that the session is anything but fun—no "now the break's over, let's get back to the hard work" talk.

Lozanov called his fast-learning process "suggestopedia," from "suggestology"—but that is an unfortunate translation into English. Says Stockwell: "The name is rather unusual, but if you see 'to suggest' in the sense of 'to propose' or 'to recommend' then it is easier to understand the relationship."[22]

As we've touched on in the previous chapter, the power of suggestion is paramount in learning: we all do best what we think we can do; we fail if we expect to fail. Every adult has seen how infants' learning abilities soar in a favourable, positive atmosphere. All good Lozanov-style facilitators try to recreate the same kind of positive fun-filled atmosphere in the classroom. And like all good advertising copywriters, they go out of their way to stress how easy the project is. Japanese-language teachers may well use the "Itchy knee; sun, she go rock!" exercise we've covered on page 156. Business-seminars may well start with the story of Ray Krok, the 52-year-old seller of milkshake machines, who first visited a Californian hamburger restaurant in 1952 and saw the start of an idea that ended up as McDonald's—an example to show how great projects can grow from very modest beginnings.

Teachers will become more like facilitators, guides.

HUGH OSBORN
Director of New Media Group
at Public TV station WNET

*Quoted in *Tomorrow's Lesson: Learn or Perish,* part of
Time magazine's special issue, *The Century Ahead*
(fall 1992).

Lozanov stresses the important links between conscious and subconscious presentation. He believes each of us has an enormous reserve of brain power waiting to be tapped. He believes that by far the most important part of all learning is subconscious; and that good teachers remove the barriers to learning by making their presentations logical, ethical, enjoyable and stress-free. Hence the importance of posters and "peripherals" as part of the total presentation.

Getting the big picture first

A major presentation technique is to present "the big picture" first—to provide an overview, like the total jigsaw puzzle picture, so that all the later pieces can then fall into place. Again, posters or other classroom peripherals may well present the big picture—so it's always there as a focusing point.

Field trips are also highly recommended at the start of any study—to see the big picture in action.

Drawing Mind Maps at the start of study, including all the main "limbs," allows students to draw in the smaller branches later.

Involve all the senses

All good presentations also appeal to all individual learning styles.

The most neglected learning style in nearly every school system is kinesthetic—or movement. Every good learning experience has plenty of verbal stimulation, plenty of music, plenty of visuals—but the really great teachers make sure to have plenty of action, plenty of participation, plenty of movement. Even though students may be visual learners, everyone embeds information by doing.

Step out of the lecturing role

This is probably the major personal change required in teaching styles. All the best "teachers" are activators, facilitators, coaches, motivators, orchestrators.

Always orchestrate "non-conscious" processing

Since Lozanov practitioners say most learning is "subconscious," the room setting, posters, body language, tone of speech and positive attitude all are vital parts of the learning process.

Plenty of role playing and "identities"

Lozanov teachers also encourage students to "act the part." There are

Frequent breaks are needed in all learning sessions.
Everyone tends to remember a dramatic first impression,
the most recent part of a presentation (generally the end),
and outstanding highlights. So the more breaks you have,
the more "firsts," "lasts" and "high points."*

*Illustrations from *Present Yourself,* by Michael Gelb, published
by Jalmar Press, 2675 Skypark Drive, Torrance, CA 90505.

few faster ways to learn science than to act out the roles of famous scientists; or to learn history by putting yourself in the historical setting.

Organize plenty of "state changes"

The best teachers organize plenty of "state changes" so that students switch from singing, to action, to talking, to viewing, to rhyme, to Mind Mapping, to group discussions. This has a two-fold purpose:

1. It reinforces the information in all learning styles; and

2. It breaks up the lesson into chunks for easy learning.

Both have a major bearing on how well the information is absorbed. For example, it is now well proven that, in any presentation, students can generally remember easiest the information at the start, the end and any "outstanding" examples that gripped their imagination. Regular "state changes" provide the opportunity for many more "firsts," "lasts" and graphic examples.

Make learning-how-to-learn a key part of every course

This is probably the main overall desired result from all learning. So the techniques should be blended into all activities.

The Lozanov "concerts"

Possibly Lozanov's greatest contribution to education has again been in the sphere of music: not only to relax your mind and put it into a highly receptive state—but to use music to float new information into your amazing memory system.

Lozanov recommends two *concerts*. And again, Charles Schmid has summarized the theory and practice neatly: "If, say, a class is learning a foreign language, as the first step the teacher sets out the new vocabulary in the form of a play, and with an overview of it in pictures. The student sits there taking a 'mental movie' of it. Immediately following this comes the first concert—what Lozanov called the *active concert*. With the student looking at the text, the teacher turns on some selected music, and he reads the foreign language in time to the music. He deliberately acts out the words dramatically in time to the music.

"Now there's no magic to this; it's precisely why it is easier to learn the lyrics of a song, rather than remember all the words on a page of notes. The music is somehow a carrier and the teacher surfs along with the music—almost like catching a wave."[23]

Lozanov's second learning phase is called a *passive concert.*

According to Lozanov, a well-executed concert can do 60% of the teaching work in 5% of the time.

TERRY WYLER WEBB with DOUGLAS WEBB
Accelerated Learning With Music:
A Trainer's Manual*

*Published by Accelerated Learning Systems, 6193 Summit Trail,
Norcross, Georgia 30092.

Charles Schmid again: "The second concert follows immediately after the first. And here we use very specific slow baroque music— around 60 beats to the minute—very precise. And while the first reading of the language was very dramatic, the second is in a more natural intonation. Now the students are invited to close their eyes if they want— although they don't have to. They put the text aside, and imagine, say, that they are in a theatre in the country they're studying, and somebody is acting a story in the background. Generally this will be the last part of a particular language session—and the students will then go home—and probably skim through their foreign-language 'play' just before they go to sleep."

Overnight the subconscious goes to work—and the seemingly automatic start of the transfer to long-term memory storage.

Lozanov fans claim the use of music in this way can accomplish 60 percent of learning in 5 percent of the time.[24]

We hasten to add that even great Lozanov fans do not recommend using his full "concert" technique in every session. Even in something as clearly defined as learning a foreign language, perhaps only three "concert" sessions might be held in a week. But all the other key principles of learning would be used in other sessions.

3. Thinking about it, and deep memory storage

Education is, of course, not only about absorbing new information. It involves thinking about it and storing it into deep memory as well.

Learning how to think is a major part of every educational programme, and good facilitators use "thinking games" and "mind games" as part of synthesizing information—as well as providing "state changes." In business seminars we've found it best to introduce this by fun projects: designing "a golf ball that can't get lost" or playing the "What if?" game on subjects well divorced from the activities of each group.

For deep memory storage, Lozanov's active and passive concerts are tops. They are designed to access the long-term memory system in order to link new information subconsciously with data already stored.

4. Activate to draw out the learning

Storing information is also only one part of the learning process. The information also has to be accessed. So the next step is "activation."

And here games, skits, discussions and plays can all be used to

Lozanov's music for the two "concerts"*

ACTIVE CONCERT

Beethoven, Concerto for Piano and Orchestra No. 5 in B-flat major.

Mozart, Symphony in D major, "Haffner," and Symphony in D Major, "Prague."

Haydn, Concerto No. 1 in C Major for Violin and Orchestra; Concerto No. 2 in G Major for Violin and Orchestra.

Haydn, Symphony in C Major No. 101, "L'Horioge;" and Symphony in G Major No. 94.

Mozart, Concerto for Violin & Orchestra in A Major No. 5; Symphony in A Major No. 29; Symphony in G Minor No. 40.

Brahms, Concerto for Violin and Orchestra in D. Major, Op. 77.

PASSIVE CONCERT

Vivaldi, Five Concertos for Flute and Chamber Orchestra.

Handel, Concerto for Organ and Orchestra in B-flat Major, Op. 7, No. 6.

J. S. Bach, Prelude in G Major, "Dogmatic Chorales."

Corelli, Concerti Grossi, Op. 6, No. 4, 10, 11, 12.

J.S. Bach, Fantasia for Organ in G. Major; Fantasia in C Minor.

Couperin, Sonatas for Harpisichord: "Le Parnasse" (Apotheosis of Corelli); "L'Estree;" J.F. Rameau, Concert Pieces for Harpisichord "Pieces de clavecin" No.1 and No. 5.

*From *The Foreign Language Teacher's Suggestopedic Manual,* by Georgi Lozanov and Evalina Gateva, published by Gordon and Breach, New York, 1988. See other selections on page 174.

"activate" the memory-banks— and reinforce the learning pathways.

Again, this needn't make more work for the teacher. The opposite, in fact. Students love to organize their own plays, presentations, debates and games. Give them the chance to present their new-found information to the rest of the class or group—any way they prefer.

Schmid explains a typical activation session, after French-language students have slept on a concert-session: "The next morning, or within 48 hours, the students come in; they haven't said a word of French yet— or at least not in the new vocabulary. Now comes three or four hours of what we call activation.

"Now we play games with the vocabulary. We're feeding their brains in different ways. We've already done it consciously in showing them the words and pictures of their French play. Then we've fed it into their subconscious, with the aid of music. And now they're activating their brains in different ways to make sure it's stored. And I tell you: now I wouldn't teach in any other way"

Schmid, who unfortunately died not long after our interview, had degrees in music, psychology and foreign language instruction. He taught at the University of Texas and New York University for many years with traditional methods before "getting hooked" on the new techniques.

"I started to teach French and German and sometimes Italian with these new techniques; I wanted to see if the system worked, if it really was all it was cracked up to be. And I was amazed. I would teach students in a three and a half hour class. I'd give them 400 words of French, say, the first day. And by the end of the third day they were able to repeat them in forms of conversation. And that had never happened before.

"Previously at the university, if I gave students 25 words a day in the old way, they'd be lucky to remember ten the next day. I was convinced.

"In fact, when I first started using the techniques myself, I started dreaming in the language after about the third day. And I had never had that feedback before."

Schmid's experience left him no doubt as to the benefits of the new learning methods: "I would say the speed-up in the learning process is anywhere from five to 20 times—maybe 25 times—over what it was in traditional methods. But it's not only the acceleration; it's the quality of learning that goes on. And the feedback. They say: 'This is fun. Why didn't I learn this way in high school?'

Sample design for a learning game

Getting students to design their own learning game can in itself be an effective learning tool.

Here's one designed by Gordon Dryden to teach the basic principles of marketing. It's called *The Great Pacific Century Marketing Game:**

1. A brief but graphic colour-slide presentation introduces creative thinking and problem-solving.

2. The game is based around eight segments of a pineapple, with each segment an aspect of the marketing cycle: the product or service; the customers; presentation; pricing and profit-ability; distribution; promotion; building satisfied customers; and taking on the world through niche marketing.

3. In one version of the game, 11 key marketing tips are numbered in a workbook under each segment. Students roll two dice, and whatever the total they discuss the implications or run quiz shows to find telling examples.

4. Another version is a board game, with cards similar to *Trivial Pursuit* and Roger von Oech's *Creative Whack Pack.*

5. The marketing game generally takes students through a mythical product-problem (such as selling surplus bananas)—and the eight segments provide plenty of "state changes" and breaks—between graphic visual presentation, group workshops, discussion in pairs and quiz shows. It teaches thinking and problem-solving skills along with marketing principles.

* Copyright: Gordon Dryden Ltd., P.O. Box 87-209, Meadowbank, Auckland 1005, New Zealand.

"Recently at a New England telephone company students were using these methods to study optic fibres and some technical telecommunications work. The trainees were sitting on the floor, playing with wooden blocks, fitting them together and understanding what goes on in an optic fibre. The trainer said: 'OK, it's time for a break.' And the trainees said: 'You take a break; we're having fun; we're learning; and we're getting this finally.' That's what I mean. It works and it's fun."

5. Apply it

In our view, the real test of learning is not a written examination through multiple-choice questions. The key is to use the learning and apply it to purposeful situations, preferably real-life.

The real test of a French course is how well you can speak French. The real test of a sales course is how well you can sell.

You learn to play a piano by playing a piano, you learn to type by typing, to ride a bike by riding a bike, to speak in public by speaking in public. So the best teachers and business seminar organizers plan plenty of action sessions to back up the theory so students can purposefully use and apply the learning.

Turn your students into teachers

As in the activation phase, it makes sound sense to have students work in pairs or teams, with a free hand to prepare their own presentations of main points. Groups in a teacher-training class, for example, may each be asked to crystallize a specific aspect of educational psychology. And more and more schools are using the "buddy" system, where an older or more qualified student helps another, and both benefit.

Encourage Mind Mapping

We've already covered the principles of this and suggested you use it to preview the learning, but it is also a remarkable way to review and make notes. *It really is what it says: a map that records main points in the same way the brain stores information—like branches on a tree.* It's also a major tool in the next process.

6. Review and evaluate

Even highly efficient learners will not always be conscious of whether they "know what they know." One way to bring the learner to that awareness is through a quick Koosh-ball throw at the end of a lesson. This

Novel ways to end seminars

Here are two of the many "accelerated learning" ways to end a seminar or learning session on a high note, with plenty of fun while encouraging participants to crystallize the main points they have learned:

a. Ask each participant to write, on one sheet of paper, a sentence summing up the main message learned.

b. Participants then pair-off, and each has 45 seconds to convince the other that his or her main point is the key one.

c. Those two then pair off with another two, with the same conditions.

d. Those four participants then line up with another four, and so on until finally half the gathering appoint a spokesperson to argue their agreed main point with the other half.

Allowing about two minutes for each segment, and a little longer for the all-in debate at the end, a conference of 300 people can complete the process in under 20 minutes.

a. Give all participants five minutes to write single-sentence summaries of all the main points they have learned—each on a separate sheet of paper.

b. Each one then attaches his or her sheets to a giant noticeboard.

c. They each then start moving the sheets about, matching like with like, discussing the reasons.

The size of each selection of main points will then help crystallize the group's conclusions—and enable the facilitator to sum up.

will jog students' memories of all the important learnings of the day. Another way is a "passive concert" review, which also covers all the points handled.

And then comes one of the most crucial steps: the self-evaluation. This is where a student truly "digs within" to uncover those precious gems of the day. Self-evaluation is a tool for higher thinking: reflecting, analysing, synthesizing, then judging.

Peer-evaluation and instructor-evaluation are also important parts in culminating a lesson, but the most important is self-evaluation. And finally, another way to review is to skim over your Mind Maps or "highlighted" notes, or both:

* Before you go to sleep on the day you've been studying;

* The next morning;

* A week later;

* A month later;

* And just before you need to use it—or before an exam. Or if you're taking a one-week course with an exam at the end, spend at least 15 minutes a night on that day's Mind Map and highlights, and at least five minutes on each of the previous days'.

Or if you're on a one-week course with an examination at the end, spend at least 15 minutes a night on that day's Mind Map and highlights, and at least five minutes on each of the previous day's.

Putting it all together

And how does all this theory work in practice? Let's look at four examples: an entire school that has switched to integrative accelerated learning techniques; a high school class that has done the same for one subject; a special foreign language project in the army; and a teacher who's made the change.

The Simon Guggenheim School experiment

The first is an example of the great potential changes that can come from innovative schooling. It is also a sobering example of how that potential cannot be fully realized unless the entire social climate of a community changes, too.

Simon Guggenheim K-8 School is in one the poorest districts of Chicago, Illinois. Nearly all families are African-American, 85 percent

Our aim is still for our school to be the best . . . a school without failure, where all children leave school having identified a talent, a skill, an intelligence, through which they can become whatever they want to be.

MICHAEL ALEXANDER
Principal, Simon Guggenheim School*

*Author interview, in Chicago, Illinois, 1990.

are officially below the poverty line, with annual incomes between $9,000 and $11,000 and a large proportion live on social welfare.

Eight years ago their children's futures were bleak. Their school had one of the worst scholastic records in all the United States. Today a great deal has changed. Guggenheim School is now regarded as an international model on how school disasters can be turned into success.

When principal Michael Alexander first arrived there in 1984, the school was a failure and in danger of being shut down by the local Board of Education. Alexander's first decision was to upgrade the morale and skills of a demoralized staff. Using some State Title I funds, for schools with special needs, he offered all staff members a 30-hour retraining course with Peter Kline, the man he now describes as "the genial dynamo of integrative learning." Half the teachers went at one time, while substitutes filled their places; then the other half.

"To put it mildly," Alexander recalls, "they were sceptical at first. We agreed there would be no pressure on them to use the principles and techniques of integrative accelerated learning. It was up to them to apply what they found valuable."[25] The rest, he says, is pleasant history.

Walk into one class, and you'll find 11-year-olds learning Spanish—at their own request—by taking part in puppet shows and singing to music.

Walk into another and 13-year-olds will be learning American history by actually taking over the roles of Abraham Lincoln or Thomas Jefferson.

Walk into the computer room and parents and students will be learning together. Go into another and a happy bunch of young African-Americans are learning about hygiene through a "rap session."

The corridors are a blaze of colourful posters. Photos of black achievers adorn the walls of many classrooms.

Ask Alexander what's so unusual about his school, and his reply is direct: "This school is a fun place to be—and it's a place where people throw aside all the roles that are generally germane to education—where teachers act one way and students act another. Everybody is now focused on creating an atmosphere of joy and learning for children—and people move in any role that's necessary in order to facilitate that."[26]

That change doesn't end in the classroom. The school runs its own breakfast and lunch programme—with meals high in nutrition. At its simplest, you can't learn if you're hungry.

**The richest component of one
of our learning courses
is the activation phase.
This takes about 75 to
80 percent of the time.
We play board games,
card games, we play with
a ball, we play with
paper dolls, we play
musical chairs, we play
with construction paper.
Much like the games you
would buy in a toy shop
but adapted to
make learning fun.**

LIBYAN LABIOSA-CASSONE*

*Second-language and accelerated learning consultant to
Simon Guggenheim School; author interview, Chicago, Illinois, 1990.

"Students walk through the hall now, very polite, very respectful," says Alexander. "Overhearing children on the playgroound, they talk about their school becoming the school of the future. 'We use accelerated learning. We're gonna be the most sophisticated school in the city with computer technology. We have Spanish in our school. Wc have tai chi in our school.' They tell their friends, and they're very excited about it."

So are the parents. An average of 20 turn up each day to help out.

What about the results?

"Academically, our performance changed dramatically," says Alexander. "The year prior to our teachers being trained in integrative, accelerated learning techniques, only 27 percent of our kids were making a year's growth in a year's instruction. A year subsequent to that, the rate went up to 54 percent, and in math it went to 58 percent."

Dr. Larry Martel, President of Interlearn Integrative Learning Systems in Hilton Head, South Carolina, surveyed the results after that year. And he reported a 103 percent increase in reading scores and an 83 percent increase in math and reading combined. In two years Guggenheim went from being at the bottom of Chicago's Subdistrict 16 schools to second from the top.

It would be great to report that its efforts have completely turned around a whole community. But the district still has one of the highest homicide rates in the country. The poverty still remains. For those students who stay on at Guggenheim, the overall achievements remain high. But many transient students are there for too short a time to have other than a glimpse of their true potential. And the surrounding neighbourhood bears daily testimony to America's urgent need for the same kind of innovative approaches to social problems that Guggenheim has brought to schooling.

Fluent French in eight weeks

For a class demonstration of accelerated learning in action, let's now visit Beverley Hills High School in Sydney, Australia.

They've introduced an accelerated learning course that has seen a three-year French course compressed into eight weeks. Says teacher Sylvia Skavounos: "I was amazed. We'd had a standard French course for two-thirds of a year before we started. Yet in the two weeks after we began, the students had learned at least 200 new words, and they could say them fluently"—much better in two weeks than the previous several

Learn a language in record time

In 1993, Bridley Moor High School in Redditch, England, tested the effectiveness of accelerated learning methods for studying a foreign language.

One group of students' German study included ten weeks of accelerated learning methods, and their examination results were compared with others studying at the same level by conventional methods.

On July 16, BBC television broadcast the examination results:

	Using new methods	Using normal methods
80% pass mark or better	65%	11%
90% pass mark or better	38%	3%

Thus, using new techniques, more than ten times as many students achieved a 90 percent pass mark.

Sources:

School examination results from Mrs Val Duffy-Cross, Assistant Head, Bridley Moor High School, Redditch, U.K. Television programme on BBC Midland TV, July 16, 1993. Course materials and methods from Accelerated Learning Systems, Aston Clinton, Bucks, England: the course outlined on page 171, and used also by the Sydney high school with its French results reported on pages 329 and 331. The course is designed for do-it-yourself home study, but can be supplied with an optional kit for teachers.

months.[27] The course they chose was produced by Accelerated Learning Systems of England, mainly for self-help learning. It also comes with a teacher kit for classroom use.

Visit the Beverley Hills French class, and you'll find the students doing exactly what Charles Schmid has described: starting with relaxation exercises; clearing their mind for the session to come; learning through *active* and *passive* concerts; reactivating their learning through games and even acting out and producing their own videotape.

Sydney's Channel 7 television brought in Jean-Philippe de Voucoux, an expert from Alliance Francais, to check progress. And he was amazed "at how quickly they were able to speak without reading" and how easy it was to have a conversation with them.

As Channel 7 summed up· it's an experiment that could turn Australia's education system "on its head."

The army learns a foreign language in record time

A journalistic story, of course, is not scientific evidence. For that we turn in brief to the American army and one of the best users of the new teaching techniques, Professor Lynn Dhority, of Boston.

Dr. Dhority was already a highly successful German teacher before he studied the *suggestopedia* method with Lozanov. He then had the opportunity of testing the method and comparing it with other measured results using standard-style German teaching. All materials for the course were prepared thoroughly in advance according to Lozanov guidelines: "peripherals," including posters, music, games, songs, activities and scripts. And because of Dr. Dhority's academic training, he was able to ensure that the results could be documented.

His "control group" of 11 students studied basic German, using accelerated learning techniques, for 108 hours over three and a half weeks (18 days) at Fort Devens army base. The results were then compared with another group of 34 army students, not taught by Dr. Dhority, learning basic German under regular "audio drill" methods over a period of 360 hours, spread over 12 weeks.

The comparative results recorded levels of "listening, comprehension, reading and speaking." And they were then checked by Dr. Lyelle Palmer, Professor of Education at Winona State University, Minnesota. They disclosed that only 29 percent of the "regular course" students reached the required "level one" of basic German in the 360 hours, while

How to increase the learning rate 661% with these techniques

Boston Professor of Education Lynn Dhority specializes in teaching second languages by many of the creative learning techniques outlined in this book.

In one well-researched study:

■ **Three groups of American soldiers studied basic German for 12 weeks using standard educational methods (60 days, 360 hours).**

■ **Another group studied the same subject, using "accelerated learning" techniques, for 18 days (108 hours).**

■ **Only 29 percent of the "standard groups" reached the required level of understanding in 360 hours.**

■ **But 64 percent of the "accelerated learning" group achieved the same ability to read German in 108 hours; and 73 percent reached the required level of understanding spoken German.**

Statistically, that is a 661 per cent better learning rate: more than twice the results in one-third the time.*

*These results are summarized from: *The 661% Solution: A statistical evaluation of the extraordinary effectiveness of Lynn Dhority's U.S. Army accelerated learning German class,* by Lyelle L. Palmer, Professor of Education and Special Education Chair, Winona State University, Minnesota, in a joint paper with Professor Dhority.

73 percent achieved the required level of "listening understanding" and 64 percent the required level of reading ability in the 120 hours.

Dr. Palmer recorded the results statistically in a joint paper headed: *The 661% Solution: A statistical evaluation of the extraordinary effectiveness of Lynn Dhority's U.S. Army accelerated learning German class.* [28] And for us he summed them up even more succinctly: "Lynn Dhority achieved more than twice the results in less than one-third the time. Statistically, that was a 661 percent increase."[29] Major savings were also achieved, of course, in instructor time and expenses, daily expenses for trainees, and time away from the job.

An accelerated integrative learning teacher

To study one specific accelerated and integrative learning teacher in action we've chosen Jan McKittrick, of Chula Vista Elementary School in southern California.[30] Her students come from multi-ethnic, multi-racial, at-risk neighbourhoods in South San Diego: 67.8 percent Latino Hispanic, 4.4 percent African-American, .4 percent American Indian or Alaskan, 4.6 percent Asian and Pacific Islander, 10.1 percent Filipino and 12.8 percent Caucasian.

Even before McKittrick started accelerated learning training in 1992, for five years her school had good results with a "whole-language, literature based" programme. But she says it was the new training that "pulled all the pieces of the puzzle together for me, because the personal growth-lifeskills strategies brought self-esteem to my classroom and to my own life. It opened the door to faster and easier academic learning for the children. And I don't have the discipline problems anymore."

So what does she do that makes the difference? Very simply: most of the techniques we've covered in this chapter:

She promotes students' self-esteem by each morning getting them into a resourceful state for learning, and she weaves similar activities into the programme throughout the day.

She begins every morning with music and dancing. "Students beg to get up in front of the room and lead the dancing exercises. It brings oxygen to the brain."

She uses many reflective thinking procedures through lots of creative writing.

She applies many of the principles developed by neuro linguistic programming pioneers Richard Bandler and John Grinder; plays soft

Supernature is nature with all of its flavors intact, waiting to be tasted.

LYALL WATSON
*Supernature**

*Published by Coronet, London.

music when taking children through practice tests, and hands out popcorn at the end of those tests so that the students have positive associations with examinations.

She enrols her class, instead of controlling it. "And the discipline problems have stopped. It's as simple as that. So often, we just talk. We talk about feelings. It opens the door to communication, which opens the door to wanting to come to school. Just to get the students to the point of attending school, and not being a discipline problem, for a whole quarter, is amazing."

And she has the vital ingredient of principal, community and other staff support: the kind of community/school/family relationship that other top-performing schools have found so essential.

Although McKittrick has only launched her programme this year, and it is too early to record researched results, she is already using many of the techniques that elsewhere are making learning much faster, easier and better.

Surprisingly slow start for big breakthroughs

Given the proven results of the new techniques, in many ways they have been slow to spread. This is probably as much a result of the "cold war" atmosphere of the 1960s and 70s as it is a consequence of any conservatism in the educational establishment. Early incorrect reports of "sleep learning" in then Communist bloc countries also conjured up illusions of "brain-washing."

Lozanov's accelerated learning techniques made their biggest early impact in foreign-language training for adults. The reasons were simple:

1. His first published international results were in this field.

2. Probably more than in any other subject, the spectacular results were easy to assess. People with no knowledge of another language were obviously learning much faster and effectively.

Sheila Ostrander and Lynn Schroeder publicized some of these feats early in the 1970's with their book *Psychic Discoveries Behind the Iron Curtain.* And their use of the word "psychic" probably turned-off as many people as it inspired. Soon afterwards, Lyall Watson answered much of the scepticism with *Supernature.* In it he mounted fact after fact to prove that what many people regard as "supernatural" is really "supernature;" that we all have hidden reserves of talent.[31]

School should be the best party in town.

PETER KLINE
*The Everyday Genius**

*Published by Great Ocean Publishers, 1823 North Lincoln Street, Arlington, VA 22207.

In North America, some of the first interest came from Canada, with its concentration on bilingual education. Dr. Jane Bancroft, Associate Professor of French at the University of Toronto, brought Lozanov to Canada in 1971. And a year later Dr. Donald Schuster, Professor of Psychology at Iowa State University, and a colleague, Ray Benitez-Bordon of Des Moines, began some of the first United States experiments. By 1975 Benitez-Bordon was reporting classes learning more than a full year's Spanish in 10 days—with four hours' study a day.[32]

But many of the early American results did not live up to the pre-publicity, largely because of misunderstandings over the role of music in the process. Many early enthusiasts thought any relaxing music would do. And the cause of good learning was not helped by many early spurious claims of spectacular results.

Fortunately the early development of the techniques coincided with some major American breakthroughs in brain-research, especially in California.

■ Dr. Roger Sperry, of the California Institute of Technology, won a Nobel Prize for his pioneering work in split-brain research.

■ Dr. Robert Ornstein, of Stanford University, played a big part in popularizing the enormous potential of the human brain.

■ And Professor Marian Diamond continued the long record of research work at Berkeley to prove the rapid growth of brain-dendrites in an environment of enriched experiences.

That brain research coincided in turn with equally startling developments in silicon-chip technology, and the proven ability of electronic inventions to speed up and simplify thousands of different processes.

Thus, while Lozanov was a seminal influence in the movement toward more efficient learning, the subsequent techniques we've described add much more. And it would be almost impossible to list all the innovators who have made valuable additions to his early work or who have made significant breakthroughs in other important ways.

Fortunately, America is at the cutting edge of research and practice in one other major allied field that could have a crucial impact on a world facing big changes in employment prospects: the analysis of learning and working styles.

Key points on learning styles

Every human being has a learning style and every human being has strengths.[1]

It's as individual as a signature.[2]

No learning style is better– or worse—than any other style.[3]

All groups—cultural, academic, male, female—include all types of learning styles.[4]

Within each culture, socio-economic strata or classroom, there are as many differences as there are between groups.[5]

Quotations from research by
*Professors Ken and Rita Dunn**

*The sources for the quotations on this page are cited in the chapter notes for chapter 10, to which they refer.
To obtain details of the Dunns' learning and working style checks, contact Learning Styles Network, School of Education and Human Services, St. Johns University, Grand Central and Utopia Parkways, Jamaica, NY 11439.

How to find your own learning style and use your many intelligences

Albert Einstein was a day-dreamer.

He even failed mathematics early in his high school life. Yet he went on to become the greatest scientist of his age.

Winston Churchill did poorly at schoolwork. He talked with a stutter and a lisp. Yet he became one of the greatest leaders and orators of the century.

Thomas Alva Edison was beaten at school with a heavy leather strap because his teacher considered him "addled" for asking so many questions. He was chastised so much that his mother took him out of school after only three months' formal education. He went on to become probably the most prolific inventor of all time. Even late in life he claimed he could not understand mathematics.

Fortunately Edison's mother—a former school teacher herself—was a pioneer in true learning. Says *The World Book Encyclopedia:* "She had the notion, unusual for those times, that learning could be fun. She made a game of teaching him—she called it exploring—the exciting world of knowledge. The boy was surprised at first, and then delighted. Soon he began to learn so fast that his mother could no longer teach him." But he continued to explore, experiment and teach himself.

Einstein, Churchill and Edison had learning styles that were not suited to their school styles.

And that same mismatch continues today for millions of others. It is possibly the biggest single cause of school failure.

It's also obvious that everyone has different talents. Pablo Picasso

The seven intelligences

Personal and professional uses

1. Linguistic intelligence.

Commonly found in: Novelists, poets, copywriters, scriptwriters, orators, political leaders, editors, publicists, journalists and speech writers.

Example of famous person: Winston Churchill, British journalist turned orator, political leader and writer.

Likely traits:

* Sensitive to patterns
* Orderly
* Systematic
* Ability to reason
* Likes to listen
* Likes to read
* Likes to write
* Spells easily
* Likes word games
* Has good memory for trivia
* May be good public speaker and debater although some linguistic specialists may prefer either oral or written communication

How to strengthen for learning:

* Tell stories
* Play memory games with names, places
* Read stories, jokes
* Write stories, jokes
* Do vocabulary skits
* Use journal writing
* Interviewing
* Do puzzles, spelling games
* Integrate writing and reading with other subject areas
* Produce, edit and supervise class magazine
* Debate
* Discussions
* Use word processor as introduction to computers

ACKNOWLEDGEMENT:

This page and pages 342, 344, 346, 348, 350 and 352 have been based on and adapted from the original research of Howard Gardner, David Thornburg, Thomas Armstrong, David Lazier, Linda Campbell, Bruce Campbell and Dee Dickinson.

was obviously a great painter, William Shakespeare a phenomenal writer, Joe Louis and Babe Ruth great sportsmen, Enrico Caruso a brilliant tenor, Anna Pavlova an outstanding ballet dancer and Katharine Hepburn a fine actress.

Some people, such as Leonardo da Vinci, have combined many talents.

Every person reading this page has a different *lifestyle* and a different *workstyle*. Successful businesses depend on their ability to cater to those different lifestyles. And human-resource consultants spend their lives matching workstyle talents to jobs.

Yet many of our schools operate as if each person is identical. Even worse: most operate with an evaluation or testing system that rewards only a limited number of abilities. And those rewards early in life often separate the allegedly gifted and intelligent from those who are claimed to be less intelligent and underachievers.

Possibly the worst educational innovation of his century was the so-called intelligence test. Two French psychologists, Alfred Binet and Theodore Simon, developed the first modern tests in 1905. Two American psychologists, Lewis M. Terman and Maud A. Merrill, both of Stanford University, later adapted the French work into what became known as the Stanford-Binet tests.

These did a good job of testing *certain* abilities. But they didn't test *all* abilities. And, worse, they gave rise to the concept that intelligence is fixed at birth. It's impossible now to say how many millions of people have had their lives ruined by this appalling myth.

So let us put the record straight: *we all have the ability to improve and expand our own intelligence. It is not fixed.*

Better still: we each have access to many different "intelligences" or intelligence traits.

And if the current authors had to choose any one step needed to transform the world's high-school systems in particular it would be this: find out each student's combination of learning styles and talents—and cater to it; and at the same time encourage the well-rounded development of all potential abilities.

The major fault with so-called I.Q., or intelligent quotient, tests is that they *confuse logic with overall intelligence*—when logic, as we've seen, is only one form of thinking skill. They also confuse linguistic ability with overall ability.

The seven intelligences

Personal and professional uses

2. Logical-mathematical intelligence.

Commonly found in: Mathematicians, scientists, engineers, animal trackers, police investigators, lawyers and accountants.

Example of prominent person: Marian Diamond, Professor of Neuroanatomy at the University of California at Berkeley.

Likely traits:

* Likes abstract thinking
* Likes being precise
* Enjoys counting
* Likes being organized
* Uses logical structure
* Enjoys computers
* Enjoys problem-solving
* Enjoys experimenting in logical way
* Prefers orderly note-taking

How to strengthen for learning:

* Stimulate problem solving
* Do mathematical computation games
* Analyze and interpret data
* Use reasoning
* Encourage own strengths
* Encourage practical experiments
* Use prediction
* Integrate organization and math into other curricular areas
* Have a place for everything
* Allow things to be done step-by-step
* Use deductive thinking
* Use computers for spreadsheets, calculations

In recent years Harvard Professor of Education Howard Gardner has been one of many who have made pioneer breakthroughs in shattering the "fixed I.Q." myth.

For more than 10 years Gardner has used prolific research to prove that each person has at least seven different "intelligence centres." As we've touched on earlier, he's defined:

Linguistic intelligence as the ability to speak or write well—highly developed in such people as Winston Churchill, John. F. Kennedy and all brilliant writers.

Logical-mathematical intelligence as the ability to reason, calculate and handle logical thinking—highly developed in such people as Bertrand Russell and Barbara McClintock, Nobel Prize winner in medicine and physiology for her scientific thinking in microbiology.

Visual-spatial intelligence as the ability to paint, take great photographs or create sculpture—well advanced in such people as Rembrandt and Michelangelo, but equally well advanced, in a different way, in the native sailors of the Pacific, with their ability to navigate by the stars.

Bodily-kinesthetic intelligence as the ability to use one's hands or body—epitomized in sports achievers and great actors.

Musical intelligence as the ability to compose songs, sing and play instruments.

Interpersonal intelligence—what we would prefer to call "social" intelligence—as the ability to relate to others.

And intrapersonal intelligence as the ability to access one's inner feelings.

Gardner accepts that many people might refer to all seven facets as intelligence "traits" or "talents," rather than different "intelligences." But he hurries to add: "If critics were willing to label language and logical thinking as talents as well, and to remove these from the pedestal they currently occupy, then I would be happy to speak of multiple talents. But I strongly resist any attempt to use a contrast between intelligence and talent as a veiled attempt to ignore or minimize the range of critical human abilities."[6]

The difference is much more than semantics. Children early in life are still being herded into the mythical "gifted" and "non-gifted" streams or tracks based largely on testing in only two traits.

We believe Gardner's findings have vital importance in planning the

The seven intelligences

Personal and professional uses

3. Visual-spatial intelligence.

Commonly found in: Architects, painters, sculptors, navigators, chess players, naturalists, theoretical physicists, battlefield strategists.

Example of famous person: Pablo Picasso, painter.

Likely traits:

* Thinks in pictures
* Creates mental images
* Uses metaphor
* Has sense of gestalt
* Likes art: drawing, painting and sculpting
* Easily reads maps, charts and diagrams
* Remembers with pictures
* Has good colour sense
* Uses all senses for imaging

How to use strength for learning:

* Use pictures to learn
* Create doodles, symbols
* Draw diagrams, maps
* Integrate art with other subjects
* Use mind-mapping
* Do visualization activities
* Watch videos or create your own
* Use peripheral stimuli on the walls; signs such as the posters in this book
* Use mime
* Change places in the room to gain a different perspective
* Use advance organizers or goal-setting charts
* Use clustering
* Highlight with colour
* Use computer-graphics

future of education. Every child is a potentially gifted child—but often in many different ways. Every person, too, has his or her own preferred learning style, working style and temperament. Back in 1921, Swiss psychiatrist Carl Jung outlined how people perceived things differently. He classified them as feelers, thinkers, sensors or intuitors. Jung was, as far as we know, the first to classify people also as either introverts or extroverts. It's unfortunate that many of Jung's perspectives were dropped by 1930 and relatively ignored until recently.

We all know people who embody many of the concepts he defined, and New Zealand professor of theology Lloyd Geering has summarized them in his excellent book *In The World Today,*[7] which seeks to bridge the gap between religion and science:

The extroverted thinkers, who abound in management, military strategy and some forms of science. People such as automotive pathfinder Lee Iacocca or British wartime military leader Bernard Montgomery.

The introverted thinkers, often interested in ideas for their own sake: philosophers such as Charles Darwin, Rene Descartes and Jung himself.

The extroverted feeling types, interested deeply in other people—the Mother Teresas of the world.

The introverted feeling types, including those who agonize over the world's problems but internalize them and assume them as a burden.

The extroverted sensation types, the sports-loving, thrill-seeking, pleasure-seekers.

The introverted sensation types "who find the outer world uninteresting and unsatisfying and turn inwardly to seek fulfilment"—including some of the great mystics.

The extroverted intuitive people "who enter new relationships with great gusto but do not always prove dependable. They can move quickly from one new interest to another, especially if it is not immediately fruitful. They have visions of new worlds to conquer or to build. They are promoters of new causes. We may name as examples Alexander the Great, Julius Caesar, Napoleon, Hitler, Henry Ford and builders of today's economic empires."

The introverted intuitive people, including the visionaries and dreamers who draw from their own hidden resources. Geering lists among the candidates for this category "the anonymous author of the Book of Revelation."

The seven intelligences

Personal and professional uses

4. Musical intelligence.

Commonly found in: Performers, composers, conductors, musical audiences, recording engineers, makers of musical instruments, piano-tuners, cultures without traditional written language.

Example of famous person: Mozart.

Likely traits:

* Sensitive to pitch, rhythm, timbre
* Sensitive to emotional power of music
* Sensitive to complex organization of music
* May be deeply spiritual

How to strengthen for learning:

* Play a musical instrument
* Learn through songs
* Use active and passive concerts for learning
* Study with baroque music
* Workout with music
* Join choir or choral group
* Write music
* Integrate music with other subject areas
* Change your mood with music
* Use music to get relaxed
* Image/make pictures with music
* Learn through raps such as timetables, whole language poems, choral reading
* Compose music on computer

And Geering says "the acknowledgment of psychological types is an essential first step if we are to appreciate Jung's concept of individuation, the process by which each of us becomes the one unique and whole human person we have the potential to become."

Many educators have now built on these concepts. Rudolph Steiner schools, for instance, place great emphasis on identifying and catering to individual temperaments.

There are currently about 20 different methods of identifying learning styles. And research by Professors Ken and Rita Dunn, from St. John's University, New York, provides one of the most comprehensive models. They've also produced a simple questionnaire which anyone can complete to obtain a computerized learning-style printout.[8]

Determining your learning style

Your learning style is a combination of three factors:

* *How you perceive information most easily*—whether you are mainly a visual, auditory, kinesthetic or tactile learner; whether you learn best by seeing, hearing, moving or touching. (The ability to taste and smell can be important in some work-styles, such as wine-tasting and perfume-blending, but these two senses are not major ones in most learning styles.)

* *How you organize and process information*—whether predominantly left-brain or right-brain, analytical or global.

* *What conditions are necessary to help you take in and store the information you are learning*—emotional, social, physical and environmental.

How you take in information

In the Dunns' research, they discovered that:

* Only 30 percent of students remember even 75 percent of what they *hear* during a normal class period.

* Forty percent retain three-quarters of what they *read* or *see.* These visual learners are of two types: some process information in word-form, while others retain what they see in diagram or picture-form.

* Fifteen percent learn best *tactually.* They need to *handle* materials, to write, draw and be involved with concrete experiences.

* Another 15 percent are kinesthetic. They learn best by *physically*

The seven intelligences

Personal and professional uses

5. Bodily-kinesthetic intelligence.

Commonly found in: Dancers, actors, athletes and sporting achievers, inventors, mimists, surgeons, karate teachers, racing car drivers, outdoor workers and the mechanically gifted.

Examples: Jayne Torvill and Christopher Dean, ice-skaters.

Likely traits:

* Exceptional control of one's body
* Control of objects
* Good timing
* Trained responses
* Good reflexes
* Learns best by moving
* Likes to engage in physical sports
* Likes to touch
* Skilled at handicrafts
* Likes to act
* Likes to use manipulatives
* Learns by participating in the learning process
* Remembers what was done rather than what was said or observed
* Very responsive to physical environment
* Plays around with objects while listening
* Fidgety if there are few breaks
* Mechanically minded

How to strengthen for learning:

* Use physical encoding exercises wherein you become object you are learning about
* Use dancing to learn
* Use movement to learn
* Act out the learning
* Use manipulatives in science, math
* Take lots of "state changes" and breaks
* Integrate movement into all curricula areas
* Mentally review while you are swimming, jogging
* Use models, machines, Technic Lego, handicrafts
* Use karate for focusing
* Use field trips
* Use classroom games
* Use drama, role-plays
* Finger snapping, clapping, stamping, jumping, climbing

doing—by participating in real experiences that generally have direct application to their lives.

According to the Dunns, we each usually have one dominant strength and also a secondary one. And, in a classroom or seminar, if our main perceptual strength is not matched with the teaching method, we may have difficulty learning, unless we can compensate with our secondary perceptual strengths.

This has major implications for solving the high-school dropout problem. In our experience, kinesthetic and tactile learners are the main candidates for failure in traditional school classrooms. They need to move, to feel, to touch, to do—and if the teaching method does not allow them to do this they feel left out, uninvolved, bored.

Neuro linguistic programming specialist Michael Grinder says that of a typical class of 30 students, 22 will be fairly balanced in their ability to take in information in a variety of ways. They will generally be able to cope when the information is presented in either visual, auditory or kinesthetic ways.

Two to three of the youngsters will have difficulty learning because of factors outside the classroom. And the remaining youngsters—up to six in a class of 30, or 20 per cent—will be "visual only," "auditory only" or "kinesthetic only" learners. They have great difficulty in absorbing information unless it is presented in the favoured style.

Grinder dubs them VO's, AO's and KO's. And he says, "It's not just a coincidence that the initials 'KO' stand for 'knockout.' These kids are 'knocked out' of the educational system. In every study I have seen regarding 'kids at risk,' kinesthetics make up the vast majority of the 26 percent dropout rate."[9]

How you organize and process information

People with strong left-brain traits take information in logically—they can absorb it easily if it is presented in a logical, linear sequence.

People with right-brain dominance generally like to take in the big global picture first; they're much more comfortable with presentations that involve visualization, imagination, music, art and intuition.

And if you can link together the powers of both hemispheres, and tap into those "seven intelligence centres," you'll obviously be able to absorb and process information more effectively.

The seven intelligences

Personal and professional uses

6. Interpersonal or "social" intelligence.

Commonly found in: Politicians, teachers, religious leaders, counsellors, sales people, managers, public relations and "people people."

Example of famous person: Oprah Winfrey, talk-show host.

Likely traits:

* Negotiates well
* Relates well, mixes well
* Able to read others' intentions
* Enjoys being with people
* Has many friends
* Communicates well, sometimes manipulates
* Enjoys group activities
* Likes to mediate disputes
* Likes to cooperate
* "Reads" social situations well

How to strengthen for learning:

* Do learning activities cooperatively
* Take lots of breaks to socialize
* Use "pair and share" learning activities
* Use relationships and communication skills
* Do "partner talks" on the phone
* Have parties and celebration of learning
* Make learning fun
* Integrate socialization into all curricular areas
* Use "People Search" activities where you have to talk to others to get answers
* Work in teams
* Learn through service
* Tutor others
* Use cause and effect

The conditions that affect your learning ability

The physical environment obviously affects learning. Sound, light, temperature, seating and body posture are all important.

People also have different *emotional needs.* And emotion plays a vital part in learning. It is in many ways the key to the brain's memory system. And the emotional content of any presentation can play a big part in how readily learners absorb information and ideas.

People also have different *social needs.* Some like to learn by themselves. Others prefer to work with a partner or their peers. Still others, in teams. Some children want an adult present or like to work with adults only. The Dunns say most underachievers are very peer-motivated.[10]

Physical and biological needs that affect learning

Eating times, time-of-day energy levels and the need for mobility can also affect learning ability.

Try learning, for instance, when you are hungry. It's hard for most of us. And some people need to constantly nibble.

Some people are morning people. Others are night owls. Again, the Dunns have found that students do better when their class-times match their own "time-clocks." [11] Significantly, they've found that most students are not morning people. "Only about one-third of more than a million students we have tested prefer learning in the first part of the morning," they report. "The majority prefer late morning or afternoon. In fact, many do not begin to be capable of concentrating on difficult material until after 10 a.m." For daytime learning, the Dunns recommend 10 a.m. to 3 p.m. But who says high schools shouldn't be open evenings for the night-owls?

The Dunns confirm that "the tactile-kinesthetics" face most learning difficulties in traditional schools.[12] They often drop out because they can't focus well sitting down hour after hour. Those that stay often "get into trouble" and get suspended. Others are often unfortunately classified as "learning disabled" and put into "special education" classes— where they do more of the same: lots of seatwork activity, paying little attention to their true strengths and learning styles.

Every top learning environment we have seen caters to a variety of intelligence-traits and a variety of learning styles. But many high schools

The seven intelligences

Personal and professional uses

7. Intrapersonal or intuitive* intelligence.

Commonly found in: Novelists, counsellors, wise elders, philosophers, gurus, persons with a deep sense of self, mystics.

Example of famous person: Plato, philosopher.

Likely traits:

* Self-knowledge
* Sensitivity to one's own values
* Deeply aware of one's own feelings
* Sensitivity to one's purpose in life
* Has a well-developed sense of self
* Intuitive ability
* Self motivated
* Deeply aware of own strengths and weaknesses
* Very private person
* Wants to be different from mainstream

* The core capacity of "intrapersonal" intelligence is the ability to access one's inner self. Some feel intuition is a separate intelligence trait: a seemingly innate ability to know about others or events.

How strengthen for learning:

* Have personal "heart-to-heart" talks
* Use personal growth activities to break learning blocks
* Debrief activities
* Think about your thinking through "Pair and Shares" and "Think and Listen"
* Take time for inner reflection
* Do independent study
* Listen to your intuition
* Discuss, reflect or write what you experienced and how you felt
* Permit freedom to be different from the group
* Make "My Books" and journals of life story
* Take control of own learning
* Teach personal affirmations
* Teach questioning

in particular still seem geared to "academic" two-dimensional teaching—directed mainly at linguistic and logical learners. Not surprisingly, many of the people involved in school administration were themselves high-achievers in logical-mathematical and linguistic ability—so to them that type of environment naturally seems best.

How to determine students' preferred learning styles

Again, one simple way is to ask. A simple request and discussion on learning styles and preferences is also often one of the simplest ways to break down barriers between teacher and students. You can also often tell a person's preferred style by listening to them talk.

Ask a visual learner for instructions and she'll tend to draw a map. If she is starting to grasp an otherwise difficult subject, she'll say "I see what you mean." Read her a menu in a restaurant and she'll have to look at it herself. Buy her a present and you can't go too wrong with a book—but check to see whether she's print oriented or prefers pictures. If the latter, she might even prefer a videotape. Most visual learners, but not all, tend to be organized, tidy and well dressed.

An auditory learner generally couldn't care less about reading a book or an instruction manual. He'll have to ask for information. He doesn't buy a car for its looks—he buys it for its stereo system. In a plane he'll immediately strike up a conversation with his new neighbour. And when he grasps new information, he says something like: "I hear what you're saying." If you buy him a present, make it a tape recorder, not a book.

A kinesthetic, tactile learner always wants to be on the move. If she bumps into to you accidentally, she'll want to give you a reassuring hug. When she grasps a new principle, "it feels right" to her. And for her Christmas present: a laptop computer?

Schools, businesses and parents should arrange for more accurate analyses of both learning and work styles. Checks using the Dunn model, for instance, can be arranged through The Learning Styles Network which operates out of St. Johns University in New York.[13] Schools can obtain from the network supplies of questionnaires covering all factors that can determine learning models. After students have completed individual questionnaires, these are returned to the network for a computerized printout, detailing each person's preferred learning environment and method. The network is co-sponsored by the American Association of Secondary School Principals. And in *Learning Styles: Quiet Revolu-*

Today we can test any secondary student and, within minutes, describe exactly how that person is likely to learn more easily and remember longer.

RITA DUNN and SHIRLEY A. GRIGGS
Learning Styles:
Quiet Revolution in American Secondary Schools*

*Published by National Association of Secondary School Principals, 1904 Association Drive, Reston, Virginia 22091.

tion in American Secondary Schools, published by the association, co-authors Rita Dunn and Shirley A. Griggs say: "Today we can test any secondary student and, within minutes, describe exactly how that person is likely to learn more easily and remember longer."

Four types of thinking style

Not only do we have preferred learning styles, we also have favourite thinking styles. Anthony Gregorc, professor of curriculum and instruction at the University of Connecticut, has divided these into four separate groups:[14]

* **Concrete sequential.**
* **Concrete random.**
* **Abstract random.**
* **Abstract sequential.**

We're indebted to SuperCamp consultant John LeTellier for adapting the Gregorc model and providing the checklist on the next three pages.[15]

We stress, however, that no thinking style is superior; they are simply different. Each style can be effective in its own way. The important thing is that you become more aware of which learning style and thinking style works best for you. Once you know your own style, you can then analyse the others. This will help you understand other people better. It will make you more flexible. And perhaps we can all pick up tips from each other on how to be more effective.

Once you've made a graph for yourself on page 358, consider these explanations to improve your own ability to learn, think, study, work and enjoy life:

Concrete sequential thinkers are based in reality, according to SuperCamp co-founder and president Bobbi DePorter. They process information in an ordered, sequential, linear way. To them, "reality consists of what they can detect through their physical sense of sight, touch, sound, taste and smell. They notice and recall details easily and remember facts specific information, formulas and rules with ease. 'Hands on' is a good way for these people to learn."[16] If you're concrete sequential—a CS—build on your organizational strengths. Provide yourself with details. Break your projects down into specific steps. Set up quiet work environments.

Concrete random thinkers are experimenters. Says DePorter: "Like

To test your own thinking style
read each set of words and mark
the two that best describe you

1.	a.	imaginative
	b.	investigative
	c.	realistic
	d.	analytical
2.	a.	organized
	b.	adaptable
	c.	critical
	d.	inquisitive
3.	a.	debating
	b.	getting to the point
	c.	creating
	d.	relating
4.	a.	personal
	b.	practical
	c.	academic
	d.	adventurous
5.	a.	precise
	b.	flexible
	c.	systematic
	d.	inventive
6.	a.	sharing
	b.	orderly
	c.	sensible
	d.	independent
7.	a.	competitive
	b.	perfectionist
	c.	cooperative
	d.	logical
8.	a.	intellectual
	b.	sensitive
	c.	hardworking
	d.	risk-taking

9.	a.	reader
	b.	people person
	c.	problem solver
	d.	planner
10.	a.	memorize
	b.	associate
	c.	think-through
	d.	originate
11.	a.	changer
	b.	judger
	c.	spontaneous
	d.	wants direction
12.	a.	communicating
	b.	discovering
	c.	cautious
	d.	reasoning
13.	a.	challenging
	b.	practicing
	c.	caring
	d.	examining
14.	a.	completing work
	b.	seeing possibilities
	c.	gaining ideas
	d.	interpreting
15.	a.	doing
	b.	feeling
	c.	thinking
	d.	experimenting

After completing the test at left:

In the columns below, circle the letters of the words you chose for each number. Add your totals for columns I, II, III and IV. Multiply the total of each column by 4. The box with the highest number describes how you most often process information.

	I	II	III	IV
1.	C	D	A	B
2.	A	C	B	D
3.	B	A	D	C
4.	B	C	A	D
5.	A	C	B	D
6.	B	C	A	D
7.	B	D	C	A
8.	C	A	B	D
9.	D	A	B	C
10.	A	C	B	D
11.	D	B	C	A
12.	C	D	A	B
13.	B	D	C	A
14.	A	C	D	B
15.	A	C	B	D

TOTAL: _____

I ___ x 4 = ☐ Concrete Sequential (CS)

II ___ x 4 = ☐ Abstract Sequential (AS)

III ___ x 4 = ☐ Abstract Random (AR)

IV ___ x 4 = ☐ Concrete Random (CR)

Now graph your results on the chart on next page.

After you have completed your personal thinking-style test on the previous page chart your results below

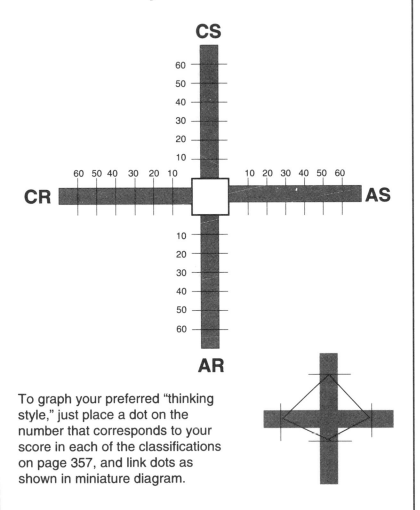

To graph your preferred "thinking style," just place a dot on the number that corresponds to your score in each of the classifications on page 357, and link dots as shown in miniature diagram.

Our thanks to John LeTellier and Dell Publishing, 666 Fifth Avenue, New York, NY 10103, for permission to reprint this test from *Quantum Learning,* by Bobbi DePorter. The test is based ، ، research by Professor Anthony Gregorc.

concrete sequentials, they're based in reality, but are willing to take more of a trial-and-error approach. Because of this, they often make the intuitive leaps necessary for true creative thought. They have a strong need to find alternatives and do things in their own way." If you're a CR, use your divergent thinking ability. Believe that it's good to see things from more than one viewpoint. Put yourself in a position to solve problems. But give yourself deadlines. Accept your need for change. Try and work with people who value divergent thinking.

Abstract random thinkers organize information through reflection, and thrive in unstructured, people-oriented environments. Says De-Porter: "The 'real' world for abstract random learners is the world of feelings and emotions. The AR's mind absorbs ideas, information and impressions and organizes them through reflection. They remember best if information is personalized. They feel constricted when they're subjected to a very structured environment." If you're an AR, use your natural ability to work with others. Recognize how strongly emotions influence your concentration. Build on your strength of learning by association. Look at the big picture first. Be careful to allow enough time to finish the job. Remind yourself to do things through plenty of visual clues, such as coloured stickers pasted up where you'll see them.

Abstract sequential thinkers love the world of theory and abstract thought. They like to think in concepts and analyse information. They make great philosophers and research scientists. DePorter again: "It's easy for them to zoom in on what's important, such as key points and significant details. Their thinking processes are logical, rational and intellectual. A favourite activity for abstract sequentials is reading, and when a project needs to be researched they are very thorough at it. Generally they prefer to work alone rather than in groups." If you're an AS, give yourself exercises in logic. Feed your intellect. Steer yourself toward highly structured situations.

The implications for schools and individuals

We believe every aspect of this research can improve learning and schooling greatly.

For personal home study, it makes great sense to know your own strengths, know your family's learning styles and build on them. If it's hard for you to sit still for a long time, you're almost certainly a kines-thetic learner. So consider starting to study by previewing your material with a giant Mind Map—on a big sheet of paper. Put it on the floor and

How to tell learning styles by the eyes

Teachers skilled in neuro linguistic programming (NLP) say that they can often tell students' preferred learning styles by looking at their eye movements and listening to them speak.*

 A student who sits still and looks straight ahead, or whose eyes look upwards when accessing information, and who is a fast talker, is generally a visual learner.

 A student who looks from side to side when accessing information, or looks down to his "offside" (right-handed student looking to the left), is probably an auditory learner. He will generally speak with a rhythmic voice.

 **A right-handed student who moves a lot, looks to the right and downwards when accessing and storing , and is a slow speaker, will probably be a kinesthetic learner.**

*Illustrations are from an inexpensive filmstrip cassette, *Teaching to Modality Strengths: A Common Sense Approach to Learning,* by Walter B. Barbe and Raymond H. Swassing, available through Zaner-Blozer, Inc., Columbus, Ohio. Copyright 1979.

*Similar points are covered in extensive detail in *Righting The Educational Conveyor Belt,* by Michael Grinder, published by Metamorphous Press, P.O. Box 10616, Portland, Oregon 97210.

use your body while you're working. After previewing the material, play some classical music—and move with its rhythm. Then do something physical. Go for a walk, a swim, or move your body while you practise mentally, through visualization, what you've just put into your brain.

Especially if you're kinesthetic, feel free to get into your favourite learning atmosphere and position. If you are an auditory learner, record your notes on to a cassette tape over baroque music. And if you are a visual learner, be sure to draw Mind Maps, doodles, symbols or pictures to represent what you are learning. For a visual learner, a picture represents a thousand words.

For taking control of your life, all people have what Dr. Robert Sternberg, Yale Professor Psychology and Education, calls *styles of managing.* "The ways in which students prefer to use their intelligences," he says, "are as important as ability. Children—in fact, all people—need to 'govern' their activities, and, in doing so, they will choose 'styles of managing themselves with which they are comfortable.' The mind carries out its activities much as a government. The *legislative* function is concerned with creating, functioning, imagining and planning. The *executive* function is concerned with implementing and with doing. The *judicial* function is concerned with judging, evaluating and comparing. Mental self-government involves all three functions, but each person will have a dominant form."[17]

For school teachers and seminar leaders, we would hope the lessons are equally obvious: analyse each student's learning style, and cater to it. You won't be able to do this for everyone all the time. But you can make sure that every style is catered for regularly throughout every learning sequence. If you do, you'll be amazed at how easily people can learn—and how much less resistance you will find.

One of the first American schools to be based almost entirely on Howard Gardner's principles is the Key Elementary School in Indianapolis. Walk into the Key School and you'll find youngsters learning in all the different "intelligences." Sure, you'll find all the traditional subject areas, such as reading and math, being covered. But you'll also find everyone involved in music, painting, drawing, physical activity and discussion. For four periods a week, children meet in multi-aged groups called pods, to explore a whole range of interests such as computers, gardening, cooking, "making money," architecture, theatre, multi-cultural games and other real-life skills.

How to go from 30% to 83% achievement

The Brightwood Elementary School in Greensboro, North Carolina, had reading and mathematics scores in the 30th percentile in 1986 when its principal, Roland Andrews, went to New York to study learning styles with Professors Rita and Ken Dunn.

Next year (1987), his school's scores on the *California Achievement Test (CAT)* rose to the 40th percentile.

So impressed were the parents in that low socioeconomic area with their children's achievement gains that they paid for sending five Brightwood teachers to New York for one week of training during the summer of 1987.

By 1989, Brightwood's CAT scores reached the 83rd percentile. Its African-American children scored as well as Caucasian youngsters.

The *only* thing that teachers did differently between 1986 and 1989 was to introduce the Dunns' model of learning styles.*

*Summarized from *Rita Dunn Answers Questions on Learning Styles* in the special issue of *Educational Leadership,* entitled *Learning Styles and The Brain,* published by the Association for Supervision and Curriculum Development (Vol. 48, No. 2, October 1990).

It is because of results like this that the present authors believe school dropout rates could be dramatically reduced by analysing and catering to each student's different learning style.

"Once a week," says Gardner, "an outside specialist visits the school and demonstrates an occupation or craft. Often the specialist is a parent, and typically the topic fits into the school theme at the time."[18]

The school is also closely involved with the Centre of Exploration at the Indianapolis Museum. "Students can enter into an apprenticeship of several months, in which they can engage in such activities as animation, shipbuilding, journalism or monitoring the weather."

Key School is also alive with projects. Says Gardner: "During any given year the school features three different themes, introduced at approximately ten-week intervals. The themes can be quite broad (such as 'Patterns' or 'Connections') or more focused ('The Renaissance— then and now' or 'Mexican heritage'). Curricula focus on these themes; desired literacies and concepts are, whenever possible, introduced as natural adjuncts to an exploration of the theme."

All projects are also videotaped so that eventually each student has a portfolio of videos to show both the work done and to reveal each one's strengths.

In brief, the Key School encourages all students to learn through all their intelligences, those where they're strong and those where they need building; it focuses on their learning styles; it encourages thinking and experimentation; and it builds apprenticeship and mentoring models.

Better yet, it shows precisely what can happen if a country finally uses its tremendous academic research skills and blends them with a well-planned school, innovative teachers, tremendous community resources and a focus that sees all children as gifted.

Great catch-up programmes

1. **Specialized kinesiology.**
2. **SMART program.**
3. **Ball/stick/bird teaching.**
4. **Four-minute reading programme.**
5. **Tape-assisted reading programme.**
6. **Peer tutoring.**
7. **"Look, Listen" method.**
8. **Reading Recovery.**
9. **Personal key vocbularies.**
10. **Beginning school mathematics.**
11. **Computerized catch-ups.**
12. **The SEED mathematics programme.**

It's easier to switch on and learn when the right button's touched

Until she was 10, Helen Keller was deaf, blind and mute.

But by 16 she had learned to read in Braille, and to write and speak well enough to go to Radcliffe College. She graduated with honours in 1904.

Fortunately her first teacher had never heard of the term "learning disabled."

Unable to use her sense of sight or hearing, Helen Keller learned first through touch. And the good news is that modern breakthroughs have now provided the tools for all of us to "switch on" to easier learning, even those who may have been labelled "backward" or "slow."

Almost a century after Keller's graduation, her message to the world is still clear: everyone is potentially gifted—in some way.

Obviously, the earlier you start to develop those talents the better. One *Fortune* survey has concluded that every dollar spent on good care before birth saved $3.38 on intensive care in a hospital neo-natal unit. And every $1 spent on the best head-start programmes before school "lowers expenditures for special education, welfare, teen pregnancy and incarceration of criminals by $6."[1]

But even if experience in infancy is poor, can children still catch up at primary school? Fortunately the evidence gives an overall "yes." This is not to deny that some people have learning difficulties. But labelling them "learning disabled" must rank with I.Q. tests as one of the great educational tragedies of the century. The very act of labelling often adds to the stress. *Our research convinces us that any person can learn— in his or her own way. And those ways are many and varied.*

One can never consent to creep when one feels an impulse to soar.

HELEN KELLER*

*Born deaf, blind and mute

Two key principles: the mind-body connection and the mind-brain connection

The first principle to restress is that learning is not only an *academic* process. Just as an infant develops his brain by sucking, grasping, crawling, creeping, walking, climbing, rocking and spinning, so too with children and adults. You will never develop another cerebral cortical brain cell after you are born, but you can keep growing those dendrites—the brain's connecting and "storage" branches—throughout life.

Professor Diamond and her co-researchers at Berkeley have proven conclusively that the more effective the physical and mental stimulation, the bigger and better the dendritic brain growth.[2] Professor Palmer has proven in Minnesota that *physical* routines at kindergarten can dramatically improve five-year olds' *academic* performance, because those concentrated physical activities actually grow the brain.[3]

Secondly, the brain and the mind are not the same. To over-simplify: if you were to compare them to a computer, the brain would be the *hardware* and the mind the *software*. The brain is biological and neurological: it has neurons, glial cells, dendrites and myelin sheathing that together provide the biological *mechanism*. In the context of this book, the mind is the *content* of the brain. It is not only possible but highly desirable to stimulate the mind through the body as well.

Again, Helen Keller is a classic case-study.[4] It took her three years merely to learn the alphabet. Her teacher, Anne Sullivan, was able to communicate with the girl's brain and mind through a sense of touch. She later spelled out words on her hand. Helen then learned to read and write in Braille, but in her own time.

Five main factors influenced Keller's *ability* to learn: time, culture, context, support and the freedom to choose.

Time was obviously vital. Her first learnings took a long time. But once she made her initial gains she was able to build on them rapidly. Learning had nothing to do with being "disabled;" it had everything to do with having handicaps and needing *her own time-clock* to overcome them. She would never have succeeded by starting in today's regimented graded classrooms.

Culture was also important. Helen Keller's culture esteemed the ability to talk and read. By comparison, in a culture without a written language, navigation might rate much higher than reading; thus culture determines the context of learning—and learning problems. "Special

80 percent of learning difficulties are related to stress. Remove the stress and you remove the difficulties.

GORDON STOKES
President, Three in One Concepts*

*This quotation is a major theme of the book *One Brain: Dyslexic Learning Correction and Brain Integration,* published by Three In One Concepts, 2001 W. Magnolia Blvd., Suite B., Burbank, CA 91506-1704. It is highly recommended as a guide to specialized kinesiology.

education" teacher and author Thomas Armstrong puts it succinctly: "Culture defines who's 'disabled' . . . a child labelled dyslexic, hyperactive or learning-disabled in our society might excel in another culture."[5]

Keller's plight was being blind, deaf and mute. She had to learn within that limited context. Had she taken an I.Q. test, with its linguistic base, her rating would have been extremely low, if she had scored at all. Without Sullivan, she may have been placed in an institution for the retarded, instead of developing as a highly gifted person.

The support of a caring and able teacher is equally essential. Sullivan never gave up on Helen, even though the girl had wild temper tantrums.

Helen Keller also had the freedom of choice. At ten she chose to want to learn to talk. There was no rush. She did it in her own time and context. Again the message is obvious: too many people in traditional education are put in no-choice situations in both conscious and subconscious ways.

Anne Sullivan discovered the brain-body and mind-body connection because she, too, had experienced difficulties in learning. Fortunately, there is now a wealth of other research to back up those discoveries.

Specialized kinesiology

Some of the most interesting research and practical applications have come from the field of specialized kinesiology. Just as *kinesthetics*, or movement, is an important aspect of many learning styles, so is *kinesiology* the science of motion, and *kinesthesia*, the sensation of position, movement and tension of parts of the body.

Kinesiology has become well known in some countries because of the way it has helped peak performance in sports. Brigitte Haas Allroggen, of the Munich Institute of Kinesiology, talks about the effectiveness of the science with Olympic teams: "All of a sudden things exploded. We began working with top Austrian athletes who later won Olympic medals and worldwide competitions. Then the Norwegian Olympic team came to us, and the Italians too. All had remarkable results."[6]

Similar techniques are now helping in education, and not just for people with learning difficulties. Says kinesiologist Kathleen Carroll, of Washington D.C., who links her training with accelerated integrative learning strategies: "Kinesiology improves academics for *anyone.*"[7]

This is, in part, because of the way the brain transmits messages both *electrically* and *chemically,* and the way in which stress causes block-

How to improve your spelling, writing, reading and listening with this simple brain exercise:

1.   **Stand up and, by raising your knees alternately, touch each hand to the opposite knee.**

2.   **Do this about ten times whenever you are stressed.**

Variations:

1.   **Do it with your eyes closed.**

2.   **Do it by raising each foot, alternately, behind you; touching each foot with the opposite hand.**

This is a typical exercise recommended by educational kinesiologists to integrate both sides of the brain, reduce stress and make learning easier. If you have difficulty with exercises like this, the authors recommend repatterning by a certified kinesiologist.

Exercises like this are covered in the highly-recommended books, *Brain Gym,* published by Edu-Kinesthetics Inc., P.O. Box 3396, Ventura, CA 93006-3396, and *One Brain: Dyslexic Learning Correction and Brain Integration,* published by Three In One Concepts, 2001 W. Magnolia Blvd., Suite B., Burbank CA 91506-1704.

We acknowledge the assistance of certified kinesiologist Kathleen Carroll, Three In One Concepts facilitator of Washington DC, in compiling this section of the book.

ages. In simple terms, educational kinesiologists say that when stress overwhelms us our brain is short-circuited—the "wiring" becomes fused. They say this is a major cause of learning problems—and labelling those problems "dyslexia" or anything else generally adds to the stress and the fusion. Often the answer lies in simple exercises which "defuse" the blockage between the left and right sides of the brain. Get rid of the blockage and you often get rid of the problem.

Some of the most outstanding work has come from specialized kinesiology researchers and practitioners Gordon Stokes and Daniel Whiteside through their Three In One Concepts organization based in Burbank, California. They say 80 percent of learning difficulties are related to stress. And this can be released by kinesiology.[8]

They have developed body exercises—using pressure-points, muscle testing and coordination patterns—to reorient the electrical patterns of the brain and thus *defuse* stress, clear the "blocked circuits" and turn on the ability to learn. By working through the body they've been able to change the state of both the brain and the mind.

Since the brain operates most effectively when both left and right sides are working in harmony, many of those kinesiology exercises can help you become more *centred*, more coordinated, less stressful and can make learning easier and natural—in the same way that Olympic athletes use centring exercises to prepare for competition.

Many of the best and simplest exercises have been developed by educational kinesiologists Paul and Gail Dennison and illustrated in *Brain Gym*, a highly-recommended handbook.[9]

These exercises were originally developed by Dr. Paul Dennison for people labelled "dyslexic"—people who supposedly see writing in reverse, like a mirror-image. But they help more than people with handicaps: they can be used at any age level and even for people who don't think they have learning problems. They're excellent, for instance, for classroom "state changes"—for any age group.

Unfortunately most schools are not yet using these tools, but where they are, the results are outstanding. A typical example comes from the Sierra Vista Junior High School in California, where Three In One Concepts worked with 11 "special education" students who were three to seven years behind their grade level. All were considered to be handi-capped by "dyslexia." A kinesiology specialist worked with the students one afternoon a week for eight weeks. And at the end of that time 73

If we insist on looking at the rainbow of intelligence through a single filter, many minds will erroneously seem devoid of light.

RENEE FULLER
inventor of ball/stick/bird teaching method*

*The quotation above is the subheading of an article entitled *Beyond IQ*, by Renee Fuller in the *In Context* magazine (winter 1988).

percent of the students showed "significant improvement" (at least one year's growth in eight weeks) in three of six learning abilities tested, 50 percent in one and 27 percent in two others.[10]

The world abounds with other excellent catch-up programmes. Among the best we have found:

SMART programme

Some teachers in San Marcos, California, are starting to use Professor Palmer's brain-stimulation programme for five-year-olds at kindergarten level. They call the programme SMART (San Marcos Accelerated Readiness Training). Walk into teacher Karen Fontana's class at the start of the day and you'll find children doing log rolls, frog hops, alligator crawls and spinning like helicopters— all part of the Palmer programme to stimulate the important vestibular system. She says these routines not only aid the learning process, they settle the children down. Later you'll find the youngsters working with eye tracking, word ladders and dotted-number flash-cards.

All activities can be integrated into regular classroom settings. And Fontana reports that by March of 1993 her young students had already completed the stipulated kindergarten curriculum for a whole year.[11]

The ball/stick/bird method

Other outstanding results have been achieved by Dr. Renee Fuller while on the staff at Rosewood Hospital Centre Psychology Department in Maryland. She worked with 26 persons who were institutionalized for retardation—ranging in age from 11 to 48 and in I.Q. tests from 28 to 72.

Fuller taught them to read. And that achievement greatly increased both their learning ability and their self-esteem. "Not only did they learn to read advanced story material with comprehension," she reports, "they also showed some unexpected emotional and behavioural changes."[12] By learning to read they learned to think. And when they learned to think, their behaviour changed and their appearance changed.

Fuller provided them with a tool to break the reading code: the ball/stick/bird method. In this method, the ball represents all the parts of letters of the alphabet having a circle; the stick represents the parts of letters with a line; and the bird the "wings" of letters, such as an "r."

She showed her students how all the letters of the alphabet consisted of just these three simple concrete forms. With that "code" and fast-paced

Students should be given choices and responsibility for their own education.

ELIZABETH SCHULZ
A Long Way To Go*

*Article in the American *Teacher Magazine* (February 1993), based on visits to several New Zealand schools.

stories, even the most retarded students were soon learning and thriving.

New Zealand breakthroughs

Other breakthroughs are often blends or developments of techniques covered in our True Learning chapter.

New Zealand's catch-up programmes, for instance, have become so successful that groups of American teachers now fly across the Pacific regularly to see how they work. New Zealand teachers are amazed to find that many American elementary schools still shuffle children around to several different teachers during a day: a reading teacher, for example, and a music teacher.

American visitors "down under" are impressed by what they call whole-language teaching. But that term is too restrictive. Whole life may well be better. The whole structure is based around the principle that students come first.

New Zealand has "a national curriculum," but that paints only in broad strokes the educational philosophy and teaching goals. Individual teachers are regarded very much as self-acting professionals, graduates of Colleges of Education which specialize in teacher training. Large blocks of all three-year teacher-training programmes are also spent in practical hands-on school experience.

Even the term *national curriculum* is probably a misnomer in that it suggests a French-style system where every year each child is learning the same set body of knowledge.

"The new national curriculum doesn't tell teachers how to run their classes," reports American *Teacher Magazine's* Elizabeth Schulz, "but it does emphasize that schools are for the students and should be organized to give them access to the skills and understanding they need to participate effectively and productively in society. School learning is meant to be relevant. Class projects should illuminate for students the interconnectedness of subjects. And, whenever possible, students should be given choices and responsibility for their own education."[13]

Four other factors play a big part in the country's highly successful catch-up programs:

1. While New Zealand education is financed by central government and the funds are distributed to schools on the basis of roll-numbers, extra money is provided for schools in low-income areas or areas with special ethnic needs.

All it takes is four minutes a day at school, four minutes at home, and a great link between home and school.*

*The key to New Zealand's "four-minute reading programme,"
as reported in the television series, *Where To Now?*
produced by the Pacific Foundation and broadcast
on the Television One network in 1991.

2. The Ministry of Education funds one of the world's best "reading recovery" programmes in elementary schools.

3. Its Learning Media division also provides to all schools an outstanding selection of free material. This includes a *Beginning School Mathematics* programme; a fast-paced, colourful *Ready To Read* series of beginner books; and a regular *School Journal,* which includes top-notch writing for children on a wide range of topics. These *Journals* have been published for years. All writing has been indexed for age groups and subjects. And that makes them ideal source-material for thematic study.

4. Teachers are also encouraged to use their own initiative.

Among the resulting breakthroughs:

The four-minute reading programme

Like many countries, New Zealand has a large number of migrant families for whom English is a second language. Not surprisingly, many of them starting school at age five have an English reading equivalent of three or four. Now many of them are catching up within a few weeks. All it takes is four minutes a day at school, and a great link between school and home.

The entire scheme is common sense and simple. When each child starts school, teachers check his or her level of understanding. If Bobby can recognize his own name and other words starting with "B," but he can't manage those starting with "P" or "W" or "K," then the teacher works out a personalized daily list of words—beginning with those letters. Those will include the recommended first 300 most-used words in the language, and others well-known to the child, such as family and local street names.

A new list of words is provided each day, hand-written on note paper. The list is taken home for study, and a carbon copy kept at school. Each morning, the teacher spends only four minutes with each child to check progress—and provide encouragement.

But the big extra ingredient is the home involvement. A "school neighbourhood worker" takes home the first list with each child, and explains to the parents, grandparents or brothers and sisters just what Bobby needs to learn—and how only four minutes a day is needed for him to flourish. If the parents have difficulty with English, a neighbourhood volunteer is found.

Educational psychologist Donna Awatere played a big part in devel-

The key ingredients of TARP:
Tape-assisted reading programme*

1 Provide a full range of books and stories
graded by age-group reading levels,
with interesting photos or pictures.

2 Encourage each child to choose stories
on subjects that interest him.

3 Have those stories recorded on audio tape,
by parents, teachers or older students.

4 The student reads the story as he listens,
at home and at school.

5 When he feels confident, he reads
the story without the tape.

6 Then he reads parts of it to his teacher,
some from his selection, some from her
choice.

On average, children on this programme
are making three years' progress
in eight to ten weeks.

*Details are covered fully in *TARP: The Tape Assisted Reading
Programme,* by John Medcalf, produced by the Flaxmere Special
Education Service, P.O. Box 5074, Flaxmere, Hastings, New Zealand.

oping the programme. She says the home-link is the real key. "It's only half as good without that."[14] Another key is the "positive reinforcement" that comes from daily success. While the programme started over ten years ago for five-year-old new entrants, it is now being used successfully in other schools for older children. As well as sending a new reading list home to parents each night, some have brought parent-helpers into the school. At Bruce McLaren Intermediate School in Auckland, for instance, 12 parents help out part-time.

Even senior reading teacher Beth Whitehead was a bit reluctant when asked by her principal to introduce the programme, saying "What can you do in four minutes?" But she tried it out. "I soon thought I'd show it wouldn't work. But when I started it, the children just zoomed in their reading. They were absolutely amazing."[15]

Whitehead stresses that the programme is built "on praise and positive reinforcement of everything that the child does correctly, however small." Obviously, the programme is slightly different for the older children, but the basic four-minute concept remains. Simple but effective.

TARP—the tape-assisted reading programme

In another part of New Zealand, schools have successfully linked together one of the simplest Japanese electronic innovations with the New Zealand *School Journal* [16] library—and used it to make spectacular progress in overcoming reading difficulties at primary school.

The innovation is the Sony Walkman cassette tape player. And in the small New Zealand suburb of Flaxmere, educational psychologist John Medcalf has taken the Walkman and used it to solve major reading problems.

The method is called TARP: tape-assisted reading programme. Basically, each child is encouraged to read stories of his own choice—based on his own interests. But when he reads each book, at home or at school, he can hear the same story on a cassette tape, through a set of Walkman headphones.

"The readers are actually selecting stories they want to read," says Medcalf, "about subjects they're interested in: reading them when they want to read them—as many times as they like before they actually try to read them to somebody else."[17]

When the student feels confident enough, the teacher checks progress.

Principles of Peer Tutoring:*

1   Students' reading levels should be checked
      first.

2   Students should be matched in pairs,
      with the tutor only a slightly better reader.

3   Books should be chosen for the right
      reading and interest levels.

4   Tutors are trained with a simple checklist,
      which shows them how to use
      "pause, prompt and praise" techniques.

5   Parents are fully informed, books taken
      home each night, and a list kept of books
      mastered.

6   Tutoring should be done daily or at least
      three times a week.

7   Each pair should record their efforts on
      a tape-recorder provided.

8   The teacher monitors the recordings to
      check progress in both reading and
      tutoring.

**Over six months the average reading gain for
tutors has been four years and for slower
learners just over two years.**

*Details are fully covered in *Peer Tutoring in Reading,* by
John Medcalf, published by the Flaxmere Special Education Service,
P.O. Box 5074, Flaxmere, Hastings, New Zealand.

"Some of the best results," says Medcalf, "have been four to five years' reading gain over approximately eight weeks on the programme." Overall the well-documented results show a three-year reading gain in eight to ten weeks.[18]

The programme is helped greatly in New Zealand through the graded *School Journal* material, backed by a regularly updated catalogue covering content, subjects and age-levels. Students may choose from a selection of taped stories that the school has built up, or may ask a teacher or parent to record onto a tape a story or article of special interest.

Where a similar programme has been used in America, the results have also been striking. Marie Garbo, Director of the National Reading Styles Institute, refers to it as "the recorded book" method. As a strong advocate of matching reading methods and materials to learning styles, she says it can even be adapted for use with highly kinesthetic youngsters: reading a book on a music stand attached to a stationary bike while listening to the tape and pedalling. Sound "far out?" Listen to the answers from two boys who tried it:

■ "When you read on that thing, all the words just come out like that. I'm serious!"

■ "When I got up there, well . . . when I started to read, I mean, I don't know, it was probably like a miracle. I started laughing because I couldn't help it because I was reading almost 100 percent better."[19]

Peer tutoring

Medcalf has also built on earlier work by Professor Ted Glynn, of the University of Otago, in developing a successful peer tutoring programme in reading, using "pause, prompt and praise" techniques.

Here one student in an primary school simply acts as a mini-teacher for another student. Generally the mini-teacher is only a little bit more advanced—so both the tutor and her buddy benefit. The tutor very definitely is not the best reader in the class—although she may end up that way. Effectively it's one-to-one teaching without taking up the time of an adult teacher. Each "tutor" is trained in "pause, prompt and praise" techniques: to praise good work in everyday language ("Neat," or "Nice one!"); to pause for ten seconds while a reader may be having difficulty (so the tutor can think of ways to help); and to prompt with suggestions.

Flaxmere Primary School teacher Rhonda Godwin sums up the results: "We've had tutors who came into the programme reading about

"Look, Listen" method for parents

- Choose a very interesting book.
- The print must be large. The younger the child, the bigger the print should be.
- A beginner likes a picture, and not too many words, on each page.
- Don't ask him to read aloud. You read to him.
- Use your finger or another pointer in unison with your reading.
- Read in phrases, with emphasis on meaning.
- Match the speed of your reading to your child's ability to follow the text.
- Both you and your child must be happy and relaxed.

Summarized from
FORBES ROBINSON'S
Look, Listen:
*Learning To Read Is Incredibly Simple**

*Distributed by J.K. Marketing, P.O. Box 366, Nelson, New Zealand.

a year to a year and a half below their chronological age, and they made up to two years' gain after working on the programme for about ten weeks."[20]

Over six months the average gain for tutors has been four years—and for the slower learners just over two years.[21]

The "Look, Listen" method

Another New Zealand innovation has made similar dramatic improvements in teaching reading to whole classes at once. Teacher Forbes Robinson has shown its effectiveness for years, and has proven it in practice around America, Britain and Canada. He calls it the "Look, Listen" method. Robinson is a fan of the Doman theory which proposes that youngsters can easily learn to read when they're exposed to big print.

For a classroom setting, Robinson recommends a piece of technology that predates television: the opaque projector. "Unlike the overhead projector, the opaque projector requires no transparencies. Its operation involves no preparation at all."[22] To use it to teach reading, you simply select a suitable book, preferably with attractive illustrations, slip it into position in the projector, turn on the power, and it projects the pages, in full colour, either one or two at a time, onto a jumbo-sized screen: preferably at least 240cm. square.

The opaque projector also comes with a "magic pointer"—and the teacher can move this quickly to follow the words as they are projected on to the screen and he reads them. Robinson says he's found this an ideal method of teaching English as a second language—and for adult literacy classes. It can also be used with previous under-achievers as part of mixed-level classes, without causing embarrassment.

The system has the added benefit of being useful for teaching any subject, so that, for instance, full-colour encyclopedia pages or graphics can be projected onto the large screen for discussion. It does, however, require a darkened room, and some schools have opted to reserve one room as a permanent projection room. In this way, more than one class can be involved at the one time with only one teacher, leaving other teachers free for preparation or one-to-one tutoring.

Where Robinson's techniques have been researched, the results have been excellent:

At Putaruru Intermediate School in New Zealand, the "Look, Listen"

To create a climate of delight that invites children to enjoy reading and writing, you will want to fill your classroom with books, books and more books.

ANNE D. FORESTER and MARGARET
REINHARD
The Learners' Way*

*Published by Peguis Publishers, 520 Hargrave St., Winnipeg,
Manitoba, Canada, R3A OX8.

method was used with 140 form one and two students, aged 11, 12 and 13. All had "reading ages" two to six years below their chronological ages. All 140 were taken in groups of about 30 in half-hour sessions four times a week for 12 weeks. The 63 students in form one were tested before and after the trial, and 40 of them made between two and three years' progress in the 12 weeks, 17 gained between one and one and a half years and five gained half a year. The school was so impressed with the results it introduced the programme for adults as well.[23]

At the Language Development Centre at Chelmsford Hall School, Eastbourne, England, the same method was used to teach reading to 106 children with severe reading difficulties—aged between four and 14. All 106 pupils averaged eight months' progress in six weeks.[24]

In several schools in Scotland, the Robinson method was used to help 15 11-to-13 year-olds diagnosed as having very low I.Q.s: between 40 and 70. They were taken for 45 to 50 minutes a day for just under six weeks, and made ten months' reading improvement.[25]

At the Fairbank Memorial Junior School in Toronto, Canada, a mid-city multi-racial school with a large proportion of youngsters learning English as a second language, after 20 minutes twice a day for only ten days, progress for children in grades 2 through 6 ranged from just under five and a half months to one year.[26]

As D.B. Routley, principal of the C.E. Webster Junior Public School in Toronto, wrote after seeing the results at his school: "During my 24 years in the field of education, I have never seen an in-service programme for teachers that has produced such a positive impact on students as the programme designed by Mr. Robinson."[27]

New Zealand's Reading Recovery programme

All those four latter programmes can be operated by normal classroom teachers. But the best-known New Zealand catch-up programme is organized by teachers who need to be specially trained. It is known as Reading Recovery, first developed by Professor Marie Clay of the University of Auckland, and outlined in her writings, *The Patterning Of Complex Behaviour, Becoming Literate: the construction of inner control,* and in the briefer core text of the programme, *The Early Detection of Reading Difficulty.*

In New Zealand, while the official age for starting school is six, nearly every child starts at five. By six, children with reading difficulties are

Release the native imagery of your child and use it for working material.

SYLVIA ASHTON-WARNER
Author of *Teacher**

*One of the keys to Ashton-Warner's success, as covered by Lynley Hood in *The Biography of Sylvia Ashton-Warner*, published by Viking, Auckland, New Zealand.

identified in the Reading Recovery programme, and helped for half an hour each day by a specially trained Reading Recovery teacher. Reading Recovery has been operating as a government-funded programme throughout New Zealand since 1984. On average, youngsters catch up within 16 weeks. And 97 percent maintain and improve their ability as they proceed through school.

The programme has been taken up by some state educational systems in Australia and the United States and by the Surrey Local Education Authority in Britain. An official British educational report on the New Zealand scheme gives it high praise—but stresses two additional points:

1. Literacy is accorded a "supremely important" place in the New Zealand education system, so "it can be no surprise that the target group of clients for Reading Recovery was identified and a programme devised for their aid "

2. "It is already clear that the New Zealand system is well on the way to identifying the next frontier, the third-wave children—that small core who do not appear able to accelerate at the rates of the majority of pupils for whom the scheme is the appropriate measure."[28]

Personal key vocabularies

Other than Marie Clay and former Director of Education, Dr. C.E. Beeby, the New Zealand educational innovator best known in other countries is probably the late Sylvia Ashton-Warner.*

She first burst to prominence internationally with her book *Teacher* in 1963. It was based largely on her work teaching primary school in New Zealand rural areas with a mainly Maori population. And her supporters would say it provides one of the main effective answers to that "third wave" reading problem. In the early 1950s, New Zealand introduced into its schools the *Janet and John* series of readers, a British modification of the American *Alice and Jerry* series. But even then teachers were encouraged to make up their own books based on children's own lives.

---

* *Those reading Sylvia Ashton-Warner's work for the first time should, in fairness, be made aware that, among her many excellent other qualities, she was also eccentric and prone to exaggeration. While she can claim credit for inventing the key vocabulary concept, many of her writings wrongly imply that she was a lone voice crying in New Zealand's educational wilderness for child-centered education. In fact, Beeby, as head of the Department of Education, was pioneering that very concept, in a very rational and effective way.*

There is no reading problem. There are problem teachers and schools.

HERBERT KOHL
Reading, How To*

*Published by Penguin, London.

In listening to young Maori children, Ashton-Warner "came to realize that some words —different words for each child—were more meaningful and memorable than others." When she asked a young child to write about a "train" he wrote about a "canoe."

She then started to listen to each child and selected the key words "which were so meaningful to him that he was able to remember them when he had seen them only once."

As Lynley Hood writes in *Sylvia,* her biography of Ashton-Warner: "Her pupils learned to read from their personal key vocabularies. Nearly every day, from their experiences at home or at school, Sylvia helped each child select a new key word. She wrote the word with heavy crayon on a stout piece of cardboard and gave it to the child. The word cards became as personal and precious to the children as the imagery they represented. Children who had laboured for months over 'See Spot run' in the new *Janet and John* readers took one look at 'corpse,' 'beer' or 'hiding' and suddenly they could read.

"The stories from which the key words were born were told in colourful Maori-English. Sylvia recorded them faithfully onto big sheets of paper and pinned them around the walls: 'I caught Uncle Monty pissing behind the tree. He got wild when I laughed at him.' 'My Dad gave my Mum a black eye.' It wasn't exactly what the Education Department had in mind when it advocated the use of children's experiences in the teaching of reading, but it certainly worked. The excitement and the sense of release created an unprecedented enthusiasm for reading."[29]

She realized that children were more interested in their own stories than hers. So she helped her students write them. She put the stories to music. And she constructed her own graphic presentations about their dreams and experiences. She regarded each child as highly creative, and encouraged them to work with clay and paint.

Above all, she summed up her philosophy in one memorable sentence: *Release the native imagery of your child and use it for working material.*

Some of the same techniques have been used by Felicity Hughes to teach English in Tanzania[30] and by Harvard-graduate Herbert Kohl to effectively teach reading to youngsters from minority cultures in California. Perhaps Kohl is right, as he puts it at the start of his common sense book *Reading, How To*: "There is no reading problem. There are problem teachers and problem schools. Most people who fail to learn

Children learn best when they are helped to discover the underlying principles for themselves.

PETER KLINE
The Everyday Genius*

*Published by Great Ocean Publishers Inc, 1823 North Lincoln Street, Arlington, VA 22207.

how to read in our society are victims of a fiercely competitive system of training that requires failure. If talking and walking were taught in most schools we might end up with as many mutes and cripples as we now have non-readers."

Beginning school mathematics

New Zealand's success in reading recovery has been matched with its innovative approach to teaching elementary mathematics.

The *Beginning School Mathematics* programme includes brightly-coloured puzzles and games.

For their first two years at school, youngsters use these and other manipulative material to learn about the main relationships that underlie mathematics.

American writer Schulz summarizes her impression of the programme in action: "As we enter the classroom, a glance at the six- and seven-year-olds tells us BSM is in full swing. Four students make geometric shapes by stretching rubber bands across pegs on a board. Children at a table draw pictures using cardboard circles, squares and triangles. One boy weighs household objects on a scale, guided by a sheet that asks, for example, if a cork is heavier than a paper clip. Six students stand in line by height and answer the teacher's questions about who is first, second and third in line, and who is standing between whom."[31]

In many ways the principles are very similar to those used by Montessori teachers in preschool.

Computerized catch-ups

Other intermediate schools have found great success by using the international *Technic Lego* programme. Others are also using some of the excellent computer maths programmes that are now readily available. Among the best are those pioneered by the Computer Curriculum Corporation, based on years of research at Stanford University in California, not just for math but for a wide variety of subjects.

Remuera Primary School in Auckland has become the first in New Zealand to introduce a computerized study programme in a joint venture with private enterprise. Its new learning centre has been established in partnership with the International College of Applied Learning, which earlier had big success using computers to teach math and basic literacy to underachieving, unemployed high-school dropouts.

Learning is the greatest game in life and the most fun.

All children are born believing this and will continue to believe this until we convince them that learning is very hard work and unpleasant.

Some kids never really learn this lesson and go through life believing that learning is fun and the only game worth playing.

We have a name for such people.

We call them geniuses.

GLENN DOMAN
Teach Your Baby Math*

*Published by the Better Baby Press, at The Institutes For The Achievement of Human Potential, 8801 Stenton Avenue, Philadelphia, Pennsylvania 19118.

The Remuera school centre, which started with ten computer work stations, offers 26 separate courses. And when it's not being used by its own pupils, the centre provides courses for other fee-paying students: at preschool, elementary and adult levels.

The SEED mathematics programme

In the United States, the best non-computer catch-up math programme we have seen is called SEED: Special Elementary Education for the Disadvantaged.[32]

In Dallas, Texas, Philadelphia, Pennsylvania and Oakland, California, teachers using the SEED method are teaching advanced high school mathematics to ten-year-old African-American children, from low-income families, who only a few months before were up to two years behind in math.

SEED teachers are themselves taught to use the Socratic method—with all classes based on questions that encourage the youngsters to solve problems by reason and logic. According to Dallas SEED director, Hamid Ebrahimi, the main objective is not math at all, but "to excel beyond their imagination."[33]

In Dallas, nine Texas Instruments engineers have served as instructors in the SEED programme at several elementary schools—and many of the youngsters have succeeded at college-level math.

In fact, Dallas provides one of the world's best educational models in business-school partnerships. More than 1,000 area businesses and civic groups have adopted nearly all of the Dallas school district's 189 schools.

But overall you'll find the most successful catch-up programmes in schools that are committed to using a wide variety of interrelated methods to try to ensure individual success for *every* student.

How to solve the dropout dilemma

■ **Adapt Japan's business methods for school.**

■ **Use the world as your classroom and study all subjects together as integrated projects.**

■ **Study in cooperative groups.**

■ **Paint the big picture first, then fill in the details.**

■ **Learn in shorter bursts, with built-in success-steps along the way.**

■ **Apply the lessons from SuperCamp.**

How to get "high" on education and not on drugs, gangs and crime

Is it really possible for nearly all students to succeed at high school?

Are there some guaranteed methods to get teenagers "high" on achievement instead of on drugs, gangs and crime? And ways to slash dropout rates even among those entering high school way behind others? Is it actually possible for nearly every student to *love* high school? Fortunately, our research says: Yes. And outstanding high schools are already achieving these results by using:

* Common sense lessons from the world's best businesses.

* Methods that captivate youngsters' emotions so they *want* to stay in school.

* Sound link-ups between university research breakthroughs, competent high school teachers and new technology.

* New group study techniques that are lifting examination "failures" into the ranks of high-achievers.

* Methods that focus on what we want for youth, not what we don't want.

* Short graduated courses where everyone can achieve step-by-step success—at any age.

* Outstanding, concentrated out-of-school SuperCamps that result in marked increases in academic results, motivation and confidence.

* New teaching techniques to make sure that all individual learning styles are catered to.

For working models of teenage success stories we've chosen examples from as far apart as the southeast panhandle of Alaska, the breath-

395

Mt. Edgecumbe's innovative teaching methods challenge students and draw raves from business leaders.

*Reading, Writing and Continuous Improvement**

*Article in *Competitive Times* magazine, published by GOAL/QPC (Number 1, 1991).

takingly beautiful national parks of New Zealand and a SuperCamp movement that has now spread from California to Russia.

1. Using Japan's business methods to improve school

If you had to nominate any American state as a revolutionary high school leader, Alaska would not top many lists. In area it's the biggest of the 50 United States—twice the size of Texas. But it has the second lowest population: about half a million people, and only one metropolitan area, Anchorage, with a population of around 200,000. Its native population is diverse: Caucasian, Eskimo, Eleuts and several Native American Indian tribes, many of them centred around small community towns of only 150 to 200 people, living on extremely low incomes, in a climate where the temperature in winter can reach -17 degrees Fahrenheit or -20 degrees Centigrade. Hardly a recipe for soaring educational success.

Yet one school in Alaska deserves an accolade as a world leader. It has also shown how great ideas can stem from other fields—in this case from Japan's quality revolution inspired originally by the American W. Edwards Deming.

TQM (Total Quality Management) and CIP (the Continuous Improvement Process or Kaizen) have been among the main processes used to transform Japan from a devastated, shattered and beaten society into a world economic leader within 40 years.

Now Mt. Edgecumbe High School, in Sitka, Alaska, has pioneered similar methods for education.[1] Mt. Edgecumbe is a public boarding school with 210 students and 13 teachers. Eighty-five percent of its students come from small villages. Most are Native Americans, descendents of the Tlingit, Haida and Tsimpshean tribes as well as Eskimo tribes and Aleuts. Forty percent of its students had struggled at other schools; now the school boasts one of America's highest levels of graduates moving on to higher education.

In many ways it owes its transformation to the vision of two people: Superintendent Larrae Rocheleau and teacher David Langford. Mt. Edgecumbe was originally opened in 1947 as a school for Native Americans. But in 1984 it was converted into an "alternative" experimental school, with Rocheleau in charge. Visitors to the school have described him as a practical idealist. One of his first objectives was "to turn these students into entrepreneurs who would go back to their villages and make a difference."[2] These dreams succeeded in part, but they really started to

W. EDWARDS DEMING'S 14 POINTS FOR QUALITY IMPROVEMENT

1. Create constancy of purpose for improvement.

2. Adapt the new philosophy of quality.

3. Cease dependence on mass inspection.

4. End the practice of awarding business on short-term costs.

5. Constantly improve the system.

6. Institute training to teach workers to do the job well.

7. Institute leadership consisting of helping people.

8. Drive out fear of asking questions.

9. Break down barriers between staff areas.

10. Eliminate workforce slogans, exhortations and targets.

11. Eliminate numerical quotas.

12. Remove barriers to pride of workmanship.

13. Institute a vigorous programme of education and retraining.

14. Take action to accomplish the transformation.

*W. Edwards Deming, *Out Of Crisis,* Massachusetts Institute of Technology Centre for Advanced Engineering Study.

take off about four years later when teacher Langford, on a visit to Phoenix, Arizona, attended a business TQM meeting. He became convinced that the same processes that had transformed Japan could transform a school. He persuaded Rocheleau to attend a further seminar, and Mt. Edgecumbe has never been the same.

How do you summarize a school that has turned nearly every other educational system upside down and inside out? Let's try:

■ *Teachers and students are all regarded as co-managers. They set their own targets and goals, individually and collectively. And they evaluate themselves regularly against agreed standards of excellence. There are no "incompletes" and "F" grades at Edgecumbe. Each task is not complete until it is regarded as meeting standards of excellence way above those ever achieved in any school examination.*

■ The first computer course begins by teaching speed typing. All students do their homework on a computer, using word processors, spreadsheets and graphic programmes to produce 100 percent perfect results—just as their future businesses will demand excellence in typing, spelling, accounting, financial and sales reports.

■ Collectively the school has identified its "internal" customers (students, teachers, administrators and other staff) and its "external" customers (universities and colleges, military, industrial and service work force, homes and society in general).

■ All activities at the school have been planned in conjunction with those "customers."

■ Students and staff have drawn up their own "mission statement." Among many other points, it stresses that: "The school places high expectations upon students, administrators and staff. Programme and curriculum are based upon a conviction that students have a great and often unrealized potential. The school prepares students to make the transition to adulthood, helping them to determine what they want to do and develop the skills and the self-confidence to accomplish their goals. Students are required to pursue rigorous academic programmes that encourage them to work at their highest levels."[3]

■ *The first week of school each year is used for building self-esteem and quality training.* Says a joint student-teacher report: "By spending the first week focusing on why students attend school, they are ready to learn and seem hungry to begin. We focus on reaching out to find out what you are truly capable of accomplishing, not just getting it done."

Mt. Edgecumbe High School's

Constancy of Purpose*

The aim of Mt. Edgecumbe High School, Sitka, Alaska, is to produce QUALITY individuals.

Our actions are based on the following beliefs:

1. Human relations are the foundation for all quality improvement.

2. All components in our organization can be improved.

3. Removing the causes of problems in the system inevitably leads to improvement.

4. The person doing the job is most knowledgeable about that job.

5. People want to be involved and do their jobs well.

6. Every person wants to feel like a valued contributor.

7. More can be accomplished by working together to improve the system than by working individually around the system.

8. A structured problem-solving process, using statistical graphic problem-solving techniques, lets you know where you are, where the variations lie, the relative importance of problems to be solved, and whether the changes made have had the desired impact.

9. Adversarial relationships are counter-productive and outmoded.

10. Every organization has undiscovered gems waiting to be developed.

11. Removing the barriers to pride of workmanship and joy of learning unlocks the true untapped potential of the organization.

12. Ongoing training, learning and experimentation is a priority for continuous improvement.

*Published by Mt. Edgecumbe High School (October 30, 1990).

■ As part of this initiation all students and all staff take part in a Ropes course—very similar to some Outward Bound courses and some Super-Camp activities. They describe it as a great confidence builder. Says TQM specialist Myron Tribus: "It does for all students what competitive athletic contests are supposed to do for a few. But it does it better. As I see it, the school is trying to develop autonomous team players."[4]

■ *Students decided it was inefficient to have seven short study periods a day, so the school switched to four 90-minute classes. This schedule allows time for lab work, hands-on projects, field trips, thorough discussions, varied teaching styles and in-depth study. The reorganized schedule also allows for an extra three hours of staff development and preparation time each week.*

■ Because students are viewed as customers, the school tries to provide what they want. Students have repeatedly requested more tech-nology, so the school has added dozens of computers, and opened the computer lab, library and science facilities at night for all pupils. As one report puts it: "Quality implementation is heavy on resources because students do the work and learning, not the teachers. The average number of hours of homework has risen to 15 per week. Studying, working together, and achievement have become a habit."[5]

■ *CIP has prompted teachers to rethink their teaching styles. One science teacher says he has changed from being an 80 percent lecturer to a 95 percent facilitator.*

■ Discipline problems? "Improving the entire education system, with student/customer needs first, has virtually eliminated classroom discipline problems . . . students acquire a sense of belonging and see the value in each class. Students help control and prevent discipline prob-lems through positive peer pressure."[6]

■ *All students set improvement goals, such as receiving all A's, avoiding conduct reports and reducing tardiness.*

■ *All students receive 90 minutes per week of quality-improvement training and school-wide problem-solving.*

■ All staff members have been trained in flow-charting. Flow charts of long-range projects are posted so that everyone can see how their part fits into the whole of each project.

■ *Because one of the school's goals is to develop "Pacific Rim entrepreneurs," the students have set up four pilot "companies":* Sitka Sound Seafoods, Alaska Premier Bait Company, Alaska's Smokehouse

Deming's 14 points

as modified by students for education*

Deming's 14 points for Total Quality Management have been applied to many businesses. But here is how one class at Mt. Edgecumbe High School in Alaska has modified them for education:

1. Create constancy of purpose toward improvement of students and service. Aim to create the best quality students capable of improving all forms of processes and entering meaningful positions in society.

2. Adopt the new philosophy. Educational management must awaken to the challenge, must learn their responsibilities and take on leadership for change.

3. Work to abolish grading and the harmful effects of rating people.

4. Cease dependence on testing to achieve quality. Eliminate the need for inspections on a mass basis (standardized achievement test, minimum graduation exams, etc.) by providing learning experiences which create quality performance.

5. Work with the educational institutions from which students come. Improve the relationships with student sources and help to improve the quality of students coming into your system.

6. Improve constantly and forever the system of student improvement and service, to improve quality and productivity.

7. Institute education and training on the job for students, teachers, classified staff and administrators.

8. Institute leadership. The aim of supervision should be to help people use machines, gadgets and materials to do a better job.

9. Drive out fear, so that everyone may work effectively for the school system. Create an environment which encourages people to speak freely.

10. Break down barriers between departments. People in teaching, special education, accounting, food service, administration, curriculum development and research, must work as a team. Develop strategies for increasing the cooperation among groups and individual people.

11. Eliminate slogans, exhortations and targets for teachers and students asking for perfect performance and new levels of productivity. Exhortations create adversarial relationships. The bulk of the causes of low quality and low productivity belong to the system and thus lie beyond the control of teachers and students.

12. Eliminate work standards (quotas) on teachers and students (e.g. raise test scores by 10% and lower dropouts by 15%). Substitute leadership.

13. Remove barriers that rob the students, teachers and management of their right to pride and joy of workmanship.

14. Institute a vigorous programme of education and self-improvement for everyone.

15. Put everybody in the school to work to accomplish the transformation. It is everybody's job.

*Published by Mt. Edgecumbe High School (October 30, 1990).

and Fish Co. and the Alaska Pulp corporation—all under the umbrella of Edgecumbe Enterprises. The "parent company" started its first salmon-processing plant in 1985, run by students themselves. The goal was to give students the skills and experience needed for running an import-export business aimed at Asian markets. By the 1988-89 year, the company was already making four annual shipments of smoked salmon to Japan. Each subsidiary company now links hands-on experience with the academic curricula. So math students calculate the dollar-yen exchange rate. Pacific Rim geography is studied in social studies. Art students design promotional brochures and package labels for products. And business and computer students learn how to develop spreadsheets to analyse costs and project prices.[7]

■ Myron Tribus provides a word picture of how the business projects link with other studies: "In the class on entrepreneurship, taught by Marty Johnson, I watched the students prepare and package smoked salmon for sale in Japan. The students had used a taste panel of local Japanese to determine the flavour and texture Japanese people liked the most. They then developed a standard procedure to produce the same taste and texture every time. To achieve the desired taste required using a certain kind of salmon, exposing it for a certain time and temperature, using a special brining solution, which they had determined experimentally yielded the proper taste, and a certain amount of time in the smoke from the right mixture of wood shavings, using slices of fish cut to a certain thickness and size. By studying the packages of smoked fish sold in Japan, they developed an attractive package which would fit in small Japanese refrigerators. They developed their own distinctive label, in Japanese of course. And they test-marketed the product in Japan."[8] That marketing includes study trips to Japan and other Pacific Rim countries.

■ *All students learn either Chinese or Japanese, and their curriculum is strong in the history, culture and languages of the Pacific Rim, English, social studies, mathematics, science, marine science, computers, business, and physical education.*

■ The school's mission statement stresses that "opportunities for leadership, public service and entrepreneurship are integrated into the programme, both during and after regular school hours."

■ Each student is assisted, guided and challenged to make choices about future academic or technical schooling and alternative methods of making a living. Enter a business class and you'll watch students preparing spreadsheets to reflect what it will cost them to live in their chosen

I wish I could find the same thirst for learning in the rest of the country.

MYRON TRIBUS*

*The Application of Quality Management Principles in Education, at Mt. Edgecumbe High School, Sitka, Alaska (1990), reproduced in An Introduction to Total Quality for Schools, published by the American Association of School Administrators (1991).

lifestyle after graduation, taking into account mortgage payments, taxes, cost of living changes and projections for such variables as the cost of transportation and schooling.

■ Frequently whole classes work without supervision—as they will be required to do in the outside world—so the teachers are free to put extra time into study and further course preparation.

■ Each curriculum is constantly being revised. As a result of student surveys and requests, Russian, physics, calculus and advanced quality training have been added to the curricula.

■ In the CIP media class, students teach other students. There is no administrator or teacher in the room. Twenty-five student trainers have assumed responsibility for training other students in the quality sciences.

■ *Staff training receives top priority. Teachers are constantly encouraged to internally challenge and justify each and every learning process.* The school has developed two research and development classes, science and technology and media CIP. These continually experiment with new technologies in equipment and human relations.

■ Each teacher has his or her own computer, with training in many applications. The school has also pioneered multiple uses for multi-media technology such as laser disks, hypercard applications and presentation software.

■ Every student receives a "Stats for Success" handbook. It is used to record homework, weekly plans, organize their time and graph progress. The entire emphasis is on self-discipline and self-motivation.

And the success ratio? Mt. Edgecumbe's simple goal is stated boldly: to produce QUALITY individuals. Almost 50 percent of all graduates have entered college and are still there or have graduated— much higher than the national average. There have been hardly any dropouts. And the school is confident that all its students will continue to grow and learn.[9]

Says *Competitive Times* magazine: "Mt. Edgecumbe's innovative teaching methods challenge students and draw raves from business leaders."[10] Adds Tribus: "I wish I could find the same thirst for learning in the rest of the country."[11]

Mt. Edgecumbe is, of course, a boarding school, but its TQM and CIP-Kaizen principles have lessons for educational systems at every level— and especially for turning previous "failures" into successes.

The old method of operating high schools is separated from the real world.

PAT NOLAN
Director of Integrated Studies Programme
at Freyberg High School*

*Author interview at Freyberg High School, Palmerston North,
New Zealand (1991). Dr. Nolan is Senior Lecturer in Education
at Massey University, Palmerston North, and Director of the
university's Educational Research and Development Centre.

2. Integrated studies use the world as a classroom

If Mt. Edgecumbe, Alaska, is an unlikely place to start a revolution, the lush, green, heavily-forested national parks and soaring mountains of New Zealand seem even further removed from the traditional schoolroom. But link them with the latest computer technology, a dedicated team of university innovators and some flexible teachers from Freyberg High School in the small city of Palmerston North, and again the result is surprising.

Every innovation has its visionary driving-force. Freyberg's was Dr. Pat Nolan, senior lecturer in education at Massey University on the outskirts of Palmerston. Massey was originally an "agricultural college" and it is closely linked with several nearby farm research institutes. So its hands on tradition is a long one. Pat Nolan marries his love of education with a passion for exploring the New Zealand outdoors: its towering volcanic snowfields, clean sparkling rivers and forests rich with native trees and birds. He's also a computer buff, who now heads Massey's Educational Research and Development Centre, a pioneer in providing data-based services to other educational institutions.

Nolan has put all his passions together in the Freyberg "integrated studies programme." But it's no mere dream. Nolan sees it as the kind of alternative educational programme that "might go the next step in providing for all high school students the kind of results previously enjoyed by only the top 30 to 40 percent."[12]

He says "the old method" of high school studies is separated from the real world. "We've all been through the school system. What we've experienced is a compartmentalized or segmented curriculum, where subjects are locked up in their little boxes, with tight little boundaries around them. So we learn mathematics, physics and English separately. Seldom do we see the connection between subjects. Yet it's by linking subjects together and seeing the interconnections that we come to understand the real world better. And that is basically what integration is all about: developing ways of teaching—and experiencing—knowledge in a way that establishes the interconnections in the minds of the students, and has them actually using that knowledge to create new solutions."

Similar arguments, of course, have been expressed for many years. In New Zealand alone five separate educational inquiries, from 1943 to 1987, have stressed the benefits of integrated studies.[13] But many high

The three elements of integrated studies*

1 Interesting out-of-class project activities, combining research and exploration.

2 Student use of computer as a tool for information processing and analysis.

3 History, geography, science, math, economics, writing, computing and other studies are linked together, not taught separately.

*Summarized from *Case Study of Curriculum Innovation in New Zealand: The Freyberg Integrated Studies Project,* by C.J. Patrick Nolan, then Associate Director of Educational Research and Development Centre, Massey University, Palmerston North, New Zealand, and David H. McKinnon, Visiting Research Fellow, Education Department, Massey University, published by Massey University (April 23, 1991).

school principals and teachers have not always been convinced. The best primary school teachers in New Zealand have been "child-centred" facilitators for many years, but many traditional high school and university teachers have been "one-subject lecturers." Integrating several subjects together means change, and change often brings fear and stress.

But it may well be the computer that forces the "integration" changes that so many reports have urged. Most computer programmes of course are very specialized. But every sensible business now integrates many of those programmes to solve interconnected problems. A finance director uses computer spreadsheets to compile a company's annual report; a designer uses the same raw data-base to produce graphics for the same report, and uses other computer programmes to produce allied artwork and camera-ready pages. Entire business plans, and quick product changes, now emerge from the bar coding flashing through thousands of different supermarkets—charting market research trends on suppliers' data bases on the other side of a continent. Customer order-forms are instantly translated into production schedules and raw-material purchase orders.

Business revolves around integrated specialists, both self-acting and working in groups. The information revolution now integrates that specialist work. And Nolan says that the real world demands changes in traditional subject-by-subject schooling. He believes changes are demanded even more by the shortage of jobs that previously required only unskilled work.

"In the past," he says, "people who have been relatively unsuccessful at school—relatively unskilled, relatively unknowledgeable—have been able to walk out in days of plenty and pick up a job and do well enough. Those days are now gone—but, not only that, the days of narrow vocational training have also gone."[14]

So Nolan's integrated studies programme has linked Massey University educational research with field-trip study projects, IBM-sponsored computer studies and the New Zealand national high school curriculum. His pilot programme started in 1986 with sixth form students at Freyberg. The first integrated studies course combined biology, computer studies, English and geography. The elements were drawn together around a central theme: preservation and management issues confronting New Zealand National Parks. And that theme was the common thread that bound the subjects together in a coherent programme. Out-of-class

So this is school: a week tramping and canoeing in some of the world's most beautiful scenery.*

*Integrated studies students at Freyberg High School in Palmerston North, New Zealand, frequently take a one-week journey down New Zealand's beautiful Wanganui River, combining the study of history, geography, ecology, the environment, land use and science, then integrating the project by computer analysis and writing projects.

Information obtained by author interviews with teachers, students and project directors, Freyberg High School (1991).

field research trips were a major part of the project. In Nolan's words: "These national park field trips confronted students not only with physical adventure and challenge, but generated the experiences, data and information needed to sustain a programme of integrated studies for a whole year. Computers also played a central role in supporting the theme; allowing the analysis of large and relatively complex data-sets not normally considered or done at this level. They also allowed extended studies in specific subjects and helped motivate students."

During that pilot programme, students' examination results were checked against a similar group taking the standard high school courses. "We had hoped to demonstrate that integrated study students would do better than those experiencing normal secondary school teaching. And that's precisely what we've been able to accomplish." Because the pilot was with senior students—normally high achievers anyway—Nolan would have been happy to say that the pilot group had done no worse. *"But what we were able to show was that their academic performance was significantly better. In English and geography, students scored 20 to 30 marks higher* and in mathematics and science they on average scored ten to 15 marks better."[15]*

For the next three years, a full programme was continued with students starting at form 3. Earlier research had shown that four different types of integrated-curriculum approaches could be used. The Freyberg team used all four: to develop student-centred inquiry, practical thinking skills, thematic studies and correlation between subjects.

The New Zealand high school curriculum also encourages students to develop positive attitudes, knowledge and skills in each subject area. So Freyberg used these as the core of their approach. And they linked that core to the four integrational themes—by out-of-class activities and computer studies.

"Over the next three years," reports Nolan, "we had out-of-class field trips, as short as one to two hours up to two to three days in junior school and seven to eight days in senior school." One class spent a week on the Wanganui River. But before it went, it split into study-groups. One researched the interconnection between the river and agriculture; another gathered information for an environmental impact report; another prepared to test the river's chemical composition and water-flow; another

* In most New Zealand school examinations, students are assessed out of a possible score of 100. "Marks" are therefore given as a percentage.

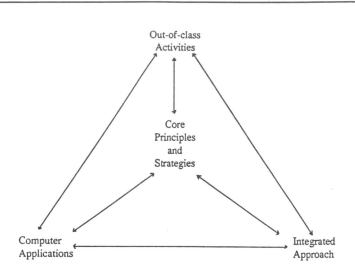

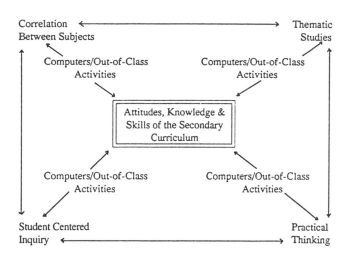

These two schematic models show how the Freyberg High School integrated studies programme integrates the core-curriculum subjects with field trips and computer studies.

Illustrations are from *Case Study of Curriculum Innovation in New Zealand: The Freyberg Integrated Studies Project,* by C.J. Patrick Nolan, then Associate Director, Educational Research and Development Centre, Massey University, and David J. McKinnon, Visiting Research Fellow, Education Department, Massey University, Palmerston North, New Zealand.

researched the Maori history of the area. "The whole project was curriculum-driven," says Nolan, "but most activities included adventure and out-door education components, learning bushcraft, camping and survival skills, as well as learning to work in groups, researching specialist subjects and then integrating them into a total report."[16]

In another project, eighth grade students investigated the feasibility of converting Palmerston's main street into a pedestrian mall. They conducted community surveys, analysed the data using computer applications, and wrote and presented a report to the city council, which found it thoroughly professional. Teachers of mathematics and English collaborated with a project researcher to develop a unit of work on ergonomics and health education. All their students became ergonomists, and took and recorded anthropometric measurements from all other students in the school. The out-of-class activities involved visits to a factory which made ergonomic furniture, and to a polytechnic ergonomics laboratory.

"As one of the sidelights," says Nolan, "we found most school furniture completely unsuitable."

Pat Nolan believes big issues are at stake with the integrated studies experiment. "For years we got away with a system where unskilled people could walk into jobs, even if they'd failed school exams. That situation has changed, and I don't believe it is ever going to return. What society demands now is the kind of knowledge and skills that we've always claimed we wanted our students to have. We've wanted them to be knowledgeable in science, in mathematics, in communication skills; we've wanted them to have political and social understanding. We've wanted them to be original thinkers—in charge of their own futures, making decisions for themselves with confidence in their own ability. Now those things are imperative. We need students who can think about issues in the round, who are holistic thinkers, who can bring knowledge and ideas from many different disciplines to bear on the problem or an issue."[17]

He says society is also "looking at the day in the very near future when computers will be as commonplace as pocket calculators are today, and where they will be nearly as affordable. Not only that, teachers won't be able to teach effectively unless they're competent and confident in using computers in virtually all subjects in the curriculum. The real power of the computer will be as a student-controlled learning tool, and our Freyberg project has been in part to anticipate that day."[18]

And the results are already in. New Zealand has a national School

Adults in the real world would never tolerate the built-in failure rate of schools.

DON BROWN
New Zealand educational consultant*

*Author interview, Kapiti College, Paraparaumu, New Zealand (1991).

Certificate examination, in specific subjects, which students can take after three years of high school. When Freyberg integrated-studies students took those specific examination subjects, they scored significantly better marks than students who had not been through the programme—up to 30 percent better.[19] And all the students we met told us that the whole integrated field-trip programme has been fun and confidence-building.

What pleases Nolan even more is that nearly all students involved in integrated studies have made this same kind of learning gain; most of those who would previously have failed examinations have now succeeded.

3. Group study and "big picture" techniques

That same motivation spurs on educational consultant Don Brown, who has also introduced two other "success" innovations to a high school near Palmerston North: Kapiti College.

"For years, 30 percent of New Zealand's population," says Brown, "have been leaving high school without a single qualification, and for years we've had a School Certificate exam which actually and deliberately failed 50 percent of youngsters. Now if we did that out in the real world we would have to say that 30 percent of the population would never get a drivers' license, and 50 percent of them would be continually sitting and resitting the exam to try and get one. Adults would never tolerate that, but that's the system we've had in schools."[20]

To change that, Kapiti College has introduced two separate American-inspired initiatives aimed at preventing dropout failures.

The first is called cooperative learning. "Very simply," says Brown, "that means that instead of working individually with everybody in competition with each other, you develop interdependence within teams." *The second innovation comes directly from the jigsaw, "big picture" example: see the pieces first and it's easier to put together.* So a Kapiti class not only works in cooperative groups—the teacher puts them in the complete picture before they start. They call the technique "the advance organizer."

Brown again: "The advance organizer gives you the picture before you have to look at the bits, and then invites you to bring the bits together to make the picture like it was presented to you in the first place."

It is, of course, the kind of thing any competent company manager

Average students have gone from 50 to 70 percent. And one-time slow-learners have gone from 37 to 63 percent.*

*Results of Cooperative Learning and "Advance Organizer" programmes working together, as summarized in New Zealand television series *Where To Now?* in 1991 and reprinted in *Pacific Network* magazine, published by the Pacific Foundation, Auckland, New Zealand (February 1992).

would do: spell out a year's programme in advance so his staff know where they fit in the picture. And at Kapiti College these two systems are showing especially good results for those who would otherwise be classed as under-achievers.   "When we have targeted that group of youngsters," says Brown, "we can demonstrate two things: first, that the overall group mark goes up, but that the bottom third mark goes up faster than that."

In one of the schools using these two systems, "average" students have increased their grade in standardized national exams from 50 percent to 70 percent. And one-time slow learners have increased their average of 37 percent to better than 63 percent. [21]

4. Six-week courses build success step by step

Another New Zealand high school has dramatically improved students' job prospects by offering a wide range of concentrated courses that each require only six weeks' study.

Tikipunga High School is in the northern city of Whangarei, centred on an area with high unemployment. Over 78 percent of its families live on welfare benefits—the typical recipe for educational disaster.

Tikipunga has reversed this outcome by planning for step-by-step success. "Our experience has shown us," says principal Edna Tait, "that even the most able students respond more positively to a short-term learning span, with a very clear set of goals, that are described, so they can achieve them; and knowing that at the end of that six weeks they will receive a statement which describes very precisely the achievements that they have made in a particular area of learning." [22]

Students take standard subjects like English, math, science and social studies, and every one learns basic computer skills in a series of six-week courses. Then they have a wide choice: they can take a six-week course in welding, cooking, car repairs, videotape production and wood-working or, for a career servicing the tourist industry, they can take a six-week course in bone-carving souvenirs. The school also has a great interest in art; original works by local painters line its corridors. And Tikipunga has an amazing 90 percent pass rate in national art examinations.

Edna Tait stresses that Tikipunga's assessment system is not a pass-fail system. The statements at the end of each six weeks explain exactly what each student has achieved.

And virtually anybody can take any unit—whether aged 15 or 50.

At this high school anyone can take a six-week study unit: from 15 to 82-year-olds.

EDNA TAIT
Principal, Tikipunga High School,
Whangarei, New Zealand*

*Abbreviated from author interview (1991).

"We've had one 82-year-old woman in a third form Maori class, and she was a joy to work with."

One big benefit of the six-week modules: it's easy to re-do a module if you feel you need more experience. In this way, the whole school works very much along similar lines to business where, say, computer staff will regularly reattend short training sessions to master a new application, or move on to a higher level.

Says Tait: "One of the real benefits is the way every student gains confidence. Success builds on success."

And the practical results? "When we did an analysis of what had happened to our leaving students, very few were either not in some form of tertiary or other learning or in paid employment."

5. SuperCamp brings it all together

What would happen if all of these approaches were linked with the world's most effective learning and self-esteem-development techniques and where students end up loving to be at school?

That answer, too, is being given decisively—and resoundingly—in a programme that started in California, has now spread to several other American states, and has been introduced in Singapore, Russia, Canada and Hong Kong. The programme is called SuperCamp. And it shows that while dramatic changes may not come overnight, they can certainly happen after ten nights.

SuperCamp is an intensive training and development programme, mainly for teenagers but also for older college students. Some students are sent by their parents—generally because of low grades or lack of motivation. Others want to come because their friends have loved it so much. After only ten days, there is increased motivation, self-esteem— and later quite remarkable achievements in academic results.

A major seven-year doctoral study[23] involving 6042 students found after only ten days that 84 percent reported having increased self esteem, 81 percent more self-confidence and 68 percent increased their motivation.

The results don't stop there. American high schools grade students A, B, C, D and F. *And after attending SuperCamp for only ten days, previously low-achieving students have reported an increase of 1 GPA (grade point average). F students have become D; D's have ave become C's; and C's have increased their ratings by half a grade point.*

Why SuperCamp works so well

SuperCamp works because of our commitment to the total experience. At the core of our programme are three important concepts:

1   **We provide an environment where maximum learning is possible—by building rapport between all participants and developing self-confidence.**

2   **We teach in a variety of learning styles so that all types of learners can understand the material.**

3   **We teach them the skills they need to learn any subject rather than specific course material.**

BOBBI DePORTER
President of SuperCamp*

*Author interview (1993)

So what are the SuperCamp's secrets? The programme, which is based on a unique prototype developed in 1982, is a dual curriculum consisting of (1) a learn-to-learn academic curriculum and (2) a personal growth and lifeskills curriculum. It uses all of the techniques we have outlined under "true learning" methods—an integrative accelerated learning model.

And it certainly is accelerated. The ten-day academic curriculum includes creative writing skills, creativity skills, speed reading, test preparation and memory-training skills in a learn-to-learn context. The personal growth/lifeskills curriculum features physical skills, values curriculum and peer and parent communication skills activities. Both the academics and the personal growth/lifeskills are embedded in music, play and emotion.

And the entire ten-day program, in our view, is an ideal model for the introduction to every high school's year—although SuperCamp's day runs from 7 a.m. to 10.30 p m.

Day 1:   Arrivals, introductions, team-building, security.

Day 2:   Memory day   an introductory day that builds confidence, safety, trust and an attitude that learning is fun—with activities that range from morning boogie to mind-mapping techniques.

Day 3:   Communications day, covering a wide range of learning-to-learn communications skills.

Day 4:   The ropes course—to give youngsters an opportunity to experience breakthroughs, stretch their self-imposed limits, work within a team to accomplish a task and to receive support.

Day 5:   Academic class day, including speed reading, academic strategies, creativity and writing.

Day 6:   Academic class day.

Day 7:   Relationship day—to learn to work on relationships with self, peers and parents; to increase self esteem.

Day 8:   Academic class day, including group projects.

Day 9:   Academic class day.

Day 10: Integration day, including personal mission statements, confidence-building exercises, team skits, goal-setting.

But that bald written summary does no justice to a ten-day adventure course of fun, games, participation and activity. Follow a teacher during her first-ever day as a SuperCamp facilitator, and you start to capture the flavour of the camp:[24]

Wings to fly

Ponder on the lives of men
What they do
Where they've been.
Stop to question
Asking why
Some men walk
Others fly.

Some are living with their lot
They live their lives and daily plot
The course which leads not up not down
But simply takes them round and round
While others hoping will not stand
For mediocrity in man
And daily striving, move ahead.

Refusing death, and all that's dead,
Again just question
Asking Why
Some men walk
Some must fly.*

Steven E. Garner

Reprinted with permission

*Typical poem used to start a goal-setting session at a
Jeannette Vos writing class at SuperCamp.

■ Overnight a bare college classroom had been transformed, decorated with live plants, neatly butcher-papered tables, pitchers of iced lemon water, peripheral posters all over the walls, an acoustically sound "ghetto blaster" in place, a "Welcome" sign and happy face on the neat flip-chart—the atmosphere already orchestrated.

■ At 10 a.m., the students arrive. No bells, only rock music—loud and energetic, the way teenagers like it.

■ A teacher poem to start the day (Steven Garner's *Wings to Fly)* as an introduction to individual goal-setting, then with direct involvement from the start as each student is asked to identify his or her overall goals in creative writing.

■ Teacher dons a chef's hat, introduces "visualization" techniques— imagining dining in a wonderful restaurant.

■ Station WIIFM (What's In It For Me) takes the air—tackling students' "hidden agendas": "If you could choose from the whole area of writing, what would be something that could really help you?" Students state the learning outcomes they'd like without realizing that they are "buying in" to the agenda on a subliminal level. The teacher puts the outcomes in "clusters"—a brainstorming technique developed by Gabriel Rico in *Writing The Natural Way.* No set piece of literature here to study; the students will learn to write from their own creative perspective.

■ The "clustered outcomes" poster goes on the wall—to add to the subconscious messages.

■ Then "future pacing"—visualizing how they would like to feel in the evening when the class is over and they've achieved their aims—with *Chariots of Fire* music playing in the background.

■ Another break; then, because many students have said how hard they feel it is to start creative writing, "cluster" and fast-writing techniques are explored—and used through the "seven intelligences."

■ But it soon becomes obvious that, as with most new creative writers, students write with static words, not picture words. So the chef-hatted teacher produces a pizza oozing with cheeses and zesty sauces— so the "picture words" can be "tasted."

■ By lunchtime, the creative writing session has become one of pleasant achievement. The teacher gets feedback from students, then a quick review and a preview of the wonderful things to come.

■ After lunch, they're "hyperactive" but after the inevitable sugar-

"Clustering" for creativity

"Clustering," like Mind Mapping, is a way of putting
thoughts down like a chain reaction—an excellent
way to encourage creativity, especially in writing.
The technique was invented by Gabriel Rico,
and is covered in her book, *WritingThe Natural Way,*
published by J.P.Tarcher, Los Angeles, CA.

intake "high" comes the early-afternoon slump. To combat it, the teacher reads a lively descriptive piece called *Lady and the Chick,* from Rebecca Kaplan's book *Writers In Training.* The students hoot and holler, as others attempt to act out the sexy parts. The emotion keeps them involved in learning.

■ More creative writing—but only after a "state change" of massaging each other's backs. Then off to building on the "cluster" and "fast write" techniques—expanding on to comparison-contrast demonstrations with Koosh-ball activity. Then another break. [Breaks and state changes play an important part in the learning process. They create more "firsts" and "lasts" and thereby better retention.]

■ Near the close of the afternoon, the teacher models a memorable childhood experience: "The forgotten immigrant"—her own version of learning English as a Second Language back in 1949.

■ The day is beautiful, so it's outside for writing exercises, after talking about story formula and visualizing possible plots, characters and settings—all to background music.

■ After the outdoor writing exercise, students evaluate their own work and feelings to date, and they're off on a two-mile run. Their teacher reads the evaluations to check progress and work out gaps that need to be plugged, needs that have to be met after dinner.

■ After the meal a quiet descends. One of the camp children's father has died. So the teacher changes pace, and reads a student composition from a previous class about a girl whose grandfather has died. "Maybe just writing about our families would help," she says, using the flexibility based on student needs that should be built into all good teaching.

■ Then the shared stories, and a run around the buildings to let off steam—typical of the "state changes" built into each session.

■ By 8 p.m.: time for some poetry readings—and their own poetry attempts, to soft background music.

■ 8:15 p.m.—time to share their efforts. A hush falls as the first student reads his poem. A 16-year-old boy begins to cry in front of the other 35 students. Then another, then all, while the students empathetically continue to share their writing and their feelings.

■ By 8:45, it's obvious the sharing could go on all night, but they have to stop for a general camp get-together to debrief the day and to talk more about beliefs, values and behaviour.

SuperCamp's report card

25%	50%	75%	100%

68% increased motivation

73% improved grades

81% developed more confidence

84% increased self-esteem

96% retained positive attitude toward SuperCamp

98% continued to use skills

Jeannette Vos's doctoral dissertation* involved a detailed survey of 6042 SuperCamp graduates, ages 12-22. Some of the highlights are above. In addition to this data, 98% of students with a GPA (grade point average) of 1.9 or less in high school improved their grades by an average of one grade point.

*An Accelerated/Integrative Learning Model Programme Evaluation: Based on Participant Perceptions of Student Attitudinal and Achievement Changes, by Jeannette Vos-Groenendal, ERIC and Northern Arizona University, Flagsaff, Arizona (1991).

■ By 10:30, they've evaluated their teachers, gone to bed—and lights are out till 7 the next morning. The teacher smiles; her ratings were good that day.

A typical day at SuperCamp, if any day could be said to be typical. Each day the staff model the key principles of self-esteem and highly motivated achievement. And the results, as we've reported, are lasting.

And how do parents feel about it? An overall positive attitude towards the learning experience is expressed by 92 percent of parents and 98 percent of students.[25]

Say Dr. and Mrs James Power, of Canton, Ohio: "We sent four children to SuperCamp. All four improved their grades, and more importantly, their self-worth and motivation."

Ninety-eight percent of students say they continue to use the skills learned. "After SuperCamp, students believe in their ability to learn," says David Blanchard, headmaster of Wellington School in Columbus, Ohio.

Says the Chicago Tribune: "SuperCamp teaches self-confidence, teamwork and especially how to recognize and surpass barriers to success."

SuperCamp has yet to start in the south Pacific, but another programme modelled on it, called Discovery, is drawing similar rave responses from teenagers who attend it in Australia and New Zealand. Discovery is operated by the Global Youth Foundation. It runs regular high-energy seven-day residential programmes, with a one-day parent workshop included on the last day. Like SuperCamp, it involves teenagers directly in esteem-building and accelerated learning techniques. The same organization is also running two-day accelerated learning programmes for seven-to-12-year-olds.

The present authors would be the first to accept that the SuperCamp and Discovery experience cannot be duplicated exactly as a formula for every school. But link the formula up with Mt. Edgecumbe, Freyberg, Kapiti and Tikipunga and you'll find most of the key principles that we believe can revolutionize high schools; principles that can not only ensure good academic grades but can build the sound base of self-esteem and confidence as an alternative to failure, dropping out, gangs, drugs and crime. Add those ingredients to other common-sense breakthroughs, and you're starting to find a recipe that will create the schools that tomorrow demands.

12 steps to a great school system

1. Plan schools as life-long year-round community resource centres.

2. Ask your customers first: your students and parents.

3. Guarantee customer success and satisfaction.

4. Cater to all intelligence traits and all learning styles.

5. Use the world's best teaching, study and learning methods.

6. Invest in your key resource: teachers as facilitators.

7. Make everyone a teacher as well as a student.

8. Plan a four-part curriculum, with personal growth, lifeskills and learning-how-to-learn linked with all content.

9. Change the assessment system.

10. Use tomorrow's technology.

11. Use your entire community as a resource.

12. Give everyone the right to choose.

The 12 steps to transform a nation's education system

Almost anything we can conceive is now possible.

And that applies equally to schools and education. So every plan to improve a school system should start with a vision of what it should be, even if that will need to be regularly updated.

Every community also has existing educational assets—land, buildings, teachers and administrators—and, like any great success story, the best educational achievements will come by starting with our assets, defining the vision, and creatively planning to link the two.

It also seems to us that any sensible vision should include these factors:

* Lifelong continual learning will be a key fact of life for everyone.

* Inside that context, everyone should be encouraged to plan his or her own curriculum for life.

* While there is no one right way to teach or learn, there are many techniques to enable anyone to learn faster, better, smarter. And an open-minded search for new ideas is central to tomorrow's world, and central to tomorrow's schools.

* Every state or country also has different school-health relationships, administrative systems, teacher training programmes. And, as in any other field, progress will often depend on the vision and drive of indiv-idual leaders: principals, teachers, parents, administrators and political leaders.

Against that background, we believe these should be the 12 main steps to an excellent school system:

We talk a good fight about wanting to have excellent schools when in fact we're content to have average ones.

DAVID GARDNER*
"Nation At Risk" Commission

*Quoted in *Newsweek* (April 19, 1993), ten years after he chaired
the National Commission on Excellence in Education.

1. Schools as lifelong, year-round community resource centres

How on earth did most schools ever become 9 a.m. to 3 p.m. teaching centres for only five days a week and often for under 200 days a year? They're probably the most under-used major resource in any country.

In many parts of the world governments, like businesses, are decentralizing, and school-based management systems are on the agenda. That agenda should include transforming the traditional school into a lifelong, year-round community resource centre.

In an age of instant information, every community will need an information resource centre. And well-organized schools can fill that role. Even if home-based, individually-paced, interactive, electronic learning methods proliferate—as we believe they will—community resource centres will be in even more demand.

And Kimi Ora Community School in West Flaxmere, Hawkes Bay, New Zealand, is a model for creating that centre. It's in the heart of a New Zealand district devastated by the closure of a major industry. In that way it typifies many of the social problems arising from a fast-changing industrial-based world. Over 50 percent of its families live on welfare benefits. But West Flaxmere is fighting back. And its new school is at the heart of that fightback.

Other suburbs may be built around industries or shopping centres. Flaxmere's rejuvenation is centred on its school. But it's much, much more than a school. "Kimi Ora could be translated from the Maori as : 'To seek total well-being,'" says initial director Lester Finch.[1]

"The people in the community named it Kimi Ora because it matched the concept that they had of the school when it was first planned—that there should be a centre, a school, which sought total well-being, and concentrated on families rather than individuals. Kimi Ora typified the approach that this community wanted this school to take, and that was an holistic approach which regarded education as a whole-of-life process and involved families."

New Zealand in recent years has turned its school administration system upside-down. A central government Department of Education has been changed into a much smaller Ministry of Education, concentrating largely on policy advice to Ggvernment, but also providing overall curriculum guidelines. School District Education Boards have been abolished. And now schools "run themselves"—each one administered

This resource centre includes a preschool with three language choices, a primary school, adult classes, doctors, nurses, a physiotherapist, a naturopath, fitness classes, parenting-skills programmes, its own minister and its own newspaper.

*Kimi Ora Community School, West Flaxmere, Hawkes Bay, New Zealand.

by a Board of Trustees, mainly elected by local parents, but with the school principal and teacher and student representatives.

West Flaxmere's plans for a new school came just before the new school-based management system was to be introduced nationally. And it has therefore been a model for many other existing schools.

Kimi Ora starts with preschool, with children from as young as two. And it starts with choices. Between 60 and 70 percent of pupils are Maori, so at preschool they can, if they wish, start in a totally Maori environment—at the kohanga reo or Maori language nest. Or they can start in an all-English class or a bilingual class.

The preschool has an array of child-development equipment, geared to each age-group: a range of colourful books, puzzles and manipulative educational playthings.

The infants grow up learning about hygiene—washing hands after each visit to the toilet and before every snack or meal. They learn about nutrition, washing and cutting up fruit and vegetables for lunch in the spotlessly clean kitchen.

The entire preschool makes full use of one of our most under-utilized resources: grandparents. Visit any of the activities each day and you'll find grandparents leading action songs, dancing and other activities.

Parents, too, are welcome—and even young babies. And not just at the play centre. The school also has a full health centre. A health nurse is always on hand. Local doctors take turns to staff the medical centre. There's a fulltime dental nurse.

At primary school, pupils can choose bilingual classes, in English and Maori, or they can learn solely in English. They've got a good range of computer equipment. And the school has an unusual design—in "pods," with groups of three classrooms spreading out from and opening on to a central core. This allows students and staff to work together on different projects and in different age groups.

"We have a whole range of activities in the adult sphere, and in the community sphere," says Finch. "There's a parenting course; a public health nurse dealing with families; a physiotherapist, a naturopath and much more."

Kimi Ora runs its own community newspaper, has its own community minister, operates its own community barter system and sports teams, has its own fitness, adult education and computer classes, and runs its own cafeteria, where parents, teachers and adult students mix every day.

Give your students and parents a Fail-Safe Guarantee

This is a greatly-reduced copy of the Fail Safe Program Guarantee issued to parents and students by the South Bay Union School District in San Diego, California.

The guarantee is on parchment with a gold embossed seal. It guarantees that all children will read at or above the national average by the time the student completes second grade. If not, the District will provide intensive one-on-one tutoring to assure that the child will reach the program goal.

For the guarantee to apply, parents must commit themselves to helping students with reading for at least 20 minutes a day.

The guarantee is published with permission from the South Bay Union School District.

Teenage mothers learn about positive parenting skills—in a 15-week course run by the Maori Women's Welfare League. That includes practical budgetary advice. "Some families are barely existing because of unemployment," says positive-parenting tutor Ellen Matthews. "And because they can't make ends meet, we try and bring in budgetary advisory people to talk to them and help them in their own personal situations. We hope to teach them to be assertive in life, to develop self-esteem, self-worth and believe in themselves."[2]

Families use Kimi Ora Community School from 8 a.m. to 10 p.m.

Says Anglican minister Ray Dunlop: "It's one of the most brilliant concepts I've ever come across. Education and learning have become the centre of the community here in West Flaxmere, rather than a commercial centre becoming that. Far more than any other school I've ever experienced, the community owns it. And that's reflected in the lack of vandalism and respect for the school."[3]

2. Ask your customers

How did a poor community come up with such an all-embracing concept as Kimi Ora?

Somebody thought to ask them! It was almost as simple as that. Concerned with a rising street-gang problem among young Maoris in New Zealand's capital city of Wellington, then Prime Minister Rob Muldoon visited some gang members and asked their advice. What they said was simple: Give us a chance to prove ourselves.

So when Muldoon learned of plans for a new school at Flaxmere, he invited the local school district administration to take up the challenge to survey the community.

If that's what can happen if an entire community is asked to plan a new school from the ground up—or the community up—what would happen if a school's other main customers were asked: the students?

Alaska's Mt. Edgecumbe High School did just that, as we've already seen. And the results are inspiring.

3. Guarantee customer satisfaction

Every successful business in the world is based on building and keeping satisfied customers. Nearly every good manufactured product comes with a written guarantee.

But very few schools offer the same type of guarantee. Why not? "If

To check your own or your students' learning styles

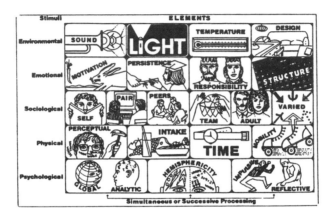

It is now easy for schools to inexpensively obtain a computerized print-out of each student's individual preferred learning style. The Learning Styles Network, operating out of St. Johns University in New York, provides such a service, based on the pioneering work of Professor Rita Dunn, Director of the Network, and her husband, Professor Ken Dunn.

The Network supplies questionnaires based on the Dunns' model (above), covering all the factors that can determine preferred learning styles, including environmental, emotional, sociological, physical and psychological considerations.

Schools or individuals organizing the learning-style check then send the forms to the Learning Styles Centre, and receive back a computer print-out detailing each person's preferred learning environment and method.

The Network is co-sponsored by the National Association of Secondary School Principals. In New Zealand, the Creative Learning Company in Auckland can arrange Dunn checks.

The Dunns' Learning Styles Inventory (above) is published with their permission.

public schools are going to survive, we have to be held accountable for the product we turn out,"[4] says innovator Phil Grignon, former Superintendent of the South Bay elementary school district in San Diego, California, where 57 percent of families are below the federal poverty line. So the district now offers a "Fail Safe" written guarantee to all its 9,500 students. That guarantee promises that "all children will read at or above grade level by the time the student completes second grade" (grade level in America is the 50 percent mark in standardized national tests). If the student does not reach that level, the district "will provide intensive one-on-one tutoring" to ensure that minimum result.[5]

To take advantage of the guarantee, each parent or guardian must in turn agree to read to students at home for at least 20 minutes each day, to check and sign homework, and to attend quarterly parent-teacher workshops. The same guarantee is being given to the district's 25 percent of students who have Spanish as a first language.

The guarantee programme is one of several innovations in the South Bay district. These include the IBM Write-to-Read program, introduced in kindergarten to link reading and writing; and a pilot Early Literacy Intervention programme adapted from New Zealand's Reading Recovery project. Of students way behind average, this pilot brought 80 percent up to grade level in a few weeks.

To help youngsters achieve even more, the district has introduced an optional programme for youngsters to attend school for up to 45 days extra each year—in the traditional school holidays. The programme is called CHOICE (Children Having Options, Innovation, Challenges and Enrichment). And like most good school achievements we've researched, CHOICE provides an enriched programme that focuses on a combination of language, arts, thematic approaches and group interaction. Says Grignon: "Extending the school year by 45 days puts our students on a par with those in Japan and Europe—and can level the academic playing field."

4. Cater to all intelligence traits and learning styles

In many ways, this is probably the most important single innovation that could be made to greatly reduce school dropout rates. In our view, Howard Gardner's and the Dunns' detailed research shows beyond doubt that most dropouts do not learn best in schools that are geared almost exclusively to only two of the seven-or-more "intelligence traits." And most, too, are unfairly handicapped in a school environment which discourages kinesthetic learning.

John Eliot is America's best elementary school model for integrative accelerated learning.

JEANNETTE VOS

The Key School in Indianapolis shows what can happen when an entire school is designed to encourage every student to develop each "intelligence"—and cater to different learning styles.

A similar example comes from Cascade Elementary School in the Washington State school district of Marysville. Teacher Bruce Campbell has been a long-time fan of Gardner's theory, and has developed a classroom set-up with seven learning centres: a building and moving centre for kinesthetics, a reading centre, a math and science centre, a working-together centre (to develop interpersonal intelligence), a personal work centre (for intrapersonal intelligence), a music centre and an art centre.[6]

Campbell is a "thematic" teacher—and his students normally divide into seven different groups to explore each day's theme, moving from centre to centre for about 20 minutes at a time. His experience has also shown that the seven-centre approach helps children develop all their talents. At the start of a typical year, most students describe only one centre as their favourite. By mid-year most have three or four favourites, and by year's end every student nominates at least six centres as preferences.

5. Use the world's best teaching techniques

No school, lifelong learning resource centre or business training and retraining unit can exist without skilled teacher-facilitators. And no changes in education will be successful without a major emphasis on teacher training and continual retraining.

John Eliot Elementary School in Needham, Massachusetts, typifies what is needed. It is the most multi-cultural school in the district. Its students include African Americans, Haitians, Hispanics, Vietnamese and many others from Asia and elsewhere—in an area where average incomes are low. Unlike Kimi Ora, it was an existing school when it started its big turn-round. Five years later its students had the top grades in Massachusetts.

One catalyst was principal Miriam Kronish. But another was her husband, Herbert, an architect. When he decided to go back temporarily to college to get a masters degree in education, fortunately that included an introduction to integrative accelerated learning techniques by Dr. John Grassi. "He was so enthused," recalls Miriam Kronish, "it got me involved."[7]

Attendance problems? We have none. Children don't want to stay away, even when they're sick. That's our problem, not non-attendance.

MIRIAM KRONISH
Principal, John Eliot Elementary School,
Needham, Massachusetts*

*Author interview by phone (1993).

Grassi was obviously another catalyst. Talk to principal Kronish by phone from halfway around the world and the enthusiasm bursts through the fibre optics: "John Grassi? He is a renaissance man, a man of the future. He is a musician, a poet, a conjuror. He's uplifting, inspirational, a change agent. And he's knowledgeable in all educational fields: preschool, elementary, high school and college; and in most areas: math, geography, science."

Kronish says the change in the school over the past five years has been dramatic. The key to those changes? "Teacher training would be the first. Our teachers have all had regular training with John Grassi. But we're not talking about lectures. We generally organize five sessions of two hours, spread over two months. In that way, each session is a practical model that can be put into action immediately. So we do one session on ideas in math, one on social science, one on language arts—and we put them into practice straight away. We experiment."

And what is the difference? "Teacher excitement. Student excitement. The teachers immediately started to write plays, music, skits. They encouraged identification and personification from the start: the students acting out the role of all people and subjects studied. And the children, they flowered."

Enter a John Eliot classroom today and you're likely to see fourth-grade students learning grammar by performing a debate as members of a baseball team: some playing the part of nouns, verbs, adverbs and adjectives, and discussing who's most important to the team. Go back the next day and you're likely to see that same group repeating the process in other classrooms.

"Every student has become a teacher," says Kronish. The barriers have been broken down. The whole programme has changed everyone in the school."

One of the keys has been the accelerated, integrative learning techniques. And how would Kronish describe them? "First, it's integrative; it integrates music, art, poetry and drama in with every other subject. And it integrates critical thinking skills across the board. I think that's a major reason we topped the MEAP* examinations: every child is involved in developing higher-level critical thinking skills. They do this from kindergarten onwards, so by fourth grade it's second nature. We've learned to use all our senses, our bodies, as part of the learning process."

Massachusetts Educational Assessment Program.

I've been
a teacher
for
20 years,
and I
genuinely
feel
reborn.

ROSEMARY GREENE
Teacher at John Eliot School,
Needham, Massachusetts*

*After experiencing training in accelerated-integrative teaching methods.
Author interview by phone (1993).

A typical classroom? "Relaxing, bright, calm, fun-filled. Each class has a tape recorder, and we regularly play relaxing music, baroque music when appropriate, and music for many other purposes."

And how might the new integrated techniques apply, say, to a science class? "Well, you might see students acting out the role of molecules, or playing the part of some endangered species. It internalizes learning. And it's fun."

John Eliot School involves the whole community. How does it do it? Says Kronish in her simple, direct, enthusiastic way: "Fully. For instance, the school has recently put on a 90-minute presentation on famous black Americans. A teacher played the role of a cable television interviewer, and students played the roles of famous people. All parents were invited. And they were amazed, thrilled, astounded, proud. Not only did the students learn history, the parents did, too. The parents also help in many other ways. We're not a rich community—far from it. But parents devote talents and time, coming into school on their days off, just being a vital part of the school, because you can't have a good school without an involved community."

The future of education in America? "Wow!" says Kronish. "If we had the power—and we do—number one would probably be teacher training. It's not enough to only read of these new techniques. You have to be trained in them, in the same way an actor or a poet is trained. Then you can transfer it to others. So we need to encourage all our universities and colleges to introduce the principles of integrative accelerative learning. It's the wave of the future.

"American education also needs to pay much more attention to research and development. Use the breakthroughs that have already been achieved.

"Next, we need much more collaboration between classroom teachers and specialists—to break down the barriers. And the whole community needs to be involved: parents, businesses, everyone."

And how have teachers reacted? Miriam Kronish practises what she enthuses. The phone is instantly handed to fourth-grade teacher Rosemary Greene: "I've been a teacher for 20 years, and I genuinely feel reborn. And the students: they've become 'invested,' excited, involved."[8]

The results, of course, speak for themselves. In part you'll find them in the examination results: overall top in a state well known for educa-

MARIAN DIAMOND
Education In The Decades Ahead*

*An essay in *Creating The Future,* edited by Dee Dickinson
and published by Accelerated Learning Systems,
Aston Clinton, Bucks, England. Dr. Diamond is Professor
of Neuroanatomy at the University of California at Berkeley.
The full quotation is: "EACH ONE—TEACH ONE
is my theme for the coming years."

tional innovations. But the real results you can see on the faces of the students, teachers and parents—if you haven't already caught them in the words of the principal.

6. Invest in your key resource: teachers

Here, too, the John Eliot experience is a model. America, in particular, has probably the world's most thorougly-researched educational break-throughs, including the teaching and learning methods covered in these pages.

Yet amazingly most of those methods are not being modelled at the university level—to train the teachers of tomorrow—let alone being used throughout elementary and high schools.

South Dakota State University—in a state renowned for its high overall scholastic attainments—is one of the few to invest in training its staff in integrative accelerated learning. It started with an intensive programme for professors in 1992. Barbara Audley, Director for Life-time Learning, received a grant to train 15 staff members in 1992. And, like John Eliot school at the elementary level, the techniques modelled were so practical the professors could put them into practice immediately, with enthusiastic results.[9]

7. Make everyone a teacher as well as a student

Again, the John Eliot experience is a model: every student, every parent and every teacher is encouraged to become not only a learner but a teacher.

Many problems of staff "burn-out" would be solved by the simple step of involving parents, grandparents and the community in the teaching process—and students too.

8. Plan a four-part curriculum

Computer-based programmes, interactive videodiscs and personal-ized telecommunications make it increasingly possible for everyone to plan one's own continuing study programme. And schools as community resource centres will provide a smorgasbord of courses and resources for a wide range of age-groups, particularly as planning one's continuing lifelong education becomes as normal and as easy as watching television.

Schools, however, will also be required to continue their present role as core-curriculum providers.

Model for an interlinked four-part curriculum

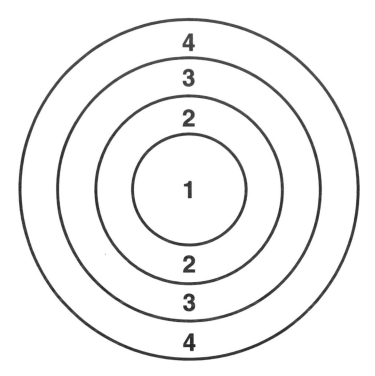

1. Personal growth curriculum, *including self-esteem and confidence-building.*
2. Lifeskills curriculum, *including creative problem-solving and self-management.*
3. Learning-to-learn curriculum, *so learning can be lifelong and fun-filled.*
4. Content curriculum, *generally with integrated themes.*

Here our own research points strongly to the need for a four-part curriculum, as important in continuing education as it is in childhood and teenage years:

1. A personal-growth curriculum, involving self-confidence, motivation, communications skills and relationship skills.

2. A lifeskills curriculum, including self-managing, creative problem-solving, career planning and replanning, economics, conflict-management and computer-based technology.

3. A learning-to-learn curriculum, including the type of brain-compatible "how to" skills covered extensively in this book, so that lifelong learning can re-emerge as fun-filled, fast and effective.

4. A content curriculum, with integrated themes.

Although all are interrelated, we have purposely placed content last—reversing most current school practices.

We have placed personal growth as first, for major reasons:

* Nearly everyone has learning blocks, but traditional schooling has succeeded in only one major way: in turning most people off, at a time when their enthusiasm for learning is vital.

* Emotion is the gateway to learning—and each person's emotional state is affected by communications skills, relationship skills, motivation and self-esteem: the personal-growth skills. If those aspects are not addressed, the gate will close.

* As Willard Daggett has put it so strongly, real listening and speaking skills are of high importance in all aspects of life and work, yet are downplayed in many educational institutions.

* Self-confidence and self-esteem are vital to all learning, and education that fails to address them will fail in its other tasks.

In a world where everyone needs to be a self-manager, practical lifeskills training also needs to be included in all education, from preschool to advanced business study. These skills include: creative problem-solving, critical thinking, leadership skills, global perspective, the confidence to play a full role in determining the future of society, and the ability to plan one's life in an era of incredible change.

Learning-how-to-learn has been a continuing theme of this book and is the bridge to all content learning. Learn how to learn and you can apply the principles to anything. Yet this most important of all specific skills is seldom taught in school.

People will over- achieve targets they set themselves.

GORDON DRYDEN
Out Of The Red*

*"Learning the importance of that sentence—and applying it—
has taught me more [about business] than any dozen textbooks
on management."   Book published by William Collins Ltd.,
Auckland, New Zealand (1978).

In specific content courses, we believe the great need is for integration: to link art with science and all other subjects; to integrate all studies into more global understanding, so that Russian or French language training, or Chinese or Italian cooking, becomes linked with an understanding of others' cultures. In this way, as Mt. Edgecumbe, Freyberg and John Eliot schools have proven in practice, the world emerges as an interactive whole.

9. Change the assessment system

It would take another book, or a large part of a book, to report on worldwide moves to gain better educational assessment systems. In a summary of key principles for school reform, these to us are the main points:

*   Too much traditional teaching and too much traditional testing have been directed to only two segments of overall intelligence.

*   Most people who have emerged successfully through the school system have been strong in those two "intelligences." These have gone on to become the arbiters of future teaching and testing methods.

*   Just as new learning methods should involve the whole person, so should assessment methods.

*   The search for excellence is a justifiable goal, in personal life, school and business—and much of our present schooling is aimed at "success" rates that fall far short of excellence.

*   Pencil-and-paper test assignments test only a very small part of anyone's ability in almost any subject, except perhaps for mental mathematics or handwriting.

*   In a world where self-management will be required of all, continuing self-assessment is needed—another reason that confidence-building should include the confidence to continually assess one's own improvement.

*   Excellence will often come from joint efforts with others, so peer-assessment should be encouraged. In fact, it can often be linked with self-assessment: evaluating yourself, then discussing that evaluation with the people you work with.

*   It is one of the great truisms that we all learn from our mistakes—and a positive attitude towards mistakes and risk-taking is a positive part of growth: seeing mistakes as steps toward excellence. No examination system should penalize risk-taking or creativity, or imply that there is

Instead of a national curriculum for education, what is really needed is an individual curriculum for every child.

CHARLES HANDY
The Age of Unreason*

*First published in Britain by Business Books Ltd.,
an imprint of Century Hutchinson Ltd, 62 Chandos Place,
Covent Garden, London WC2N 4NW (1989).

only one right answer to any problem, except perhaps for simple arithmetic (even then Einstein would not have produced his theories of relativity had he not challenged basic mathematics).

 * Critical thinking is a vital skill. Free and open-minded contributions to problem-solving are essential in all aspects of life. Any assessment methods should encourage this, not pigeon-hole anyone in the "only one right answer" mode.

 * Teacher assessment is at least as important as student assessment. Every professional seminar presenter hands out evaluation forms. They're vital self-correcting feedback. And all teachers following this pattern are modelling a positive attitude toward continual growth by the free, fair and frank exchange of opinions.

 * Competent school teachers and administrators will apply the same principles to parent-teacher relationships: sending home teacher-evaluation forms regularly as part of the school home confidence building, part of the new customer-service concept.

 * In fields where competence can be measured at specific levels, this generally involves performing the task in practice: typing at 65 words a minute, playing a piano, riding a bike, running or swimming at a certain speed. In all cases, the real test is competency in the task, not competency in writing about it.

 * The Japanese have used the excellent American-developed Deming methods of total quality management to produce cars and electronic components of excellence. Mt. Edgecumbe High School has shown how to interpret those principles into school education—and into different assessment methods. All school systems would be wise to take heed.

10. Use tomorrow's technology

We've already made our views clear on one other matter: new methods of instant communication are bringing with them the biggest change in civilization in centuries.

This revolution will soon provide each person with the tools to obtain all the information he or she needs, whenever it is needed and in whatever form: print, photograph, videotape, television screen or facsimile transmission.

River Oaks School in Oakville, Ontario, Canada, is typical of what will soon be happening at all schools. It is a primary school that has been set up with a particular vision of how it can help its students march

Sony Corporation sets goals for the company 500 years into the future. They are literally inventing the future. As a species, can we do it any differently?

NANCY J. HARTLAND
Future People:
*Where are we headed as a species?**

*Article in *Agenda* (winter, 1993).

confidently into the instant-information age.[10] Every student in every class has the opportunity to link with the school's overall computer network. CD-ROMS are a fact of life. And the school doesn't even own a printed encyclopedia. All of its big reference library is on both interactive video discs and CD-ROMS—instantly accessible to anyone in the school, and in a variety of forms: so that pictures and facts can be combined for printouts, photos can be married with information.

Through the simple marvels of Hypercard—a software programme that comes free with every Apple computer—every student at the school is already a computer programmer, and his own curriculum designer.

Highly-advanced computers have the ability to serve as both tutors and libraries, providing instant information and feedback to individual students. "Virtual reality" technology already enables anyone to participate in experiences as varied as history and space travel. It is beyond the scope of this book to predict all the changes that are coming in electronic communications, but this type of technology will make it possible for each student, of any age, to tailor an individual curriculum and eventually to actually experience each lesson.

Suffice it to say here that interactive computer-satellite-video television and electronic games technology provide the combined catalyst that will finally force a much-needed change in the teacher's role: from *information* to *transformation*. And every school in the world, if it's not already doing so, should be matching every progressive company in keeping up with the full scope of technology and its impact on society and on education.

11. Use the entire community as a resource

Again, John Eliot, Kimi Ora, Mt. Edgecumbe, Freyberg, the Key School in Indianapolis, and many of the other models we have quoted, underscore the common sense of moving schooling away from the traditional classroom. How the world ever came to confuse classroom teaching with real learning is a mystery of its own. Probably only the dedication of enthusiastic teachers, principals and administrators has enabled this system to last so long—in spite of itself. But that tradition is rapidly coming to an end. And the lessons are clear from other industries that failed to correctly analyse their future role in a world of rapid change. After opening up much of the world last century, railway company after company collapsed, because they thought they were in the railways business, not the people-moving and transport business. Holly-

The world is on the verge of a revolution, the like of which has not been seen since Gutenberg ran the first Bible off a printing press 500 years ago.

GILBERT WONG
Getting Wired*

*An article published in the New Zealand Herald, Auckland, New Zealand (July 10, 1993).

wood almost died through the start of television, because it wrongly thought it was in the moving-film business, not the entertainment business.

And if schools themselves do not lead the educational changes, and make themselves the new community resource centres for lifelong learning, then the world is well served by the other innovators waiting to fill the gap.

12. For everyone: the right to choose

The coming changes will be dictated, we believe, by another inevitable fact of life: the growing one-world economy and the consumer's right to choose.

The whole world now is not only one giant electronic, automobile, fast-food and financial services market; it is also a major one-world educational market.

It is now possible for the works of our most brilliant educators and schools to be translated into forms that can, in turn, be made available instantly to anyone who wants them, anywhere, any time. The day of the school monopoly on education is rapidly ending.

And we may well see the emergence of new forms of education-business cooperation as among the big growth industries of the next century.

The most successful corporation of the 1990s will be something called a learning organization.

Fortune International*

**Quoted by Peter M. Senge, *The Fifth Discipline,* published by Random House, Sydney, Australia (1992).*

The new learning organization as a catalyst for change

An unusual new marriage is about to be consummated.

The partners will be education and business. Already the reasons are clear and the models exist.

Mt. Edgecumbe High School in Alaska is only one of the harbingers.

"Within the next decades education will change more than it has changed since the modern school was created by the printed book three hundred years ago," says Peter Drucker, the century's most respected management writer.[1]

"Forget all your old tired ideas about leadership," says *Fortune International*. "The most successful corporation of the 1990s will be something called a learning organization."[2]

But it will be much more than that. And Bill O'Brien, Chief Executive of America's Hanover Insurance, puts one of the real challenges: "Our grandfathers worked six days a week to earn what most of us now earn by Tuesday afternoon. The ferment in management will continue until we build organizations that are more consistent with man's higher aspirations beyond food, shelter and belonging."[3]

We believe at least eight main reasons will shape the new partnership:

1. For the first time in history, the world can now produce an abundance of goods with a fraction of the previous workforce. As Charles Handy says, that requires "upside down thinking" about every aspect of society and how we organise it.[4]

2. Knowledge is the main capital of the future. And where university-based knowledge has already teamed up with innovative business, the

Philips projects that CD-I[1] sales by the end of the decade will equal current sales of CD-Audio, about a billion discs a year.

BOB SWAIN
*CD-I Unleashes Fresh Potential**

*Article in *Broadcast* (May 8, 1992).

1. Interactive compact discs.

results have changed the world. The Stanford University-venture-capital-brainpower base for Silicon Valley, the Massachusetts Institute of Technology's Media Lab and the bonds between the giant Japanese companies and their universities are striking examples.

3. The emerging super "electronic highways" are already linking business, home, school and university into an instant world information-exchange. If the computer is the engine of the new age, the electronic highways are the new century's equivalent to rail and road, but multiplied thousands of times. Their power to transform society will leave no structure untouched.

4. The blistering pace of change has set the retraining agenda for business. In the United States, "employers—business, government agencies and the military—already spend as much money and effort on the education and training of their employees, and especially the most highly educated ones, as do all the country's colleges and universities together."[5]

5. Interactive learning technology will change education as much as Nintendo, Sega and Electronic Arts games have altered youngsters' leisure-time. Imagine for a moment the full catalogue of hundreds of *New Zealand School Journal* publications that are at the heart of the tape-assisted reading program, the one that's enabling youngsters to close a three-to- five-year reading gap in a few weeks. Instead of recording those books individually on audio-cassettes, it is now possible to put the entire library—pictures and text plus sound track—on one interactive video-disc, and to sell it for a few dollars, to be played through any television screen. Soon it will be possible for anyone to dial up that information from a worldwide database and have it played on individual interactive television sets. The entire output of scores of New Zealand writers and artists, made available instantly to anyone who wants it! And not just the output of books, but the interactive material that will blend with it: the extra pictures, sounds, words, graphics and invitations to explore.

6. Lifelong education is now a dominant fact of life. Linked with the active aging of the population, it will also provide one of the big growth industries of the next decade, alongside telecommunications, multimedia interactive technology and servicing leisure needs. By the year 2000 the total number of Americans aged over 65 is likely to be between 40 and 45 million. Fully one-third of Americans—76 million people—were born between 1946 and 1964, the years of the so-called baby boom. They all turn 60 between 2006 and 2024. And as Ken Dychtwald says:

Instead of "location, location, location," "database, database, database."

STAN RAPP AND TOM COLLINS
MaxiMarketing*

*Subtitled *The New Direction in Advertising, Promotion and Marketing Strategy,* McGraw-Hill, New York (1987).

"When a few thousand people across the country share an opinion, read a book, or buy a product, that's interesting; it may even amount to a trend. But . . . when 76 million people do so, it's a revolution."[6]

7. "Databased lifestyle marketing" will alter the shape of retailing: the ability to electronically store—and service—customer preferences, lifestyle changes and learning needs. The big Kimberly-Clark disposable diaper company spends an eight-figure sum each year servicing a database that sends out direct mailings to a big majority of America's 3.5 million new mothers. Marketing experts Stan Rapp and Tom Collins say Kimberly-Clark now has "a priceless by-product, a huge and annually-growing database of . . . parents and children by name and address. This data base is as much a company asset as factories and forests."[7] They say it may well be time to replace the old property-development maxim of "location, location, location" with "database, database, database."

8. Much of the research has already been done to chart the path to the new learning society. We have summarized only some of the highlights. And in every field of that research lie opportunities for business development: to take the educational breakthroughs, in particular, and make them available to families and to businesses.

Says Drucker: "Education can no longer be confined to the schools. Every employing institution has to become a teacher."

Tom Peters talks about an "organization-as-university."[8] And more and more companies are fitting that model.

* Quad/Graphics, the Wisconsin printing company with a $500 million-a-year turnover, has been specifically set up as a learning organization. All employees sign up as students. They work a four-day, 40-hour, flex-time week. On the fifth day they're encouraged to turn up in the company's classroom—without pay; and about half do. Everyone in the company is encouraged to be both a student and a teacher. You don't get promoted until you have trained your successor.[9]

* At Johnsonville Foods, another Wisconsin company, nearly every worker is taking a company-paid economics course at the local community college. Most work in small group projects. Each is encouraged to be a self-acting manager. Says one plant manager: "We're teachers. We help people grow. That's my main goal. Each person is his or her own manager."[10]

Arie De Geus, head of planning for Royal Dutch/Shell sums up the economic imperatives: "The ability to learn faster than your competitors

Where there is genuine vision, people excel and learn, not because they are told to, but because they want to.

PETER M. SENGE
The Fifth Discipline*

*Published by Random House, Sydney, Australia (1992).

may be the only sustainable competitive advantage."[11] And according to Alvin Toffler: "Knowledge has become the ultimate resource of business because it is the ultimate substitute."[12]

Hanover's O'Brien again puts the challenge in human terms. The future manager's fundamental task, he says, is "providing the enabling conditions for people to lead the most enriching lives they can." Mt. Edgecumbe's Larrae Rochelau would smile agreement.

It is not the role of this book to document all the changes that are turning the business world upside down and inside out. Peters, Drucker, Toffler, Reich, Ohmae,[13] Akio Morita,[14] John Naisbitt,[15] Daniel Burstein[16] and dozens of other writers have spelled them out. Deming and the total quality management movement have presented some of the alternatives.

And Peter M. Senge, of the Massachusetts Institute of Technology, in his seminal book, *The Fifth Discipline,* has supplied a model for business as a learning organization—based in part around a shared vision of the future and a "systems thinking" approach to organization. "If any one idea about leadership has inspired organizations for thousands of years," he says, "it's the capacity to hold a shared picture of the future we seek to create. One is hard-pressed to think of any organization that has sustained some measure of greatness in the absence of goals, values and vision that become deeply shared throughout the organization . . . It is impossible to imagine the accomplishments of building AT and T, Ford or Apple in the absence of a shared vision. Theodore Vail had a vision of a universal telephone service that would take 50 years to bring about. Henry Ford envisioned common people, not just the wealthy, owning their own automobiles. Steven Jobs, Steve Woznak and their Apple co-founders saw the power of the computer to empower people."[17]

Senge's book is a challenge to all in business to rethink their future, as we too have urged. "Most of us at one time or another," he writes, "have been part of a great 'team,' a group of people who functioned together in an extraordinary way—who trusted each other, who complemented each others' strengths and compensated for each others' limitations, who had common goals that were larger than individual goals, and who produced extraordinary results. I have met many people who have experienced this sort of profound teamwork—in sports, or in the performing arts or in business. Many say that they have spent much of their life looking for that experience again. What they experienced was a learning organization."

As we researched this book, we too have been struck by the common

Barbara Praschnig
Creative Learning Company Ltd.
P.O. Box 5422
Wellesley Street
Auckland
New Zealand

Hello Barbara,

We have now completed our third customized training program with your very interesting company.

Thank you from all of us. What outstanding changes!

During our recent new-product launches throughout New Zealand, the staff have been using these new learning techniques with amazing results. Music, drama, mind maps, colour, creating rapport and many other techniques have all surfaced during presentations and customer demonstrations.

What has been interesting is the effect on those staff members who didn't initially accept the unusual methods incorporated in the course. They have enquired, tested and finally adopted in small ways much of what you introduced.

Above all—they remembered.

Doug Cowie
National Education Manager
Apple Computers New Zealand

*This is a typical letter to one of New Zealand's pioneer practitioners in accelerated learning.

traits that shine from great corporations, great schools and great sports organizations: the vision, the passion, the commitment to excellence, the sense of achievement, and above all, a belief that almost anything is possible.

We've also found a strong move to blend the best skills and techniques of business and education. When the current co-authors met first at the 1991 annual convention of the Society for Accelerative Learning and Teaching—one from business, one from college-teaching—it was significant that one-third of those present were from industry: at what had previously been an "educators'" conference. Two years later, former IBM senior instructor Norm Erickson is SALT president.

Laurence Martel, President of the National Academy of Integrative Learning, of Hilton Head, South Carolina, is equally at home in both worlds. And he's convinced that not only do we need learning organizations, we need learning communities.

"In recent years," he says, "organizations have asked me to help them enhance individual and organizational performance, using a new philosophy of learning, grounded in modern science, that I call integrative learning. Initially I assumed teachers and managers in schools, corporations, community agencies and universities would have different needs and concerns. But what I found with respect to creating the learning community is that all organizations are in the same boat. That boat is our common need to enhance learning performance greatly at every level, every sector, of society."[18]

Colin Rose is an English innovator who has seized on the breakthroughs in educational research and turned them into a highly successful business. Originally a specialist marketer of diet foods, he became fascinated with the psychology of weight control, and then with the psychology of "suggestion." It wasn't long before he became a keen student of Lozanov, Gardner, Dunn, Sperry, Ornstein, Diamond and Mihaly and Isabella Csikszentmihalyi.[19] And in recent years he has probably done more than anyone else in the United Kingdom to popularize accelerated learning techniques.

As Europe moved in the 1980s towards a common community, Rose realized that British business executives were generally way behind their continental competitors in foreign language skills. His Accelerated Learning Systems company filled the niche with self-study language courses based on multiple-intelligence concepts. Offered with an uncon-

Some training results with new methods

Bell Atlantic C & P Telephone Co.:

4-week and 6-week customer rep.
training course and 12-day technical course.
42, 57 and 50 percent training time reduction.
Dropout rate reduced 300 percent.
$700,000-a-year saving in training costs.

Eastman Kodak, Rochester, NY.:

Engineer-trainer Ed White reduced his training time in electronics course from 48 hours to 27 hours. Employee retention of information, 90 days later, increased from 74 percent to 96 percent.

Northeast Medical College:

Forty percent of first-year medical students failed their final exam in anatomy. The course was redesigned with integrative learning principles—and 100 percent passed.

*Information supplied by Laurence D. Martel, President,
National Academy of Integrative Learning,
Hilton Head, South Carolina.

ditional money-back guarantee, these soon became the country's biggest-selling language resources. They were designed as do-it-yourself learning kits for home instruction, but are now being used in many schools.

Rose has now designed simple learning-how-to-learn packages: booklets, video and cassettes. And he has moved into business training, again with simple kits. Sit with him at his headquarters in Aston Clinton, England, and you'll find direct-mail educational packages going off to the world. "Already over 500 organizations are benefiting from our train-the-trainer package. They span the entire spectrum of business and public service, organizations like Sony, IBM, Kelloggs, Avon Cosmetics, Esso, Proctor & Gamble, Boeing Aircraft, Telecom Australia and Saudi Arabian Airlines. We've recently put 10,000 people at the Rover car company through a learn-to-learn program."[20] Rose's company has also been involved as teacher-training consultants in Brunei.

Some of the main business breakthroughs are coming in cutting-edge industries, particularly in multi-media communications.

Laurence Martel, whose organization evaluated the Guggenheim school results, has also summarized some of the business breakthroughs using new accelerated and integrative learning techniques. Two typical results:

* Eastman Kodak, Rochester, New York: a 48-hour electronics training course reduced to 27 hours, with a 94 percent memory retention of material 90 days later.

* Bell Atlantic: six- and four-week customer service training courses for company representatives and 12-day technical training courses—42, 57 and 50 percent reductions in training times, a big increase in job performance, dropout rates reduced by over 300 percent, and a $700,000-a-year saving in training costs.[21]

Mary Jane Gill, the former Managing Director of Training Education Services with Bell Atlantic, says the really big breakthrough, however, is not only in speed. "What you really get is an 'information age' employee. You get somebody who can work independent of supervision, a better problem-solver, a person who can work by himself or herself but also work well in a team. I can't over-emphasize the importance of this. Everyone in business knows that middle-management is being replaced with communications technology. So the information-age employee has to be a skilled self-manager. And that's what the new training techniques

Learning organizations will find ways to nurture and focus the capacities within us that today we call "extraordinary."

BILL O'BRIEN,
C.E.O., Hanover Insurance*

*Quoted by Peter M. Senge in *The Fifth Discipline*, published by Random House, Sydney, Australia (1992).

are achieving. In my view, that's much more important than the obvious big reductions in training time."[22] From her home base in Maryland, U.S.A., Gill has now joined with Colin Rose to co-author a Training and Development Programme, so the kind of training proven in action at Bell Atlantic is now being used by such British companies as Glaxo, Laura Ashley, Nestle Rowntree, W.H. Smith and I.C.I.

SuperCamp experience is also benefiting business. Former SuperCamp trainers Kim Zoller and Greg Cortepassi run their own Teamworks consulting company, using similar approaches in business training to those suggested in this book: accelerated, integrative learning, a four-pronged curriculum covering personal growth skills, life skills, learn-to-learn skills and content. Says Bill Shell, Vice President of Bank I in Greeley, Colorado, after all 140 people at the bank had been through their training course: "We needed to make leaps in productivity while retaining the same resources, and while greater demands were placed on people. We needed to prepare our employees for the intense demands of systems conversion. This could have created a lot of stress, and we even expected some employees to leave. But with the accelerated integrative training, we had just the opposite. I would venture to say that even their personal lives got better."[23]

But that's not surprising. Hanover's Bill O'Brien says, "The more I understand the real skills of leadership in a learning organization, the more I become convinced that these are the skills of effective parenting. Leading in a learning organization involves supporting people in clarifying and pursuing their own visions, 'moral suasion,' helping people discover underlying causes of problems, and empowering them to make choices. What could be a better description of an effective family? The fact that many parents don't succeed especially well simply shows that we haven't created the learning environment for parenting, just as we've not created the learning environment for developing leaders."[24]

M.I.T.'s Peter Senge challenges us all to make a choice. "Choice is different from desire," he says. "Try an experiment. Say: 'I want.' Now say: 'I choose.' What's the difference? For most people, 'I want' is passive; 'I choose' is active. For most, wanting is a state of deficiency— we want what we do not have. Choosing is a state of sufficiency— electing to have what we truly want."

And that, we believe, is the real challenge of the future.

Welcome to tomorrow when computers aren't the only things that will get smarter. You will too.

SUBLIMINAL DYNAMICS*

*Headline on a pamphlet produced by Subliminal Dynamics, 14700 East Kentucky Drive, Suite 535, Aurora, CO. 80012, advertising their courses which include "subliminal photography" methods for high-speed reading and recall.

How to organize for transformation in communities, states, nations

Now it's your turn. The Learning Revolution is yours to shape.

Almost everything that idealistic dreamers ever imagined is now possible. We live in an age of potential plenty, yet millions of people even in affluent societies will go to bed hungry tonight.

We live in an age where mass literacy and higher education is possible for all, yet where 49 percent of high school seniors tested in a typical American city cannot identify on a map of the world the United States of America.[1] And where at least 23 million Americans are functionally illiterate.

In a world which has stockpiled enough nuclear weapons to blow itself to pieces several times over, countries have continued to spend around $83 million an hour on armaments and "defence"[2] while decrying their inability to finance health and education. And the biggest growth industry in many developed countries is "home security" for protection against the dispossessed.

In education, as we have seen throughout this book, the knowledge exists to bring to birth the world's first truly learned society.

Our over-riding theme is that the world needs nothing less than a learning revolution to match the cataclysmic changes that are coming with the age of instant communication. That revolution can start anywhere. And it is already happening in hundreds of different ways.

Writing soon after the early development of electronics, futurist H.G. Wells forecast revolutionary changes in the world by the end of this century. They would come, he predicted, not by armed revolution but by a "revolt of the competent." He envisaged an "open" conspiracy of

From a nation at risk to a nation of promise.

LAURENCE D. MARTEL
President, Interlearn*

*The quote was the title of his keynote address to the 50th anniversary conference of the American Council for Higher Education, reprinted in *Continuing Higher Education* (Fall 1988).

interested, intelligent and devoted people who would finally rebel at the kind of absurd contradictions we have just highlighted.

That gentle revolution is now under way. It will be guided, as we've seen, by trends that are already obvious. And leading American educationalist Dr. Laurence D. Martel has put them succinctly in a 50th anniversary keynote speech to the American Council for Higher Education. We are moving, he says:

*   *From an industrial-manufacturing economy to a high-tech service and knowledge-based economy* "where inventiveness, entrepreneurial and self-regenerative learning replace the hierarchical, controlled production model."

*   *From one lifetime career to a lifetime of careers,* probably an average of at least eight in a lifespan—requiring "a life of continuous adaptability and refocussing."

*   *From manpower to mind-power—a shift from "a labour force to a learning force"* where capital and wealth will be generated from the mental performance and inventiveness of persons as opposed to traditional labour.

*   *From retooling the workforce to regenerating the learning force*—where work itself involves continuous learning.

*   *From a fulltime workforce to part-time labour.*

*   *From a narrow view of intelligence as verbal and mathematical ability to the theory of multiple intelligences*—a view that permits "redefinition of learning opportunities."

*   *From a dominant-race, male, single-language society to a multi-cultural, diverse, multi-lingual, humane-centred one.*

*   *From central control to decentralized consensus.*

*   *From a youthful society to a greying society*—where by 2007 the largest voting block in the United States will be 65 years and older. ("Imagine," says Martel, "the resulting legislation if priorities shift from national defence to health care, from welfare to homecare.")

*   *From seven workers supporting one retiree to three workers underwriting one retiree*—at a time when many new entrants to the labour force are unskilled and disadvantaged.

Martel headlined his address, significantly, *From a Nation at Risk to a Nation of Promise.* And he challenged his audience of academic leaders to "declare the 20th century over and start the new century now,

Never have the possibilities for human development been more remarkable.

The motto of the
New Horizons for Learning network,
based on a speech by Jean Houston*

*Reported in *New Horizons for Learning: Creating an
Educational Network,* by Dee Dickinson—the story of New Horizons
for Learning; available through New Horizons,
4649 Sunnyside North, Seattle, WA 98108.

with a new vision of continuing higher education as a leading force in economic revitalization, educational reform and community renewal."[3]

We agree. In our view, the change is already coming from the drive, and enthusiasm of thousands of different initiatives in communities, states and nations, in schools, businesses and homes:

* Dee Dickinson was a mid-life Seattle educator with a highly active mind when she attended an education conference organized by the World Futures Society in Minneapolis in 1979. Two people inspired her at that conference: Luis Alberto Machado, Venezuela's first Minister for the Development of Human Intelligence, and Jean Houston, director of the Foundation for Mind Research in New York.

Said Machado: "We do not know to what lengths human beings may go along the path of personal development. Possible achievements surpass the limits of our own imagination." Said Houston: "Never have the possibilities for human development been more remarkable."

Dickinson and two other Seattle enthusiasts, Joan Oates and Mary Carson, were then writing a "Futures Paper" for their school district. And the Minneapolis conference excited them so much "we hardly needed a plane to fly home." Their paper was to sound a theme that is as true today as then: "Imagine a school system," it began, "where students dance to illustrate parts of a sentence; learn basic math through music; learn geography by cooking a country's cuisine, sewing their clothes, acting their dramas, and playing their games; learn how to write by working with practising journalists; where students' science projects are criticized by industrial scientists; where they learn plane geometry through choreography; learn history through dramatic and visual arts; learn how to honour a contract by developing learning agreements with teachers; learn physical skills through mental imagery; learn work-related skills by practising them in the work place; learn foreign languages in physical education classes; and learn about labour-management relations in vocational cooperative education classes.

"Such a school system would seek to stimulate and cultivate all of the senses, not just some of them." And further: "We believe this kind of education will prepare our young people to live in a future world that will be characterized by increasing complexity and uncertainty, value conflicts, technological advances and global interdependency."[4]

Soon afterwards Dickinson's embryo group, joined by school psychologist Sue Leskinen, used the same dream as the basis for a new educational network, New Horizons for Learning. It's one of dozens of

The Edison Project

We need a complete redesign of the way we teach our children.

When Thomas Edison invented electric illumination, he didn't tinker with candles to make them burn better.

Instead he created something brilliantly new: the light bulb.

In the same fashion, American education needs a fundamental breakthrough, a new dynamic that will light the way to a transformed educational system.

CHRIS WHITTLE
Conceiver of The Edison Project*

*The Edison Project is a long-term research and development initiative to design an operate "a new generation of American schools." Contact adddress: The Edison Project, 388 Main Street, Knoxville, Tennessee 37902. Phone (615) 595-3000.

networks now linking around the world to promote new concepts for organizing tomorrow's education.

* Brian Picot was a semi-retired Auckland supermarket executive when the government asked him to chair a panel to recommend changes in New Zealand schools. His report was to turn their administration upside down, challenging each community to organize for excellence in its own way. About 3000 community-elected Boards of Trustees are now doing precisely that: parents linking with teachers, principals and students to control their own future schooling.

* Minnesota was the first American state to do the same: giving panels of parents and teachers the right to run their own charter schools.

* From Minnesota also, Mary Regnier is typical of a new style of entrepreneur, active in planning change. But in her case she starts with families and communities. Says Regnier: "Designing the future *begins* by listening to the children themselves. They know what they need."[5] And her Vision for New Life company acts as the catalyst and facilitator for bringing communities together to plan their own future.

* When communications specialist Chris Whittle pondered the poor state of many American schools, he decided to redesign them. With colleagues like Sylvia W. Peters and Benno C. Schmidt, former president of Yale University, Whittle has set up The Edison Project: a research and development initiative based in Knoxville, Tennessee, to design and operate "a new generation of American schools." They have a team from education, business, government, technology and communications working on the project, and the first of the new schools will open in 1996.[6]

* In San Diego, California, other educators have formed an organization to promote in-depth substantive learning about global systems and diverse cultures. They call it ISTEP: International Studies Education Project of San Diego, and they have raised substantial funds from sponsors for seminars and workshops to train teachers.

* In Eugene, Oregon, Superintendent of Public Schools Margaret Nichols in 1985 commissioned an extensive three-year study of alternative learning programs. Betty Shoemaker, a curriculum specialist, was the facilitator for the task-force—and the result is Eugene's "Education 2000 Integrated Curriculum," a major attempt to apply on a district-wide basis what Miriam Kronish has achieved with John Eliot School in Massachusetts.

* Dr. Richard Paul became so concerned a few years back at the lack

Now go out and change the world.

CHARLES KRAUTHAMMER
Time magazine*

*Essay (June 28, 1993), based on his commencement
address at McGill University, Montreal, Canada.

of critical thinking skills, in the world in general and in education in particular, that he set up a Foundation for Critical Thinking. The movement has rapidly grown to be an international one, based in Sonoma in the heart of California's wine country—and its concepts are spreading in schools around America and the world.

* In Wichita, Kansas, financial services executive Robert Hernandez was so appalled at his children's lack of geographic knowledge that he linked with a printing company and they have now launched a company specializing in educational games. In the past year alone, Hernandez has been on 250 radio talkshows promoting his message of parent-involvement with youngsters' education.

* Since he became the sixth man to walk on the moon, astronaut Dr. Edgar Mitchell has spent 20 years researching and testing the brain's outstanding abilities. Entrepreneur Richard Welch has spent almost as long developing and improving a system of "subliminal dynamics" that results in some remarkable increases in reading speeds: thousands of words a minute. Now the two are working together with their Colorado-based company, Subliminal Dynamics, to take that message to the world.[7]

So the catalyst can be anyone, anywhere: in business, at school, in a community or a family. And it needs to be, for the evidence is overwhelming:

* The world is racing into an era that is changing every aspect of the way we communicate, learn, live, work and play.

* These changes demand a complete rethink on how we learn; how we can rekindle the learning enthusiasm we embraced as small children; how we can go on learning and relearning throughout life; how we can provide the same stimulation to those coming after us; and how we can reshape the world.

* The tools are here. The time is now. The script is yours to write — or dance, or sing, or play, or act, or draw, or orchestrate. Welcome to tomorrow.

Chapter reference notes ▬▬▬▬▬▬▬▬▬▬

Note:

Where the same reference source is used more than once, subsequent references are abbreviated in this way:

6: 1.2 — meaning: see chapter 1, note number 2.

G.D. is Gordon Dryden, and J.V. is Jeannette Vos.

Preface

1. "The Gentle Revolution" is the registered title of a series of books published by Glenn Doman and The Institutes For The Achievement of Human Potential, Philadelphia, PA. Throughout this book, the term "learning revolution" is used in the same sense as the "agricultural" and "industrial" revolutions.

2. American family statistics from *Children in Crisis,* a series of reports in *Fortune International* (August 10, 1992).

3. World armaments and defence spending, for all countries excluding the former Soviet Union and China, extracted from the SIPRI Yearbook 1992 (Stockholm International Peace Research Institute), and China and USSR figures from *The Military Balance 1992-93,* published by The Institute for Strategic Studies, London (1993). SIPRI figures, however, are quoted in 1988 dollar values, and the others in 1985 dollar values. Taking all figures for 1991 or the most recent year recorded, the world's defence and armaments spending reached $731,012 million for a full year, which works out at $2,002 million a day and therefore $83 million an hour. The ac-

tual figure would be higher if quoted in 1993 dollars.

4. National Commission on Children's report, *Beyond Rhetoric* (1991).

5. Skills-knowledge estimate by Secretary's Commission on Achieving Necessary Skills (SCANS), *What Work Requires of America's Schools,* U.S. Department of Labour (1991).

6. Georgi Lozanov, *Suggestology and Outlines of Suggestopedy,* Gordon and Breach, New York (1978); Donald Schuster and Charles Gritton, *Suggestive Accelerative Learning and Teaching,* Gordon and Breach, New York (1985); Lynn Dhority, *The ACT Approach: The Artful Use of Suggestion for Integrative Learning,* Gordon and Breach, New York (1991: expanded edition); Richard Bandler and John Grinder, *Using Your Brain For a Change,* Real People Press, Moab, Utah (1986); Georgi Lozanov and Evalina Gateva, *The Foreign Language Teachers' Suggestopedic Manual,* Gordon and Breach, New York (1988); Tony Stockwell, *Accelerated Learning: in Theory and Practice,* EFFECT, Liechtenstein (1992); Terry Wyler Webb, with Douglas Webb, *Accelerated Learning With Music: Trainer's Manual,* Accelerated Learning Systems, Norcross, Georgia (1990); Win Wengler, *Beyond Teaching and Learning,* Project Renaissance, Singapore (1992).

7. Wording paraphrased from Rabbi Hillel: *If I am not for myself, who will be for me? If I am for myself alone, what am I? And if not now, when?* From *Ethics of The Fathers* (the ancient Pirke *Avot).*

Introduction

1. From Robert Reich, *The Work Of Nations,* Simon & Schuster, New York (1991).

2. All Robert Reich quotations are from *The Work Of Nations.*

3. Reich's estimates for present earnings-percentages are supported by John Kenneth Galbraith, *The Culture of Contentment,* Houghton Mifflin Company (1992), from U.S. Government data.

4. SuperCamp research by Jeannette Vos-Groenendal, *An Accelerative/Integrative Learning Model Program: Based on Participant Perceptions of Student Attitudinal and Achievement Changes,* unpublished doctoral dissertation, ERIC and Northern Arizona University, Flagstaff, Arizona (1991).

Chapter 1: The future

1. Sources for most information are cited at the foot of page 40.

2. Fibre optic predictions: John Naisbitt and Patricia Aburdene, *Megatrends 2000,* William Morrow, New York (1990).

3. Stewart Brand, *The Media Lab: Inventing the Future at M.I.T.,* Viking Penguin, New York (1987).

4. Total number of book-titles published in the world in 1990: 842,000, according to the UNESCO Statistical Yearbook (1992).

5. Dr. Willard Daggett speaks frequently on the changing shape of education. His reference here was taken from a tape-recorded speech to Colorado school administrators (1992).

6. The $7.6 trillion figure for world trade in goods: *Time* magazine (July 3, 1993). The $114 trillion figure for electronic money transfers: Scott Cunningham and Alan L. Porter, *Communications Networks: a dozen ways they'll change our lives,* article in *The Futurist* (January-February 1992).

7. John Naisbitt predictions in this chapter, unless sourced to a book, are from a Gordon Dryden interview in Cambridge, Mass., soon after the publication of *Megatrends 2000* (1990).

8. Peter Drucker's forecasts are in *The New Realities,* Harper & Row, New York (1989); John Naisbitt's in *Megatrends 2000,* Kenichi Ohmae's in *The Borderless World,* Fontana, London (1990); and Robert Reich's in *The Work of Nations,* Simon & Schuster, New York (1991).

9. Franchising predictions from Steven S. Raab, with Gregory Matusky, in *Blue print For Franchising a Business,* John Wiley & Sons, New York (1987).

10. World tourist predictions: 1.2.

11. Japanese tourist goals, from Maarten Wevers, *Japan, its Future and New Zealand,* Victoria University Press (1988).

12. New Zealand tourist targets: from chairman of New Zealand Tourism Board, Norman Geary, interview in Auckland, N.Z., with G.D. (1991).

13. Norman McCrae: interview in London, U.K., with G.D. (1990).

14. 1.7.

15. Tony Buzan: interview in Marlow, England, with G.D. (1990).

16. Karen Pitman: interview in Washington, D.C., with G.D. (1990).

17. Lisbeth B. Schorr: interview in Washington, D.C., with G.D. (1990).

18. Most data on the aging of the population from Ken Dychtwald, *Age Wave,* Bantam, New York (1990).

Chapter 2: Why not the best?

1. British report: by Sir Christopher Ball, *More Means Different: Wider Access to Higher Education,* Royal Society for the encouragement of Arts, Manufacturers and Commerce (RSA), London (May, 1990).

2. In July, 1993, the New Zealand Ministry of Education circulated for widespread public discussion a new document, *Education for the 21st Century,*

Learning Media Ltd., Box 3293, Wellington, New Zealand.

3. In 1993 the New Zealand Government has also established a World Communications Laboratory Secretariat, based on the concept that New Zealand—as a country that is small and isolated, but with a superior telecommunications system and high public acceptance of new technology—could well become a communications laboratory for the world.

4. Gil Simpson: interview in Christchurch, N.Z., with G.D. (1991).

5. Early childhood brain development: see more detailed research, pages 223-227.

6. New Zealand hearing problems: *Child Hearing in New Zealand, Strategic Directions,* N.Z. Health Department (1991).

7. Prof. Crawford: interview in London, with G.D. (1990).

8. University study showing percentage of new mothers "at risk": a 10-year research project carried out by the Psychology Department, University of Otago Medical School, Dunedin, New Zealand, and summarized in *Pacific Network,* Pacific Foundation, Auckland, New Zealand (February, 1992).

9. New Zealand educational spending, from Ministry of Education, *Education for the 21st Century,* Learning Media, Wellington (1993). This report lists estimated expenditure per preschooler in 1990 as $NZ3,236. The Ministry's Data Management and Analysis Section divides this figure by 2.23 to estimate costs for individual youngsters at kindergarten as most attend part-time; we have used that calculation (supplied by Ministry, August 3, 1993)

10. 1.5.

11. Lincoln Unified School District project summarized from *The Lincoln Plan,* by Steve Bingler, in *New Horizons For Learning* (Winter 1992 edition, Volume XIII, No. 2).

12. Kimi Ora Community school report from personal visits by Gordon Dryden (1991 and 1992).

13. Stuart McNaughton, in an essay entitled *The Face of Instruction* in *Growing Up: The Politics of Human Learning,* edited by John Moss and Tim Linzey, published by Longman Paul, Auckland, New Zealand (1991).

Chapter 3: Meet your amazing brain

1. 1.15.

2. Preface 6.

3. Robert Ornstein and Richard F. Thompson, with illustrations by David Macauley, *The Amazing Brain,* Houghton Mifflin Company, Boston (1984).

4. 3.3.

5. Paul D. MacLean, *The Triune Brain in Evolution,* Plenum, New York (1990).

6. Howard Gardner, *Frames of Mind,* Basic Books (1983).

7. Colin Rose, interview in Aston Clinton, Bucks, England, with G.D. (1990).

8. Marian Diamond, interview in Berkeley, CA, with G.D. (1990). For more scientific data, see Marian Cleeves Diamond, *Enriching Heredity,* Macmillan, New York (1988).

9. For excellent coverage of the history of Polynesian Pacific explorations, see the Australian Broadcasting Commission's television series, *Man On The Rim,* especially episode 11, *The Last Horizon.*

10. According to the BBC television series, *The Story of English,* the English language has over 550,000 words, but the number continues to increase. The TV series has been adapted as an excellent book: Robert Crum, William Cran and Robert MacNeil, *The Story of English,* Faber and Faber/BBC Books, London (1986).

11. Specific Diagnostic Studies Inc.

analyses student profiles through its Learning Channel Preference Checklist. It has now collated results from 5,300 students, grades 5 through 12, in the United States, Hong Kong and Japan. "Every student profile showed a certain percentage in each of the three categories," reports Valerie Barlous, Director of Programme Services, in a letter to the present authors (1993). "The average student profile from this sample population: haptic, 37 percent; auditory, 34 percent; and visual, 29 percent." Most studies of students with pronounced learning styles show up to 40 per cent are strong haptic or kinesthetic learners, 35 to 40 per cent are visual learners (generally preferring pictures and graphics rather than being "print-oriented") and the remainder auditory learners. See fuller coverage and references, chapter 10.

12 Wilder Penfield and Herbert Jasper, *Epilepsy and the Functional Anatomy of the Human Brain,* Little Brown, Boston (1954).

Chapter 4: A do-it-yourself guide

1. Marilyn King, from *Dare To Imagine,* an article in *On The Beam,* published by New Horizons for Learning, Seattle, W.A. (Fall, 1991).

2. Colin Rose, *Accelerated Learning,* Dell, New York (1985). For brainwave activity and its impact on learning, see also Preface 6, and Terry Wyler Webb, with Douglas Webb, *Accelerated Learning With Music—a Trainer's Manual,* Accelerated Learning Systems, Norcross, Georgia (1990).

3. 3.2.

4. Tony Buzan, *Make The Most Of Your Mind,* Linden, New York (1984).

5. 3.8.

6. Accelerated Learning Systems, 50 Aylesbury Road, Aston Clinton, Aylesbury, Bucks HP22 5AH, England.

7. 3.10.

8. In its planning for a United Europe,

the Council of Europe produced official guidelines confirming the 2000 most-used words. These form the basis for most introductory courses in foreign languages, according to Accelerated Learning Systems, of England.

9. The 12-act play system is used by Accelerated Learning Systems, of U.K.

10. Preface 6.

Chapter 5: How to think for successful ideas

1. *The World Book Encyclopedia.*

2. Frank Rose, *East of Eden: The End of Innocence at Apple Computer,* Arrow Books, London (1989).

3. John F. Love, *McDonald's: Behind The Arches,* Bantam, New York (1986).

4. Part of this chapter originally appeared in Gordon Dryden's *Out Of The Red,* William Collins, Auckland (1978).

5. *The Illustrated Encyclopedia of New Zealand,* David Bateman, Auckland (1986).

6. Graham T. Crocombe, Michael J. Enright and Michael E. Porter, *Upgrading New Zealand's Competitive Advantage,* Oxford, New Zealand (1991).

7. Ogilvy, David, *Ogilvy on Advertising,* Crown Publishers, New York (1983).

8. Peter Ellyard, speech to New Zealand school principals (1992).

9. William J.J. Gordon is the founder of Synetics Educational Systems Inc.

10: Peter Evans and Geoff Deehan, *The Keys to Creativity,* Grafton, London (1988).

11. Alex Osborn, *Applied Imagination,* Charles Schribner's Sons, New York (1953).

12. James L. Adams, *Conceptual Blockbusting,* Penguin, New York (1987).

13. Toshihiko Yamashita, *The Panasonic Way,* Kohansha International, New York (1987).

14. Masaaki Imai, *Kaizen: The Key To*

Japan's Competitive Success, Random House, New York (1986).

15. 5.14.

16. Masaaki Imai's book (5.14) is excellent. See also: Mary Wilson, *The Deming Management Method,* Dodd Mead & Company Inc., U.S.A., (1986); and W. Edwards Deming, *Out Of Crisis,* Massachusetts Institute of Technology Centre for Advanced Engineering Study (1986).

17. Edward de Bono has been a prolific writer since he first published *Lateral Thinking,* Penguin, London (1970). For extensive but brief coverage of his approach: Edward de Bono, *De Bono's Thinking Course,* BBC Books, London (1982).

18. Roger von Oech, *A Whack On The Side Of The Head,* Warner Books, New York (1983).

19. 5.12.

20. 5.17.

21. Edward de Bono, *Teaching Thinking,* Penguin, London (1977).

Chapter 6: Right from the start

1. Professor Marian Diamond points out (letter to authors, June, 1993) that, while no one develops another cortical brain-cell from the time of birth, brain-cells do continue to multiply after birth in the dentate gyrus of the hippocampal complex; granule cells in the cerebellum; and nerve cells in the olfactory epithelium.

2. 2.7.

3. Dr. Ian James, interview in New York, with G.D. (1990).

4. Jane M. Healy, *Your Child's Growing Mind,* Doubleday, New York (1987).

5. 2.8.

6. Preface 2.

7. Preface 2.

8. Speed of messages around the brain: 4.3, and The Diagram Group, *The Brain: A User's Manual,* Berkley Books, New York (1983); Richard M. Restak, *The*

Brain: The Last Frontier, Warner Books, New York (1979).

9. 3.3.

10. Gordon Dryden, *Where To Now?* television series, produced by Pacific Foundation, New Zealand (1991), scripts reproduced in *Pacific Network* (February, 1992).

Chapter 7: The vital years

1. Benjamin S. Bloom, *Stability and Change in Human Characteristics,* John Wiley, New York (1964).

2. 1.15.

3. 7.1.

4. Dr. Phil Silva, Director of the Dunedin Multidisciplinary Health and Development Research Unit, University of Otago Medical School, interview in Dunedin New Zealand, with G.D. (1991).

5. The Christchurch study is financed by the New Zealand Medical Research Council. Percentages are from Dr. David Fergusson, Program Director, in interview with G.D. (1991).

6. 3.7.

7. Research by Jack Canfield, 1982, covering 100 children each assigned to a researcher for a day; results summarized by Bobbi DePorter, *Quantum Learning,* Dell, New York (1992).

8. Prof. Diamond interview in Berkeley, California, with G.D. (1990).

9. Richard M. Restak, *The Infant Mind,* Doubleday, New York (1986).

10. Ruth Rice, *The Effects of Tactile-Kinesthetic Stimulation on the Subsequent Development of Premature Infants,* University of Texas (1975).

11. Prof. Lyelle L. Palmer, *Kindergarten Maxi-Stimulation: Results over Four Years,* at Westwood School, Irving, Texas (1971-75); *A Chance to Learn: Intensive Neuro-Stimulation in Transition Kindergarten,* at Shingle Creek Elementary School, Minneapolis (1989-90); and *Smooth Eye Pursuit Stimula-*

tion Readiness in Kindergarten, at Shingle Creek Elementary School, Minneapolis (1990-91)

12. Palmer interview and correspondence with J.V. (1993).

13. 7.12.

14. Janet Doman interview in Philadelphia with G.D. (1990).

15. Shinichi Suzuki, *Nurtured By Love,* Exposition Press, New York (1975).

16. Gordon Dryden first interviewed Glenn Doman, in Melbourne, Australia, for New Zealand radio and television in 1974; he has studied the Doman method in action in Australia, New Zealand and especially at The Institutes for the Achievement of Human Potential in Philadelphia, in 1988 (for one week), 1989 (for one week), in 1990 (during a three-day television recording session) and during the preparation of this book (1992). Dryden has yet to meet one published critic of Doman who has actually visited The Institutes or studied his work at first hand.

17. Glenn Doman interview in Philadelphia, PA, with G.D. (1990).

18. Felicity Hughes, *Reading and Writing Before School,* Jonathan Cape, London (1971): an excellent and sensible summary.

19. Dr. Noor Laily Dato' Abu Bakar and Mansor Haji Sukaimi, *The Child of Excellence,* The Nury Institute, Malaysia (1991).

20. Dorothy Butler, *Babies Need Books,* Penguin, London (1984).

21. 3.8.

22. All details of the Missouri Parents As Teachers program obtained by G.D. during videotaping visit to St. Louis, Missouri (1990).

23. 7.22.

24. 2.2.

25. Ferguson Florissant School District data from visit to the district by G.D. (1990).

26. Article, *Forward* (October 9, 1992).

27. The HIPPY programme has been introduced into New Zealand by the Pacific Foundation, of which Gordon Dryden was co-founder and chief executive from 1990 to 1992. Details have come from that association, including visits to Israel by Foundation executives Lesley Max and Telesia McDonald.

28. Amy J.L. Baker and Cyaya S. Piotrikowski, in *The Effects of Participation in HIPPY on Children's Classroom Adaptation: Teacher Ratings,* published by the National Council of Jewish Women, Center for the Child, and available through the NCJW, 53 West 23rd Street, New York, NY 10010.

29. 7.19.

30. Of several reports on the Venezuela project, we are indebted to the excellent summary by Dee Dickinson, *New Horizons for Learning: Creating an Educational Network,* New Horizons for Learning, Seattle (1990).

31. 7.30.

32. Rarotonga experience, from personal visit by G.D. to Rarotonga, Cook Islands, in 1977, and later interviews with Dr. Joseph Williams in Auckland, New Zealand, 1991. During the time Dr. Williams was Director of Health and later Minister of Health, child occupancy of hospital beds dropped from an average of 50 a day to an average of four, a reduction of 92 percent.

33. G.D. visit to Sweden (1990).

34. Daniel Goleman, Paul Kaufman and Michael Ray, *The Creative Spirit,* Dutton, New York (1992).

35. Details of the Foundation Centre for Phenomenological Research gained on a visit by G.D. to the Artesia II Montessori center, at French Camp, CA. (1990).

36. 7.35.

37. Maria Montessori, *The Montessori Method,* Schocken Books, New York (1964): first published in English in 1912.

38. Pauline Pertab interview with Gordon Dryden in Auckland, New Zealand (1993).

39. 7.35. Prof. Wong-Filmore's comparisons are based on personal research into both the California project and the New Zealand kohanga reo movement.

40. 2.9.

41. California early-childhood attendance figures as at 1992.

Chapter 8: The secret heart of learning

1. *What Work Requires of Schools: A SCANS Report for America 2000,* The Secretary's Commission on Achieving Necessary Skills, U.S. Department of Labour (June 1991).

2. 2.1.

3. Preface 2.

4. Preface 2.

5. 6.10.

6. 6.10, including Lesley Max quotation.

7. Georgi Lozanov, *Suggestology and Outlines of Suggestopedy,* Gordon and Breach, New York (1978).

8. Joseph Romanos, *Makers of Champions: Great New Zealand Coaches,* Mills Publications, Lower Hutt, New Zealand (1987).

9. Tom Peters, *Thriving on Chaos,* Pan, London (1989).

10. Hewlett Packard, from personal visit by G.D. to Silicon Valley headquarters (1982).

11. Toshihiko Yamashita, *The Panasonic Way,* Kodansha, New York (1987).

12. 8.9.

13. Akio Morita, *Made In Japan,* Signet-Dutton, New York (1986).

14. 8.9.

15. Many versions have been attributed to Edison; this one from *The World Book Encyclopedia.*

16. 3.7.

17. Northview Elementary School information, originally from *Schools in America,* PBS TV documentary, produced by MacNeil Lehrer (1990). Amended grade-average figures supplied by Dr. Yunk to authors (1993).

18. 8.17.

19. All information, including quotations concerning Monrad Intermediate School, from personal interviews by G.D. (1991).

20. Robert C. Christopher, *The Japanese Mind,* Pan, London (1984).

21. Japanese experiences, unless otherwise attributed, from Jeannette Vos research visit to Japan as a Stanford University Japan Project Fellow (1991).

22. Katherine Lewis, *Cooperation and Control in Japanese Nursery Schools,* published in comparative Education Review (Vol. 28, No. 1, 1984).

23. 8.20.

Chapter 9: True learning

1. Guggenheim School information collected by G.D. during videotaping of *Where To Now?* TV programme in Chicago (1990) and follow-up interview with Nancy Ellis, Guggenheim senior teacher, by J.V. (1993).

2. *The Accounting Game,* Educational Discoveries, 2511 55th Street, Boulder, CO 80301.

3. French course at Beverley Hills High School, Sydney, Australia, from Seven Network TV magazine programme, Sydney (1990).

4. 240 teaching games, by Tony Stockwell, of Liechtenstein. See his summary in *Accelerated Learning in Theory and Practice,* EFFECT, Liechtenstein (1992). The book is written in the form of a Lozanov-type presentation. Both co-authors have attended Stockwell training programmes.

5. *The Great Pacific Century Marketing Game,* devised by G.D.

6. The Creative Learning Company, Auckland, N.Z., has been using accelerated learning techniques in prison.

7. J.V. is one of the facilitators at this programme, organized by Dr. John Grassi.

8. From Glenn Capelli seminar at SALT Convention in Minneapolis, MN. (1992).

9. 9.4.

10. Preface 6.

11. Interview with G.D., Washington, D.C. (1990).

12. Interview at Sodertalji High School, Sweden, with G.D. (1990).

13. Interview in San Francisco, California, with G.D. (1990).

14. In Stockwell's book, 9.4.

15. Capelli *Attitude* tape from Youth Mastermind, Perth, Australia.

16. 4.2.

17. Preface 6, and 4.2.

18. 9.13.

19. Terry Wyler Webb, with Douglas Webb, *Accelerated Learning With Music: A Trainer's Manual*, Accelerated Learning Systems, Norcross, Georgia (1992).

20. Sheila Ostrander and Lynn Schroeder, *Superlearning*, Dell, New York (1979), reported claims that some students had learned up to 3,000 foreign words in a day. Lozanov in 8.7 records 1,000 to 1,200 words being learned per day, with a recall rate of 96.1% (see graph, page 306). The present co-authors have seen no authenticated research evidence to justify higher claims than this, and have seen no evidence outside Bulgaria of figures as high as 1,000 to 1,200.

21. 9.19.

22. Book, 9.4.

23. 9.13.

24. Preface 6.

25. Introduction to Peter Kline's *The Everyday Genius*, Great Ocean Publishers, Arlington, Virginia (1988).

26. 9.1.

27. 9.3.

28. Written analysis of Dr. Dhority's results, provided by Dr. Palmer.

29. Conversation with J.V. (1993).

30. Jan McKittrick did a 40-hour accelerated integrative learning extension course with co-author Vos at the California State University at San Marcos, California; information here from interviews with J.V. (1993).

31. Lyall Watson, *Supernature,* Coronet, London (1973). A three-hour G.D. interview with Watson on Radio i in Auckland, New Zealand, in 1974 (plus an interview with Glenn Doman in Melbourne, Australia, the same year) provided the initial catalyst for the research by G.D. that eventually led to this book.

32. 9.20.

Chapter 10: Do it in style

1. From *Learning and Teaching Styles and Brain Behaviour,* newsletter of the Association for Supervision and Curriculum Development and the Oklahoma State Department of Education, Oklahoma (1988).

2. *Survey of Research on Learning Styles,* in *Educational Leadership* (Vol. 46, No. 6, March 1989).

3. 10.1.

4. 10.1.

5. 10.1.

6. Howard Gardner, *Frames Of Mind,* Basic Books, New York (1983).

7. Lloyd Geering, *In The World Today,* Allen & Unwin and Port Nicholson Press, Wellington (1988), and a programme with G.D. in *Gordon Dryden's Summer Seminars,* Radio IZB, Auckland (1989): programme subtitle: *Reinventing Religion, From The Best of the World's Philosophies.*

8. For details of the Dunns' *Learning Styles Inventory,* contact Learning Styles Network, School of Education and Human Services, St. Johns University, Grand Canal and Utopia Parkways, Jamaica, NY 11439. Of all the Dunns' extensive research, we recommend in particular: Rita and Kenn Dunn and Donald Treffinger, *Bringing Out the Giftedness in Your Child,* John Wiley

and Sons, New York (1992); and Marie Carbo and Rita and Keith Dunn, *Teaching Students To Read Through Their Individual Learning Styles,* Allyn and Bacon, Boston (1991).

9. Michael Grinder, *Righting The Educational Conveyor Belt,* Metamorphous Press, Portland, Oregon (1989).

10. Rita Dunn, Jeffrey S. Beadry and Angela Klavas, *Survey of Research on Learning Styles,* in *Educational Leadership* (Vol. 46, No. 6, pages 53-58).

11. 10.10.

12. From a summary of the Dunns' research, *Learning and Teaching Styles and Brain Behaviour,* published by the Association for Supervision and Curriculum Development and the Oklahoma Department of Education Newsletter (1988) and reported by Laurence Martel, in *Seminar on Innovative Approaches to Meeting Basic Learning Needs,* United Nations Development Programme, New York (January 10-11, 1991). The Dunns say many tactile-kinesthetic learners face major learning problems because teachers wrongly think they are hyperactive. Ninety-five percent of these children are males.

13. 10.8.

14. Anthony Gregorc, *An Adult's Guide to Style,* Gabriel Systems, Maynard, Mass. (1982). See also his article, *Style as a Symptom: a Phenomenological Perspective,* in *Theory Into Practice* (Vol. 23, No. 1, page 51).

15. This test, while adapted from Anthony Gregorc's, first appeared in this form in: Bobbi DePorter, with Mike Hernacki, *Quantum Learning,* Dell Publishing, New York (1992).

16. Adapted from book in 10.15.

17. Robert Sternberg, *Beyond I.Q.,* Cambridge University Press, U.S.A. (1985).

18. Howard Gardner, *The Unschooled Mind,* Basic Books, New York (1991).

Chapter 11: Catching up quick

1. Preface 2.

2. 3.8.

3. 7.11.

4. Helen Keller, *The Story Of My Life,* Doubleday, New York (1954); Helen E. Waite, *Valiant Companions: Helen Keller and Anne Sullivan Macy,* Macrae (1959); Norman Richards, *Helen Keller,* Children's Press (1968).

5. Thomas Armstrong, *In Their Own Way,* J.P. Tarcher, Los Angeles (1987).

6. Brigette Allroggen, *Munich Institute of Technology,* in *Three In One Concepts Newsletter,* Three In One Concepts, Burbank, CA. (1993).

7. Kathy Carroll, interview with J.V. (1993).

8. Gordon Stokes and Daniel Whiteside, *One Brain: Dyslexic Learning Correction and Brain Integration,* Three In One Concepts, Burbank, CA. (1984).

9. Paul and Gail Dennison, *Brain Gym,* Edu-Kinesthetics, Ventura, CA. (1988).

10. Sierra Vista Junior School results reported in *Diffusing Dyslexia,* by Lee Wasserwald, special education teacher, in *1985 Grant Results Report,* available through Three In One Concepts, Burbank, CA.

11. San Marcos School SMART program, based on interviews by J.V. (1993),

12 Renee Fuller, *In Search of the I.Q. Correlation* and *Ball-Stick-Bird Series,* Ball-Stick-Bird Publications, Stony Brook, New York; and *Beyond I.Q.,* an article by Fuller summarizing her work, *In Context* magazine (winter 1988).

13. Elizabeth Schulz, *A Long Way To Go,* article in *American Teacher* magazine (February 1993).

14. Four-minute reading programme, and Donna Awatere quotation, from *Pacific News,* magazine of Radio Pacific, Auckland, New Zealand (1981).

15. Interview with G.D. (1991).

16. *The New Zealand School Journal* is published by Learning Media Ltd., part of the New Zealand Government's Ministry of Education. It provides an extensive range of books and journals to all New Zealand schools, and all stories are listed, by age and interest groups, in *School Journal Catalogue, 1974-1989,* and in regular *Learning Media Catalogues.*

17. John Medcalf, quotes from interview with G.D. (1991), and some material summarized from his book, *TARP: The Tape Assisted Reading Programme,* Flaxmere Special Education Service, Flaxmere, New Zealand.

18. John Medcalf, *TARP: An Individualized Tape-Assisted Reading Programme,* in *Reading Forum N.Z.,* N.Z. Reading Association (Term One 1989).

19. Marie Garbo, *Igniting The Literacy Revolution Through Reading Styles,* article in *Educational Leadership,* Association for Supervision and Curriculum Development, Alexandria, VA. (October, 1990).

20. Rhonda Godwin, interview with G.D. (1991).

21. Research data gathered by John Medcalf and related to G.D. in interview (1991).

22. Forbes Robinson, *Look, Listen: Learning To Read Is Incredibly Simple,* J.K. Marketing, Nelson, New Zealand (1986). Robinson recommends the Vu Lyte (Model 4) opaque projector, produced by Da-Lite Screen Company Inc., P.O. Box 137, Warsaw, Indiana 46580. Robinson's book includes an appendix with the 220 basic "sight words" a child will need (originally defined by Professor E.W. Dolch); and another appendix of word games.

23. 11.22, and in *The Putaruru Experiment,* a Television New Zealand documentary, TVNZ archives.

24. 11.22. Eastbourne children's reading ability tested before and after the experiment, using the Schonell Graded Word Recognition Test.

25. 11.22. Scottish results evaluated using Burt Word Reading Test.

26. 11.22. Canadian results derived from the Schonell Graded Word Recognition Test.

27. 11.22.

28. *Reading Recovery in New Zealand,* a report from the Office of Her Majesty's Chief Inspector of Schools, published by the British Government Office for Standards in Education, London (1993).

29. Lynley Hood, *Sylvia: The Biography of Sylvia Ashton-Warner,* Viking, Auckland, N.Z. (1988). Sylvia Ashton-Warner, *Teacher,* Penguin, London (1966).

30. 7.18.

31. 11.13.

32. SEED information, mainly collected by G.D. on visit to SEED office in Oakland, CA (1989).

33. John Naisbitt and Patricia Aburdene, *Re-inventing The Corporation,* Macdonald, London (1986).

Chapter 12: Solving the dropout dilemma

1. Our thanks to The Management Edge Ltd., P.O. Box 12461, Wellington, New Zealand, and especially to Ross Peddler, Director, for assembling various reports on Mt. Edgecumbe High School. Several New Zealand and New South Wales, Australia, schools are introducing TQM projects, with The Management Edge as consultants.

2. Myron Tribus, *The Application of Quality Management Principles in Education at Mt. Edgecumbe High School, Sitka, Alaska, (1990),* reprinted in *An Introduction to Total Quality for Schools,* American Association of School Administrators (1991). While Larrae Rocheleau is still Superintendent at Sitka, David Langford has moved on.

3. Mission Statement supplied by the school.

4. 12.2.

5. *Opportunity and Solution Overview,* report by Mt. Edgecumbe High School (October 30, 1990), available through the school.

6. 12.5.

7. 12.2, and pilot-company organizational graphics from the school.

8. 12.2.

9. The goal to produce quality individuals, from the school's *Constancy of Purpose* statement (October 30, 1990). 12.5: 46 percent of school graduates are attending post-secondary school.

10. *Reading, Writing and Continuous Improvement,* an article in *Competitive Times,* the Total Quality Management Newsletter, published by GOAL/QPC (Number 1, 1991). Several of the facts quoted in our summary are from this article.

11. 12.2.

12. Dr. Nolan: interview in Palmerston North with G.D. (1991).

13. C.J. Patrick Nolan and David H. McKinnon, *Case Study of Curriculum Innovation in New Zealand: The Freyberg Integrated Studies Project,* Massey University, Palmerston North (April 23, 1991).

14. 12.12.

15. 12.12.

16. 12.12, with background information from 12.13.

17. 12.12.

18. 12.12.

19. Detailed results are in 12.13, but brief summary is from *Pacific Network Magazine,* Pacific Foundation, Auckland (February, 1992).

20. Don Brown, interview with G.D. at Kapiti College, Paraparaumu, New Zealand (1991).

21. 12.20.

22. Edna Tait interview, with G.D. at Tikipunga High School, Whangarei, New Zealand (1991).

23. Jeannette Vos-Groenendal, *An Accelerated/Integrative Learning Model Program Evaluation:* Based on Participant Perceptions of Student Attitudinal and Achievement Changes, ERIC and Northern Arizona University, Flagstaff, Arizona (1991).

24. From J.V. diary notes of her first day as instructor at SuperCamp.

25. 12.23, with specific parent comments from SuperCamp files.

Chapter 13. Planning tomorrow's schools

1. Lester Finch: interview in West Flaxmere, New Zealand, with G.D. (1991).

2. Ellen Matthews, interview in West Flaxmere, New Zealand, with G.D. (1991).

3. Ray Duncan: interview, in West Flaxmere, New Zealand, with G.D. (1991).

4. *South Bay Schools Go Extra Mile For Reading Success,* article in Los Angeles Times (June 1, 1992). Phil Grignon is no longer superintendent of the district.

5. Information from J.V. and G.D. interview with Dr. Susan Schmidt, of the South Bay School District, San Diego (1992).

6. Information on Cascade Elementary School from *A Teachers' Perspective,* by Bruce Campbell, in *Creating The Future,* edited by Dee Dickinson, Accelerated Learning Systems, England (1991).

7. Miriam Kronish: interviews from Needham, Massachusetts, by phone with G.D. and J.V. (1993). J.V. also has firsthand experience with John Eliot School's accelerated integrative learning program. Dr. John Grassi engags her each summer to teach "Whole brain techniques for the reluctant learner" in his masters programme seminars. She considers John Eliot America's finest elementary school success model to date, and

SuperCamp the finest high school model, in integrative accelerated learning.

8. Rosemary Green: interview by phone from Needham, Massachusetts, with G.D. (1993).

9. J.V. was engaged for the first five days to take staff through the main principles.

10: River Oaks School information: from Apple Computer presentation at Auckland College of Education, New Zealand (1992).

Chapter 14: Tomorrow's business world

1. 1.8.

2. Peter M. Senge, *The Fifth Discipline*, Random House, Sydney, Australia (1992).

3. 14.2.

4. Charles Handy, *The Age of Unreason*, Hutchinson, London (1989).

5. 1.8.

6. 1.18.

7. Stan Rapp and Tom Collins, *Maxi-Market-ng: The New Directions in Advertising, Promotion and Marketing Strategy*, McGraw-Hill, New York (1987).

8. Tom Peters, *Liberation Management*, Knopf, New York (1992).

9. 14.8.

10. 14.8.

11. 14.2.

12. Alvin Toffler, *Powershift*, Bantam, New York (1990).

13. 1.8.

14.. Akio Morita, *Made In Japan*, Signet-Dutton, New York (1986).

15. John Naisbitt, *Megatrends*, Warner Books, New York (1982); John Naisbitt and Patricia Aburdene, *Re-Inventing The Corporation*, Macdonald, London (1986), and *Megatrends 2000*, William Morrow, New York (1990).

16. Daniel Burstein, *Yen!* Bantam,

Morebank, Australia (1989), and *Euroquake*, Bantam, Australia (1991).

17. 14.2.

18. Laurence Martel, *Building a Learning Community*, article in *The School Administrator* (June, 1993).

19. Mihaly and Isabella Csikszentmihalyi, *Optimal Experience*, Cambridge: Harvard University Press (1988), and *Flow: The Psychology of Optimal Experience*, Harper and Row, New York (1990).

20: Colin Rose data obtained from interviews in Aston Clinton, U.K., with G.D. (1990), and phone interviews (1993).

21: Data supplied by Dr. Martel to authors (1993).

22. Mary Jane Gill, interview in Maryland, with G.D. (1990).

23. Quotations and information supplied by Kim Zoller and Greg Cortepassi to J.V. (1993).

24. 14.2

Chapter 15. Taking control of the future

1. Laurence D. Martel, *From a Nation at Risk to a Nation of Promise*, reprinted in *Continuing Higher Education* (Fall 1988), quoting the National Geographic Society Research which led to the society's $60 million education foundation.

2. Preface 3.

3. 15.1.

4. 7.30.

5. Interview with J.V. (1992).

6. Information from The Edison Project.

7. From Subliminal Dynamics research data supplied to authors (1993).

Acknowledgements and thanks ■■■■■■■■■■■■■

For all who helped

Both authors thank:

* The pioneers in many fields on whose shoulders this work stands. These include Georgi Lozanov, Roger Sperry, Robert Ornstein, Marian Diamond, Paul MacLean, Howard Gardner, W. Edwards Deming, Don Schuster, John Grassi, Peter Kline, Laurence Martel, Rita and Ken Dunn, Paul and Gail Dennison, C.E. Beeby, Daniel Whiteside, Gordon Stokes, Bobbi DePorter, Eric Jensen, Charles Schmid, Richard Bandler, John Grinder, Michael Grinder, Lynn Dhority, Anthony Gregorc, John Le Tellier, Peter Senge, Bettie B. Youngs, Tony Buzan and Glenn Doman. Special thanks to Lyelle Palmer for insisting that we verify and cite all quotations and research, and assisting us to do that. Our appreciation to those who permitted us to reproduce quotations and illustrations. And our thanks to those involved in the publishing venture, especially Susanna Polmares, Bradley Winch Sr., Bradley Winch Jr., Jeanne Iler, Susan Remkus, Colin Rose and Diana Rose.

Jeannette Vos thanks:

* Co-author Gordon Dryden for his zest, persistence and true partnership, as visionary, crystallizer, writer, editor and interpreter.

* My immediate family members and friends for their support: Leisha, Summer and Ed Groenendal, Elly and John Van Barneveld, Carol Kuchta, Marilyn Gill, Pat Tanagon, Bob Ewalt, Phyllis Gigi, Melanie Bower, Don Lucas, Robert Jones, Jan McKittrick, Mark Cornell and Sandi Hendrickson. And to Gordon's wife, Margaret, for the strength she must have given him during this challenging project.

* My professional friends and colleagues and those who helped with research: Kathleen Carroll, Bill Mammal, Katharine Kertesz, Mary Regnier, Robin Smith, Richard Packard, Mary Dereshiwsky, Anne

Nevin, Rolf Parta, Elsie Begler, Steven Garner, Donald Treffinger, Miriam Kronish, Kim Zoller, Greg Cortepassi, Edgar Mitchell, Richard Welch, Nancy Ellis, Miriam Kronish and Betty Shoemaker.

Gordon Dryden thanks:

* Jeannette Vos, for suggesting this book, for her idealism, superb seven-year research project into new methods of learning, outstanding practical experience in the classroom at all levels, painstaking checking and amazing tolerance as she reeled from seeing dozens of pages of extra research slashed to a few sentences in an editor's drive for simplicity.

* To all the people around the world who have helped with interviews and in other ways, including:

* The United States: Glenn and Katie Doman, Marian Diamond, John Naisbitt, Lisbeth Schorr, Dan Schorr, Jane Healy, Karen Pitman, Janet Doman, Dawn Price, Mary Jane Gill, Barbara Montgomery, Judith Jones, Michael Alexander, Libyan Labiosa-Cassone, Philip Cassone, Joy Rowse, Sue Treffeison, Dee Dickinson, Nancy Margulies, Marilyn King, Lily Wong-Filmore, Susan Schmidt, Antonia Lopez, Lynn O'Brien, Valerie Barlous and Jayn Zopf.

* The United Kingdom: Sheila Kitzinger, Norman Macrae, David Lewis, Michael Crawford, Tony Buzan and Vanda North.

* Sweden: Ingemar Svantesson, Christopher Gudmundsson, Agnetta Nilsson, Bengt-Eric Andersson, Bengt Lindquist, Barbara Martin, Bo Naesland, Agneta Borg, Barbro Martensson and Anders Larsson.

* Liechtenstein: Tony Stockwell.

* Australia: Glenn Capelli.

* Malaysia: Noor Laily Dato' Abu Bakar, Mansor Haji Sukaimi.

* Spain: Juan Sanchez-Muliterno and Eduardo Reyes.

* New Zealand: Barbara Praschnig, Lesley Max and all trustees of the Pacific Foundation, the ASB Charitable Trust, Joe Williams, Edna Tait, John Fleming, Pat Nolan, Phil Silva, Lester Finch, Bruce Kirk, Tony Hewett, Mike Gifford, Noah Gordon, John Medcalf, Lloyd Geering, Murray Brown, Don Brown, Bob Elliott, David Fergusson, Di Hay, Kay Bradford, Patrick Eisdell Moore, Peter Allen, Bruce Green, Pita Sharples, Pauline Pertab, Colin Follas, Ken Booth, Joy Clarke, Gordon McLauchlan, Barry Fenn, Dave Delay and Graye Shattky.

* Margaret Dryden, for understanding, help and tolerance (as ever), and the Groenendal family for patience.

Invitation to join an international learning network

Even before this book was published, both authors have been delighted at the reception.

* The first draft was released at the American Booksellers' Convention in Miami at the end of May, 1993. Swedish publisher Ingemar Svantesson read it overnight, and was back the next day to declare 1994 "The Year of the Learning Revolution" in Scandinavia. He's planning three separate *Learning Revolution* conventions in Sweden , with both authors closely involved.

* In New Zealand, the Auckland College of Education is also planning a major international *Learning Revolution* convention.

* Plans are underway to produce an international telvision series on *The Learning Revolution.*

It has also become obvious as we've worked on the book that closer contacts need to be forged between interested parties around the world..

So if you would like to join a "Learning Network" to follow up ideas presented in this book, you're invited to contact the authors.

Both are very interested in helping with other international conventions.

As the start of the network, we have compiled a list of the resources that we have found most useful—books, music and tapes—and you will find that from page 496.

We're also aware that many key resources may not always be in general bookstores. We have therefore arranged for certain recommended programmes to be made available on request through the publishers of *The Learning Revolution.* They include programmes on:

* Mind Mapping.
* Learning how to learn.
* Music for accelerated learning.
* Foreign language learning.
* Teaching.
* Activities to enhance children's learning.
* Business training.

If you would like to be part of the network, please duplicate the coupon below and fax or mail.

Gordon Dryden and Jeannette Vos
The Learning Revolution Network
through our publishers in these countries:

Accelerated Learning Systems Ltd, 50 Aylesbury Road, Aston Clinton,
Aylesbury, Bucks, HP22 5AH, United Kingdom.
Phone (0296) 631177.   Fax (0296) 631074.

Accelerated Learning System 2000 Pty. Ltd, P.O. Box 618, Mt. Ommaney,
Queensland, Australia 4074.
Phone (07) 2790799. Fax (07) 2793505.

Accelerated Learning Systems (Pty) Ltd, 14 Milner Road Tamboerskloof,
Capetown, South Africa 8001.
Phone (021) 221738. Fax (021) 261827.

Please include my name on your mailing list. I'm also interested in:

a. Books and tapes on Mind Mapping and drawing _____ ☐
b. *Accelerated Learning with Music* _____ ☐
c. *Accelerate Your Learning* courses (learning how to learn) ___ ☐
d. Learning a foreign language quickly at home _____ ☐
e. Videotapes of *The Learning Revolution* _____ ☐
f. Subscribing to a Network newsletter _____ ☐
g. Learning activities for pre-schoolers _____ ☐
h. Learning activities for 6-to-9-year-olds _____ ☐
i. Learning more effective methods of teaching _____ ☐
j. Business training programmes _____ ☐

NAME _____

ADDRESS _____

_____

PHONE (   ) _____ FAX (   ) _____

Networks, books, tapes, music

SELF-STUDY PROGRAMMES

Accelerated Learning Systems

A wide range of self-study programmes, based on the accelerated learning method, are now available through Accelerated Learning Systems Ltd. These include:

* Foreign language courses (French, German, Spanish and Italian, and — coming soon — Japanese and English as a foreign language).

* *Accelerate Your Learning.* A very comprehensive course for 12- to 18-year-olds that shows students how to discover and use their preferred way of learning.

* *Yes, You Can Draw.* An art course by Nancy Margulies.

* *Training and Development Programme.* How to adapt an organisation's training to incorporate accelerated learning methods, and how to build a learning organisation.

The company is completing a Pre-School Learning Programme, Games for Learning for 6-to-9-year-olds, language courses on CD-ROM, and a Teacher Training Programme designed to enable schools to implement the principles discussed in this book in a practical way. Free brochures available from Accelerated Learning Systems, through addresses listed on previous page.

Tony Buzan material

The Buzan Centre, Suites 2/3, Cardigan House, 37 Waterloo Road, Winton, Bournemouth, Dorset, BH9 1BD, UK. Phone (0202) 533593. Fax (0202) 534572.

NETWORKS

SEAL

Society for Effective and Affective Learning, 49 Henley Road, Ipswich, IPI 35J, UK. Phone (0473) 226525.

SALT

Society for Accelerative Learning and Teaching, 1725 South Hill Street, Oceanside, CA 92054-5319, USA. Phone 1 (800) 228-5327. Fax (619) 722-3507.

New Horizons

New Horizons for Learning, 4649 Sunnyside North, Seattle, WA 98103, USA. Excellent international newsletter.

BOOKS AND TAPES

This first selection includes a sample of good introductory books. A more detailed bibliography then follows.

Mind Mapping

Buzan, Tony, *The Mind Map Book— Radiant Thinking,* BBC Books, London (1993).

North, Vanda, *Get Ahead,* Buzan Centre, England.

Israel, Lana, *Brain Power For Kids,* Buzan Centre, England.

Mindscapes and drawing

Margulies, Nancy, *Mapping Inner Space,* Zephyr Press, Tucson, AZ. (1991), with videotape.

Margulies, Nancy, *Yes, You Can Draw!,* Accelerated Learning Systems, England (1991), with videotape.

The future

Reich, Robert B., *The Work Of Nations,* Simon & Schuster, New York (1991).

Handy, Charles, *The Age Of Unreason,* Hutchinson, London (1989).

Naisbitt, John; and Aburdene, Patricia, *Megatrends 2000,* Morrow, New York (1990).

Drucker, Peter, *The New Realities,* Harper & Row, New York (1989).

Business

Peters, Tom, *Liberation Management,* Knopf, New York (1992).

Peters, Tom, *Thriving On Chaos,* Pan, London (1989).

Covey, Stephen, *The 7 Habits Of Highly Effective People,* Simon & Schuster, New York (1989)

The brain

Ornstein, Robert; and Thomas, Richard F., *The Amazing Brain,* Houghton Mifflin, Boston (1984).

Morgan, Brian and Roberta, *Brain Food,* Pan (1987).

Restak, Richard M. *The Mind,* Bantam, New York (1988).

Creating new ideas

Michalko, Michael, *Thinkertoys,* Ten Speed Press, Berkeley, California (1991).

von Oech, Roger, *A Whack On The Side Of The Head,* Warner, New York (1990).

von Oech, Roger, *Creative Whack Pack* (playing cards), U.S. Games Systems, Stamford, CT.

Memory training

Buzan, Tony, *Use Your Perfect Memory,* Plume-Penguin, New York (1991).

Yepson, Roger B., *How to Boost Your Brain Power,* Thorsons, England (1987).

Minninger, Joan, *Total Recall,* Thorsons, England (1989).

Accelerated learning

Rose, Colin, *Accelerated Learning,* Dell, New York (1985).

DePorter, Bobbi; with Hernacki, Mike, *Quantum Learning,* Dell, New York (1992).

Stockwell, Tony, *Accelerated Learning In Theory and Practice,* EFFECT, Liechtenstein (1992).

Intelligence

Gardner, Howard, *Frames Of Mind,*

Basic Books, New York (1983).

Gardner, Howard, *The Unschooled Mind,* Basic Books, New York (1991).

Sternberg, Robert, *Beyond I.Q.,* Cambridge University Press, New York (1985).

Critical thinking

Paul, Richard, *Critical Thinking: What Every Person Needs to Survive In a Rapidly Changing World,* The Foundation for Critical Thinking, Santa Rosa CA (1992).

Teaching techniques

Jensen, Eric, *SuperTeaching,* Kendall/Hunt, Dubuque, Iowa (1988).

Pritchard, Allyn; and Taylor, Jean, *The Use of Suggestion in the Classroom,* Academy Therapy Publications, Navato, California (1980).

Campbell, Linda and Bruce; and Dickinson, Dee, *Teaching and Learning Through Multiple Intelligences,* New Horizons for Learning, Seattle, Washington (1992).

Integrative learning curriculum in the classroom

Dhority, Lynn, *The ACT approach: The Artful Use of Suggestion for Integrative Learning,* Gordon and Breach, New York (1991, expanded edition).

Caine, Renate Nummela and Geoffrey, *Making Connections: Teaching and the Human Brain,* Association for Supervision and Curriculum Development, Alexandria, VA (1991).

Clark, Barbara, *Optimizing Learning: The Integrative Educational Model In The Classroom,* Merrill, Columbus, Ohio (1986).

Grassi, John, *The Accelerated Learning Process in Science,* ALPS Products, Framingham, Mass (1985).

Educational kinesiology

Dennison, Paul and Gail, *Brain Gym: Simple Activities For Whole Brain Learning,* Edu-Kinesthetics Inc., Glendale, California (1985).

Stokes, Gordon; Whiteside, Daniel, *One Brain: Dyslexic Learning Correction and Brain Integration,* Three In One Concepts, Burbank (1987).

Great for students

Martel, Laurence, *School Success,* Learning Matters, Arlington, Virginia (1992).

Saperstein, Rose; and Joseph, James, *Read Your Way To The Top,* Bluechip Publishers, Seattle, Washington (1987).

Great for parents

Kline, Peter, *The Everyday Genius,* Great Ocean Publishers, Arlington, Virginia (1988).

Armstrong, Thomas, *In Their Own Way,* Jeremy Tarcher, LA (1987).

Clark, Faith and Cecil, *Hassle-Free Homework,* Doubleday, New York (1989).

Early parenting

Britton, Lesley, *Montessori: Play & Learn,* Vermilion-Random Century, London (1992).

White, Burton L., *The First Three Years of Life,* Prentice Hall, New York, NY (1985),

Beck, Joan, *How To Raise a Brighter Child,* Fontana, London (1985).

Marzolla, Jean; and Lloyd, Janice,

Learning Through Play, Harper & Row, New York (1972).

Early reading and math

Doman, Glenn, *Teach Your Baby To Read,* Better Baby Press, Philadelphia (1970), with videotape and kit.

Doman, Glenn, *Teach Your Baby Math,* Better Baby Press, Philadelphia (1979) with kit.

Hughes, Felicity, *Reading and Writing Before School,* Jonathan Cape, London (1971).

Learning difficulties

Vitale, Marbara Meister, *Unicorns Are Real: A Right Brained Approach to Learning,* Jalmar Press, Rolling Hills Estates, California (1982).

Learning styles

Dunn, Rita and Ken; Treffinger, Donald, *Bringing Out The Giftedness In Your Child,* John Wiley, New York (1992).

Carbo, Marie; Dunn, Rita and Ken, *Teaching Students to Learn Through Their Individual Learning Styles,* Allyn and Bacon, Boston (1991).

Self esteem

Youngs, Bettie, *The Vital 6 Ingredients of Self Esteem: How to Develop Them In Your Students,* Jalmar Press, Rolling Hills CA (1992). For teachers, primary and secondary.

Borba, Michele, *Esteem-Builders,* Jalmar Press, Rolling Hills Estates, California (1989). For primary teachers.

McDaniel, Sandy; and Bielen, Peggy, *Project Self-Esteem,* Jalmar Press, Rolling Hills Estates, California. For

primary teachers: parent involvement programme.

Atkin, Terri; Cowan, David; Dumne, Gerry; Palomares, Susanna; Schilling, Dianne; and Schuster, Sandy, *Creating Success: A Program for Behaviourally and Academically At Risk Children,* Innerchoice Publishing, Spring Valley CA (1990).

Music for learning

Webb, Terry Wyler; with Webb, Douglas, *Accelerated Learning With Music: A Trainer's Manual,* Accelerated Learning Systems, Norcross, Georgia (1990) with cassette tapes.

Campbell, Don, *Rhythms of Learning,* Zephyr Press, Tucson (1990).

Campbell, Don, *100 Ways to Improve Teaching with Your Voice and Music,* Zephyr Press, Tucson (1992).

Neuro linguistic programming

Bandler, Richard; and Grinder, John, *Using Your Brain For a Change,* Real People Press, Moab, Utah (1986).

Grinder, Michael, *ENVoY: Your Personal Guide to Classroom Management, Michael Grinder,* Battleground WA (1993).

Grinder, Michael, *Righting The Educational Conveyor Belt,* Metamorphous Press, Portland (1989).

Building learning organizations

Senge, Peter M., *The Fifth Discipline,* Random House, Sydney (1992).

Educational overview

Dickinson, Dee (editor), *Creating The Future,* Accelerated Learning Systems, England (1991).

Other recommended reading

Adams, James L., *Conceptual Blockbusting*, Penguin, New York (1987).

Adams, James L., *The Care and Feeding of Ideas*, Penguin, London (1986).

Alroggen, Brigette, *Munich Institute of Technology*, Three In One Concepts Newsletter, Three In One Concepts, Burbank, CA (March 1993).

American Association of School Administrators, *Learning Styles: Putting Them In Research and Common Sense into Practice*. AASA Publications, 1801 North Moore St., Arlington, Virginia, 22209 (1991).

Andreas, Connirae and Steve; *Heart Of The Mind: Engaging Your Inner Power to Change*, Real People Press, Moab, Utah (1989)

Ashton-Warner, Sylvia, *Teacher*, Penguin, London (1966).

Assogioli, Thomas, *Psychosynthesis*, Viking Press, New York (1965).

Ball, Christopher, *More Means Different: Widening Access to Higher Education*, Royal Society for the Encouragement of Arts, Manufactuers & Commerce, London (1990).

Ball, Gerry, *Circle Of Warmth*, Human Development Training Institute, San Diego, California, (1980).

Bandler, Richard; and Grinder, John; *Transformations*, Real People Press, Moab, Utah (1981).

Beadle, Muriel, *A Child's Mind*, MacGibbon & Kee, London (1971).

Beeby, C.E., *The Biography of an Idea: Beeby on Education*, New Zealand Council for Educational Research, Wellington, New Zealand (1992).

Bensen, Herbert, *Your Maximum Mind*, Avon Books, New York (1987).

Blakemore, Colin, *The Mind Machine*, BBC Books, London (1990), accompanies television series.

Bloom, Benjamin (Editor), *Developing Talent In Young People*, McGraw Hill, New York (1981).

Bloom, Benjamin, *Stability and Characteristics in Human Change*, John Wiley, New York (1964).

Brand, Stewart, *The Media Lab: Inventing the Future at M.I.T.*, Penguin, New York (1987).

Brown, Barbara, *Between Health and Illness*, Houghton Mifflin Co., Boston (1984).

Brown, Barbara, *SuperMind, the Ultimate Energy*, Harper & Row, New York (1980).

Butler, Dorothy, *Babies Need Books*, Penguin, London (1984).

Caine, Renate Nummela and Geoffrey, *Making Connections: Teaching and the Human Brain*, Association for Supervision and Curriculum Development, Alexandria, Virginia (1991).

Campbell, Don, *Music, Physician for Times to Come*, Quest Books, Wheaton (1991).

Campbell, Linda; Campbell, Bruce; and Dickinson, Dee, *Teaching and Learning Through Multiple Intelligences*, New Horizons for Learning, Seattle, WA (1992).

Caples, John, *How To Make Your Advertising Make Money,* Prentice Hall, Englewood Cliffs, New Jersey (1983).

Caples, John, *Tested Advertising Methods,* Prentice Hall, Englewood Cliffs, New Jersey (1974).

Carlzon, Jan, *Moments of Truth,* Harper & Row, Sydney, Australia (1987).

Cherry, Clare; Godwin, Douglas; and Staples, Jesse, *Is The Left Brain Always Right?* Fearon Teacher Aids, Belmont, California (1989).

Chopra, Deepak, *Perfect Health: The Complete Mind-Body Guide,* Harmony Books, New York (1990).

Chopra, Deepak, *Quantum Healing,* Bantam, New York (1989).

Christopher, Robert C., *The Japanese Mind,* Pan, London (1984).

Clark, Cecil, *Learning Disability, Attention Deficit and Hyperactivity,* interviewed by Francis Hendry in *The Learning Bulletin,* National Learning Laboratory (Vol 2, No. 2, February 1990).

Clay, Marie, *The Patterning Of Complex Behaviour,* Heinemann, Auckland (1979).

Costa, Arthur, *Supervision for Teaching Thinking,* Pacific Grove, California (1989).

Crocombe, Graham T.; Enright, Michael J.; and Porter, Michael E.; *Upgrading New Zealand's Competitive Advantage,* Oxford, New Zealand (1991).

Crum, Robert; Cran, William; and MacNeil, Robert, *The Story of English,* Faber & Faber/BBC Books, London (1986).

Csikszentmihalyi, Mihaly and Isabella, *Flow: The Psychology of Optimal Experience,* Harper & Row, New York (1991).

Csikszentmihalyi, Mihaly and Isabella, *Optimal Experience,* Harvard University Press, Cambridge (1988).

De Bono, Edward, *De Bono's Thinking Course,* BBC Books, London (1982).

De Bono, Edward, *Handbook for the Positive Revolution,* Viking Penguin, New York (1985).

De Bono, Edward, *Lateral Thinking,* Harper & Row, New York (1979).

Deming, W. Edwards, *Out of Crisis,* Massachusetts Institute of Technology Centre for Advanced Engineering Study (1986).

Diagram Group, The, *The Brain: A User's Manual,* Berkley Books, New York (1983).

Diamond, Marian, *Enriching Heredity,* Macmillan, New York (1988).

Dickinson, Dee, *New Horizons for Learning: Creating an Educational Network,* New Horizons for Learning, Seattle (1990).

Dickinson, Dee, *Positive Trends in Learning;* IBM Educational Systems, Atlanta, Georgia (1991).

Doman, Glenn, *What To Do About Your Brain-Injured Child,* Better Baby Press, Philadelphia (1974).

Doman, Glenn; and Armentrout, Michael J., *The Universal Multiplication of Intelligence* (report for Government of Venezuela), The Better Baby Press, Philadelphia (1980).

Doman, Glenn; Doman, Douglas; and Hagy, Bruce, *How To Teach Your Baby To Be Physically Superb,* The Better Baby Press, Philadelphia (1988).

Doman, Glenn; Doman, Janet; and Susan Aisen, *How To Give Your Baby Encyclopedic Knowledge,* The Better Baby Press, Philadelphia (1984).

Dreikurs, Rudolph, *Happy Children,* Fontana, London (1972).

Drucker, Peter, *The Age of Discontinuity,* Pan, London (1972).

Dryden, Gordon, *Out Of The Red,* Collins, Auckland (1978).

Dunn, Rita and Ken; and Price, G.E., *Learning Style Inventory,* Price Systems Inc, P.O. Box 1818, Lawrence, KA 66044.

Dunn, Rita; and Griggs, Shirley A., *Learning Styles: Quiet Revolution in American Secondary Schools,* National Association of Secondary School Principals, Reston, Virginia (1988).

Dychtwald, Ken, *Age Wave,* Bantam, New York (1990).

Ellison, Launa, *What Does The Brain Have To Do With Learning?* Holistic Education Review (Fall 1991).

Evans, Peter; and Deehan, Geoff, *The Keys To Creativity,* Grafton, London (1988), with BBC radio series.

Fabun, Don, *Three Roads to Awareness,* Glencoe Press (1970).

Forester, Anne D.; and Reinhard, Margaret, *The Learners' Way,* Peguis, Manitoba, Canada (1990).

Fortune, *Children In Crisis,* special issue of Fortune (August 10, 1992).

Fraiberg, Selma H., *The Magic Years,* Charles Scribner's Sons, New York (1959).

Fritz, Robert, *The Path of Least Resistance,* Stillpoint, Salem, MA (1984).

Fuller, Renee; Shuman, Joyce; Schmell, Judith; Lutkus, Anthony; and Noyes, Elizabeth, *Reading as Therapy in Patients with Severe IQ Deficits,* Journal of Cliical Child Psychology (1975, Spring, Volume IV, No. 1).

Galbraith, John Kenneth, *The Culture of Contentment,* Houghton Mifflin, Boston (1992).

Gallwey, W. Timothy, *The Inner Game of Golf,* Pan, London (1979).

Gallwey, W. Timothy, *The Inner Game of Tennis,* Random House, New York (1974).

Goleman, Daniel; Kaufman, Paul; and

Ray, Michael, *The Creative Spirit,* Dutton, New York (1992).

Goodlad, John, *A Place Called School,* McGraw-Hill, New York (1984).

Gore, Al, *Earth In The Balance,* Plume, New York (1993).

Gorney, Roderic, *The Human Agenda,* Guild of Tutors Press, Los Angeles (1979).

Grassi, John, *Introduction to Geometry: A Curriculum Guide For Elementary Teachers,* ALPS Products, Framingham, Mass (1985).

Gregorc, Anthony, *An Adult's Guide To Style,* Gabriel Systems, Maynard (1982).

Gross, Ronald, *Peak Learning,* Jeremy Tarcher Inc, Los Angeles (1991).

Healy, Jane M., *Endangered Minds,* Simon & Schuster, New York (1990).

Healy, Jane M., *Your Child's Growing Mind,* Doubleday, New York (1987).

Her Majesty's Chief Inspector of Schools, *Reading Recovery In New Zealand,* HMSO, London (1993).

Herbert, Nick, *Quantum Reality,* Doubleday, New York (1987).

Herrmann, Ned, *The Creative Brain,* Brain Books, Lake Lure, North Carolina (1989).

Hewitt-Gleeson, Michael, *Software For The Brain,* Wrightbooks, Victoria, Australia (1989).

Hewitt-Gleeson, Michael, *Software For The Brain 2,* Wrightbooks, Victoria, Australia (1991).

Higbee, Kenneth, L., *Your Memory: How it Works and How to Improve it,* Piatkus, London (19890.

Hirsch, E.D. Jr, *Cultural Literacy,* Bantam/Schwartz, Moorebank, NSW, Australia (1988).

Holt, John, *How Children Fail,* Pitman, New York (1968).

Hood, Lynley, *Sylvia: The Biography of Sylvia Ashton-Warner,* Viking, Auckland, New Zealand (1988).

Hughes, Felicity, *Reading and Writing Before School,* Jonathan Cape, London (1971).

Hutchinson, Michael, *Mega Brain,* Ballantine, New York (1986).

Imai, Masaaki, *Kaizen: The Key to Japan's Competitive Success,* Random House (1986).

John-Roger; and McWilliams, Peter, *Do it! Let's Get Off Our Buts,* Prelude Press, Los Angeles (1991).

John-Roger; and McWilliams, Peter, *Life 101: Everything We Wish We Had Learned About Life In School – But Didn't,* Prelude Press, Los Angeles (1991).

Jung, Carl, *Man And His Symbols,* Doubleday, New York (1964).

Kantrowitz, Barbara; Takayama, Hideko, *In Japan, First Grade Isn't Boot Camp,* Newsweek (April 17, 1989).

Kantrowitz, Barbara; and Wingert, Pat, *An "F" in World Competition,* Newsweek (February 17, 1992).

Keller, Helen, *The Story of My Life,* Doubleday, New York (1954).

Khalsa, S., *Edu-K for Everybody,* Edu-Kinesthetics Publications, Glendale, CA.

Kiyosaki, Robert T., *If You Want to Be Rich and Happy, Don't Go To School?* Excellerated Learning Publishing, San Diego, CA (1991).

Kohl, Herbert, *Reading, How To,* Penguin, London (1973).

Levering, Robert; Moskowitz, Milton; and Katz, Michael, *The 100 Best Companies To Work For In America,* Signet (1985).

Lewis, David, *You Can Teach Your Child Intelligence,* Souvenir Press, London (1981).

Lewis, Katherine, *Cooperation and Control In Japanese Nursery Schools,* Comparative Education Review, (Vol 28, No. 1, 1984).

Lindgreen, Henry, *Educational Psychology In The Classroom,* John Wiley, New York (1962).

Lorayne, Harry, *The Page-a-Minute Memory Book,* Angus & Robertson, Sydney, Australia (1986).

Lorayne, Harry; and Lucas, Jerry, *The Memory Book,* Ballantine Books, New York (1975).

Love, John F., *McDonald's: Behind The Scenes,* Bantam, New York (1986).

Lozanov, Georgi; and Gateva, Evalina, *The Foreign Language Teachers' Suggestopedic Manual,* Gordon and Breach, New York (1988).

Lozanov, Georgi, *Suggestology and Outlines of Suggestopedy,* Gordon and Breach, New York (1978).

MacLean, Paul D., *The Triune Brain in Evolution,* Plenum, New York (1990).

Macrae, Norman, *The 2024 Report,* Sidgwick & Jackson, London (1986).

Maguire, Jack, *Care and Feeding of The Brain,* Doubleday, New York (1990).

Maltz, Maxwell, *Psycho-Cybernetics,* Pocket Books, New York (1966).

Martel, Laurence, *A Working Solution For The Nation's Schools* (validation report on integrative learning at Simon Guggenheim School), Interlearn, Hilton Head Island, South Carolina (1989).

Martel, Laurence, *Seminar on Innovative Approaches to Meeting Basic Learning Needs,* prepared for United Nations Development Programme, Interlearn, South Carolina (1991).

Martel, Laurence, *Testimonials and Comments from Corporate Customers,* Interlearn, South Carolina (1991).

Martel, Laurence, *The Effectiveness of the Integrative Learning System as Perceived by New York Teachers and Administrators,* prepared for the New York State Department of Education, Interlearn, South Carolina (1991).

Max, Lesley, *Children: Endangered Species?* Penguin, Auckland (1990).

Medcalf, John, *Peer Tutoring in Reading,* Flaxmere Special Education Service, Hastings, New Zealand.

Medcalf, John, T.A.R.P.: *The Tape Assisted Reading Programme,* Flaxmere Special Education Service, Hastings, New Zealand (1990).

Montessori, Maria, *The Montessori Method,* Schocken Books, New York (1964; first published in English in 1912).

Montessori, Maria, *Spontaneous Activity in Education,* Schocken Books, New York (1965; first published in English in 1917).

Montessori, Maria, *The Absorbent Mind,* Delta, New York (1967; based on Dr. Montessori's last lecturers, in India, after the end of World War II.)

Morgan, Brian and Roberta, *Brain Food,* Pan (1987).

Morita, Akio, *Made In Japan,* Signet-Dutton, New York (1986).

Myers, Norman (general editor), *The Gaia Atlas of Planet Management,* Pan, London (1985).

Naisbitt, John, *Megatrends,* Warner Books, New York (1982).

Naisbitt, John; and Aburdene, Patricia, *Re-inventing The Corporation,* Macdonald, London (1986).

New Zealand Department of Health, *Child Hearing in New Zealand: Strategic Directions,* N.Z. Department of Health, Wellington (1991).

New Zealand Ministry of Education, *Education For the 21st Century,* Learning Media, Wellington (1983).

Newsweek, *The Best Schools in the World* (December 2, 1991).

Nolan, Pat; and McKinnon, David H., *Case Study of Curriculum Innovation in New Zealand: The Freyberg Integrated Studies Project,* Massey University, Palmerston North, New Zealand (1991).

Noor, Laily Dato' Abu Bakar; and Sukaimi, Mansor Haji, *The Child of Excellence,* Nury Institute, Malaysia (1991).

Ogilvy, David, *Ogilvy on Advertising,* Crown Publishers, New York (1983).

Ohmae, Kenichi, *The Borderless World,* Fontana, London (1990).

Ornstein, Robert, *Multimind,* Houghton Mifflin, Boston (1986).

Ornstein, Robert, *The Nature of Human Consciousness,* W.H. Freeman, New York (1973).

Ornstein, Robert, *The Psychology of Consciousness,* Penguin, New York (1977).

Ornstein, Robert; and Ehrlich, Paul, *New World, New Mind,* Simon & Schuster, New York (1989).

Ornstein, Robert; and Sobel, David, *The Healing Brain,* Simon & Schuster, New York (1987).

Osborn, Alex, *Applied Imagination,* Charles Scribner's Sons (1953).

Pacific Foundation, *Right From The Start, From Day One,* and *Growing Up Great* (three 36-page parent-education booklets in full colour), Pacific Foundation, P.O. Box 28-346, Remuera, Auckland, New Zealand (1992).

Palmer, Lyelle, *Kindergarten Maxi-Stimulation: Results Over Four Years,* at Westwood School, Irving, Texas (1971-75), *A Chance to Learn: Intensive Neuro-Stimulation in Transition Kindergarten,* at Shingle Creek Elementary School, Minneapolis (1989-90); and *Smooth Eye Pursuit Stimula-*

tion *Readiness in Kindergarten, at Shingle Creek Elementary School Minneapolis* (1990-91).

Parnes, Sidney, *Creativity: Unlocking Human Potential,* Dok Publications, New York (1972).

Penfield, Wilder; and Jasper, Herbert, *Epilepsy and the Functional Anatomy of the Human Brain,* Little Brown, Boston (1954).

Peters, Thomas J.; and Waterman, Robert H. Jr., *In Search of Excellence,* Harper & Row, New York (1982).

Peters, Tom; and Austin, Nancy, *A Passion for Excellence,* Collins, London (1985).

Pibrum, Karl, *The Neurophysiology of Remembering,* Scientific American (January 1969).

Pibrum, Karl; and Coleman, Daniel, *Holographic Memory,* Psychology Today (February 1979).

Polk Lillard, Paula, *Montessori: A Modern Approach,* Schocken Books Inc, New York (1972).

Postman, Neil, and Weingartner, Charles, *Teaching as a Subversive Activity,* Dell, (1987).

Raab, Steven S., and Matursky, *Blueprint for Franchising a Business,* John Wiley, New York (1987).

Rapp, Stan; and Collins, Tom, *MaxiMarketing: The New Directions in Advertising, Promotion and Marketing Strategy,* McGraw-Hill, New York (1987).

Rattray Taylor, Gordon, introduction to *Inventions That Changed The World,* Reader's Digest, London (1983).

Restak, Richard M., *The Brain: The Last Frontier,* Warner, New York (1979).

Restak, Richard M., *The Infant Mind,* Doubleday, New York (1986).

Rico, Gabrielle, *Writing The Natural Way,* J.P. Tarcher, Los Angeles (1983).

Robbins, Anthony, *Unlimited Power,* Simon & Schuster, New York (1986).

Roberts, Gwilym, *Boost Your Child's Brain Power: How to Use Good Nutrition,* Thorsons, England (1988).

Robinson, Forbes, *Look, Listen: Learning to read is incredibly simple,* J.K. Marketing, P.O. Box 366, Nelson, New Zealand (1986).

Roddick, Anita, *Body and Soul,* Ebury Press, London (1991).

Rogers, Carl, *Freedom to Learn,* Charles E. Merrill, Columbus, Ohio (1969).

Romanos, Joseph, *Makers of Champions: Great New Zealand Coaches,* Mills Publications, Lower Hutt (1987).

Rose, Frank, *East of Eden: The End of Innocence as Apple Computer,* Arrow, London (1989).

Russell, Peter, *The Brain Book,* E.P. Dutton, New York (1979).

Schorr, Lisbeth B. with Dan, *Within Our Reach,* Doubleday, New York (1988).

Schulz, Elizabeth, *A Long Way To Go,* Teacher Magazine (February 1993).

Schwartz, David J., *The Magic of Thinking Success,* Melvin Powers, North Hollywood (1987).

Sculley, John, *Odyssey: Pepsi to Apple,* Fontana, London (1989).

Secretary's Commission on Achieving Necessary Skills (SCANS), *What Work Requires of America's Schools,* U.S. Department of Labour, Washington D.C. (1991).

Shoemaker, Betty, *Education 2000: District 4J Integrated Curriculum and Planning Guide, K-4,* Eugene Oregon School District, 4J Public Schools.

South Dakota State University, *The Wave of the Future Splashes SDSU: Faculty Rides the Crest to Brain Friendly Learning,* SDSU Update (1993).

Sperry, Roger, *Some Effects of Disconnecting the Cerebral Hemispheres,* Science (September 1982).

Sperry, Roger, *The Great Commissure,* Scientific American (January 1964).

Steinbeck, John, *The Grapes of Wrath,* William Heinemann, London (first published 1939).

Stevenson, Harold, *Learning From Asian Schools,* Scientific American, (December 1992).

Sutton-Smith, Brian, *How to Play with Your Children,* Hawthorne Press, New York (1974).

Suzuki, Shinichi, *Nurtured By Love,* Exposition Press, New York (1975).

Svantesson, Ingemar, *Mind Mapping and Memory,* Swan, Auckland (1989).

Thornburg, David, *Multiple Intelligence Inventory,* Thornburg Centre for Creative Development.

Toffler, Alvin, *PowerShift,* Bantam, New York (1990).

Townsend, Robert, *Further Up The Organization,* Michael Joseph, London (1984).

Treffinger, Donald, *Programming for Giftedness: Needed Directions,* Innotech Journal, Republic of the Philippines, Department of Education, Manila (January-June, 1992).

Tribus, Myron, *The Application of Quality Management Principles in Education at Mt. Edgecumbe High School, Sitka, Alaska,* in *An Introduction to Total Quality for Schools,* American Association of School Administrators (1991).

Vos-Groenendal, Jeannette, *An Accelerated/Integrative Learning Model Program Evaluation: Based on Participant Perceptions of Student Attitudinal and Achievement Changes,* unpublished dissertation, ERIC and Northern Arizona University, Flagstaff, Arizona (1991).

Waite, Helen E., *Valiant Companions: Helen Keller and Anne Sullivan Macy,* Macrae (1959).

Wallace, Rosella R., *Active Learning: Rappin' and Rhymin',* Upbeat Publishing, Anchor Point, Alaska (1990).

Watson, Lyall, *Supernature,* Coronet, London (1973).

Wenger, Win, *Image Streaming: An Easy Way To Inservice Your Intelligence,* Success (April 1991).

Wenger, Win, *Beyond Teaching and Learning,* Project Renaissance, Singapore (1992).

Wevers, Maartin, *Japan, its Future and New Zealand,* Victoria University Press, Wellington (1988).

Wilson, Mary, *The Deming Management Method,* Dodd Mead, U.S.A. (1986).

Wujec, Tom, *Pumping Ions: Games and Exercises To Flex Your Mind,* Doubleday, Toronto (1990).

Yamashita, Toshihiko, *The Panasonic Way,* Kohansha, New York (1987).

Young, Elaine, *I Am A Blade Of Grass,* Jalmar Press, Rolling Hills Estates, California (1989).

Index